Centre and Periphery

ONE WORLD ARCHAEOLOGY

Series Editor: P. J. Ucko

Animals into Art
H. Morphy (ed.), vol. 7

Archaeological Approaches to Cultural Identity
S. J. Shennan (ed.), vol. 10

Archaeological Heritage Management in the Modern World
H. F. Cleere (ed.), vol. 9

Archaeology and the Information Age: a global perspective
P. Reilly & S. Rahtz (eds), vol. 21

The Archaeology of Africa: food, metals and towns
T. Shaw, P. Sinclair, B. Andah & A. Okpoko (eds), vol. 20

Conflict in the Archaeology of Living Traditions
R. Layton (ed.), vol. 8

Domination and Resistance
D. Miller, M. J. Rowlands & C. Tilley (eds), vol. 3

The Excluded Past: archaeology in education
P. Stone & R. MacKenzie (eds), vol. 17

Foraging and Farming: the evolution of plant exploitation
D. R. Harris & G. C. Hillman (eds), vol. 13

From the Baltic to the Black Sea: studies in medieval archaeology
D. Austin & L. Alcock (eds), vol. 18

Hunters of the Recent Past
L. B. Davis & B. O. K. Reeves (eds), vol. 15

The Meanings of Things: material culture and symbolic expression
I. Hodder (ed.), vol. 6

The Origins of Human Behaviour
R. A. Foley (ed.), vol. 19

The Politics of the Past
P. Gathercole & D. Lowenthal (eds), vol. 12

Sacred Sites, Sacred Places
D. L. Carmichael, J. Hubert, B. Reeves & A. Schanche (eds), vol. 23

Signifying Animals: human meaning in the natural world
R. G. Willis (ed.), vol. 16

Social Construction of the Past: representation as power
G. C. Bond & A. Gilliam (eds), vol. 24

State and Society: the emergence and development of social hierarchy and political centralization
J. Gledhill, B. Bender & M. T. Larsen (eds), vol. 4

Tropical Archaeobotany: applications and developments
J. G. Hather (ed.), vol. 22

The Walking Larder: patterns of domestication, pastoralism, and predation
J. Clutton-Brock (ed.), vol. 2

What is an Animal?
T. Ingold (ed.), vol. 1

What's New? A closer look at the process of innovation
S. E. Van der Leeuw & R. Torrence (eds), vol. 14

Who Needs the Past? Indigenous values and archaeology
R. Layton (ed.), vol. 5

Centre and Periphery

Comparative Studies in Archaeology

Edited by T. C. Champion

London and New York

First published in 1989 by Unwin Hyman Ltd

First published in paperback 1995
by Routledge
11 New Fetter Lane, London EC4P 4EE

Simultaneously published in the USA and Canada
by Routledge
29 West 35th Street, New York, NY 10001

Typeset in 10 on 11 Bembo by Computape (Pickering) Ltd,
Pickering, North Yorkshire

Printed and bound in Great Britain at the University Press, Cambridge

British Library Cataloguing in Publication Data
A catalogue record for this book is available from the British Library

Library of Congress Cataloguing in Publication Data
A catalogue record for this book has been requested

ISBN 0-415-12253-8

List of contributors

H. Arthur Bankoff, Department of Classics, Brooklyn College of the City University of New York, USA.

Brad Bartel, Department of Anthropology, San Diego University, California, USA.

James A. Boutilier, Department of History and Political Economy, Royal Roads Military College, Victoria, British Columbia, Canada.

Timothy C. Champion, Department of Archaeology, University of Southampton, UK.

Michael Dietler, Department of Anthropology, University of California, Berkeley, USA.

Dena F. Dincauze, Department of Anthropology, University of Massachusetts, USA.

Paul Farnsworth, Archaeology Program, University of California, Los Angeles, USA.

Robert J. Hasenstab, Department of Anthropology, University of Massachusetts, USA.

Lubomír E. Havlík, Czechoslovak Academy of Sciences, Brno, Czechoslovakia.

Randall H. McGuire, Department of Anthropology, State University of New York, Binghamton, New York, USA.

Klavs Randsborg, Institute of Archaeology, Copenhagen University, Denmark.

Simon Stoddart, Magdalene College, Cambridge, UK.

Slawoj Szynkiewicz, Institute for the History of Material Culture, Polish Academy of Sciences, Warsaw, Poland.

Ruth D. Whitehouse, Department of Classics, Queen Mary College, University of London, UK.

John B. Wilkins, Department of Classics, Queen Mary College, University of London, UK.

David F. Williams, Department of Archaeology, University of Southampton, UK.

Frederick A. Winter, Department of Classics, Brooklyn College of the City University of New York, USA.

List of contributors

Foreword

This book is one of a major series of more than 20 volumes resulting from the World Archaeological Congress held in Southampton, England, in September 1986. The series reflects the enormous academic impact of the Congress, which was attended by 850 people from more than 70 countries, and attracted many additional contributions from others who were unable to attend in person.

The *One World Archaeology* series is the result of a determined and highly successful attempt to bring together for the first time not only archaeologists and anthropologists from many different parts of the world, as well as academics from a host of contingent disciplines, but also non-academics from a wide range of cultural backgrounds, who could lend their own expertise to the discussions at the Congress. Many of the latter, accustomed to being treated as the 'subjects' of archaeological and anthropological observation, had never before been admitted as equal participants in the discussion of their own (cultural) past or present, with their own particularly vital contribution to make towards global, cross-cultural understanding.

The Congress therefore really addressed world archaeology in its widest sense. Central to a world archaeological approach is the investigation not only of how people lived in the past but also of how, and why, changes took place resulting in the forms of society and culture which exist today. Contrary to popular belief, and the archaeology of some 20 years ago, world archaeology is much more than the mere recording of specific historical events, embracing as it does the study of social and cultural change in its entirety. All the books in the *One World Archaeology* series are the result of meetings and discussions which took place within a context that encouraged a feeling of self-criticism and humility in the participants about their own interpretations and concepts of the past. Many participants experienced a new self-awareness, as well as a degree of awe about past and present human endeavours, all of which is reflected in this unique series.

The Congress was organized around major themes. Several of these themes were based on the discussion of full-length papers which had been circulated some months previously to all who had indicated a special interest in them. Other sessions, including some dealing with areas of specialization defined by period or geographical region, were based on oral addresses, or a combination of precirculated papers and lectures. In all cases, the entire sessions were recorded on cassette, and all contributors were presented with the recordings of the discussion of their papers. A major part of the thinking behind the Congress was that a meeting of many hundreds of participants that did not leave behind a published record of its academic discussions would be little more than an exercise in tourism.

Thus, from the very beginning of the detailed planning for the World Archaeological Congress, in 1982, the intention was to produce post-Congress books containing a selection only of the contributions, revised in the light of discussions during the sessions themselves as well as during subsequent consultations with the academic editors appointed for each book. From the outset, contributors to the Congress knew that if their papers were selected for publication, they would have only a few months to revise them according to editorial specifications, and that they would become authors in an important academic volume scheduled to appear within a reasonable period following the Southampton meeting.

The publication of the series reflects the intense planning which took place before the Congress. Not only were all contributors aware of the subsequent production schedules, but also session organizers were already planning their books before and during the Congress. The editors were entitled to commission additional chapters for their books when they felt that there were significant gaps in the coverage of a topic during the Congress, or where discussion at the Congress indicated a need for additional contributions.

One of the main themes of the Congress was devoted to 'Comparative Studies in the Development of Complex Societies'. The theme was based on discussion of precirculated full-length papers, covering three and a half days, and was under the overall control of Dr Tim Champion, Senior Lecturer in the Department of Archaeology, University of Southamption, and Dr Michael Rowlands, Reader in the Department of Anthropology, University College London. The choice of this topic for a major theme arose from a desire to explore, from a worldwide and interdisciplinary perspective, the assumptions that are embodied in the common use by archaeologists and others of concepts such as 'complex societies', a supposed stage in social development often also assumed to be marked by the invention and wide usage of literacy.

This awareness of the dangers of assuming that archaeological terminology is a precise language consisting of terms which have a single accepted meaning, with well authenticated qualitative connotations, derived, at least in part, from lessons learnt from the last major interdisciplinary consideration of urbanization in 1970 (Ucko *et al*. 1972). At that time discussion led Stuart Piggott (1972, pp. 948–9) to stress

> that we must avoid semantic confusion when we use certain words and names for things. We use the word 'town' or 'city', and in the classical world this was *polis* or *urbs*, and what we have to consider is whether we are falling into that well-known trap of confusing names with actual things, and while using the name embodying modern concepts, we forget that these concepts were not those of literate antiquity, and therefore by reasonable assumption not of non-literate antiquity. Consider for instance the Latin use of *urbs* in relation to the Celtic population of barbarian Europe. What did a Latin writer really mean when he called

> a hill-fort, *urbs*, as indeed on occasion they did? It did not mean it was like Rome, although he used the same word for the city, the Imperial City, as he would for this barbarian earthwork enclosure, the functions of which, or the functions of any hill-fort, we very imperfectly understand. Let us avoid the ancient belief in the magic power of words, which can make us turn names into real things, and so fulfil a primitive conviction that when you have given a thing a name you have a command over it, like knowing someone's secret name. It is possible to persuade oneself that having named a concept, therefore, it actually exists and can be dealt with accordingly.

The overall theme therefore took as its starting point the assumption that the concept of social complexity needed to be re-examined and probably refined. A narrow parochial approach to the past, which simply assumes a European development to urbanization and literacy as the valid criterion for defining a complex society, totally ignores the complexity of non-literate civilizations and cultures such as the Inca of Peru or that of Benin in Nigeria. However, a world archaeological approach to a concept such as that of social complexity focuses attention on precisely those features which archaeologists all too often take for granted.

Discussions during the Congress were grouped around five main headings, and have led to the publication of three books. The first subtheme, organized by Barbara Bender, Department of Anthropology, University College London, was concerned with 'The Development of Complexity', the second, under the control of Daniel Miller, also of the Department of Anthropology, University College London, and Christopher Tilley of Trinity Hall, Cambridge, was on 'Modes of Domination', and the third, organized by Michael Rowlands, was on 'European Expansion and the Archaeology of Capitalism'. Contributions from these three subthemes, which were discussed on two different days, form the book *Domination and resistance*, edited by Miller, Rowlands and Tilley. The fourth subtheme on 'Centre–Periphery Relations', which was discussed for one day, has resulted in this volume. More than a day was devoted to the fifth subtheme, 'State and Society; the Emergence, Development and Transformation of Forms of Social Hierarchy, Class Relations and Political Centralization'. This has been edited by its organizers John Gledhill of the Department of Anthropology, University College London, and Mogens Larsen of the Centre for Research in the Humanities, Copenhagen, Denmark, with Barbara Bender, under the title *State and society*.

The approach adopted within the overall theme of 'Comparative Studies in the Development of Complex Societies' was based on a consideration of the *processes* involved in the creation and establishment of the elements of social organization, and social activities, which archaeologists and others commonly claim to be the visible end results of the activities of complex societies. In a comparative context, attention is focused on the reasons why, and mechanisms by which, the non-literate civilizations of, for example, the

Inca of Peru, built and maintained some 23 000 kilometres of 'roads' and what their function was within the sociopolitical state system of some 6 to 12 million peoples with diverse backgrounds and identities who lived in environmental conditions as different as the desert and the High Andes. Within the non-literate Inca state, political control of heterogeneous social groups was achieved by an hierarchical system of regional administrative centres with an inevitable complexity of relations existing between centres and the hinterland. Given this complexity, which exists in the absence of literacy in the Inca state, the traditional focus of the study of complex societies on the better-known literate 'civilizations' of the Old World appears odd and misguided.

If the traditional assumptions about 'complexity' can thus be discarded, so too can the equally traditional, and virtually exclusive, emphasis on development and evolution. The conventional concern with determining where and when 'state' and 'class' originated gives way to more fundamental questions about the processes of long-term social change and the very complex relationships which exist between social and cultural identity and perception, order, and development.

Key concepts in such an approach, essential to our understanding of the relevant social processes, are those of 'authority' and 'power'. Contributors to the theme on 'Comparative Studies of the Development of Complex Societies' examined both concepts in an attempt to disentangle any Eurocentric assumptions embedded in the terms themselves, and also to describe precisely the forms which power and authority may take in other societies, both today and in the past.

Inherent in all of the contributions is the assumption that social relations have never been any more equal and symmetrical in societies in the past than they are in contemporary societies. Many of the perspectives adopted in these books explore the details of these asymmetrical relations, considering not only the variety of forms that have been adopted over different times and in different parts of the world, but also the different mechanisms which have been employed to bolster and reinforce such inequalities. With such inequalities in the distribution of power, and in access to knowledge, come equally varied forms of control over symbolism, ritual, religious cults, and even literacy.

A particular focus of interest therefore lies in the detailed exploration of the different forms and functions of literacy in different societies, an exploration that clearly reveals that these were in no way uniform and that literacy, in itself, cannot be used as a clear marker of social qualitative development (see *Who needs the past?*, edited by R. Layton) – to be able to read and write is not, in itself, to be a member of a qualitatively complex society.

Another form of inherent asymmetry in human societies derives from centre–periphery relations. The presence at the Congress of so many participants from the so-called Third and Fourth Worlds made it possible to examine in detail these relations in a very wide variety of forms, in particular those frequently glossed over in the archaeological literature under rubrics such as 'civilized'–'barbarian', 'urban'–'non-urban', sedentary–nomadic, and agriculturalist–pastoralist.

In focusing on the nature of the varying relationships that can develop between centre and periphery, one is led inevitably to detailed questions about imperialism, colonialism, and acculturation. In part these forms of relationships are a matter of ideology (of 'empire', of 'nation', and of ethnic groups), but it is the mechanisms of expansion, incorporation, and maintenance which are clearly vital to our understanding of the past and present, and which are examined in some detail.

The main themes in *Centre and periphery* have been discussed in detail in its editorial Introduction (pp. 1–21). My aim in what follows is to examine a few of the points which have struck me personally as being of particular note or fascination.

In this book Timothy Champion and his contributors are confronted with the phenomenon of ethnicity, either in the form of groups of people claiming a special and separate identity from the majority population and its social subgroupings, or being recognized by 'outsiders' as constituting a distinctive cultural grouping. The nature of such groupings, and the difficulty of securely identifying them in the archaeological record, is discussed in several chapters of *Archaeological approaches to cultural identity* (edited by S. J. Shennan). In *Centre and periphery* it is argued that, at least in certain cases, such groupings, with their attendant strength of emotions and feelings of 'belonging', are a result of the pressures and politics of complex societies, including the integration of peoples within a wider society. In other words, the view can be taken that such special ethnic groupings are a form of resistance to the interests and aims of the centre and that the nature of their compositions has been far from static (and see *State and society*, edited by J. Gledhill *et al.*). According to this argument, what particular nomenclature is applied to whom is very much a matter of the power politics of any particular time – whether it be the all-embracing category of 'barbarians' as described by the Romans, or the invention, by Europeans, of a unitary group called (Australian) 'Aborigines' to camouflage a large number of distinct cultural and linguistic groups.

The implications for the archaeology of complex and hierarchical societies are far reaching. The variety of actual material culture evidence discovered by the archaeologist may hide the fact that in real social and political terms the peoples with distinctive material culture were in fact treated as homogeneous and that they themselves may have considered such differences as secondary in importance to their shared commonalities. Equally, a shared material culture at some level of generality may give the impression of homogeneity when the peoples themselves consider they are culturally distinct from one another. It is easy, therefore, for the archaeologist to be misled. It is also, of course, easy to overlook the importance of research designs being formulated with the specific aim of acting as possible correctives to 'official' ideology and dogma which may have been promulgated, in text and statuary, by the powerful centres of politics, administration, and influence. It is important to recognize, as is made clear in this book, that much archaeological data, such as portraiture, may often be the selective evidence of those in power, whose products were conceived of in the context of proving and demonstrating legitimacy. Nor is it irrelevant to appreciate that one of the main tools of domination and influence from a centre is control of the educational (and propaganda) system (see also *State and society*, edited by J. Gledhill *et al.* and *The excluded past*, edited by P. Stone & R. MacKenzie), which may mean that what is ostentatious and widespread in the archaeological record may in fact be a far cry from the occupations and activities of the majority within any given society.

It is the concern of several of the chapters of this book to disentangle what may have been the mechanics of a centre–periphery relationship at any particular time. In practice, this is often strikingly difficult to accomplish. On the one hand, the problems involve the way that the 'noise' of any official propaganda machine must be checked and evaluated against the actual evidence revealed by archaeological investigation. On the other, it may be that it is only the recognition of patterning in the archaeological record which suggests that centre–periphery relationships may have existed. Unfortunately, it is often the case that crucial archaeological evidence which might otherwise be able to 'make sense' of the centre–periphery balance of relations must often be postulated as being absent. In the past, use of 'negative evidence' such as the postulated control by early urban centres such as Jericho, of salt trading routes, has found little favour, just because the postulate can never be demonstrated. In the case of the economics of complex societies and their hinterlands, it is now accepted that it is impossible to attempt to reconstruct the trading processes involved without assuming the existence of imports and exports of archaeologically invisible materials. Such commodities should not be thought of in purely materialistic and physical terms – for example, goods of organic substances such as food, wood, feathers, woven textiles, and so on – but also in terms of all the invisible activities – religious, political, and so on – which must have accompanied such transactions and contracts. As *Centre and periphery* makes clear through various case studies, the nature and organization of such invisible production and exchange of even materialistic items – in one example it being the business of individual households and, in another, exclusively concerned with non-luxury goods – may completely alter the nature of our understanding of the complexities of the systems under review. We must, in any case, realize that the nature of any centre–periphery relationship is likely to have been based at least as much on the intangible elements of allegiances and social intercourse as on the exclusively economic. The enormously difficult task of the archaeologist attempting to unravel the details of a complex system of past economic distribution and trade and of a past political system making use of political ideology and persuasion as well as effective power, can be sampled in this book from many different cultures of the ancient world, not least when the expectations from the Roman literature about relations with pre-Roman Britain are confounded by the actual archaeological evidence of the traded amphorae themselves.

Centre and periphery reviews the several alternative parameters of explanation within which archaeologists have attempted to operate, including several of Marxist derivation which are those that perhaps appear to be the most useful in this astonishingly difficult area of investigation. One of the interesting points which emerges most clearly from many of the accounts and analyses in this book is that many of the concepts commonly employed as if they were of self-evident significance and capable of only one interpretation are in fact, and in practice, essentially relative concepts. This is not only the case with regard to the changing nature of who is classified at any particular time as a member of a particular ethnic grouping, but it also applies to what should be called a 'centre' in a centre–periphery relationship. The nature of such a centre, and where exactly it is to be located, is not a simple matter of fact and physical location, but of attitude and perception. What constitutes the centre of influence and power is a relative matter dependent on the viewpoint of a particular actor in the assessment. In archaeological terms, the effective centre as revealed by the evidence of past material culture may well not have been the solitary emic perception of one and the same centre as seen by all those within an archaeological periphery. It is even possible that the model of 'centre–periphery' is a Eurocentric, and oversimplified, one and that the very diverse interactions which are often subsumed within the term would be better expressed in different ways.

Another of the important points to emerge from this book is that a 'periphery' is also a relative concept whose actual nature and make-up may be very varied. Very often such undifferentiated concepts are found to correlate with stereotypical characterizations of the inhabitants of such an undifferentiated 'periphery', such as the presumed war-like nature of nomads inhabiting the 'space' around the complex central 'civilization'. In fact it becomes clear from reading *Centre and periphery* that the 'periphery' will be a very different kind of entity with which the 'centre' has to interact depending on whether it is composed of settled agricultural villages or of mobile nomadic groups. Furthermore, the nature of a centre–periphery relationship is not only far from being a static one in terms of membership of its constituent groups, but it is also dynamic and multidirectional in terms of the flow of goods and people from a presumed 'centre' to a presumed 'periphery' and vice versa. As the nature of peripheries is variable and their composition is usually heterogeneous, so too will be the patterns of trade and influence between their component parts and any dominating external centre.

In the context of all these problems of interpretation – many of which are a direct consequence of the nature of archaeological evidence and the relationship between such evidence derived from the usage and subsequent disposal of waste materials, and the literary records produced by outside observers or by the dominant central authorities – it is perhaps not surprising that archaeologists have been forced to attempt subtle statistical analyses of their data in an attempt to grasp the possible complexities of that data. Such sophistication of analytical tools appears to be in danger of outstripping the sophistication of explanatory models of interpretation.

Centre and periphery makes it clear that there is in fact no one simple polarity and distinction between a centre and a periphery, and that there is an urgent need for reconsideration of acculturation models, which can be applied to societies of the past. It is an important message of this book that such frameworks will have to be able to accommodate not only the dynamics of changing compositions of the units under scrutiny at any time, but also the relative importance of differing emic views in different types of any presumed periphery. Above all, such models of acculturation will have to be able to accommodate both the propaganda of rulers and the realities of actual practice as revealed by the archaeological record.

P. J. Ucko
Southampton

References

Piggott, S. 1972. Conclusion. In *Man, settlement and urbanism*, P. J. Ucko, R. Tringham & G. W. Dimbleby (eds), 947–53. London: Duckworth.

Ucko, P. J., R. Tringham & G.W. Dimbleby (eds) 1972. *Man, settlement and urbanism*. London: Duckworth.

Contents

Preface

The chapters that make up this book were originally given as papers in the World Archaeological Congress in Southampton in 1986. Chapter 4 by Simon Stoddart was originally discussed in a session on 'State and Society', and Chapter 10 by Brad Bartel in the session entitled 'Identity Maintenance and Cultural Assimilation in Complex Societies' within the theme on 'Archaeological "Objectivity" in Interpretation'; all the other chapters derive from papers within the 'Centre–Periphery Relations' discussion sessions. One of the aims of the theme devoted to 'Comparative Studies in the Development of Complex Societies' was to find ways of initiating new forms of debate within archaeology and to situate it more firmly within a broader field of debate embracing anthropology, sociology, and history as well. Some of the attempts to reforge the links between archaeology and these other disciplines, by concentrating on methods of meaningful debate about social relations in past societies, have been incorporated in the other two books arising from that session, *Domination and resistance* (edited by Daniel Miller, Michael Rowlands & Christopher Tilley) and *State and society* (edited by John Gledhill, Barbara Bender & Mogens Larsen). These published books should give a good indication of the breadth of the discussion, which in 4½ days never seemed in danger of drying up and embraced scholars from many countries and many disciplines.

I am particularly grateful to my fellow organizers for their unflagging determination not to let the organization of a very big session get out of hand or on top of us, and to the many participants who turned up and took part; above all to the contributors to this book, who have made the editor's job a lot easier than it might have been.

As a member of the Executive Committee which was responsible for the organization of the Congress, I am only too well aware of some of the problems that had to be faced. All of us who took part in the academic sessions and benefited so much from them therefore owe a great debt to Peter Ucko, the National Secretary, without whose untiring efforts over many years we would never have had such an opportunity to meet and talk to so large and varied a group.

Timothy C. Champion
Southampton

Preface

Introduction

TIMOTHY C. CHAMPION

In recent years there have been signs, among archaeologists studying the development of social complexity, of increasing dissatisfaction with the evolutionary theories of the Anglo-American 'New Archaeology' of the 1960s and 1970s as full explanations. Much has been learnt from this phase of archaeological enquiry. The focusing of attention on a society's relationship to its environment, on the complicated interrelationships of internal factors such as subsistence economy, exchange, technology and population, and on the potential for small-scale change in one area to initiate major restructuring of the whole social system, has been most fruitful. Attempts to use the concepts of chiefdom and state have led not only to discussion of the applicability of such terms in prehistoric contexts, but also to debate about the proper identification of such social concepts, or indeed other concepts of complexity with material correlates in the archaeological record. Above all there has been the recognition of the very wide range of forms of social organization which is largely masked by lumping them into such grossly oversimplified categories as chiefdom and state. Because of the evident success of this conceptual framework in stimulating archaeological enquiry, its shortcomings have also become increasingly obvious. There has been a reliance on functionalist and adaptationist explanations, and an obsession with the adaptively successful reorganizations which enable societies to incorporate ever larger quantities of territory, population or energy. There has been a tendency to adopt a stadial approach within a theory of unilinear social evolution which can frequently descend into sterile debate about the correct attribution of a particular social formation to one category or another, or the search for process to transform social formation from one stage to the next. Finally, there has been an excessively abstract modelling of social factors which pays little attention to the realities of social relations in historical societies. The rich diversity of forms taken by societies with complex organization is given scant attention in the search for generalized evolutionary models.

The concern of this book is to explore one particular alternative framework – the analysis of long-distance relationships, especially between societies with markedly different patterns of social or economic organization, and the potential of such asymmetric interactions to bring about major transformations of social relations. In one sense, a recognition of such long-distance relationships has been present in archaeology for a considerable time, as frequent references to such concepts as 'diffusion', 'influence' or 'trade' testify. Connections of this sort have frequently been invoked as no more than a simplistic sort of explanation of observed similarity in material culture. They have also been used to give an account, or even an intended explanation, of economic, social and political development, though mostly without a systematic analysis of how the relationships might have operated, and sometimes in a quite irresponsible manner, as with the hyperdiffusionist attempts to derive all human civilization from Egypt. In the present case, however, we are dealing not with the explanation of observed similarity, but with the investigation of the social consequences of long-distance interaction, in a debate moulded specifically by the concept of the relationships between centres and peripheries. Like so much else in archaeology, this theme has been taken up from elsewhere, in particular from political theory and geography, but we should regard this not so much as a 'borrowing' which shows archaeology's own intellectual impoverishment, but as sign of archaeology's close connection to contemporary debate in other important areas of social enquiry, and of its ability to contribute meaningfully to that debate.

Centre and periphery

The concepts of centre and periphery, in various ways and in various degrees of specificity, have had a long history in western European thought. Such opposed ideas as town and country, civilized and barbarian, long engrained in our thinking, implicitly embody them. The Western construction of history, with its emphasis on the rise and fall of the classical world, the emergence of its north and west European successor states and their rise to world dominance, also incorporates a contrast between an innovative, developing, dynamic and dominant region and others which are backward and ultimately subjected. This contrast is both a spatial one, with the dynamic region of western Europe surrounded on all sides by less developed territories, and a cultural one, defining western Europe as an area of particular interest and values, to be studied, appreciated and maintained in a way very different from the regions beyond. This spatial contrast may also be given a temporal dimension, in theories of social evolution which stress the backward or retarded nature of non-European societies. Though the European historical tradition may not always be couched in the specific terminology of centre and periphery, it does nonetheless by its very Eurocentric nature reflect them.

More specifically, the centre and periphery model has figured in a variety of ways in the geographical analysis of the spatial organization of human society. The German geographer von Thuenen's study (1826) of the intellectual fiction of the isolated city in a featureless plain demonstrated the theoretical relationship between distance from the centre and increasing economic disadvantage, and was the ultimate intellectual ancestor of the specifically archaeological theory of site-catchment analysis (Higgs and

Vita-Finzi 1970). Christaller's work (1966) on least-cost solutions to the problem of the spatial organization of functional hierarchies of settlement systems in an industrialized society represented a rather different approach to centrality, but it was the stimulus for a great period of growth in academic interest in such problems and for the emergence of a geographical theory of central places. These ideas were the starting point for several different lines of enquiry in recent archaeology, and anthropology too (Cherry 1987, Hodges 1987), including attempts to modify central place theory for application to the regional analysis of ethnohistoric settlement systems (Smith 1976) or to prehistoric societies (Steponaitis 1978), or to use rank–size correlation as a measure of the emergence of centralized political authority (Johnson 1981). Underlying this work in archaeology there is an attempt to find a means of translating social concepts of power and authority into terms appropriate to the analysis of the actual archaeological data, among which settlement evidence is comparatively plentiful (Renfrew 1982). Much of this work suffers from being too concerned with the spatial patterning rather than the social reality, and from weaknesses in moving from one frame of reference to another. Furthermore, the kind of relationship typically analysed in this way has been comparatively small-scale, within a defined zone, whether that is a geographical entity such as an island or river drainage or a historically defined polity, and focused on a single central point, whether a small settlement in relation to the resources in its catchment area or a large urban centre in relation to its hinterland.

A broader frame of vision was not common, but some work did point to the recognition of patterns on a larger scale. Smith's (1976) typology of regional settlement systems included a dendritic pattern stemming from a single focus or gateway community (Hirth 1978), which could serve to integrate two rather differently ordered societies, somewhat comparable to Polanyi's concept of a port-of-trade (1957). Rather earlier Toynbee (1954) had drawn attention to the tendency for new and dynamic societies to emerge on the fringes of old and declining ones, as did Macedonia on the northern borders of the Greek world, or the Manchu in the case of China, in a pattern of progressive shifting of power from the centre to the periphery. This not only applied the concept of centre and periphery on a larger scale and within a frame that was not clearly defined by any natural or historical boundaries, but also conceived of the centre itself in a different way; not as a single point, but as a large polity or even a cluster of polities. Despite the underlying patterns of historical and geographical thinking, however, and the occasional specific formulation of the ideas of centre and periphery, there does not seem to have been much explicit theoretical development of the concept at a large scale, appropriate to the analysis of relations between polities.

From the early 1970s this picture rapidly changed as the idea of centre and periphery achieved considerable intellectual popularity in a variety of related academic fields such as political, historical, and economic geography, political theory, and historical sociology (e.g. Gottmann 1980). Strassoldo

(1980, p. 53) has suggested that this new interest in the relationships of centre and periphery at a global scale was linked to broader changes in Western thinking about the human environment and social development: a realization of the limits to technological growth, a concern for the environment and its resources, an unwillingness to accept centralized power structures uncritically, a concern with apparently insoluble problems of famine and impoverishment, with the political transformation of former colonies, and with the changing nature of American and Western European world dominance. However that may be, the centre and periphery model came to the fore in several disciplines, even to the point of being an academic 'fashion'. The scale of its application and the precise meaning given to the terms naturally varied somewhat with the context. The model was most often adopted to analyse contemporary political structures, but could also have a historical dimension, and be applied not just to the analysis of contemporary patterns but also to the historical processes through which they had arisen. The widespread discussion of the idea therefore provided an alternative framework for understanding the processes through which the stark contrasts in economic and political development in the modern world had come about, at a time when the traditional perception of those processes was being called into question.

Development and underdevelopment

Throughout the 19th century and the first half of the 20th the prevailing response of the Western intellectual tradition to the contrasts between the more 'advanced' societies of western Europe and the less 'advanced' ones of the rest of the world with whom they were increasingly coming into contact was an appeal to the concept of social evolution. The progress of western Europe to its dominant world role, politically, economically, technologically, and militarily, was based on a specific conjunction of circumstances; other societies had not been so fortunate and had been left stranded at lower points on the evolutionary ladder. The metaphors used to characterize this inequality draw heavily on the language and imagery of a biological organism, in particular the human body. Concepts such as 'advanced' or 'backward', applied to the development of society, have unfortunate overtones of mental retardation, but the most common metaphors, 'development' and 'underdevelopment', suggest that the proper maturation of the human body is analogous to the growth of western European society to some inherently ordained form, while failures to achieve this normal pattern are somehow to be diagnosed as problems for treatment. Even the term 'aid' for such treatment offered by the developed to the underdeveloped world perpetuates the imagery of a condition to be cured by the appropriate injection of cash or technology. Constant pictures of famine in the Third World may also serve to reinforce this imagery of a parallelism between the malnutrition and underdevelopment of the individual, and the underdevelopment of the social or political group, both to be cured in similar ways.

Since World War II, however, the existence of a systematic structural connection between the growth of western Europe and the underdevelopment of other societies, and the precise nature of such a connection, has been the subject of growing debate. It was initiated in the first place by the development theorists such as Frank (1967), who argued that the underdevelopment of the Third World was the result of its exploitation by expanding European capitalism, perpetuated through the creation of an international division of labour, the extraction of surplus, and the creation of a market for the products of the technologically advanced producers in the developed core area. In the end, as Boutilier explains in his discussion of the Solomon Islands in Chapter 1, early theories of dependency failed to deal adequately with the nature of the structural connection between centre and periphery, and the variety of response to capitalist penetration displayed by the periphery. The course of the debate had, however, been firmly set.

Wallerstein and world systems

The same theme of the structured growth of inequality was taken up in a rather different way in Immanuel Wallerstein's *The modern world-system* (1974), which expanded the historical and geographical scale of the currently prevailing model of centre and periphery. His aim was to describe and account for the condition of the modern world, especially the emergence of the current political and economic structure of capitalist world domination. In so doing, he raised questions not only about the precise formulation of such an account of recent history, but also about the correct scale of analysis and the correct units to form its basis. Though he was not, as will be seen, primarily concerned with the pre-capitalist world, and indeed explicitly excluded it from his analysis, it is appropriate to raise his fundamental methodological questions in an earlier chronological context, and to ask whether, or to what extent, he was right to limit the applicability of his concept so narrowly.

Wallerstein's analysis is based on the asserted importance of studying the individual social system, which is characterized by 'the fact that life within it is largely self-contained and that the dynamics of its development are largely internal' (Wallerstein 1974, p. 347). No society, of course, is ever entirely isolated, so the lack of an absolute definition need not pose serious problems. On this basis, Wallerstein distinguishes two types of social system: not the tribes and states of much archaeological and anthropological discussion, but only 'the relatively small, highly autonomous subsistence economies not part of some regular tribute-demanding system' (1974, p. 348), and the much larger-scale world systems, containing a multiplicity of cultures and based on a geographical division of labour in accordance with the principle of most efficient location of production within the system as a whole.

Wallerstein argues further that thus far there have only been two types of world system, though a third form, a socialist world government, is envisaged as a theoretical but currently unattainable possibility. The two types are the world empire, in which a single political system dominates, however weakly, more or less the entire area of interrelated societies, and the world economy, in which no such single political structure exists.

It is furthermore an integral part of Wallerstein's thesis that the growth of a stable and long-lived world economy is a unique event of the modern world, specifically related to the rise of the European capitalist economies, which has given capitalist entrepreneurs the ability to operate over, and to dominate, a far wider territory than could ever be controlled by a single political unit. Capitalism has 'invented the technology that makes it possible to increase the flow of surplus from the lower strata to the upper strata, from the periphery to the center, from the majority to the minority by eliminating the "waste" of too cumbersome a political structure'; world empires, on the other hand, were a 'primitive means of economic domination' (Wallerstein 1974, pp. 15–16).

World economies operate within an external arena with which they have little or no contact, and are themselves characterized by a division into core states and peripheral areas. The core comprises an area of strong state machinery, typically a cluster of states rather than a single state, and of high technological advance and sophisticated economic institutions, which enable it to extract surplus from the periphery. That is an area where those features are correspondingly weak, and which is regarded mainly as a source of raw materials. Another important element in the structure is the semi-periphery, which forms a link between the core and the periphery, but also a buffer; it serves to integrate core and periphery economically as well as geographically, but also to provide a means of moderating political pressures that might be brought to bear on the core. Such semi-peripheries do not have access to the political opportunities offered by being part of the core.

One important feature of Wallerstein's model is its ability to cope with diachronic change. Though the existence of a core is a stable and permanent feature, the set of states which comprise the core may vary through time, and indeed there can be significant shifts of membership and of geographical centre of gravity in quite short periods. Similarly, individual states may 'decline' from semi-peripheral to peripheral status, while others are correspondingly 'promoted'. The whole world economy is potentially expansive, so areas in the external arena may themselves in time be incorporated in the periphery.

This is not the place to discuss the details of Wallerstein's account of European capitalist expansion since the 'great transformation' of European economies, which he places in the 16th century, though it should be noted that it has sparked a considerable debate. What is of more relevance here is the applicability of Wallerstein's model and its concepts to earlier, pre-capitalist societies. These were not Wallerstein's main concern; indeed in places he seems to regard the world economy model as inappropriate to them. 'We have insisted that the modern world economy is, and can only be, a capitalist world economy' (Wallerstein 1974, p. 350). He is, however, prepared to admit that there were some, presumably very few, pre-capitalist, pre-modern world economies, though he argues that they were all transformed into world empires by political expansion; he cites in particular China, Persia and Rome (Wallerstein 1974, p. 16). The contrast is therefore between the economic integration of modern world systems in the form of world economies, and the essentially political nature of those in pre-modern times.

In extending the debate on centre–periphery relations to archaeology, and attempting to assess the utility of the model for pre-modern societies, we clearly have to consider the validity of Wallerstein's simple division of social systems into an opposition between small-scale subsistence economies which are not part of a tribute-demanding structure on the one hand, and world systems on the other. This is particularly important in the light of his insistence that the only form of world system to have existed to any significant degree in pre-modern times was the world empire. It would not take long to think of a variety of possible asymmetric relationships between social groups, and of historical examples of them, which do not fit easily into such a simple dichotomous classification. We also have to ask whether there might not in the past have been world systems with the economic structures of world economies which were not coterminous with world empires and did not resolve themselves into world empires. In any case, even if only a few such pre-capitalist world economies did exist, then the circumstances in which they came into being, and in which they were in turn transformed into world empires, are also matters of considerable interest.

The crux of the question is whether Wallerstein was right in asserting that the modern pre-capitalist world economy was the only true embodiment of the world economy version of the world system, or whether he did not thereby exclude large tracts of past human existence from a potentially meaningful analysis. Clearly, though, if the concept of a world economy were to be applied to pre-capitalist societies, it would need to be generalized and freed from the culture-specific capitalist formulations of centre and periphery, and of the relationships between them, which dominate Wallerstein's discussion.

Posed in this way, the question can be situated in the long-standing, but somewhat sterile, debates about substantivist or formalist approaches to the discussion of past economies and about primitivist or modernist assessments of their scale. Wallerstein's view of pre-capitalist economies would place him firmly in the substantivist and primitivist camps; he would hold that the nature of pre-modern economies was qualitatively different from that of modern economies and hence cannot be analysed in the terms developed appropriately for the contemporary world, and in particular that the degree of commercial activity in the ancient economy was minimal. It would be futile to argue that there were not major differences between modern capitalist economies and those of past pre-capitalist societies, but in our desire to emphasize the differentness of the past, we should not lose sight of the possibility of similarity and continuity. After all, the world economy which Wallerstein saw developing in the 16th century itself grew out of a network of economic relationships centred on the Mediterranean (Hodges & Whitehouse 1983), which was certainly of a qualitatively different nature but was nonetheless of critical importance in the emergence of early medieval Europe. There do not in fact seem to be any a priori grounds why we should not expect to find world economies of a non-capitalist kind in the pre-capitalist world; Wallerstein did not find any because he was not concerned to look for them.

In a perceptive review of Wallerstein's original book, Schneider (1977) has suggested that Wallerstein gave too great an emphasis to the uniqueness of the western European expansion, and that his work 'suffers from too narrow an application of its own theory'. Her own main concern was with the period immediately prior to that of Wallerstein's study, and she argued that he systematically underestimated the scale and consequences of pre-capitalist exchanges, and in particular that he had misconceived the critical importance of luxury goods. Wallerstein (1974, p. 306) had, for instance, described the Russian fur trade of the 16th century, one of the 'rich trades', as 'an exchange of preciosities, a method of consuming surplus rather than producing it, hence dispensable at moments of contraction, and consequently not central to the functioning of the economic system'. Schneider argues that this denial of the importance of the rôle of so-called luxury goods led to a failure by Wallerstein to understand the process of initial European expansion in search of such items as spices. To archaeologists familiar with the debate over the rôle of prestige goods in the structuring of social relations, and the close connection between such luxury goods and other items of production, even if they are not mutually exchangeable, any denial of their importance is even stranger.

The contrast between luxury and utilitarian goods is not in fact an absolute one; they are, rather, two opposite ends of a spectrum. Individual items are not to be categorized as either luxury or utilitarian on the basis of any immutable physical property or necessity for biological survival: meaning is given to them by the rôle they play in the social relations of a specific society at a specific time. Furs and textiles do not only fulfil a functional, utilitarian need for clothing, but can take on a variety of social-specific meanings. Similarly, consumable items such as wine or spices, or particular types of meat or fish, can be valued both as nutrition and as a social statement. Nor should we assume that even the category of 'utilitarian' is unproblematic; as Rowlands (1987) has argued, Mesopotamia's shortage of basic raw materials such as stone and metal would not necessarily imply a need to ensure regular imports, unless we knew the purposes to which they were put and their importance for the social reproduction of the state. Equally, the critical rôle played by 'luxury goods' in the economic system is not to be measured in purely quantitative terms of volume, nor does it determine the degree to which they can be considered utilitarian rather than luxury goods. Some luxuries have the potential to be transformed into more utilitarian products, and themselves to transform social relations. In many prehistoric Near Eastern and European societies copper seems to have followed such a course, while more recently, as Mintz (1985) has shown, sugar has passed from being a 'luxury' used for medicinal, flavouring, and decorative purposes to become the basis of plantation economies in the periphery and a key element in the new patterns of diet, employment, and social relations of the industrial world in the core. To raise a graded distinction between luxury and utilitarian goods to the level of absolute opposition and then to deny the economic importance of luxury goods may, as Schneider argued, have misrepresented the medieval and modern picture, but its effect is potentially much more serious for our understanding of pre-capitalist societies.

Diffusionism reinvented?

It has been suggested by Renfrew (1986, p. 6) that the concept of centre and periphery is an example of the diffusionist thinking of the old-fashioned culture–historical school in a new guise, with its emphasis on exogenous change. It is, of course, much more than that: as already mentioned, it is one way of proceeding in an attempt to escape the aridity of neo-evolutionary theories of social development, and to recognize the importance of the specific context of social and political relationships in which real historical actors operated. Somewhat similar aims could also be claimed for Renfrew's own concept of peer polity interaction, which recognizes that social change can be produced not only endogenously but also through external relationships, though here the emphasis is on connections within a cluster of autonomous polities equal in structural terms if not equal in actual economic, political, or military power. It is significant than many of the case studies analysed to assess the utility of the peer polity concept (Renfrew & Cherry 1986) in fact concern clusters of polities which were peripheral to more developed regions (e.g. Iron Age Europe). It was suggested that those external relationships had an important rôle to play in initiating or maintaining the internal processes of development through peer polity interaction; competitive emulation or a network of alliances among peer polities might well produce a marked similarity of socio-economic development or a shared set of political or ideological values, but the stimulus to such change among the cluster of polities as a whole came from interactions with an area outside that cluster. There does not seem to be any a priori reason to reject what those empirical examples as well as many other historical situations would suggest, namely that processes of endogenous change can include relationships between polities of unequal status as well as those of equal status (in terms of the structure of the model, if not on any scale of 'evolution' or 'development').

The fundamental question concerns the correct scale of analysis. Whereas evolutionary explanations have emphasized the trajectory followed by a single polity, and have sought to find the causes of change internally, the centre and periphery model, like the peer polity model, recognizes a larger framework of social organization which can generate its own internal patterns of change. In the terminology of systems, centre–periphery relations should not be regarded as exogenous, either to the centre or to the periphery; rather, the system itself is larger than any single society or polity. Centre–periphery relations are integral to it, and explanations which rely on the historical elucidation of such relations are themselves dealing with endogenous change, not invoking external causes.

It is nevertheless instructive to try to specify in what ways an analysis of centre–periphery relationships is superior to an old-fashioned diffusionist explanation. The arguments against diffusionist thinking were partly empirical, in that they simply did not fit the pattern of facts which archaeology was progressively revealing, as Renfrew (1973), for instance, argued in the case of the impact of radiocarbon dating on our perception of the traditional chronological relationships of European prehistory. They also arose partly from a realization of the theoretical importance of endogenous factors. In both cases, however, the objections were to the inappropriate or exaggerated reliance on diffusionist ideas to the exclusion of others, rather than to the inadequacy of such ideas in general. Far more serious was the failure of diffusionist explanations to offer any description in real social terms of the precise social context in which the relationships were played out. Diffusion could either be elevated to some suprahistorical force which did not need further analysis, or it could be provided with some mechanism such as migration, invasion, or acculturation, which was in turn frequently felt not to need any more detailed account. The transformation of diffusion as the observation of static patterns of similarities in the archaeological record into diffusion as the explanation of dynamic social change was easy but fundamentally flawed, since it failed to give an adequate account of change in terms appropriate to the nature of prehistoric societies.

It is important that centre–periphery analyses do not share the same flaws; core and periphery or the world economy are not to be elevated to suprahistorical forces, operating universally and not in need of specific analysis in any given context. On the other hand, these concepts do provide a general framework within which it is possible to analyse in very precise terms the specific conditions in which the relationships between polities at different levels of economic, political or technological development did, in specific cases, produce changes in those polities. That is the aim of the various chapters in this book, and it is clear from the insights they provide that the concept, either as a framework for understanding past social change or as a heuristic device for investigating it, has great utility. It is not just a tried and discredited idea in new terminological clothes, but an intellectually stimulating theme for elucidating a detailed understanding of past social change.

Archaeological applications

Wallerstein's concept of core and periphery is, as discussed above, an integral part of his theory of a uniquely capitalist world economy. To develop its application to archaeological examples of pre-capitalist societies, it is clearly necessary to free it from this culturally specific form and to generalize it. The broader idea of a world system, embodying a centre and a periphery, will then provide a conceptual framework for the analysis of past societies, but will need to be defined in specific terms appropriate to each historical context. The very concept of a world system implies a scale of analysis far larger than a single polity or cluster of polities, and the contrast inherent in the concept of core and periphery, differentiating two aspects of a relationship which is itself the primary entity of archaeological interest, implies not just a spatial separation but a difference in the nature of social organization. The precise form that the system takes, and the nature of the relationships which structure it, are likely to have been very varied in the past.

The centre–periphery model has already been a fruitful source of archaeological insight, as is shown in the chapters in this book and elsewhere (see e.g. Rowlands *et al.* 1987 for an important series of Old World studies). In much of this work, the interest has moved away from Wallerstein's concern with trade, and has concentrated more on the growth and nature of long-distance interactions and their capacity for producing social transformations, on the interrelationship of cycles of economic activity in spatially distant areas, and on diachronic patterns in the location of power centres (Frankenstein & Rowlands 1978, Gledhill 1978, Kristiansen 1982). This is not due to the technical problems of quantifying the level of prehistoric and early historic exchange, though these are without doubt considerable. Even in those areas where substantial bodies of documentary evidence exist, for example in the Near East (Larsen 1987), the record can be very patchy; for those areas where no documents ever existed, or none survive today, the problem is far worse. The only source of evidence is archaeology, and recovery of relevant information will depend not only on modern excavation techniques and strategies, but also on past behavioural practices with regard to the deposition of such materials in an archaeologically recoverable way, and on the very nature of the exchanged items themselves. Many of these were organic, such as furs, timber, textiles, or slaves, and hence only rarely survive in an archaeologically recognizable form, making any estimate of the scale of 'trade' or the accumulation of capital impossible.

Nor is this shift of emphasis due to some espousal of a simple primitivist view that exchange was not materially important in the ancient economies. Rather, it follows from an assessment of the different possibilities of exploiting economic activities in the ancient and modern worlds. Kohl (1987, p. 23), for example, has argued that economic development and dependency could not be linked in the ancient world as they can now, because of specific differences in the nature of technologies, such as metallurgy, which could not be so easily limited to create spatial variations in technological competence, or in the nature of transport facilities, or in the availability of sources of power, such as the horse, which could be exploited on the periphery to change the structure of the system. The specific nature of ancient economy and technology in many cases simply did not allow economic power to be wielded in the way that is possible in the modern world. As Kohl has argued, the development of underdevelopment was itself underdeveloped in Bronze Age Asia. Hence archaeological interest, though still focused on exchange, both for its importance in social and political relations, and for its visibility in the archaeological record (at least in the case of some items), has also turned to broader questions of political dependence.

At the same time, archaeology has shown a greater interest in the historical development of the periphery. Wallerstein himself was little concerned with the actual transformations of societies outside the core of his world economy, though something of this history as seen from the periphery has been provided by Wolf (1982). Similar studies in the nature of reaction to the expansion of the core and the transformation of local peripheral institutions through interaction with it have been undertaken in archaeology, for instance by Hedaeger (1987) and Haselgrove (1982, 1987) for northern and northwestern Europe outside the Roman world. As several of the chapters in this book show – McGuire's Chapter 2 on the American Southwest, Dincauze and Hasenstab's Chapter 3 on the Iroquois, Whitehouse and Wilkins's Chapter 5 on south Italian responses to Greek colonization – concepts of centre and periphery in a world system can provide an insight into the nature of social change in the periphery.

To allow such an analysis to proceed beyond the banal invocation of centre–periphery relations as an explanation for observed change, a procedure no better than an appeal to diffusion, it is necessary to develop analytical concepts appropriate to these archaeological cases that will allow these general ideas to be made specific and put into practice. One such concept of importance is that of a prestige-goods economy (Ekholm 1977, Frankenstein & Rowlands 1978, Gledhill 1978). Such economies, indeed, seem particularly common on the fringe of early states and empires, and are a regular means of articulating societies with very different structures of economic and social organization. Within such economies, prestige goods circulate in a variety of contexts, in a system which associates them closely with status. The nature of the relationship between exchange and hierarchy may be complex; Rowlands (1987), for example, has discussed the rôle of the circulation of prestige items in societies which stress inalienable rights as a means of creating social dependencies. Nor can it be assumed that the nature of the exchanges within which such goods circulate will necessarily be clear-cut; Larsen (1987) has argued that many of the commodities exchanged in Mesopotamia were both a source of commercial profit and a means of defining social statuses. The coexistence of different types of exchange within a single society has long been recognized, but the particular problems of characterizing the nature of prestige-goods systems and their relationship to other systems is a major question for archaeology.

Nevertheless, the concept of prestige-goods economies has proved a valuable one. Both Dietler in Chapter 6, dealing with the export of wine from southern France to central Europe in the early Iron Age, and Williams in Chapter 7, studying the wine trade beyond the frontiers of the early Roman empire, stress the rôle played by this item in the reorganization of hierarchical societies in the periphery. McGuire too, in his study of the American Southwest in Chapter 2, stresses the vital nature of the supply of prestige goods from the south for the social reproduction of Anasazi communities.

It is necessary not only to develop an appropriate analysis for the relationship of the prestige goods exchanges to the rest of the economy, but also to find ways of characterizing the economy of the periphery and describing transformations in it. Wolf (1982) has suggested the concept of mode of production, and in particular the specific formulation of kin-ordered and tributary modes, as being appropriate for the analysis of the economies of such peripheral societies. Following Wolf, McGuire in Chapter 2 develops the notion of a kin-ordered mode of production, and the varieties of relationship within it, in the context of the American Southwest. The importance of these concepts is that they offer a far more useful way of discussing the social and economic organization of peripheral societies than the notion of redistribution associated with the chiefdom level of political organization proposed by Service (1962), and criticized by Earle (1977) and Carneiro (1981). Wolf (1982, pp. 97–9) stresses the possibility for chiefs to transcend the limitations of the kin-ordered mode and transform their status differential into one of class in a tributary mode, if they can acquire some independent power over resources and some new mechanism of power. The new possibilities opened up for such chiefs by interactions with an expanding periphery, with the possibility of control over new resources or new forms of prestige goods or knowledge, or new sources of political power through alliances, provide exactly the sort of context in which such transformations might occur.

In addition to the prestige goods systems already mentioned, Dincauze and Hasenstab in Chapter 3 discuss the importance of maize agriculture and the skills it requires, while Havlík in Chapter 13 describes the rôle of the introduction of Christianity into early medieval Moravia. The new religion was closely associated with the recently consolidated kingship, as the physical proximity of palace and churches and the burial of royalty in the nave of a church testify, and was a powerful instrument in legitimating and expanding royal power.

Recognizing centre and periphery

The concept of centre and periphery has now been so widely used that it is necessary to think about its definition in specific contexts. Even in the modern world there is no automatic correlation between political centres and areas of highest economic investment or technological advance; indeed, the peripheral areas will often be the most technologically advanced, as the capitalist economy seeks to take advantage of variations in the costs of labour and raw materials and to promote a geographical specialization and division of labour. Similarly in Wallerstein's world economies it was control of the investment and of the economic institutions by the core areas, and the channelling to them of the produced surplus, that characterized their status, rather than the physical location of any of these things at a geographical centre. In modifying Wallerstein's model to suit the conditions of pre-capitalist societies, we would still expect the core areas to be net consumers of the products of the periphery, and to be the dominant partners in the network of political relationships of which the exchange may be the visible manifestation, while the peripheries are the net providers and the dominated partners. How, though, are we to recognize such patterns in the archaeological record?

As mentioned above, archaeology has been only minimally concerned with questions of the volume of trade in centre–periphery relationships. Quantifying the volume may be difficult, but the making of comparisons in order to estimate the extent of inequality in the exchange is going to be even more so. In any case the exchanges may have been subjectively seen by the participants as being fair and balanced, if not of particular advantage to their own side. The amazement of the Greeks, for instance, recorded by Diodorus Siculus (V. 26, 2–3), at the willingness of the barbarian Celts to accept as little as one amphora of wine for a slave was probably matched by a similar surprise on the part of the Celts. For most archaeological analyses the exchanged items and the balance between them have been of less importance than the actual exchanges and the political relationships within which they took place. But how are those relationships to be recognized, and how is the nature of domination in the relationship to be defined if the archaeologically visible material is not an adequate source of evidence? This may not be a problem if the centre–periphery model is being used as a heuristic framework for organizing and furthering our understanding of the past, but if it is not to become totally vacuous, the question of domination and inequality must be faced. The inequality may lie not in the balance of trade, nor in the costs of participating, but more in the costs that would be incurred in trying to extricate oneself from the relationship. Just as the capitalist economy can create an economic dependency through the establishment of a geographical division of labour and the export of goods from the centre, so the political structures involved in pre-capitalist centre–periphery systems can ensnare the periphery ever more firmly and make it dependent on the centre for social, or even biological, reproduction, because of a lack of any suitable alternative. It is a characteristic of many, though by no means all, peripheries that they are not presented with opportunities for similar interactions with a plurality of centres, while the centre may well have other possibilities for meeting its needs; hence there is an asymmetry in the relationship, which leads to dependence. Both Randsborg in Chapter 12 on Denmark and Szynkiewicz in Chapter 8 on nomadic relationships with China discuss the oscillation between trading and raiding, as peripheries turn to military force to maintain the access to items from the centre on which they have come to depend. In the latter case, the nomadic dependence on China for essential foodstuffs was such that it could be used as an overt mechanism of political control. McGuire's treatment (Ch. 2) of the Anasazi *katsina* religion as a crisis cult which arose in the face of cessation of contacts with the south again underlines the strength of the dependence that had been produced.

One question implicit in the discussion in several of the chapters in this book is the extent to which we impose a pattern of centre and periphery analysis, in which the centre is defined as much by the preconceptions of our own culturally determined vision of the past and other societies as by any objective set of criteria for defining it and recognizing it in the archaeological record. As has already been remarked, the concept of the centre is well established in Western thought, and the centre is frequently endowed with culture-specific values. Oppositions such as town/country, urban/provincial, civilized/uncivilized, classical/barbarian, are heavily value-laden and structure many of our patterns of thought. In particular, they influence our expectations about the nature of interactions in the prehistoric and early historic world, where metaphors such as 'ex oriente lux' and 'la rayonnement de la civilisation hellénique' are not uncommon, and clearly betray our attitudes to the past.

Thus in the case of the archaeologically and historically documented expansion of the Mediterranean world it has become common to speak in terms of 'hellenization' or 'romanization', as if such processes were natural, and Greece and Rome were naturally to be thought of as centres. Stoddart, in Chapter 4 on the emergence of Etruscan society, is at pains to refute this 'natural' assumption of an external causation for the development of a non-classical world, though it ultimately came to share much of classical civilization. His argument raises questions about the definition of the Mediterranean centre of European civilization in the first millennium BC; about whether, in fact, we are right to think exclusively in terms of a Greek centre, or whether there was a much more diffuse centre, including also Etruscans and Phoenicians, who have been excluded for reasons that have more to do with recent European perceptions of the true development of their history and culture. Similarly, Whitehouse and Wilkins in Chapter 5 question the notion of 'hellenization' and draw attention to the very limited spheres of interaction between the Greek colonies of southern Italy and their immediate neighbours. At a rather different level, Szynkiewicz in Chapter 8 raises the question of whether the characterization of the mutual dependence between the nomadic cultures and China as a centre–periphery relationship is derived from the Chinese view of the world as sharply divided into themselves and the outside. We might also ask whether our own culturally determined attitude to sedentary farmers predisposes us to regard the Chinese state as a centre, and the extent to which this is a useful description of the reality of their external relations.

One quite specific problem raised by our own perception of historical development concerns the terminology to be applied to interacting populations, especially where a centre is expanding. As Whitehouse and Wilkins point out in Chapter 5, the term 'native' carries colonial overtones of either a romantic or a pejorative nature, while 'indigenous' suggests permanent and everlasting presence; 'aboriginal' has the same problems, while other terms such as 'local' are vague. It does not seem appropriate, or even possible, to fix on a single term to describe all the varied contexts discussed in this book, so usage will inevitably vary. If we cannot remove all the cultural overtones from our terminology, we must be aware of them, and prevent them from allowing our language to influence the way we view other societies.

The rôle of the semi-periphery

The concept of the semi-periphery has played little part in the archaeological adaptation of Wallerstein's ideas, though it was an important part of his world system. It served to protect the core from pressures from the periphery, and bore some of the costs of running the system. Dietler's analysis (Ch. 6) of the wine trade in the south of France pays full attention to the zone lying between the prime producers on the coast and the ultimate destination of some of the wine in central Europe. He stresses its economic and social, as well as its geographical, centrality – a centrality characterized by a different pattern of consumption and discard in the archaeological record.

Dincauze and Hasenstab (Ch. 3) raise similar questions concerning the actual nature of long-distance connections and the rôle of the sites on the fringe of the Cahokia region. Their estimate of a 40-day travel time from the centre to the Iroquoian periphery corresponds with Wallerstein's discussion (1974, pp. 16–17) of 60 days as a possible upper limit (whatever the transport technology available at any time or place), and Braudel's (1972, p. 355) estimate of 70–80 days for communication between the eastern and western peripheries of the Mediterranean world. Within such a large system, the sub-centres of the Cahokia world, intermediate between the centre and the Iroquoian periphery, may perhaps be regarded as a form of semi-periphery.

The power of the semi-periphery to divert exchange in its own interest is well exemplified by McGuire's discussion (Ch. 2) of the consequences of the rise of Casas Grandes. Archaeological research will have to pay much more attention to the social and political rôle of such intermediate communities and their capacity for inducing very significant changes in the nature of their peripheries.

The incorporation of the periphery

As Wallerstein emphasized, centre–periphery systems are not static. Recent archaeological debate has paid comparatively little attention to the questions involved in the diachronic development of such systems, though Nash (1987) and Haselgrove (1987) have explored the political expansion of Rome into western Europe and the establishment of ever more remote peripheries. Some of the systems described in this book were comparatively short-lived, such as the Mississippian system in the eastern United States (Ch. 3) and the Southwestern link to Mesoamerica (Ch. 2), but others were more enduring. Szynkiewicz (Ch. 8) describes one process of expansion, that of the Chinese state; administrative and military costs prohibited further political expansion, and the periphery was subordinated by the strategic control of trade. By contrast, the nomadic pastoralists of the periphery could regularly pose a severe military threat to the centre, but could not for long administer any gains they might make.

The process of Roman expansion and incorporation in western Europe does not serve as a model for the rest of the Empire. Two chapters in this book discuss one particular region of southeastern Europe. Winter and Bankoff (Ch. 9) explore the changing nature of the relationship of Serbia in modern Yugoslavia to the Mediterranean world. They argue that after the first penetration of the region in search of raw materials, it was the specific nature of the local economy, with a primary importance placed on the extraction of raw materials, especially metals, rather than on the growth of productive industries, that determined the course of later social development. Bartel's study of Roman expansion in the same region (Ch. 10) concentrates on the variety of policies implemented in response to the varying economic and strategic importance of different zones. This produces an elegant general model, widely applicable in situations of colonial and imperial expansion, which could be tested in other areas with potentially interesting results. Farnsworth's detailed study (Ch. 11) of material culture change in the Franciscan missions of California in the wake of military and religious enforcement of a European economy represents one example of Bartel's model of acculturation. These chapters show clearly how the precise nature of the mechanisms by which the centre seeks to penetrate and subject the periphery will affect the transformations wrought on peripheral society.

The decline of the core

Spatio-temporal shifts in the location of power, with the decline of an old core and the emergence of a new one on the periphery, are an accepted part of our vision of the historical development of the Western world, if not of elsewhere. The shift westward in the Mediterranean, then to northern and northwestern Europe, then to the United States is well known, if not precisely formulated in so many words. The emergence of Europe is indeed a major theme of historical and sociological writing (e.g. Jones 1981, Hall 1985, Mann 1986), but archaeology too has its rôle to play. Randsborg's study (Ch. 12) is concerned with the correlations of the cycles of economic activity within the Empire and its northern periphery, and the interplay of local development within northern Europe and external connections. Havlík's Chapter 13 highlights the critical rôle of Christianity in providing a means of integrating politically autonomous societies over a wide area and in offering norms for the whole social order, a point made more generally by Hall (1985, pp. 121–6). On the other hand, the lack of an overarching political authority, and even more the presence of two competing cores in the Eastern and Western Empires, allowed Moravia a period of competitive aggression through which it achieved a position of considerable power.

An assessment

As the chapters in this book demonstrate, archaeologists have found the concept of centre and periphery to be a fruitful one in analysing a wide variety of specific historical cases. Though it raises many detailed questions concerning the precise formulation of the relationships involved, and in particular concerning the connection between exchange and hierarchy and the articulation of different systems of exchange inside and outside a society, it offers a potential framework for understanding the processes of economic and political development in many different societies. Such explanations could, in theory, offer an account of a variety of processes familiar to archaeologists, including the emergence of states, cyclic patterns of very extensive cultural homogeneity, especially in prestige items, and spatio-temporal shifts in power centres.

For this potential to be realized, however, there are some important prerequisites. The very large scale of the appropriate unit of analysis, the world system, will in many cases embrace archaeological evidence which is traditionally separated into different spatial, chronological, or cultural specialisms. Thus the later prehistory of Europe cannot be sensibly split into Bronze Age and Iron Age compartments, since the patterns of cyclic growth and contraction ignore such divisions; equally, it may be impossible to understand temperate Europe without the Mediterranean world or the Near East. Research programmes will have to face this difficulty, and also the very different standards of data recovery and presentation that exist within established disciplinary subdivisions.

At the same time, the widening of the scale of enquiry should not blind us to the subtleties of regional variations within the system. More attention will have to be paid to the variations in the regional patterns of production, consumption, and discard to form a proper social context for the observed archaeological remains. Distribution maps will not reveal world systems unless it is possible to give a detailed account of how the material being mapped was produced and consumed throughout the entire system.

These, however, are challenges that archaeology should face. For archaeology alone has the potential to reveal the processes of the development of human society throughout most of its past, and many of the most useful types of evidence for this kind of enquiry, especially prestige goods, are precisely the kind of thing that archaeology is best equipped to study.

References

Braudel, F. 1972. *The Mediterranean and the Mediterranean world in the age of Philip II*. 2nd edition. London: Collins.

Carneiro, R. L. 1981. The chiefdom: precursor of the state. In *The transition to statehood in the New World*, G. D. Jones & P. R. Kautz (eds), 37–79. Cambridge: Cambridge University Press.

Cherry, J. F. 1987. Power in space: studies of the state. In *Landscape and culture: geographical and archaeological perspectives*, J. M. Wagstaff (ed.), 146–72. Oxford: Basil Blackwell.

Christaller, W. 1966. *Central places in southern Germany*. Englewood Cliffs, NJ: Prentice Hall.

Earle, T. K. 1977. A reappraisal of redistribution: complex Hawaiian chiefdoms. In *Exchange systems in prehistory*, T. K. Earle & J. E. Ericson (eds), 213–32. New York: Academic Press.

Ekholm, K. 1977. External exchange and the transformation of central African social systems. In *The evolution of social systems*, J. Friedman & M. J. Rowlands (eds), 115–36. London: Duckworth.

Frank, A. G. 1967. *Capitalism and underdevelopment in Latin America: historical studies of Chile and Brazil*. New York: Monthly Review Press.

Frankenstein, S. & M. Rowlands 1978. The internal structure and regional context of Early Iron Age society in southwest Germany. *Bulletin of the Institute of Archaeology, London University* **15**, 73–112.

Gledhill, J. 1978. Formative development in the North American Southwest. In *Social organisation and settlement*, D. Green, C. Haselgrove & M. Spriggs (eds), 241–90. British Archaeological Reports International Series **47**, Oxford.

Gottmann, J. 1980. *Centre and periphery: spatial variation in politics*. Beverly Hills and London: Sage.

Hall, J. 1985. *Powers and liberties: the causes and consequences of the rise of the West*. Oxford: Basil Blackwell.

Haselgrove, C. 1982. Wealth, prestige and power: the dynamics of political centralisation in south-east England. In *Ranking, resource and exchange*, A. C. Renfrew & S. J. Shennan (eds), 79–88. Cambridge: Cambridge University Press.

Haselgrove, C. 1987. Culture process on the periphery: Belgic Gaul and Rome during the late Republic and early Empire. In *Centre and periphery in the ancient world*, M. Rowlands, M. Larsen & K. Kristiansen (eds), 104–24. Cambridge: Cambridge University Press.

Hedaeger, L. 1987. Empire, frontier and the barbarian hinterland: Rome and northern Europe from AD 1–400. In *Centre and periphery in the ancient world*, M. Rowlands, M. Larsen & K. Kristiansen (eds), 125–40. Cambridge: Cambridge University Press.

Higgs, E. & C. Vita-Finzi 1970. Prehistoric economy in the Mount Carmel area of Palestine: site catchment analysis. *Proceedings of the Prehistoric Society* **36**, 1–37.

Hirth, K. G. 1978. Inter-regional trade and the formulation of prehistoric gateway communities. *American Antiquity* **43**, 25–45.

Hodges, R. 1987. Spatial models, anthropology and archaeology. In *Landscape and culture: geographical and archaeological perspectives*, J. M. Wagstaff (ed.), 118–33. Oxford: Basil Blackwell.

Hodges, R. & D. Whitehouse 1983. *Muhammad, Charlemagne and the rise of Europe*. London: Duckworth.

Johnson, G. A. 1981. Monitoring complex system integration and boundary phenomena with settlement data. In *Archaeological approaches to the study of complexity*, S. E. van der Leeuw (ed.), 143–88. Amsterdam: University of Amsterdam.

Jones, E. L. 1981. *The European miracle*. Cambridge: Cambridge University Press.

Kohl, P. 1987. The ancient economy, transferable technologies and the Bronze Age world system: a view from the northeastern frontier of the ancient Near East. In *Centre and periphery in the ancient world*, M. Rowlands, M. Larsen & K. Kristiansen (eds), 13–24. Cambridge: Cambridge University Press.

Kristiansen, K. 1982. The formation of tribal systems in later European prehistory: northern Europe 4000–500 BC. In *Theory and explanation in archaeology*, A. C. Renfrew, M. Rowlands & B. A. Segraves (eds), 241–80. New York and London: Academic Press.

Larsen, M. 1987. Commercial networks in the ancient Near East. In *Centre and periphery in the ancient world*, M. Rowlands, M. Larsen & K. Kristiansen (eds), 47–56. Cambridge: Cambridge University Press.

Mann, M. 1986. *The sources of social power: a history of power from the beginning to AD 1760*. Cambridge: Cambridge University Press.

Mintz, S. 1985. *Sweetness and power: the place of sugar in modern history*. New York: Viking.

Nash, D. 1987. Imperial expansion under the Roman Republic. In *Centre and periphery in the ancient world*, M. Rowlands, M. Larsen & K. Kristiansen (eds), 87–103. Cambridge: Cambridge University Press.

Polanyi, K. 1957. *Trade and markets in the early empires*. Chicago: Chicago University Press.

Renfrew, A. C. 1973. *Before civilisation: the radiocarbon revolution and prehistoric Europe*. London: Cape.

Renfrew, A. C. 1982. Socio-economic change in ranked societies. In *Ranking, resource and exchange*, A. C. Renfrew & S. J. Shennan (eds), 1–8. Cambridge: Cambridge University Press.

Renfrew, A. C. 1986. Introduction: peer polity interaction and socio-political change. In *Peer polity interaction and socio-political change*, A. C. Renfrew & J. F. Cherry (eds), 1–18. Cambridge: Cambridge University Press.

Renfrew, A. C. & J. F. Cherry (eds) 1986. *Peer polity interaction and socio-political change*. Cambridge: Cambridge University Press.

Rowlands, M. 1987. Centre and periphery: a review of the concept. In *Centre and periphery in the ancient world*, M. Rowlands, M. Larsen & K. Kristiansen (eds), 1–11. Cambridge: Cambridge University Press.

Rowlands, M., M. Larsen & K. Kristiansen (eds) 1987. *Centre and periphery in the ancient world*. Cambridge: Cambridge University Press.

Schneider, J. 1977. Was there a pre-capitalist world system? *Peasant Studies* **6** (1), 20–9.

Service, E. R. 1962. *Primitive social organisation: an evolutionary perspective*. New York: Random House.

Smith, C. A. 1976. *Regional analysis*. New York and London: Academic Press.

Steponaitis, V. 1978. Location theory and complex chiefdoms: a Mississippian example. In *Mississippian settlement patterns*, B. D. Smith (ed.), 417–53. New York: Academic Press.

Strassoldo, R. 1980. Centre–periphery and system–boundary: culturological perspectives. In *Centre and periphery: spatial variation in politics*, J. Gottmann (ed.), 27–61. Beverly Hills and London: Sage.

von Thuenen, W. 1826. *Die isolierte Staat in Beziehung auf Landwirtschaft und Nationaloekonomie*. Hamburg.

Toynbee, A. 1954. *A study of history*, vol. 8. Oxford: Oxford University Press.

Wallerstein, I. 1974. *The modern world-system*, vol. 1. New York: Academic Press.

Wolf, E. R. 1982. *Europe and the people without history*. Berkeley: University of California Press.

1 *Metropole and margin: the dependency theory and the political economy of the Solomon Islands, 1880–1980*

JAMES A. BOUTILIER

Introduction

The Solomon Islands are one of the major island groups of the south Pacific with a population of 225 000 and a land area of 28 530 square km. They were a British protectorate for 85 years from 1893 to 1978, when they gained their political independence. Outwardly, the history of the islands accords closely with the neo-Marxist dependency theory which maintains, *inter alia*, that colonial territories were exploited for their human and natural resources in order to advance the welfare of the metropolitan power. The establishment of a large-scale plantation economy by international firms and the recruitment of Solomon Islanders for labour service at home and abroad seems to fit this classic model. Furthermore, the dependency theory argues that the current state of underdevelopment of Third World nations is directly attributable to the continued economic imbalance in the relationship between the imperial centre and the territorial periphery.

To what extent, however, was this actually the case with respect to the Solomon Islands? Was their experience really congruent with the dependency model? I attempt to answer this question below. While I focus on the political economy of the islands, particularly in the period prior to World War II, I do not wish to imply that the imperial and post-imperial relationship was a purely economic one. Like Galtung, I would argue that political and social forces can be converted into economic ones and vice-versa (Blomström & Hettne 1984, p. 177), although the scope of this chapter does not permit extended reference to these other forces.

Traditional Solomon Islands 'society'

The Solomon Islands are for the most part high, rugged, jungle-clad islands. The inhabitants on the eve of sustained contact with the European world were mainly of Melanesian stock, living in scattered hamlets in the interior or in tiny settlements by the sea. They were slash-and-burn horticulturalists and fisherfolk whose 'society' was fragmented into dozens of societies by differences in language, culture, and social organization (Lasaqa 1972, p. 7). Their economy was a subsistence one capable of generating modest surpluses for ceremonial purposes. There was relatively little division of labour and what there was was mainly along gender lines (Howard 1983a, p. 6). The islanders had a highly developed sense of place and commitment to kin and those who had gone before. Propitiation of ghosts and spirits was part of the daily round and in this they were encouraged and assisted by the principal political figure in the community, the big-man. Melanesian politics was essentially egalitarian. In theory any man could aspire to big-man status and big-men achieved and retained their positions of authority by virtue of their demonstrated leadership and largess. Members of the community were bound by bonds of blood and the demands of complex networks of reciprocal obligation.

What is significant is that while there were trade networks linking communities (which otherwise would have viewed one another with hostility), Solomon Islands societies were very nearly self-sustaining economically, and the ethos of production was one of collectivism (Keesing n.d., p. 7). There was no tradition of wage labour. There was, of course, wealth but that was of a largely ceremonial sort. And there was no sense of societal divisions in terms of class. Solomon Islands societies were conservative, autonomous, and limited in their areal horizons. It was this world then – 100 000 or so islanders scattered in isolated communities over 1500 km – that was drawn unwillingly into the world capitalist system.

Dependency theory: the 'development of underdevelopment'

Over the past 40 years social scientists have tried with varying degrees of success to develop models which would explain the workings of the global economy with reference to the relationship between the developed and underdeveloped world. That relationship was the result of three phases of European commercial expansion extending over a period of 500 years. The first or merchant capital phase was largely synonymous with the first age of European empire-building and lasted from the 15th to the 18th century. The principal motivation of this phase was the search for foreign produce, and the overseas trade generated thereby constituted an 'exogenous contribution to western Europe's capital accumulation' (Hoogvelt 1976, p. 69) which fuelled the Industrial Revolution and set the stage for the second or colonial phase of expansion.

The hallmark of the second phase was the desire to control markets. The emphasis was on administering dependencies in such a way that their produce and labour was harnessed for the benefit of the mother country. In Hoogvelt's words, colonialism involved 'subjugation by integration and integration by subjugation' (1976, p. 66). Planters, traders, missionaries, administrators, and businessmen were the principal actors in these processes. They employed a variety of strategies to effect the penetration and transformation of the traditional economies of the dependencies, and to render them subservient to metropolitan control (Brookfield 1972, p. 72). They inaugurated tax systems, intended ostensibly to render the colonial territories self-supporting economically, but designed in practice to drive the indigenes into the labour and cash-cropping markets. They promoted ideologies which were antithetical to the world view of collectively-oriented, subsistence agriculturalists and supportive of the individualistic, work ethic-related, capitalist system (Howard 1983a, p. 2). And they gained monopoly control over the production and marketing of a territory's produce on the one hand, and the introduction and sale of consumer goods therein on the other.

On a micro-scale, the effect of these changes was the abrupt undermining of local self-sufficiency and cultural integrity, and the creation of a dual economy consisting of a steadily diminishing subsistence sector and a lopsided 'modern' sector based upon the production of one or two primary products subject to volatile market conditions. On a macro-scale, the effect was global polarization, with the peoples of the world divided into developed and underdeveloped blocs and the capitalist–proletarian relationship replicated on a worldwide basis.

The third phase of capitalist expansion was the so-called neocolonial phase. During this phase (confined largely to the second half of the 20th century) former dependencies regained their political independence while remaining subject to high degrees of economic control by their one-time colonial masters and often also by transnational corporations and financial agencies. Ironically, most newly independent states were committed – voluntarily or involuntarily – to development programmes based on emulating Western achievements, a fact which further reinforced their dependence on the First World (Hoyle 1976, p. 81).

Development theories in the 1950s and early 1960s were 'grounded in the conservative and liberal ideologies of neo-classical and functional and diffusionist sociology' (Gardezi 1986, p. 136). The 'Blue' paradigm of development, as advanced by Walt Rostow, the author of *The stages of economic growth: a non-communist manifesto* (1960), chose to ignore 'the development implications of the co-existence of dominant rich and dependent poor countries in one integrated international economy and offer[ed] instead a linear conception of development in which poor countries were simply late starters' (Knapman 1986, p. 94).

This vision reflected the West's belief in progress. Development theories were simplistic, optimistic, and fashionable. The United Nations labelled the 1960s the Development Decade, and planners and practitioners alike awaited the moment when Third World economies, suitably stimulated by the new international division of labour (the 'branch plant' exodus of capital and of labour-intensive manufacturing from the developed world), would reach a point of 'take-off' and enjoy 'sustained growth'. Governments in ex-colonies embraced this vision and sought to achieve economic diversification and self-reliance by promoting exports and relying on foreign investment and aid.

'Take-off' and autarky, however, proved elusive. It soon became obvious that there was a fundamental incompatibility between the demands of economic rationality – on which the development plans were predicated – and the maintenance of traditional values. What was needed, it appeared, was an alternative model which would enable developing countries to achieve their goals. The very structure of the world economy seemed to be retarding their economies.

The evolution of that model, or paradigm shift, is best understood in its historical context. During the 1960s, as European empires were being dismantled and the Americans were being drawn deeper into Vietnam, there was not only a clear diminution of Western political dominance but an increased awareness of the illegitimacy of imperial mandates. That awareness was fostered in part by the remarkable growth in the number of Third World universities. The naïve optimism of the early 1960s gave way to pessimism and scepticism. There was a growing, and frequently uncritical, fascination on the part of Western observers with major exercises in social engineering and self-reliance like the Great Proletarian Cultural Revolution in China. A demand arose in the Western intellectual community to decolonize the social sciences and to view affairs in a holistic, interdisciplinary manner.

What emerged from this tumultuous decade was the dependency theory. That theory, the apparent answer to the inadequacy of existing developmental theories, owed its origins to economists in Latin America and particularly in Chile, the *dependentistas*. According to Smith (1978, p. 209):

> [the] dependency theory represents the intellectual meeting ground of Marxism and certain important forms of nationalism in the Third World, and it thereby serves as the ideological underpinning of a 'united front' among these groups directed against what it sees as the local power of northern imperialism.

There are several major features of the dependency theory that require highlighting. First, Smith's observations notwithstanding, the theory reflects a recognition of the theoretical poverty of Marxism *vis-à-vis* a study of non-European cultures (Blomström & Hettne 1984, p. 180). The mechanistic, linear, Eurocentric aspects of orthodox Marxism were practically demolished by Latin American neo-Marxists and their colleagues in the Caribbean and Africa. In keeping with Myrdal's call (cited in Blomström & Hettne 1984, p. 71) for broader analysis, the *dependentistas* embraced the holism of Hegel, who argued that the whole has a logic greater than the sum of the parts. Henceforth, the phenomenon of Third World underdevelopment was to be seen in a global context.

From that it followed that the relationship between the developed and underdeveloped world could no longer be overlooked, and further that the global economic system as promoted by the developed world was seen as the root of Third World underdevelopment. The neo-Marxist belief argued that:

> Western capitalism causes the development of underdevelopment in the dependent periphery of the world economy it has created. The underdevelopment mechanism invoked is elegantly simple. Monopoly capital profits, inflated by manipulation of terms of trade and repatriated to metropolitan capitalist countries or reinvested in the periphery in pursuit of future profit repatriation: and income, distributed unequally domestically, is spent on imports from metropolitan capitalist countries. On both counts the capitalist West received a development stimulus denied the periphery (Knapman 1986, p. 97).

The concept of 'centre' and 'periphery' was an analytical construct at the heart of the dependency theory. The centre represented the imperial power or metropole, the periphery its colonial handmaiden on the margin, and a dialectical flow existed between them which benefited the former and acted to the detriment of the latter. This construct was useful to a degree (and was taken up in a slightly altered form in the post-dependency, world system theory) but in a number of accounts it was treated too simplistically. One line of argument suggested, for example, that a periphery could simultaneously be a centre for a subsequent stage in an economic relationship. Furthermore, it was possible for territory to be on the intersection of two peripheries, one administrative and the other economic.

Raúl Prebisch was at the forefront in terms of elaborating the centre–periphery concept. He argued that for a number of reasons (the constraints of traditional land tenure, rapid population growth, premature imitation of the centre's consumption patterns, and political developments which were incongruent with economic performance) peripheral capitalism was 'unique' (Blomström & Hettne 1984, p. 172). Peripheral capitalism, according to Prebisch, was dual in nature.

> A large portion of the population finds itself outside the modern, dynamic sector (or in the terminology of the dependency school, it is 'marginalized') because it lacks the power to increase wages at the same rate as it increases productivity. This dualism in which a modern sector, with a dynamic of its own, has been placed 'on top of' a traditional sector, will continue to exist as long as there is peripheral capitalism which precludes any development that will benefit the entire population (Prebisch, cited in Blomström & Hettne 1984, p. 174).

Viewed another way, peripheral capitalism lacked organic legitimacy and was essentially imitative, while central capitalism, having evolved over an extended period, enjoyed organic stability and was innovative in character.

One thing which makes the dependency theory difficult to grasp is that there are almost as many variations on the theory as there are theorists. Put at its simplest, neo-Marxists disagree among themselves about the manner in which imperialism is to be held responsible for the continued underdevelopment of the Third World (Hoogvelt 1976, p. 83). Their positions, however, can generally be reduced to two points of view. The first maintains that the continued underdevelopment of the Third World is the result of the concentration of capital within the advanced world; that underdevelopment results from the invasion of too little capital rather than too much. The second maintains that 'it is no longer the imperialist rivalries between capitalist states, but that between the modern transnational corporations which determine the economic, political, and indeed the social reality of the world today' (*op. cit.* p. 84). As Hoogvelt notes, 'the secret behind the riddle of modern imperialism lies in the organization of giant transnational corporations and their practice to associate themselves in joint ventures with local – private as well as state – capital in underdeveloped countries' (*ibid.*).

Sunkel suggests that the theory of transnationalization provides a useful conceptual framework because it helps to explain a number of aspects of Third World underdevelopment (see Blomström & Hettne 1984, p. 175). One such aspect is the emergence of new political and commercial élites in ex-colonies. In many cases the members of these élites were carefully selected and groomed by the colonial authorities for their post-Independence responsibilities. Howard (1983a), Keesing (n.d.), and others argue that those élites act like Fanon's 'black colonials', advancing their own cause in association with transnationals at the expense of their own people and their traditional cultures.

In order to attract transnationals and support from international agencies like the Asian Development Bank, the Commonwealth Development Corporation, and the European Economic Community, it is necessary for those élites to create an appropriate investment climate in the host nation. This means, in practice, ensuring political stability by discouraging unions and opposition to government development schemes, promising cheap co-operative labour, and providing financial and infrastructural inducements. The upshot of this élite–transnational alignment is that nations on the periphery remain answerable to distant centres, and that development performance must be viewed critically. All too frequently there is growth without development, and the élites benefit while the people do not.

By the late 1970s the dependency school was virtually dead. The result was, in Blomström & Hettne's words, 'an awkward theoretical vacuum' (1984, p. 163). Perhaps the most significant new model to emerge is the world system model. Wallerstein (1974), previously a proponent of the dependency theory, has promoted the concept of a world system in an effort to avoid some of the theoretical pitfalls associated, for example, with Prebisch's two types of capitalism. Furthermore, the world system approach seeks to avoid the dependency theory's exaggerated emphasis on external factors.

Paradoxically, Third World dependency theorists tended to ignore the internal workings of their own societies in their eagerness to focus on the manipulative activities of First World capitalists. The world system theory redirects our attention to the internal workings, though, having said that, it is important to note that Wallerstein tries to avoid some of the polarities that characterized previous models. Thus there is only one kind of capitalism, namely that of the world system. He does retain the centre–periphery relationship, but he expands the range of possibilities and alters the labels. What was the centre or metropole for the *dependentistas* becomes the core state, while the periphery is subdivided into semi-periphery, periphery, and external arena in order to allow nations to move in graduated steps from beyond the world system (the external arena) via the periphery and semi-periphery until they achieve core state status.

Having outlined the evolution of the dependency theory as well as the centre–periphery construct and established a theoretical framework within which to view the political economy of the Solomon Islands, we must now return to the initial question: to what extent did the Solomon Islands fit these models during the period 1880 to 1980?

The labour trade and smallholder era

Melanesia was one of the last corners of the globe to be subject to capitalist penetration and thus the Solomons were not drawn into the world economy until the end of the merchant capital phase. The islanders enjoyed fleeting contact with whalers, *bêche-de-mer* fishers, and missionaries during the first half of the 19th century, but the economic impact of such associations was negligible.

The real threshold, in terms of the islanders' integration into the world economy, came with the inauguration of the labour trade in the southwest Pacific in the 1860s. Labour-recruiting schooners plied the waters of Melanesia, recruiting islanders for three-year periods of indentured labour service on the sugar estates of Queensland and the coconut plantations of Fiji. During the 1880s and 1890s the Solomons became the principal focus for such recruitment, and tens of thousands of Solomon Islanders saw service overseas (Newbury 1979, p. 11). That service, which lasted until 1911, introduced the islanders to Western material and non-material culture, and acquainted them with the workings of the capitalist economy (Shlomowitz 1985, p. 41). Returned islanders acted as agents of penetration, bringing with them European trade goods and ideas which altered traditional societies and created a condition of dependence on Western goods like tobacco, firearms, and metal implements (Boutilier 1979, p. 47).

The European presence in the islands was minimal at this time. Schooners from the Royal Navy's Australian station visited the Solomons occasionally to investigate outrages associated with the labour trade, but as the archipelago appeared to have only limited economic potential Her Majesty's

Government was disinclined to add the Solomons to its list of imperial possessions. The largely unregulated nature of the labour trade and the likelihood of French territorial expansion in the southwest Pacific did, however, prompt the British to change their minds and they declared a protectorate over the islands in 1893.

They did so ostensibly to afford protection to the islanders but, in fact, to forestall the French. There appears to have been little if any economic motive involved. British nationals in the Solomons were few and, while they operated in a hostile environment, they had not agitated – as their colleagues in Fiji had done 20 years before – for the islands to be incorporated within the Empire. In this instance, at least, we appear to have a case of trade following the flag rather than the other way around.

The first resident commissioner, Charles Woodford, arrived in the Solomons in 1896. He had two interrelated priorities: to establish law and order, and to promote the protectorate's economy. Not only were activities like headhunting, cannibalism and raiding repugnant to European sensibilities and dangerous to the inhabitants of the protectorate, but they created a climate which was not conducive to European investment. While the vast majority of the islanders were barely aware that they were now protected subjects of the Crown, Woodford was answerable to Whitehall and felt obliged to embark on a programme of pacification (that is to say, the violent reduction of opposition to the British presence and the imposition of an alien system of values) and commercial development. Thus Treasury policy, the expectations of the British legal system, the demands of expatriate residents, and the exigencies of local administration combined to draw these remote islands deeper into the capitalist system.

Commercial development took place in two stages, and was directly affected by the colonial administration's policies on land and labour. The first stage involved the acquisition of free or leasehold land by undercapitalized smallholders, while the second stage involved the acquisition of those lands by three major companies and the economic marginalization of the original smallholders.

One or two examples will suffice to illustrate the first stage just described. Five traders bought a total of 22 720 acres of land on the Guadalcanal Plains during this pioneering period for £171, while Oscar Svenson purchased 2446 acres of land at Berande on the Guadalcanal coast for 3000 porpoise teeth, some tobacco, and trade goods worth £5. There was nothing unusual about these acquisitions, in the sense that they replicated similar examples of land alienation at the same stage in the imperial penetrative process elsewhere, but they do give an indication of the relative ease with which a handful of Europeans succeeded in acquiring potentially valuable agricultural land (Lasaqa 1972, pp. 29, 304).

At the same time the colonial authorities began formulating a land policy ostensibly intended to prevent land speculation, but in practice designed to divest the islanders of more and more of their land in order to generate leasehold revenues. That policy came into effect with the promulgation of the Solomons (Waste Lands) Regulation of 1900 (and a subsequent regulation in 1904). Central to that regulation, as the title suggests, was the concept of waste land. This concept enabled the colonial administration to assume ownership (in complete defiance of traditional systems of land tenure, which did not recognize the idea of ownerless land) over 'all unoccupied lands in the absence of evidence of native ownership' (Lasaqa 1972, p. 31), and to lease that land to expatriate applicants.

The era of the major companies

The first major company to invest in the Solomons was Lever Brothers, after 1929 part of Unilever, the giant Anglo-Dutch combine which manufactured soap and margarine (Beckford 1972, p. 111). The firm's involvement in the protectorate resulted from two unrelated though fortuitous developments: the end, in the early 1900s, of a twenty-year slump in the world oils and fats market, and the Pacific Island Company's (PIC) desperate need for funding to enable it to invest in phosphate mining on Nauru and Ocean Island. Lever Brothers established Lever's Pacific Plantations Ltd (LPPL) in 1902, and in 1906 acquired roughly 200 000 acres of land from the restructured PIC (1902) Ltd. Shortly thereafter LPPL acquired a further 90 000 acres, roughly 51 000 acres of which had previously been owned by Oscar Svenson.

The magnitude of LPPL's land holdings reflected three conclusions that William Lever had reached about commodity production: first, that it must be on the largest scale possible; second, that the profitability of plantations must be taken one year with another; and third, that:

> the overall objective of creating vegetable [coconut/copra] oil plantations from the standpoint of the industrialist who used them must be to increase the total supply so as to tilt the balance in his favour rather than to supply his own factories direct from his plantations (Fieldhouse 1978, p. 459).

The colonial government also had to take a long-term view of economic development. As Lasaqa has noted, coconut plantations require 'an extensive initial outlay of capital over a ten year period during which direct financial returns to the planter are nil' (1972, p. 34). LPPL paid no rent to the protectorate before 1930 and thereafter its direct contribution to the economy in the form of rents was slight. The real benefit to the protectorate accrued 'from LPPL's investment, the trade it generated, the duties it paid on imports, the stimulus it would provide to the cash economy through payment of wages and the encouragement its entry might give to other potential investors and traders . . .' (Fieldhouse 1978, p. 463).

The second company to enter the Solomons in the period prior to World War I was the Australian-based shipping and merchandising firm, Burns Philp (BP). Concerned that LPPL might dominate the protectorate's economy, Woodford encouraged BP to invest in the group. This it did, acquiring a lease in 1908 to more than 10 000 acres at Muvia on the Guadalcanal Plains, which was transferred subsequently to its holding company, Solomon Islands Development Corporation (SIDC). SIDC also purchased Berande estate from Svenson. In addition BP formed what were to all intents and purposes two subsidiaries, Shortland Island Plantations Ltd and Choiseul Plantations Ltd, to develop coconut estates in the western half of the protectorate.

BP's relationship with the colonial authorities is an interesting one. While Woodford encouraged the company initially, he was loath to grant them the concessions they requested for fear of being accused of favouritism by LPPL (Buckley & Klugman 1981, p. 173). There is an interesting passage in the BP files which illustrates the way in which island governments could be manipulated by major firms if need be. It relates to a proposal to allow a Chinese banana merchant in Sydney to lease land from BP in the Solomons. While BP, LPPL, and the Australian firm of W. R. Carpenter (the third company which entered the Solomons in 1914) avoided destructive rounds of competition by gentlemen's agreements, they were particularly nervous about competition from Indian and Chinese merchants.

> If we want them there [Chinese in the Solomons] we can introduce them without difficulty; if we do not want them we can easily arrange for them to be restricted. There is power under the Pacific Orders-in-Council to issue prohibitions, and we could move the Resident Commissioner or [Western Pacific] High Commissioner to block it or we could get the men and have them established before the authorities woke up to the position (cited in Buckley & Klugman 1981, p. 249).

The statistics with respect to freehold or certificate of occupation (lease) land have to be treated with care. While there were provisions on the books that empowered the colonial government to reclaim land that had not been developed within a certain period of time, these regulations were seldom enforced and only a modest proportion of the vast acreage held by LPPL, BP, and Carpenters was ever developed. Eight years after entering the Solomons LPPL had only 8000 acres under nuts and only 2000 of those were bearing. By 1920 the firm had 20 000 acres under nuts, but that was the largest area it ever used effectively. LPPL's greatest annual production was 7850 tons (1937), and when that figure is set against the 1 million tons produced globally it reveals that Lever never produced enough copra to decisively influence the world market price for vegetable oils and fats. In short, in the words of Unilever's official historian, Fieldhouse, the mountain gave birth to a mouse (1978, p. 465).

The factor which, above all others, determined the size and profitability of company plantations in the protectorate was the availability of labour. Although the colonial authorities introduced a head tax in 1922 (resisted in varying degrees by the islanders who felt, quite rightly, that they were getting almost nothing in return for their money) which had the effect of driving men into the plantation work force, the maximum number available at any one time was usually about 5000. This was the number LPPL would have required to plant and maintain one-third of its 300 000-acre holdings. LPPL, however, was not alone in the field. There were other companies and individuals competing for labour, and the situation was exacerbated when in 1934 the colonial authorities, faced with the catastrophic decline in commodity prices occasioned by the Depression, reduced plantation wages from £24 to £12 per annum. Although it could be and was argued that this decision was intended to provide hard-pressed concerns with some relief, it had the opposite effect in practice.

There was, as Buckley & Klugman observe, 'virtually no proletariat dependent upon working for wages for its livelihood' (1981, p. 277). Cushioned from the economic impact of the Depression by recourse to the traditional subsistence economy, the Solomon Islanders withdrew in increasing numbers from the labour force. The number of plantation workers fell from 6115 in 1927 to 3927 in 1932. What is more, the islanders reduced their own not insubstantial production of copra from 3000 tons in 1931 to 300 tons in 1932 (Lasaqa 1972, p. 42). Experience suggested that no alteration of wage scales (within the limits of profitability) or provision of incentives could increase the number of labourers sufficiently to allow substantial new areas to be brought into production. The colonial authorities were acutely aware of this problem, but sympathetic as they were they resolutely refused, decade after decade, to consider any proposal for recruiting labour from outside the group. Thus, as Fieldhouse (1978, p. 473) concludes, it was not the miserable returns of the Depression years nor the ravages of coconut pests but the lack of labour which throttled LPPL.

Things were no better during this period for BP. Their trading stations at Makambo, Gizo and Faisi were crippled by debt, and a number of smallholders were obliged to mortgage their plantations to the company and begin managing their own estates on behalf of their creditors. The average value of copra fell from a high of $53.96 per ton in 1921 to $5.97 in 1935 (Lasaqa 1972, p. 41). The price was so low, in fact, that BP decided to forfeit practically all of the profit on copra in order to encourage continued production.

World War II and reconstruction

The Japanese occupied the western and central Solomons early in 1942. They advanced as far as Tulagi, the capital of the protectorate, and Guadalcanal. European residents, with the exception of a handful of planters, traders, administrators, and missionaries, were evacuated from the group and most of the major plantations were abandoned. Cattle, which had been introduced in the interwar years to keep down the undergrowth on plantations (and thereby effect a saving in wages), were killed or ran wild. The plantation labourers made their way home by a variety of means, and the economy ground to a halt. The resident commissioner went into hiding on the island of Malaita and in this way the fiction of unbroken British rule was maintained.

The Americans began the reoccupation of the Solomons in August 1942, landing at Tulagi and on Guadalcanal. For the next 18 months the majority of the fighting took place on plantation lands on Guadalcanal, the Russell Islands, and New Georgia. Most plantations were rendered derelict, and buildings, wharves, and other prewar installations were destroyed (Belshaw 1950, p. 81).

The problem of economic reconstruction at the end of the war was enormous. There was an acute lack of shipping, the British government refused to pay war compensation, firms like BP decided not to return to the Solomons, and the administration was deeply alarmed by a popular politico-religious movement centred on Malaita known as Maasina or Marching Rule, which lasted from 1944 to 1952.

The war constituted a major psychological threshold for the islanders. The myth of white invincibility was shattered, anti-colonial sentiments were imbibed from the Americans, and service with the Solomon Islands Labour Corps introduced a large number of islanders to undreamt of quantities of goods or 'cargo' (thereby highlighting the apparent niggardliness of the colonial regime) and wage scales which no postwar employer could hope to match. The war destroyed the old economic order and acquainted the islanders with the real magnitude and power of the global economy.

Maasina Rule's ideology focused on 'community re-organization, communal work, political organization in hierarchies of chiefs and their collective bargaining with the colonial government over the terms of administration, plantation labour and law' (Keesing 1982, p. 359). Maasina Rule had short-term and long-term implications for economic reconstruction. In the short term it created a degree of political uncertainty which did not encourage new commercial ventures, and it reduced the flow of labour from the most populous island in the protectorate. In the long term it marked the growth of a new political consciousness within the group which altered the colonial government's economic policies and marked the beginning of the end of colonial rule.

Postwar development programmes

The government advanced a number of conventional 'Blue paradigm' development schemes in the 1950s but it was hamstrung by a lack of assured transportation, administrative infrastructure, and basic knowledge about the protectorate's economic potential. There was no systematic analysis of island resources until the 1950s, when forestry and geological departments were established and the colonial authorities attempted to arrive at a comprehensive picture of traditional land tenure. Adequate knowledge, however, was only part of the problem. As Hoyle has demonstrated, development schemes tended to be viewed in 'partial rather than holistic terms' (1976, p. 84), and relatively little thought was given to the fact that new crops like cocoa would have to compete against much larger and more established cocoa-growing regions nearer world markets (Belshaw 1950, p. 87).

In the meantime LPPL, buoyed by the high prices enjoyed by copra in the early 1950s, decided to return to the Solomons and concentrate most of its efforts on rehabilitating the high-yield, pest-free plantations on the Russell Islands in the centre of the group. However, by the late 1950s the company was faced once again with low profitability as a result of falling oil prices and a government policy of one-year labour contracts. Because this policy militated against the efficient utilization of labour, the company decided in 1961 to begin divesting itself of most of its acreage once the holdings had been exploited for their timber reserves. For its part the government was 'increasingly aware that it was politically undesirable in an age of nascent political consciousness among the islanders that an expatriate company should lock up so much land without making any attempt to develop it' (Fieldhouse 1978, p. 484). The colonial authorities were anxious to 'eradicate the long-term political and economic consequences of the concessionary policy adopted by the Colonial Office sixty years earlier' (Fieldhouse 1978, p. 486) and to ensure that the land was returned to the people.

Lever's Pacific Timbers was established in late 1963, but it took five years of negotiations before a settlement was reached with the colonial government and the company agreed to surrender its occupation leases in return for permission to extract timber without payment of royalties or obligation to replant the land. Since then several other timber companies have entered the field and timber is now the Solomon Islands' second biggest export earner (27% in 1979), with unprocessed logs – the least valuable form – constituting about 80% of exports (SPEC 1982; Solomons section, p. 19).

During the 1970s, as the Solomon Islands moved towards independence, the colonial government embarked on a further series of development schemes designed to diversify the narrowly-based economy and provide an element of import substitution. The three most important projects involved joint venture arrangements with major transnationals or aid agencies. Outwardly at least these arrangements were very much in keeping with the dependency theory's predicted shift from metropolitan to transnational control.

The largest joint venture involved the Japanese conglomerate Taiyo Gyogyo (the world's biggest fishing company), and the Solomon Islands government in 1972. Solomon Taiyo Ltd and the various fisheries initiatives that it has given rise to accounted for roughly 38% of the value of the microstate's exports in 1979. The second scheme involved a joint venture between the Commonwealth Development Corporation and the Solomon Islands' Government (CDC 70%; government 26%; and landowners 4%) to establish an extensive palm-oil plantation on the Guadalcanal Plains in 1971 (PIM 1984, p. 377). The oil is exported to Japan, Britain and the

European Economic Community where it benefits from a preferential tariff.

The third scheme involved a similar joint venture with one of Hawaii's 'Big Five' companies, C. Brewer and Co. Ltd, which is a subsidiary of the giant US conglomerate I. U. International Corporation. The firm which was created, Brewer Solomons Associates, began large-scale rice production on the Guadalcanal Plains in the 1970s but sold out to the government in 1982 as a result of problems caused by 'overexpansion and a vanished overseas market' (PIM 1984, p. 376, Howard 1983b, p. 284).

Conclusion

Where does all this leave us in terms of the dependency theory, which postulates that the centre retarded the periphery's development by siphoning off its wealth and drawing it into a consumer economy which it could not afford? Do the Solomons fit these presumptions with respect to the development of underdevelopment?

The labour trade of the late 19th century constituted the first real penetration of Solomon Island societies and their gradual linkage with the world capitalist system. Queensland became the centre and the Solomons the periphery, with the latter serving as a reservoir of cheap, tractable labour in accordance with the customary profile of plantation economies (Beckford 1972, p. 33). Although large numbers of islanders were involved and indigenous societies, particularly on Malaita, were altered by the experience, the customary mode of production remained relatively unchanged.

The British, as we have seen, extended their protection over the Solomons for political rather than economic reasons in 1893. During the next 10 to 15 years there was a reasonable amount of land alienation on the part of planters and traders living primarily on Guadalcanal and New Georgia. Land 'sales' were generally at variance with indigenous visions of ownership and were fostered by the colonial land policy. Subsequently, the colonial administration encouraged the commercial involvement of major companies like LPPL and BP. From an administrative and commercial point of view the Solomons came to lie on the point of intersection of two peripheral arcs, one centred on Sydney and the other on London. Burns Philp steamers served as commercial and cultural conduits linking the protectorate's economy to Australia, while imperial administrative–legal links ran from the smallest hamlet via district officers, the resident commissioner (Tulagi), and the Western Pacific high commissioner (Suva) to Whitehall and back. Within the archipelago Tulagi was the administrative and commercial centre for which Guadalcanal, New Georgia, and other locations acted as the periphery.

All the evidence suggests that the economic history of the Solomons prior to World War II (when the slate was very nearly wiped clean) does not accord closely with the basic premises of the dependency theory. It is true that a dual economy came into existence and that a lopsided 'modern' sector was created which was characterized by near-monopoly control of production, marketing and sales, but for the most part firms like LPPL, BP, and Carpenters enjoyed meagre to non-existent returns on their investments. The Solomons simply were not profitable, least of all in the rapacious way suggested by the theorists. More money appears to have flowed into the Solomons than flowed out in terms of company operations. And if we look at the second premise, the impoverishment of underdeveloped territories by virtue of what Beckford calls the 'high import propensity of consumption in plantation society' (1972, p. 210), the import–export figures for the period 1919 to 1937 suggest that exports exceeded imports by roughly 20% in value (£4 937 304 to £3 823 367). To that extent at least the protectorate was not living beyond its means even during the grim Depression years.

It could, of course, be argued that those imports were unequally distributed. This, I think, is beyond doubt. The tiny expatriate community utilized the bulk of the imports, although it is of interest that 10% of the imports for 1936–37 consisted of rice, primarily for plantation workers, and 5% of tobacco, much of which was undoubtedly bound for the islanders. What is important to note, however, is that plantation operations did not create land hunger, that food supplies (in the overall sense) were never in jeopardy, and that the introduced cattle, far from competing for land as they did in New Caledonia and elsewhere, had the effect of reducing the demand for labour and thus safeguarding the traditional agricultural sector.

The labour pool in the Solomons proved to be relatively inelastic. Right up to the present day 80% of the population supports itself by subsistence agriculture and has never been reduced to a landless peasantry or a rootless proletariat. Islanders did provide the labour essential to the plantation economy but they did it very much on their own terms, withdrawing their services during the Depression and the period of Maasina Rule.

While sympathetic to big business, government was not always in league with it as some dependency theory advocates would have us believe. Indeed government decisions helped destroy the very profits the theory anticipated. Government labour policies before and after the war undermined big business, while the administration's approach to timber extraction did not favour LPPL. 'On any matter in which the interests of the islanders seemed to clash with those of LPPL,' Fieldhouse notes, 'officialdom became resolute. It had no doubt that its primary obligation was to its subjects rather than to a British multinational . . . .' (1978, p. 489).

It is more difficult to arrive at a balance sheet for the postwar era. For a variety of internal rather than external reasons economic development was slow and haphazard in the late 1940s and 1950s. From the perspective of the centre, London, the Solomons were literally and figuratively peripheral during this period. As the empire began to disintegrate in Africa more and more British administrators (so-called 'Africa retreads') fetched up in the new colonial capital, Honiara, bringing with them 'African' notions of development and administration. Development initiatives were orthodox and accorded with the 'development equals good' outlook of the early 1960s. The approach was paternalistic and there was hardly any debate about the larger meaning of development as there was in Latin America. The University of the South Pacific came into existence in Fiji in 1968 and began educating a handful of Solomon Islanders, but it was an institution charged with colonial values which did not produce home-grown dependency theorists. Instead, in the eyes of those theorists, it began producing members of those élites that were seen to be contributors to the development of underdevelopment phenomenon.

Roger Keesing and Francis Bugotu were among the few who made tentative assessments of Solomon Islands 'society' on the eve of independence in 1978. Bugotu chaired an education committee which produced a report entitled *Education for what?* (1972), a title which reflected a modest debate on the rôle of the individual in Solomon Islands society and the future direction of that society. This was one of a number of educational policy statements that looked at the dialectical tension between rural development and urban-based, élite-benefiting development. Although rhetorical recognition was paid to rural development by the education and other ministries, the emphasis, in practice, was on agribusiness schemes like rice and palm-oil and not on village-level development.

Keesing attacked the native bourgeoisie – limited in number but like all such élites disproportionately powerful – and lamented the way in which 'the quality, the texture of Solomons village life has been progressively corroded by the money economy that has brought greed and acquisitiveness to a society predicated on sharing . . . .' (n.d., p. 7). His is a standard dependency viewpoint, that 'colonialism has produced in the Solomons an economy of exploitation and "underdevelopment" characteristic of the tropical Third World, albeit on a small scale' (n.d., p. 5). Like Howard (1983a, p. 4), he calls for 'strong collective action' in order to 'shape a new world' (n.d., p. 14), but does not provide a practical blueprint outlining how this is to be accomplished.

There are those who would argue that nations like the Solomons have displayed increased sophistication in their dealings with transnational corporations like Taiyo Gyogyo because they have achieved, among other things, increased indigenous control, promises of localization, and access to advanced technologies (Hoogvelt 1976, p. 79). The counter-argument is that a government which offers a considerable array of inducements to transnational corporations and highlights 'the relatively calm state of labour relations' (SPEC 1982; Solomons section, p. 16) is simply forging fresh bonds of dependence with new centres. There is a good deal of validity in this second point of view because the Taiyo experience has revealed that joint-ownership and training schemes for indigenes do not give the Solomon Islands government access to, or control over, the vital mechanisms of global marketing. Without these they are almost powerless.

I do not have the data to argue strongly one way or the other whether the postwar economy of the Solomons fits the development or underdevelopment model. Superficially it does. Certainly the dominant position of transnationals in the Solomons economy fits the expectations of the dependency theory. But unlike other peripheral regions the Solomons have virtually no industry, have never been drawn into a 'branch plant' economy, have almost no sense of class consciousness, have no impoverished peasantry in the thrall of landlord-gentry, and have relatively little foreign debt. In the final analysis it was the Solomon Islands' very peripheralness that saved them from the intense inequities which have characterized centre–periphery relations within the world economy elsewhere.

References

Beckford, G. 1972. *Persistent poverty: underdevelopment in plantation economies in the Third World*. New York: Oxford University Press.

Belshaw, C. S. 1950. *Island administration in the south west Pacific: government and reconstruction in New Caledonia, the New Hebrides and the British Solomon Islands*. London: Royal Institute of International Affairs.

Blomström, M. & B. Hettne 1984. *Development theory in transition: the dependency debate and beyond: the Third World responses*. London: Zed Books.

Boutilier, J. 1979. Killing the Government: Imperial policy and the pacification of Malaita. In *The pacification of Melanesia*, M. Rodman & M. Cooper (eds), 43–88. Ann Arbor: University of Michigan Press.

Brookfield, H. C. 1972. *Colonialism, development and independence: the case of the Melanesian islands in the South Pacific*. Cambridge: Cambridge University Press.

Buckley, K. & K. Klugman 1981. *The history of Burns Philp: the Australian company in the South Pacific*. Sydney: Burns, Philp and Co. Ltd.

Fieldhouse, D. K. 1978. *Unilever overseas: the anatomy of a multi-national, 1895–1965*. London: Croom Helm.

Gardezi, H. H. 1986. Review of *The political economy of Fiji* by Jay Narayan (Suva: South Pacific Review Press, 1984). *Canadian Review of Sociology and Anthropology* **23**(1), 136–7.

Hoogvelt, A. M. M. 1976. *The sociology of developing societies*. London: Macmillan.

Howard, M. 1983a. *The political economy of the South Pacific*. Townsville: James Cook University.

Howard, M. 1983b. Transnational corporations: the influence of the capitalist world economy. In *Foreign forces in the Pacific*, M. Howard (ed.), 264–89. Suva: University of the South Pacific.

Hoyle, A. R. 1976. Development in the South Pacific: success and failure. *Journal of Administration Overseas* **15**(3), 77–84.

Keesing, R. M. 1982. Kastom and anti-colonialism on Malaita: 'culture' as political symbol. *Mankind* **13**(4), 357–73.

Keesing, R. M. n.d. Seeking paths for Solomons development. Paper presented at the Seventh Waigani Seminar (Law and Development in Melanesia).

Knapman, B. 1986. Merchant capital in the extreme periphery: Burns Philp (South Seas) Co. Ltd in Fiji, 1920–1939. *Historical Studies* **22**(86), 93–115.

Lasaqa, I. Q. 1972. Melanesians' choice: Tadhimboko participation in the Solomon Islands cash economy. *New Guinea Research Unit Bulletin*. Canberra: Australian National University Press.

Newbury, C. 1979. Imperial history or development history? some reflections on Pacific labour markets in the nineteenth century. Paper presented at the 1979 ANZAAS Conference.

Pacific Islands Monthly (PIM) 1984. *Pacific Islands Yearbook*, J. Carter (ed.). Sydney: Pacific Publications.

Schlomowitz, R. 1985. Time-expired Melanesian labour in Queensland: an investigation in job turnover 1884–1906. *Pacific Studies* **8**(2), 25–44.

Smith, A. 1978. The case of dependency theory. In *The Third World: premises of U.S. policy*, W. Scott Thompson (ed.), 207–26. San Francisco: Institute for Contemporary Studies.

South Pacific Bureau of Economic Cooperation (SPEC) 1982. *South Pacific Bureau of Economic Cooperation trade and investment guide*. Suva: SPEC.

Wallerstein, I. 1974. *The modern world-system I*. New York: Academic Press.

2 *The greater Southwest as a periphery of Mesoamerica*

RANDALL H. MCGUIRE

To the extent that any society must interact with other societies in consumption and production, it is necessary for archaeologists to consider the larger system of relationships in an account of its reproduction. This raises both empirical and theoretical issues in the study of prehistory. How interdependent were prehistoric societies at different points in time, and how extensive was the larger system of relationships into which these societies entered? Perhaps more importantly, what conceptual tools best allow us to understand and account for variability and change in these relationships? Consideration of each of these issues leads us away from models for prehistory which treat societies or cultures as hard-bounded objects explicable in terms of local adaptive processes.

This chapter ponders the theoretical issues of: (a) how we can integrate local relations of production (adaptation) and long-range interactions in our reconstructions of prehistory, and (b) how we can incorporate the rôle of ideology and human action in these reconstructions. The prehistoric Southwest and its interaction with Mesoamerica provides the empirical context for considering these issues.

The Southwest and Mesoamerica

The American Southwest[1] is one of the most intensely studied archaeological zones in the world. It includes the modern states of Arizona, New Mexico, southeast Utah, southwest Colorado, and trans-Pecos Texas in the United States, and the states of Sonora and Chihuahua in Mexico (Fig. 2.1). Archaeologists usually divide the Formative (Neolithic) Southwest into four major cultural/spatial units; the Anasazi, the Mogollon, the Patayan and the Hohokam. In this chapter I am only concerned with the Anasazi and a late manifestation of the Mogollon at the site of Casas Grandes, Chihuahua.

Anasazi remains occur on the Colorado plateau in Arizona, New Mexico, Utah, and Colorado and in the Rio Grande valley of New Mexico. The Anasazi were corn agriculturalists who initially lived in pithouses and later in multi-storeyed, apartment-like complexes called pueblos. Archaeologists have divided the temporal sequence for the Anasazi into seven numbered periods, Basketmaker II–III and Pueblo I–V. The descendants of the Anasazi,

Figure 2.1 Map of the greater Southwest and northern Mesoamerica.

the Zuni, Hopi, Keres, Tewa, and Tiwa, and Towa live today in Arizona and New Mexico.

Mogollon remains occur in a mountainous band that starts in the middle of Arizona and arches through western New Mexico into Chihuahua. Late in the Mogollon sequence at about AD 1200 the site of Casas Grandes in northwestern Chihuahua began developing into a major centre. At its height from AD 1300 to 1400, Casas Grandes was one of the largest settlements in the New World, with a ceremonial complex including tombs, platform mounds, and a ballcourt and a series of over 1000 pueblo-like rooms built around compounds. Of all the sites in the Southwest, Casas Grandes is the most Mesoamerican-looking and has yielded the most Mesoamerican artefacts.

Mesoamerica refers to the prehistoric high-culture area of central America, the home of the Olmecs, Aztecs, Mayas, and Toltecs. The northern boundary of Mesoamerica shifted through time but at its northernmost extent between AD 1000 and 1520 it extended to the southern edge of the Southwest. There is little or no evidence of direct contact between the Southwest and the core of highland Mesoamerica, but items from the northern edge of Mesoamerica (copper bells, macaws, and ceramics) occur in the Southwest and Southwestern turquoise occurs in Mesoamerica.

The nature of interactions between the Southwest and Mesoamerica has been a key point of debate in Southwestern archaeology (see Mathien & McGuire 1986, Wilcox 1986). Some archaeologists have seen the Southwest as simply the northernmost edge of Mesoamerica and Southwestern prehistory as explainable in terms of the ebbs and flows of Mesoamerican prehistory. Others have discounted the importance of contacts with Mesoamerica for an understanding of Southwestern prehistory. Many of the advocates of a strong Mesoamerican influence on Southwestern prehistory have recently adopted Wallerstein's world systems theory and these attempts have exhibited both the strengths and weaknesses of this theory for the study of prehistory.

The world system perspective

The work of Wallerstein (1974, 1978, 1980) and his concept of core and periphery have had a major impact on how archaeologists currently conceptualize prehistory. He leads us to examine how the development of cores derives from the creation of peripheries, shifting our focus from diffusion or adaptation to interaction and dependencies. There are, however, a number of general shortcomings to Wallerstein's theory, and these limit our insights concerning prehistory. Wallerstein directs us to the right questions, but his work does not provide us with the conceptual tools to answer those questions in non-capitalist economies.

In many ways Wallerstein's theory represents a quantum leap in the study of prehistory. It allows us to look at regional relationships instead of focusing only on human–environmental relations in a single river valley or basin. Societies are no longer bounded objects but dynamic entities defined and transformed by unequal relationships in a larger system. Core areas dominate this system and forge the relationships which create the great diversity necessary for linking a region as a whole.

The theoretical value of the world systems perspective has attracted many archaeologists. Some, such as Kohl (1979), Whitecotton and Pailes (1986), and Ekholm and Friedman (1982), have attempted to map Wallerstein's theory directly onto prehistory. Other archaeologists have found the world systems model heuristically useful but analytically inappropriate to their prehistoric cases (Blanton *et al.* 1981, Upham 1982, Plog 1983).

Wallerstein (1974, 1980) does not present a general theory of cultural evolution but instead a historical theory for the rise of capitalism. He writes modestly about the empires that preceded the capitalist world economy and extensively on the rise of the capitalist world economy. He has, however, only slight concern with the non-capitalist world economies which characterize most of human existence and nearly all of prehistory. More importantly, Wallerstein's theory is historical and not evolutionary. Wallerstein's concepts refer to specific developments in the history of the world and are not generalizable to all times and places.

Wallerstein (1978) identifies four possible modes of production in world history: reciprocal mini-systems, redistributive empires, a capitalist world economy, and a hoped for socialist world government. In reciprocal mini-systems all able-bodied individuals engage in production, and processes of reciprocal exchange create inequalities favouring senior males. World empires contain a stratum of non-producers who pre-empt the surplus of others through a tribute network controlled by a centralized political system. The non-producing capitalist bourgeoisie secures surplus from the workers via market exchanges. In these formulations Wallerstein draws his understandings of non-capitalist economics almost exclusively from Polanyi (1957).

Prehistoric archaeologists have primarily utilized Wallerstein's concept of world economy as a mode of production (Plog *et al.* 1982, Upham 1982, Plog 1983, Whitecotton & Pailes 1986). Wallerstein, however, has made no original contributions to the study of pre-capitalist world economies. When he discusses world economies he inevitably moves immediately to the discussion of the capitalist world economy. World economies derive from a functional and geographic division of labour but differ from world empires in their lack of an overarching centralized government. Wallerstein indicates that world economies are inherently unstable and short-lived entities; the capitalist world economy is anomalous because it has lasted 500 years. Clearly the dynamics of the capitalist world economy must be markedly different from those of earlier world economies. Wallerstein does not provide us with discussions of those earlier dynamics.

Wallerstein's approach emphasizes how the core subjugates the periphery, but it does not adequately deal with the unique aspects and developments of peripheries, or with how peripheries affect the core (Wolf 1982, p. 23). Archaeological interpreters of Wallerstein identify regional interaction as important to uneven development, but accounting for how this interaction leads to particular prehistorical sequences is another matter. We must be able to interpret the variation in societies that are not cores. Simply identifying all such societies as peripheries obscures both the variability and the rôle of these societies in determining prehistoric developments.

The concept of 'core and periphery' itself presents some operational problems for the prehistorian. It has great heuristic value, helping us to interpret prehistory as the result of unbalanced interaction within a region. But how do we decide if a prehistoric area was a core, periphery, or semi-periphery? There also exists a problem of scale. In the context of Southwestern prehistory we may wish to speak of Chaco Canyon as a core; but in terms of the Southwest and Mesoamerica the entire Southwest must be considered a periphery. These concepts may function well at the macro-level of explaining the rise of capitalism as a worldwide phenomenon, but they are too broad and imprecise for understanding the specifics of development of a region.

A consideration of Southwestern prehistory clearly illustrates these problems. Several different cores existed in the prehistory of highland Mesoamerica; the northernmost lay at Tula on the upper edge of the Valley of Mexico. Little or no evidence exists for direct contact between the Southwest and any Mesoamerican core (McGuire 1980). The Southwest did interact with the societies of west Mexico, such as the prehistoric cultures of Durango, Nayarit, Jalisco, and Sinaloa. Most archaeologists consider this area a part of Mesoamerica only between AD 1100 and 1300 (Weaver 1972). Even during this time-period west Mexico was a periphery first of the Toltec and then of the world economy that followed. The Southwest, therefore, was the hinterland of a periphery.

When we step back from our examination of the Southwestern situation to examine the larger Mesoamerican scheme, we realize that the Southwest was never more than a very distant and minor part of the Mesoamerican world system. Identifying the Southwest as a periphery does not fully describe its position in the system, nor does it reveal the dynamics which link particular changes in the Southwest to alterations in the larger world system.

Relations of production and exchange

Wallerstein's is not the only model that directs us to seek answers in the dependencies that exist between societies and individuals. A number of other contemporary scholars have advanced equally insightful theories. The French Marxists have developed an approach to the study of primitive economics based on the concept of modes of production (Terray 1975, Meillassoux 1981, Godelier 1982). Others have discussed the concept of a prestige-goods economy (Frankenstein & Rowlands 1978, Gledhill 1978). Eric Wolf's (1982) penetrating analysis of the rise of capitalism reveals the global interconnectedness of this phenomenon, yet manages to do so without relying on the simplistic opposition of core and periphery. A new formulation can be drawn from a synthesis of these ideas, with the addition of insights derived from Laclau (1977) and Ollman (1976).

This formulation focuses primarily on relations of dependency and on how these relations link and oppose social groups. As long as social units are independent and self-sustaining, there exists no social mechanism for domination and exploitation (Marx 1964, pp. 67–120). Changes in dependencies result from the competition among individuals or groups within and between societies. Changes in material conditions affecting production and exchange, such as population growth, environmental change, and technological change, will confer advantages on some groups or individuals at the expense of others. Change in the nature of dependencies and in the structure of societies, however, only occurs if individuals manipulate these advantages to their own gain. The results of such competition are not pre-ordained, and failings of human judgement and action affect the outcome, as do the material conditions that structure the competition.

Two types of relations create dependencies: (a) relations of production and (b) relations of exchange and distribution. Production and exchange are interconnected and interdependent processes. Production in a social context requires the distribution of the product, and exchange cannot exist without a product to transfer. The existence of one of these sets of relations both determines and demands the existence of the other; paradoxically, however, focusing on one often leads to different perceptions of social life than does focusing on the other.

Productive processes create dependencies insofar as individuals must depend on others for access to the technology, energy, or natural resources necessary for production. The exact nature of these relations and the magnitude of the dependencies they create vary greatly in human history.

Relations of exchange and distribution link productive activities to the biological and social reproduction of households. Both the biological necessities of human existence and the goods essential for social existence are prerequisites for reproduction. Relations of exchange determine a household's access to those biological and social necessities that it does not itself produce. The greater the number of such essentials and the fewer the sources for them, the more dependent households will be on others for their reproduction.

Many researchers have emphasized either production or exchange, subsuming one relation under the other. While this avoids artificially separating these two aspects, it raises a false issue of which relation is primary in determining cultural change. Although it seems reasonable to suggest that in certain cases production or exchange may be primary, it seems equally unreasonable to assume that one will always dominate the other as a determinant of social forms. In the following discussion of production and exchange neither will be considered as necessarily dominant over the other, but a holistic understanding of their interrelationship will nevertheless be maintained.

Modes of production

The concept 'modes of production' originated in the work of Karl Marx, and modern scholars interpret it in various ways. Researchers generally include the means of production (i.e. the materials, energy, human labour, and knowledge necessary for production) and the relations of production (i.e. the reciprocal relations between people producing goods) within a mode of production. Marx and Engels used the concept in an ambiguous manner, sometimes suggesting that modes occurred in an evolutionary sequence and at other times treating modes as generic types following no set pattern of evolution (Wolf 1982, pp. 400–2, Hobsbawm 1964). Soviet-bloc scholars and the so-called vulgar Marxists have accepted modes as evolutionary stages (Friedman 1974, Block 1983), while French researchers analyse modes of production as systems in their own right rather than as evolutionary stages (Althusser & Balibar 1970, Seddon 1974, Terray 1975, Meillassoux 1981, Godelier 1982).

My use of modes of production follows Wolf's (1982, pp. 400–2) eclectic formulation, which incorporates the French view with Ollman's (1976) emphasis on modes of production as sets of relations, not sets of dependent variables. In this manner, a mode of production is 'a specific, historically occurring set of social relations through which labor is deployed to wrest energy from the environment' (Wolf 1982, p. 75). In each mode a distinctive ideology mystifies or obscures the true nature of these social relations from the participants in the mode.

The value of this concept lies not in the classification of cases but in its elucidation of the strategic relations which structure social life. Wolf (1982) defines three modes of production; Marx defined five at one time, seven at another (Marx & Engels 1947, Marx 1968). There exists no universal list of modes; the scale of an analysis or the problems being addressed will determine what distinctions are usefully drawn and how many modes are constituted.

Nor should modes be construed as evolutionary stages. Modes of production are historically and not evolutionarily related (Wolf 1982, p. 76). There exists no inherent ordering to modes of production and, more important, multiple modes may exist at any point of time. This does not mean that any mode may be transformed into any other but that such transformations do not follow a set developmental sequence.

It is important to realize that modes of production refer to social relations between individuals and groups and are not therefore characteristics of a social unit. Multiple modes of production may exist in a society, or several societies may be involved in a single mode of production (Wolf 1982, p. 76). Modes of production create the social units we see; they are not products of these units.

Each mode of production contains within it internal contradictions which are the basis for transforming that mode into another. Productive relations change gradually in modes until these contradictions can no longer be obscured by the existing ideology. The ideological crisis ultimately moves people to action, and this action transforms the mode (Godelier 1982). Cultural change is, therefore, gradual and developmental within modes and revolutionary in the transformation of modes.

Wolf (1982, pp. 77–100) defines three modes of production: the capitalist, the tributary, and the kin-ordered. Only the last two are potentially relevant to discussions of prehistoric Southwestern–Mesoamerican interactions.

In the tributary mode of production the primary producer retains access to the means of production while members of the élite extract surplus from the producers through the use of political or military means (Wolf 1982, pp. 79–80). A ruling élite in this mode will be strongest when it controls a key productive element, such as irrigation, and some means of coercion, such as a standing army. Considerable variability exists in the degree of centralized power that can exist in modes of this type. At one extreme the local élite holds power, producing what anthropologists have previously called chiefdoms or feudalism. At the other extreme, power is centralized in one ruling élite, a situation characteristic of the Asiatic mode of production or empires (Wolf 1982, pp. 80–1). Tributary modes of production probably characterized the high-culture centres of Mesoamerica, from the Olmec to the Aztec (Blanton *et al.* 1981, p. 226).

In a kin-ordered mode of production, kinship relations define the relations of production and are both the locus and the form of the economy (Wolf 1981, p. 52, 1982, p. 91, Godelier 1982, p. 23). 'Kinship can be understood as a way of committing social labor to the transformation of nature through appeals to filiation and marriage and consanguinity and affinity' (Wolf 1982, p. 91). Individuals achieve power and prestige through the manipulation of their lineage's productive power and by establishing, through marriage, alliances with other lineages. Over time gains in power can produce real and lasting inequalities and the ideological ranking of lineages.

The very characteristics that define a kin-ordered mode of production also limit the extent of inequalities that can exist and the scale of political control possible. As a leader develops a following through the judicious management of redistribution and alliance, he reaches a limit in the extent of his power and influence. This can only be transcended by developing access to production independent of kinship (Wolf 1982, pp. 95–6). Cumulative conflict can often exceed the integrative abilities of kin-based mechanisms, leading to a fragmentation of groups. With no control that transcends kinship, the kin-ordered mode of production organizes groups like stacks of blocks, which are easily decomposable into lower-level constituent kin groups (McGuire 1983a, pp. 117–19).

Even when kinship is the dominant means of establishing rights to resources and labour, the way in which these rights are established and the extent of inequalities can vary greatly between groups. Following Wolf (1982, p. 91), kinship itself works in two different ways depending on the availability of resources and how people obtain these resources. When resources are generally available and access to them is unrestricted – a situation characteristic of many hunting and gathering groups – kinship serves primarily to create relationships between people and distribute social labour. Kinship in these situations is fluid, incorporating newcomers and excluding existing members as the dynamics of production require. Real inequalities evolve based on seniority, sex and pioneer status. When resources are limited and access to them is restricted – a situation characteristic of groups that transform nature through mechanisms such as agriculture – then kinship serves to define rights of access to resources. Kinship boundaries are drawn tightly around rights to production, including and excluding individuals from production. Mythological ancestors legitimize membership in groups, and inequalities arise as a result of the ranking of lineages or clans. Many of the societies that anthropologists call chiefdoms lie at the extreme of this type of relationship.

This conceptualization of modes of production does not parallel traditional evolutionary classifications used in archaeology. For example, societies that anthropologists have labelled as chiefdoms include cultural groups involved in kin-ordered modes of production, tributary modes of production, or some combination of modes. The emphasis in this analysis is on the productive relations between individuals and groups, not on the forms of political organization.

The prehistoric Southwest included both extremes of the kin-ordered mode. Cultures in the Phoenix Basin (Wilcox & Shenk 1977) and Chaco Canyon (Grebinger 1973, Judge 1979, Tainter & Gillio 1980) exhibited the levels of inequality and types of organization that characterize chiefdoms within a kin-ordered mode of production. At no point in the prehistoric Southwest is there evidence of standing armies or coercive force adequate to infer a tributary mode of production.

Economic systems

Whereas modes of production refer to the relations that organize production, economic systems define the relations of exchange that link different sectors of an economy or different productive units (Laclau 1977, pp. 34–5). Such systems operate on a local, regional, and even a global scale, as in the case of the modern capitalist economic system. An economic system may link different modes of production and societies into a whole, thereby creating a unity without which those modes and societies would not exist (Laclau 1977, p. 35).

Economic systems should not be confused with the archaeological concept of modes of exchange (Renfrew 1975). Archaeologists have utilized modes of exchange as a classificatory scheme in order to pigeonhole societies in an evolutionary sequence based on the organization of long-distance exchange (Findlow & Bolognese 1982). Modes of exchange are the mechanisms by which goods are moved across a landscape and inform only indirectly on the relations that create dependencies between individuals and groups.

Just as production and exchange each determine and demand the existence of the other, so too are modes of production and economic systems related. Certain types of economic systems require the existence of certain modes of production. For example, a capitalist economic system would not be possible if the only existing modes of production were kin-ordered modes.

A capitalist economic system, however, incorporates modes in addition to the capitalist mode of production, including both tributary and kin-ordered modes (Laclau 1977, Wolf 1982).

Economic systems should not be equated with evolutionary stages. Like modes of production, economic systems represent specific historically occurring relations (Laclau 1977, p. 43). There does not exist and could not exist an exhaustive list of types of economic systems; the scale of the analysis and the problems at hand will determine what systems are constituted. Finally, human groups do not pass through any necessary developmental progression from one type of economic system to another.

A variety of different economic systems have been constituted in the past, including the capitalist (Laclau 1977, Marx 1967), the mercantile (Marx 1967, p. 331, Wolf 1982, pp. 83–8), and the prestige-goods (Frankenstein & Rowlands 1978, Gledhill 1978). The last of these types is the most relevant to the discussion of Southwestern–Mesoamerican interactions.

Prestige-goods economies are based on the association of political power with control of access to foreign goods, which assume meaning as social valuables. The concept of such economies is derived from recent work in primitive economics (Strathern 1971, Sahlins 1972, Schneider 1974), and from the archaeological work of Frankenstein and Rowlands (1978) and Gledhill (1978). Such economies are most commonly associated with kin-ordered modes of production and may link kin-ordered and tributary modes.

In a prestige-goods economy, élites – usually male lineage heads – obtain power by controlling access to goods obtainable only through external exchange. Individuals do not require these goods for their physical well-being, but the items are social valuables essential for the reproduction of the group. Individuals in the society must have these valuables in order to validate the major social and religious transitions of their lives, including births, marriages, deaths, and other major life events. Subordinate individuals become dependent upon lineage heads for access to these valuables. The lineage heads in turn extract surplus production of both utilitarian goods and valuables in return for the provisioning of these social necessities. The lineage heads use this surplus production in status competitions with other lineage heads, and to obtain more valuables from outside the society. The relationship is asymmetrical in that the individual has only one source of valuables, whereas the lineage head can draw surplus production from a variety of subordinates.

The lineage head must also enter into subordinate relationships in order to maintain his position in this system. When multiple levels of dependency exist, as they do in societies labelled as chiefdoms, lower-level lineage heads depend on higher-level lineage heads to provide them with the goods they need to maintain their social position. These include valuables for distribution to their followers and items which symbolically legitimize lower-level lineage head status *vis à vis* their superiors and subordinates. High-value goods and lesser valuables for distribution to subordinates are linked at this point in the exchange system so that any disruption in the supply or flow of one affects the other. Ultimately the paramount élites must depend on others, outside their society, for the goods that allow them to maintain the system of dependencies within their own society.

By controlling the valuables required for social reproduction, the lineage head pre-empts the surplus production of a society. This appropriation derives primarily from the social meaning of the artefacts involved and not from the use of force. This meaning is an integral part of an ideology that serves to deny the exploitative rôle of the lineage head and to legitimize the broader system of inequalities that exist. The artefacts derive their power from ideology, and their exchange and distribution maintains the ideology. Goods that are rare, that require unusual skill to produce, or that are associated with more powerful social systems provide the best candidates for valuables (Flannery 1968).

Inequality increases in this kind of system where lineage heads exploit small advantages in competition to increase the number of individuals dependent upon them. Descent groups that have inferior productive resources are disadvantaged in competition and may become dependent upon the lineage head of a different descent group for their valuables. In this case the dominant group may compel the poorer descent group to produce goods that serve the needs of the dominant group. Lineage heads gain power relative to their subordinates when they come to control the production or source of the valuables used in the system. The greater this control the less dependent the lineage heads are on foreign lineage heads, and the more they are able to monopolize access to valuables. This means less redistribution to dependents and an increasingly restricted circulation of valuables, only to those within the élite group (Frankenstein & Rowlands 1978).

The lineage head may exploit distinctions drawn between richer and poorer descent groups to create real differences in the access to the means of production. Poorer descent groups may become indebted to richer ones for valuables, and this may be used as a justification for the dominant group's usurping of the resources and labour power of the poorer. The lineage head may also manipulate the symbolic, mythological, and genealogical differences between richer and poorer descent groups to create ideologically sanctioned rankings of kin groups.

These processes can ultimately transform a kin-ordered mode of production to an even more exploitative form, and also transform the economic system. As lineage heads come to control access to production as well as to the distribution of valuables, they acquire retainers dependent upon them not just for access to social necessities but also for their livelihoods. The lineage heads obtain followers whose allegiance transcends kin obligations. Both internal contradictions and external dependencies make prestige-goods economies inherently unstable.

The lineage heads' access to foreign valuables and their ability to compete with other lineage heads ultimately depend on the productive capabilities of their dependents. Here we are concerned with the traditional variables of an ecological archaeology: population size, environment, and technology. The lineage heads possess a potentially unlimited demand for surplus, but material conditions ultimately limit the productive capabilities of the society. If the lineage head attempts to exceed this limitation or coerce greater labour investments than subordinates are willing to expend, either the economy must collapse or the producers will overthrow the lineage head. Only if the productive power of the society increases or the lineage heads obtain a source for coercive force may this contradiction be overcome and the system transformed to a more exploitative mode of production.

The dependency of such economies on external lineage heads contributes to their instability, since individuals within the society or from competing social groups may break the lineage heads' monopoly on foreign valuables, thereby displacing them. This may be done by establishing new sources of valuables or by renegotiating social meanings and introducing new valuables. The external trade connections of the lineage head provide an even greater source of instability. The supply of foreign valuables normally depends on trade connections which link the lineage heads to faraway societies, over which they have no control. Environmental, political, or social perturbations several hundred miles away can disrupt the flow of valuables to the lineage head.

A prestige-goods economy existed in the Southwest among the Hohokam at least as early as AD 700 (McGuire 1983b), and such a system clearly existed in the Chaco by approximately AD 950 (Gledhill 1978, Akins & Schelberg 1981). Blanton *et al.* (1981, p. 250) have argued that a prestige-goods economy existed in Mesoamerica from 1000 BC until the final two centuries before the Spanish conquest. This economic system was notably more elaborate than that of the Southwest, with the movement of many utilitarian commodities, such as obsidian. According to Blanton *et al.* (1981, p. 248) a prestige-goods economy structured this exchange and there is no evidence of regular inter-regional dependencies for food before the 15th century.

The Pueblo III collapse and the Anasazi *katsina* religion

The theory presented here attempts to delineate the significant elements at work in processes of cultural change. It does not seek to specify universal causes, but rather to identify the key structural relations we should examine in any given instance of change. Explanation comes from the revelation of the relations and contradictions that produce change in a specific prehistoric case. To illustrate how this consideration of production and exchange allows us to understand particular events in prehistory, I employ the model to analyse the abandonment of the San Juan Basin and the subsequent appearance of the Anasazi *katsina* religion.[2]

One of the most dramatic events in Anasazi prehistory was the abandonment of Mesa Verde and the San Juan river basin at about AD 1300 and the subsequent concentration of Anasazi populations in the Rio Grande

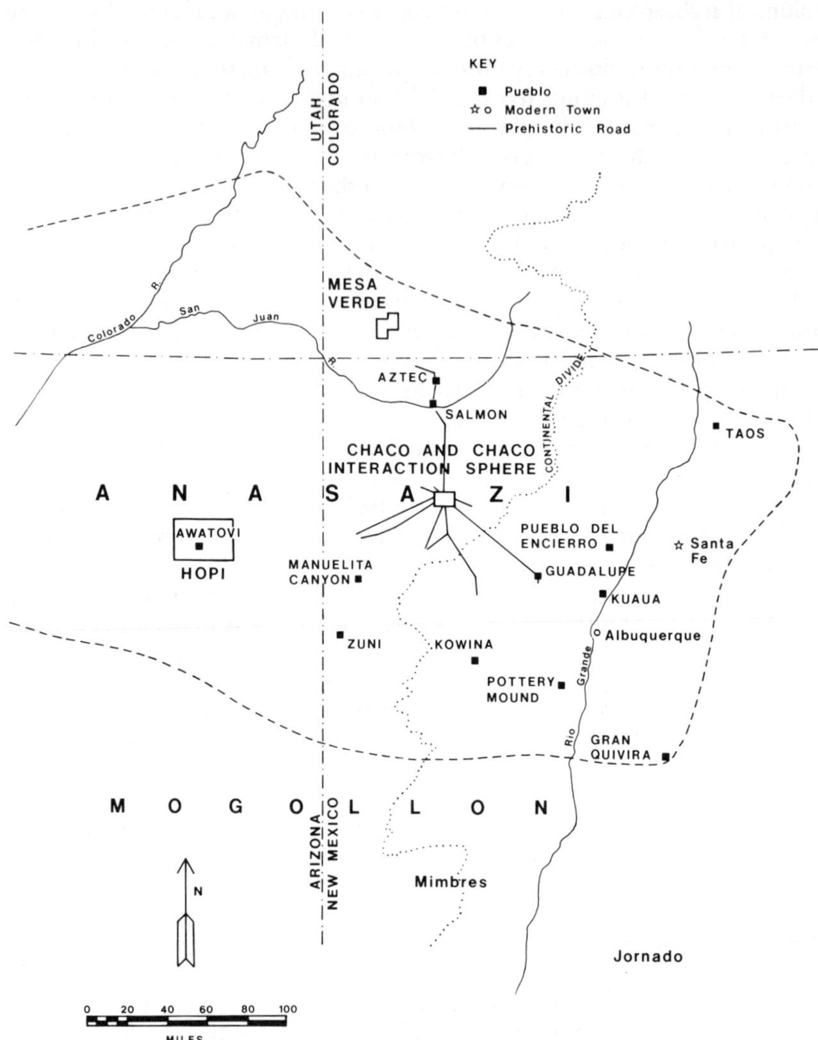

Figure 2.2 Map of the Anasazi region with selected sites.

valley, Zuni, Acoma, and at scattered locales in northwestern Arizona (Fig. 2.2). The abandonment of individual sites and river valleys was a common occurrence in Anasazi prehistory, but the emptying of an area the size of the San Juan Basin was a rare event (Cordell 1979, pp. 102–3). The Pueblo III to Pueblo IV transition marked the greatest demographic shift in Anasazi prehistory, and so has been of major interest to Southwestern archaeologists.

Interestingly, this demographic shift occurred at a time of extreme drought in the Colorado Plateau (Dean & Robinson 1977, Euler *et al.* 1979). The congruence between this drought and the abandonments has not been lost on Southwestern archaeologists, many of whom cite a general environmental deterioriation resulting from the drought as the cause for abandonment (Hayes 1964, Lister 1966, Dean 1970, Bradfield 1971, Zubrow 1971). Numerous other researchers have indicated the inadequacy of simple environmental explanations that do not take into account the internal social dynamics of the societies involved (Martin & Plog 1973, pp. 318–33, Cordell 1979, p. 150, Tainter & Gillio 1980). Kelley (1981) points to alternative events that correspond to this period of abandonment: the exclusion of the Anasazi from a Mesoamerican world system. After AD 1200 Mesoamerican goods, such as copper bells and macaws, become scarce or disappear altogether from Anasazi sites (Schroeder 1966, McGuire 1980).

If we are to explain the abandonment of the San Juan Basin, we must examine the effects of both environmental stress and the ending of long-distance trade on Anasazi kin-ordered modes of production, and on the prestige-goods economy linking societies in the Southwest to each other and to Mesoamerica. For production, this requires defining the means of production, the limitations to production inherent in the means of production, and the organization of production. For exchange, we must consider what was being exchanged, what were the values of goods, and what were the linkages in the exchange network. Finally, both kin-ordered modes of production and prestige-goods economies are maintained not by coercive force but by an ideology embodied in kin relations and material goods. Events which reveal the contradictions in this ideology move people to transform these relations, and no such transformation could occur without a renegotiation of the ideology. The relations of production and exchange in the late 13th century developed from patterns of organization inherited from the past, and some discussion of this past facilitates our understanding of the Pueblo III (AD 1150 to 1350) to Pueblo IV (AD 1350 to 1540) transition.

Production in Anasazi prehistory centred on the cultivation of corn, beans, and squash. Wild resources, both plants and animals, almost certainly provided a significant portion of the diet in all periods (Cordell 1979, pp. 67–8). Cordell and Plog's (1979) summary of Puebloan prehistory suggests that the Anasazi dependence on agriculture increased through time, with a marked increase in agricultural intensification during Pueblo II (AD 900 to 1150). Despite the importance of wild resources for survival, only corn agriculture provided a basis for the population aggregation and societal complexity of the Pueblo III period. Increasing emphasis on corn agriculture, however, ultimately led to an environmental crisis (Plog 1983, p. 325).

The modern San Juan Basin is environmentally marginal for corn agriculture because both the rate of summer precipitation and the number of frost-free days only slightly exceed the minimal requirements for corn growth (Hack 1942, p. 20, Vivian 1974, Cordell 1979, p. 68, Tainter & Gillio 1980, p. 11). Modern climatic conditions did not characterize all of Anasazi prehistory, and the key climatic factors of precipitation and growing season varied through time (Euler *et al.* 1979). However, because of the marginality of the area, even slight fluctuations in climate could significantly expand or contract the number of areas suitable for corn agriculture, and Anasazi populations reacted to these variations by expanding and contracting their range (Euler *et al.* 1979).

These expansions and contractions would have had a profound influence on the productive relations in a kin-ordered mode of production. With low population densities such as those that characterize Anasazi populations in the Basketmaker II to Pueblo I periods (AD 400 to 900) (Cordell & Plog 1979), expansion would have made a prime productive resource – agricultural land – more generally available. This increase in access would have weakened lineage control of resources and, concurrently, the power of lineage heads. On the other hand, contraction without population loss would have decreased access to the means of production, strengthening lineage control and the power of lineage heads. Furthermore, contraction would have revealed an internal contradiction in this type of mode. While strengthening the power of lineage heads, contraction also would have increased the chances of conflict, straining the ability of lineage heads to hold societies together.

The widespread appearance of features designed to concentrate and store water after around AD 1000 suggests a general intensification of agricultural production over much of the San Juan Basin (Vivian 1974). The intensification appears to have been related both to environmental change and to population growth (Vivian 1974, Cordell & Plog 1979, Euler *et al.* 1979). These changes would have strengthened lineage control of production. The technology required for production (water-control features) would have become part of lineage lands and provided lineage heads with greater control of the technology needed for production.

The grandest and perhaps most complex expression of Anasazi culture occurred in Chaco Canyon between about AD 1030 and 1150 (Vivian & Mathews 1965, Judge 1979). The Anasazi built at least 13 multi-storeyed great houses in the canyon itself and a network of roads linking outlying settlements, scattered across the San Juan Basin and beyond to a Chacoan interaction sphere (Lyons & Hitchcock 1977, Altschul 1978, Tainter & Gillio 1980, pp. 98–113, Obenauf 1983, Powers *et al.* 1983). Most researchers now agree that Chaco society contained ranked lineages centred on the main towns in the canyon (Grebinger 1973, Altschul 1978, Judge 1979, Tainter & Gillio 1980). The collapse of the Chaco system at the end of Pueblo II resulted in a reorganization of San Juan Basin Anasazi populations, with many large pueblos built or expanded, and a shift in stylistic dominance from Chaco to Mesa Verde.

Production in the late Pueblo III period was organized around widely scattered large pueblos, usually on major streams with associated water-control features. The preference for locations near major streams and the general aggregation of population reflects a series of droughts starting in AD 1215 and culminating in the great drought of AD 1280 (Euler *et al.* 1979). This organization coalesced during the mid-1200s and lasted until about AD 1300. In the Mesa Verde region the large cliff dwellings, including Long House, Cliff Palace, Mug House, and Spruce Tree House, reached their peak in this period, and along the Mancos and other rivers below the mesa even larger pueblos arose (Rohn 1971, Cattanach 1980). On the San Juan river the Anasazi reoccupied former Chacoan outliers, including Aztec and the Salmon ruin (Morris 1919, Irwin-Williams 1972). Near Zuni, at El Morro, seven pueblos of several hundred rooms each were constructed in the mid-1200s and abandoned by 1300 (LeBlanc 1978). In the Manuelito Canyon population increased and large pueblos were built in the mid-1200s and abandoned by AD 1325 (Weaver 1978). On the upper Puerco the Guadalupe site grew during the late 1200s, only to be abandoned by AD 1300 (Pippin 1979). Around Acoma, on the Cebolleta Mesa, the Kowina ruin grew to over 300 rooms in the late 1200s, but the Anasazi abandoned it by AD 1300 (Dittert 1959, p. 558). At each of these site complexes there are large pueblos with associated water-control features, as well as small pueblos which are economically linked to them.

A commanding centre such as Chaco Canyon did not exist during the late Pueblo III period. Mesa Verde forms dominated ceramic and architectural styles but available evidence does not suggest that Mesa Verde controlled an economic network like Chaco's or that a single polity united Mesa Verde. Instead of one centre, there existed numerous competing centres each with its own supporting area. The relations of exchange in the late Pueblo III period reflect these changes in the organization of production.

During Pueblo II Chaco Canyon linked an Anasazi prestige-goods economy to the prestige-goods economy of Mesoamerica. At Pueblo Bonito in Chaco Canyon, Pepper's (1920) and Judd's (1954) excavations recovered the largest number of Mesoamerican items located from an Anasazi site: 38 macaws, 34 copper bells, and a handful of pseudo-cloisonné items. In addition to these goods they recovered large quantities of Southwestern prestige goods, including marine shell, turquoise, painted wood, and ceramic cylinder jars.

In the Chaco interaction sphere Mesoamerican goods have been recovered only from large canyon towns, while other indigenous prestige goods also occur at outliers (Tainter & Gillio 1980, pp. 100–13). This suggests that the Mesoamerican goods were high-value goods used in exchanges between the Chaco leaders and other leaders of Southwest and west Mexico, and that they provided the material basis for linkages between these lineage heads and were the legitimizing symbols for lineage-head status. The linkages maintained by the prestige exchange of Mesoamerican goods structured the exchange of Southwestern lower-valued prestige goods, which the leaders distributed as social valuables to their dependents. The Chacoans probably traded turquoise south for the Mesoamerican items (Weigand *et al.* 1977).

A recent reappraisal and reanalysis of the tree-ring dates from Casas Grandes suggests that construction began at the site in the beginning of the 13th century and peaked in the 14th century (Ravesloot *et al.* 1986).[3] During the Medio period (AD 1200 to 1450) Casas Grandes became the major node for Mesoamerican exchanges and the strongest link to Mesoamerican prestige-goods economies in the Southwest (Di Peso 1974). Casas Grandes appears to have controlled the flow of Mesoamerican prestige goods into the Southwest and indeed some of these goods, including copper bells and macaws, were produced or raised in the town (Di Peso *et al.* 1974b). The bulk of trade, however, was in Southwestern prestige goods, including shell and ceramics, exchanged to lineage heads north of Casas Grandes (McGuire 1980, pp. 19–22).

The distribution of copper bells and macaws in this period suggests that Casas Grandes interacted primarily with the Mogollon and passed few Mesoamerican goods on to the Anasazi of the San Juan Basin. We have located a total of 108 macaws from Mogollon, Salado, and Sinagua[4] sites dating between AD 1200 and 1450, but only 9 from contemporary Anasazi sites (Di Peso *et al.* 1974b, p. 185). Medio period Mogollon sites have yielded over 110 copper bells, with no Anasazi bells securely dated to this time period (Di Peso *et al.* 1974a, pp. 508–9).[5] Casas Grandes also appears to have played a predominant rôle in the exchange of shell within the Southwest. During Pueblo III times the Anasazi lineage heads became dependent upon a foreign centre, Casas Grandes, for their prestige goods and this centre apparently favoured other groups in its exchange. The supply of high-value Mesoamerican goods and lower-value Southwestern valuables declined and became more erratic.

The relations of production and exchange in the prehistory of the San Juan Basin were quite dynamic, with several major shifts in the nature of these relations. This discussion only concerns the final and most dramatic shift, the one that led to the abandonment of the basin. Both events which have been advanced to account for this abandonment, environmental deterioration and the breakdown of linkages to Mesoamerica, might have led to the collapse of the late Pueblo III Anasazi economy. They would have strained the relations of production and exchange and revealed the contradictions in the ideology which supported these relations, resulting in a transformation of the mode of production and the economy.

In the absence of technological innovations to increase production, or of population decline, environmental deterioration might have created a crisis for a kin-ordered mode of production. Such deterioration would have deprived lineages with marginal lands of their means of production and would have decreased the volume of production even for more affluent lineages. These changes would have increased the level of conflict within societies, possibly in excess of the mediating potential of kinship relations. A decrease in production would have also threatened the prestige-goods economy linking the San Juan Basin Anasazi societies. Lower rates of production would have forced lineage heads to moderate their expenditures and lose power, or to become more demanding in their extraction of surplus from the primary producers. The existence of many competing communities in the Pueblo III San Juan Basin would have militated against the first option, and the second could have led the populace to dispose of their leadership.

The interruption in the flow of precious items resulting from the rise of Casas Grandes might have created a crisis even in the absence of the productive crisis. The cut-off of Mesoamerican goods would have deprived the highest-level leaders of the material symbols they needed to legitimize their status, and of the valuables they needed to maintain exchange relations with other leaders. Since exchange in prestige-goods economies tends to be organized from the top to the bottom, this disruption in the flow of high-level valuables would have disrupted the exchange of lower-level valuables, effectively denying all lineage heads the means of enforcing the contributions of their subordinates. Thus, the lineage heads' hold over the system of asymmetrical exchanges would have been weakened or destroyed, leaving the door open for an effective challenge to the existing order.

The crisis of the late 13th century was not only environmental and social but also ideological. The resolution of this ideological crisis set in motion the transformation of Pueblo III society to Pueblo IV forms and the abandonment of the San Juan Basin. The productive and distributional crises undermined the sustaining ideology of the San Juan Anasazi to an extent that had not occurred in the past. The droughts probably resulted in real material hardship for the Anasazi, perhaps because of population densities greater than any in the past. The loss or erratic supply of social valuables would have thrown the system of social reproduction into chaos, requiring people to renegotiate the symbolic exchanges which legitimized their social lives in terms of a new set of social meanings with a new set of artefacts. Individuals would have perceived both the material deprivation and the social chaos as a failure of the lineage heads to fulfil their obligations, a view reinforced by the lineage heads' loss of their symbols of power and legitimization. The contradictions in the existing moral order would have been laid bare for all to see.

The demystification of a legitimizing ideology creates the necessary prerequisite for social transformation, the motivation needed before social action can occur. In prestige-goods economies power derives from the social meaning of valuables controlled by the lineage head and in a kin-ordered mode of production the lineage head's control of production derives from ideologically sanctioned kin relations. The creation of a new ideology transforms social meanings, destroying the advantage of the old leadership. The new leadership would be made up of those who could manipulate the new ideology and transform the system of dependencies to serve their own ends. Anthropologists commonly refer to such ideological transformations as crisis cults (LaBarre 1971). I propose that the appearance, rapid spread, and popularity of the *katsina* religion among the Anasazi by AD 1300 can be explained in terms of this concept.

All such cults include prophets who promise a return to the happiness of the past if people reject the ways of the present and perform certain rituals. The promised rewards may come in the near future or lie in a foreign land. The ideal moves people to action and this action transforms reality (Godelier 1982).

Drawing on the anthropological literature concerning crisis cults, we can identify a number of archaeologically visible characteristics of such cults (Wallace 1956, Worsley 1957, Hobsbawm 1959, LaBarre 1971). Material deprivation and social disintegration precede the appearance of these cults. They spread rapidly, especially within the boundaries of cultural systems. The cults integrate existing beliefs and symbolic forms in new ways, and they borrow elements from other ideologies, especially those of dominant societies. They commonly incorporate imitative magic; individuals imitate in ritual and through objects the new and better world promised by the cult.

The Anasazi *katsina* religion manifests all of these characteristics. I have already discussed in some detail the collapse of social order and material stress that preceded the cult, and identified the contradictions in the late Pueblo III San Juan Anasazi world. The mural and rock art of the cult commonly includes warriors and shields, interpreted by many researchers as evidence of cultural disequilibrium associated with the cult (Ellis & Hammack 1968, Hibben 1975, pp. 130–2, Peckham 1981, p. 34, Adams 1983). I will now consider each of the other characteristics in their turn.[6]

The *katsina* religion appeared suddenly among the late 13th-century Anasazi of southern New Mexico and rapidly spread throughout the Anasazi region, except for the Taos archaeological district. Rock art associated with the cult manifested itself abruptly in southern New Mexico by AD 1325 and radiated swiftly to all Anasazi areas except Taos (Schaafsma & Schaafsma 1974, p. 543, Schaafsma 1980, pp. 243–301). Archaeologists have reported *kiva* murals at a number of widely dispersed Pueblo IV pueblos, including Awatovi (Smith 1952), Pottery Mound (Hibben 1967, 1975), Kuaua (Dutton 1963), Pueblo del Encierro (Schaafsma 1965), and Gran Quivira (Peckham 1981).

The Anasazi *katsina* religion incorporates a number of existing ritual features combined with innovations derived ultimately from Mesoamerica (Adams 1983). *Kivas* remained the centres of ritual life and the cult incorporated traditional *kiva* features such as the *sipapu*. Most researchers accept the ultimate Mesoamerican origin of the basic symbols and features of the cult, including masked rain dancers, the feathered serpent, macaws, and jaguars (Parsons 1939, Beals 1943, Brew 1943). The Anasazi began incorporating many of these features and symbols during the AD 1200s: Ferdon (1955, pp. 8–12) reported a plumed serpent from a Pueblo III tower in McElmo canyon; macaws occurred in larger Pueblo III sites (Hargrave 1970), and masked dancers appear in the Southwest both in the rock art of the Jornada Mogollon, as early as AD 1000 (Schaafsma & Schaafsma 1974, Schaafsma 1980, pp. 235–42), and on Classic Mimbres ceramics (Carlson 1982). The Pueblo IV cult was not a totally original phenomenon but a unique recombination of existing symbols and features, many of which were derived from Mesoamerica.

Pueblo IV *kiva* murals depict the rituals of the religion. Masked figures dance with representations of the lost valuables of the past: macaws, marine shells, copper bells and tropical bird feathers (Smith 1952, Hibben 1975). The murals themselves appear to have been part of renewal rituals. *Kivas* contain from 1 to 100 separate murals painted one on top of the other, as repetitive imitative magic (Smith 1952, pp. 19–20, Hibben 1975, pp. 30–4, Peckham 1981, p. 34). In the pueblos, archaeologists find little or no marine shell (Smith 1952, Hibben 1975, pp. 60, 89, Hayes *et al.* 1981, p. 163), no copper bells, and rarely macaws (Hargrave 1970). Instead they recover clay copies of copper bells and representations of macaws and marine shells on murals and ceramics (Kidder 1932, p. 138, Smith 1952, Lambert 1958, Hibben 1975, pp. 60, 89, Hayes *et al.* 1981, p. 162). The wealth of the past, no longer attainable because of the collapse of the earlier prestige-goods economy, lives on on *kiva* walls, on ceramic vessels, and in clay copies – imitative magic to recover the glories of the past and ensure the cycle of the universe.

The *katsina* religion spread rapidly to all areas of the Anasazi except the northern Tiwa around Taos (Adams 1983, Schaafsma & Schaafsma 1974, p. 536). The modern northern Tiwa lack the religion (Parsons 1939) and there are no historic accounts of the religion among them (Smith 1952, pp. 75, 92). Prehistoric *kiva* murals do not appear in archaeological sites in the region, and Schaafsma (1980, pp. 285–6) explicitly reports that *katsina* religion rock art rarely occurs in the Taos region. If the religion did exist among the northern Tiwa, it must have been far weaker and less elaborate than in the other pueblo groups.

According to most researchers the Tiwa were the original inhabitants of the Rio Grande valley and the split into northern and southern groups occurred long before the early 1300s (Ford *et al.* 1972, p. 30). The northern Tiwa probably lived in the Taos area by AD 1000 and the archaeology of this region shows far greater continuity in occupation and style than any other region in the Rio Grande (Wetherington 1968, Ford *et al.* 1972). The only area in the Anasazi range where the Pueblo IV *katsina* religion was absent or very weak was also the area least affected by the stresses and migrations of the late 13th century. Considering that this was a crisis cult, it is not surprising that it apparently failed to take hold in the area where a crisis had not occurred.

Conclusion

I have proposed a complex scenario integrating material, social, and ideological factors to account for the transformation of Pueblo III Anasazi society. First, drought strained the Anasazi's productive capabilities. Given the population densities of the late Pueblo III period, this would have challenged the organizational capabilities of the Anasazi lineage heads to mitigate conflicts between competing lineage groups. Though Anasazi societies had survived drought in the San Juan Basin before, this time the rise of Casas Grandes interrupted the high-level exchange networks linking the Anasazi to west Mexico. Through the AD 1200s lineage heads would have had increasing difficulty sustaining the prestige-goods economy which maintained social reproduction in the region and the ideology that supported it. Anasazi populations faced real material deprivation and cultural breakdown. The stage was set for the rise of a crisis cult to transform the social and ideological order. Prophets of a new religion, incorporating some features familiar to the people and new features derived ultimately from Mesoamerican models and proximally from the masked dances of the Jornada, promised a better life. A utopia lay to the east with much rain and a fertile river valley; the people should go there and dance to ensure the cycle of the world and perform magic to recover the wealth of the past.

My purpose in this chapter has been to examine how we might come to a new understanding of Southwestern prehistory; an understanding that does not treat social units as self-contained billiard balls spinning off each other; an understanding that gives weight to both local adaptations and interactions in a field greater than a single river valley or even the Southwest; an understanding that does not invoke the spectre of Mesoamerican domination of the Southwest or deny the connectedness of the two regions. I have reviewed the application of Wallerstein's theory to this issue and found it limited in the insights it gives us. In its stead I propose that we must integrate considerations of production, exchange, and ideology. An examination of the Pueblo III to Pueblo IV transition illustrates how this approach allows us to link changes in the Southwest to changes in Mesoamerica without overly simplistic appeals to Mesoamerican domination of the Southwest. Equally important, it allows us to speak of prehistoric cultural change in terms of the interaction of material, social, and ideological forces without reducing any of these factors to epiphenomena.

Acknowledgements

This chapter benefited from the assistance of many people. Conversations with Immanuel Wallerstein, Edward Ferdon, R. Gwinn Vivian, and Catherine Lutz helped me in the formulation of my ideas. Michael Schiffer, Jane Collins, Vincas Steponaitis, Richard Nelson, J. Charles Kelley, Emlin Myers, and Margaret Conkey reviewed earlier drafts of it. It was Wes Jernigan who first suggested to me that the Pueblo *katsina* religion originated as a crisis cult; correspondence with Chuck Adams concerning the *katsina* religion was very helpful. I must thank two people for telling me I was wrong in earlier versions of this work; Albert Schroeder for pointing out I had the origins of the *katsina* religion too early and John Ravesloot for correcting the dating of Casas Grandes. Finally, I appreciated the friendship, help, and encouragement of the late Charles Di Peso.

Notes

1 The use of the term 'Southwest' for this region is somewhat problematic because the area is the southwest of the USA but the northwest of Mexico. At this time no other label for the region has been widely accepted and more descriptive expressions such as the Mexican–American west are awkward when used in text. For these reasons the parochial use of 'Southwest' has been continued in this chapter.

2 The *katsina* (*kachina*) religion of the Southwestern pueblos is characterized by the public performances of masked dancers, or *katsinas*. It is an aesthetic religion that requires its practitioners to make material sacrifices and regularly perform the rituals of the religion. The rituals function to maintain the cycle of the world necessary for agriculture and the continuance of all life.

3 This new dating for the Casas Grandes Medio period shifts the period from AD 1150–1350 to AD 1200–1400. Because of the new dates, I had to rethink my previous interpretation of the P III to P IV transition (McGuire 1986a, 1986b). Through a re-examination of the data I realized that Mesoamerican goods stopped appearing in Anasazi sites in the AD 1200s, not at AD 1300, suggesting that Casas Grandes should be seen as a blockage to Anasazi exchange and not a facilitator. The change also caused me to decide that the processes of ideological transformation would have had to have occurred in the 13th century and not the 14th.

4 Sinagua and Salado refer to archaeological complexes that occur in the mountains of Arizona and western New Mexico. Some researchers treat them as manifestations of a late Mogollon culture and others regard them as separate cultures.

5 The number of sites excavated in the Anasazi area for this time period exceeds the number excavated for the Mogollon. It is highly unlikely that the relative frequencies of macaws and bells result from excavation bias.

6 Adams (1983) provides a detailed consideration of the spread and variability of the *katsina* religion in the ethnographic and prehistoric pueblos. His discussion differs from my own most notably in terms of its scope. Whereas Adams seeks to explain the variety and detail of the religion, my emphasis is on accounting for those similarities that unify the religion. I primarily wish to answer the questions of why the religion appeared when it did and why it gained popularity and spread so rapidly. Researchers seriously interested in the Pueblo *katsina* religion should consult Adams's work for a more in-depth consideration than I have presented here.

References

Adams, E. C. 1983. The appearance, evolution, and meaning of the katsina cult to the pre-hispanic world of the Southwestern United States. Paper presented at the 11th International Congress of Anthropological and Ethnological Sciences, Vancouver.

Akins, N. J. & J. D. Schelberg 1981. Evidence for organizational complexity as seen from the mortuary practices at Chaco Canyon. Paper presented at the Annual Meeting of the Society for American Archaeology, San Diego.

Althusser, L. & E. Balibar 1970. *Reading Capital*. New York: Pantheon Books.

Altschul, J. H. 1978. The development of the Chacoan interaction sphere. *Journal of Anthropological Research* **34**, 109–46.

Beals, R. L. 1943. Relations between Mesoamerica and the Southwest. In *El Norte de*

Mexico y el Sur de los Estados Unidos, 245–52. Proceedings of La Tercera Reunión de Mesa Redonda sobre Problemas Antropologicos de Mexico y Centro America. Sociedad Mexicana de Antropologia, Mexico, D.F.

Blanton, R. E. & G. Feinman 1984. The Mesoamerican world system. *American Anthropologist* **86**, 673–82.

Blanton, R. E., S. A. Kowalewski, G. Feinman & J. Appel 1981. *Ancient Mesoamerica*. Cambridge: Cambridge University Press.

Bloch, M. 1983. *Marxism and anthropology*. Oxford: Oxford University Press.

Bradfield, R. M. 1971. *The changing pattern of Hopi agriculture*. Royal Anthropological Institute of Great Britain and Northern Ireland Occasional Papers **30**, London.

Brew, J. O. 1943. On the Pueblo IV and on the katchina–Tlaloc relations. In *El Norte de Mexico y el Sur de los Estados Unidos*, 241–5. Proceedings of La Tercera Reunion de Mesa Redonda sobre Problemas Antropologicos de Mexico y Centro America. Sociedad Mexicana de Antropologia, Mexico, D.F.

Carlson, R. L. 1982. The Mimbres katchina cult. In *Mogollon Archaeology: Proceedings of the 1980 Mogollon Conference*, P. H. Beckett (ed.), 147–56. Ramona: Acoma Books.

Cattanach, G. S., Jr. 1980. *Long House, Mesa Verde National Park, Colorado*. National Park Service Publications in Archeology no. 7H, Washington, D.C.

Cordell, L. S. 1979. *Cultural resources overview: middle Rio Grande Valley, New Mexico*. Albuquerque: USDA Forest Service.

Cordell, L. S. & F. Plog 1979. Escaping the confines of normative thought: a reevaluation of Puebloan prehistory. *American Antiquity* **44**, 405–29.

Dean, J. 1970. Aspects of Tsegi phase social organization: a trial reconstruction. In *Reconstructing prehistoric Pueblo societies*, W. A. Longacre (ed.), 140–74. Albuquerque: University of New Mexico Press.

Dean, J. & W. Robinson 1977. *Dendroclimatic variability in the American Southwest, A.D. 680 to 1970*. Laboratory of Tree-Ring Research, University of Arizona, Tucson.

Di Peso, C. C. 1974. *Casas Grandes, a fallen trading center of the Gran Chichimeca*. Vol. 2: *The Medio period*. Dragoon: The Amerind Foundation.

Di Peso, C. C., J. B. Rinaldo & G. J. Fenner 1974a. *Casas Grandes, a fallen trading center of the Gran Chichimeca*. Vol. 7: *Stone and metal*. Dragoon: The Amerind Foundation.

Di Peso, C. C., J. B. Rinaldo & G. J. Fenner 1974b. *Casas Grandes, a fallen trading center of the Gran Chichimeca*. Vol. 8: *Bone, perishables, commerce, subsistence, and burials*. Dragoon: The Amerind Foundation.

Dittert, A. E. 1959. *Culture change in the Cebolleta Mesa region, New Mexico*. Unpublished PhD dissertation, Department of Anthropology, University of Arizona, Tucson.

Dutton, B. P. 1963. *Sun Father's way, the kiva murals of Kuaua*. Albuquerque: University of New Mexico Press.

Ekholm, K. & J. Friedman 1982. 'Capital', imperialism and exploitation in ancient world systems. *Review* **4**, 87–109.

Ellis, F. H. & L. Hammack 1968. The inner sanctum of Feather Cave, a Mogollon sun and earth shrine linking Mexico and the Southwest. *American Antiquity* **33**, 25–44.

Euler, R. C., G. J. Gumerman, T. N. V. Karlstrom, J. S. Dean & H. H. Richard 1979. The Colorado Plateaus: cultural dynamics and paleoenvironments. *Science* **205**, 1089–101.

Ferdon, E. N., Jr. 1955. *A trial survey of Mexican–Southwestern architectural parallels*. School of American Research Monograph **11**, Sante Fe.

Findlow, F. J. & M. Bolognese 1982. Regional modeling of obsidian procurement in the American Southwest. In *Contexts for prehistoric exchange*, J. E. Ericson & T. K. Earle (eds), 53–82. New York: Academic Press.

Flannery, K. V. 1968. The Olmecs and the valley of Oaxaca: a model for interaction in Formative times. In *Dumbarton Oaks Conference on the Olmec*, E. P. Benson (ed.), 79–110. Washington, D.C.: Dumbarton Oaks.

Ford, R. I., A. H. Schroeder & S. L. Peckham 1972. Three perspectives on Pueblo prehistory. In *New perspectives on the Pueblos*, Alfonso Ortiz (ed.), 19–39. Albuquerque: University of New Mexico Press.

Frankenstein, S. & M. J. Rowlands 1978. The internal structure and regional context of Early Iron Age society in south-western Germany. *Bulletin of the Institute of Archaeology, London University* **15**, 73–112.

Friedman, J. 1974. Marxism, structuralism and vulgar materialism. *Man* **9**, 444–69.

Gledhill, J. 1978. Formative development in the North American Southwest. In *Social Organisation and Settlement*, D. Green, C. Haselgrove & M. Spriggs (eds), 241–84. British Archaeological Reports International Series 47, Oxford.

Godelier, M. 1982. The ideal in the real. In *Culture, ideology and politics*, R. Samuel & G. S. Jones (eds), 12–38. London: Routledge and Kegan Paul.

Grebinger, P. 1973. Prehistoric social organization in Chaco Canyon, New Mexico: an alternative reconstruction. *The Kiva* **39**, 3–23.

Hack, J. T. 1942. The changing physical environment of the Hopi Indians of Arizona. *Papers of the Peabody Museum of American Archaeology and Ethnology* **35**, 1–85.

Hargrave, L. 1970. *Mexican macaws*. Anthropological Papers of the University of Arizona no. 20, Tucson.

Hayes, A. C. 1964. *The archaeological survey of Wetherill Mesa, Mesa Verde National Park, Colorado*. U.S. National Park Service Archeological Series no. 7A, Washington, D.C.

Hayes, A. C., J. N. Young & A. H. Warren 1981. *Excavation of Mound 7, Gran Quivira National Monument, New Mexico*. National Park Service Publications in Archeology no. 16, Washington, D.C.

Hibben, F. C. 1967. Mexican features of mural paintings at Pottery Mound. *Archaeology* **20**, 84–7.

Hibben, F. C. 1975. *Kiva art of the Anasazi at Pottery Mound*. Las Vegas: KC Publications.

Hobsbawm, E. J. 1959. *Primitive rebels*. New York: W. W. Norton.

Hobsbawm, E. J. 1964. Introduction. In *Pre-capitalist economic formations*, K. Marx, 1–67. New York: International Publishers.

Irwin-Williams, C. (ed.) 1972. *The structure of Chacoan society in the northern Southwest: investigations at the Salmon site 1972*. Eastern New Mexico University Contributions in Anthropology no. 4, Portales.

Judd, N. M. 1954. *The material culture of Pueblo Bonito*. Smithsonian Miscellaneous Collections no. 147, Washington, D.C.

Judge, W. J. 1979. The development of a complex cultural ecosystem in the Chaco Basin, New Mexico. In *Proceedings of the First Conference on Scientific Research in the National Parks*, R. Linn (ed.), Vol. 2, 901–5. National Park Service Transactions and Proceedings Series no. 5.

Kelley, J. C. 1981. Discussion. In *The proto-historic period in the North American Southwest, A.D. 1450–1700*, D. R. Wilcox & W. B. Masse (eds), 434–9. Arizona State University Anthropological Research Papers no. 24, Tempe.

Kidder, A. V. 1932. *The artifacts of Pecos*. Andover: Robert S. Peabody Foundation for Archaeology.

Kohl, P. 1979. The 'world economy' of west Asia in the third millennium B.C., In *South Asian Archaeology 1977*, M. Taddei (ed.), 55–85. Naples: Istituto Universitario Orientale.

LaBarre, W. 1971. Materials for a history of studies of crisis cults: a bibliographic essay. *Current Anthropology* **12**, 3–27.

Laclau, E. 1977. *Politics and ideology in Marxist theory*. London: New Left Books.

Lambert, M. F. 1958. A pottery bell from northwestern New Mexico. *American Antiquity* **24**, 184–5.

LeBlanc, S. A. 1978. Settlement patterns in the El Morro Valley, New Mexico. In *Investigations of the Southwestern Anthropological Research Group: an experiment in archaeological cooperation*, R. C. Euler & G. J. Gumerman (eds), 45–51. Flagstaff: Museum of Northern Arizona.

Lister, R. H. 1966. *Contributions to Mesa Verde archeology III: Site 866, and the cultural sequence at four villages in the Far View group, Mesa Verde National Park, Colorado*. University of Colorado Studies Series in Anthropology no. 12, Boulder.

Lyons, T. R. & R. K. Hitchcock 1977. Remote sensing interpretation of an Anasazi land route system. In *Aerial and remote sensing techniques in archaeology*, T. R. Lyons & R. K. Hitchcock (eds), 111–34. Reports of the Chaco Center no. 2, National Parks Service, Albuquerque.

McGuire, R. H. 1980. The Mesoamerican connection in the Southwest. *The Kiva* **46**, 3–38.

McGuire, R. H. 1983a. Breaking down cultural complexity: inequality and heterogeneity. *Advances in Archaeological Method and Theory* **6**, 91–142.

McGuire, R. H. 1983b. *The role of shell trade in the explanation of Hohokam prehistory*. Paper presented at the 1983 Hohokam Conference, Tempe.

McGuire, R. H. 1986a. Economies and modes of production in the prehistoric Southwestern periphery. In *Ripples in the Chichimec Sea: new considerations of Southwestern–Mesoamerican interactions*, F. J. Mathien & R. H. McGuire (eds), 243–69. Carbondale: Southern Illinois University Press.

McGuire, R. H. 1986b. *The Mexican–American West as a periphery of Mesoamerica*: precirculated paper, in *Comparative studies in the development of complex societies*, World Archaeological Congress Vol. 3 (mimeo).

Martin, P. S. & F. Plog 1973. *The archaeology of Arizona: a study of the Southwest region*. Garden City: Doubleday Natural History Press.

Marx, K. 1964. *Pre-capitalist economic formations* (edited by E. J. Hobsbawm, translated by J. Cohen). New York: International Publishers.

Marx, K. 1967. *Capital*, Vol. 3 (translated by S. Moore & E. Aveling). New York: International Publishers.

Marx, K. 1968. Preface to a *Contribution to the critique of political economy*. In *Selected works*, K. Marx & F. Engels (translated by S. W. Ryazanskaya), 123–32. London: Lawrence and Wishart.

Marx, K. & F. Engels 1947. *The German ideology* (translated by R. Pascal). New York: International Publishers.

Mathien, F. J. & R. H. McGuire (eds) 1986. *Ripples in the Chichimec Sea: new considerations of Southwestern–Mesoamerican interactions*. Carbondale: Southern Illinois University Press.

Meillassoux, C. 1981. *Maidens, meal and money*. Cambridge: Cambridge University Press.

Morris, E. H. 1919. *The Aztec ruin*. Anthropological Papers of the American Museum of Natural History no. 26, New York.

Obenauf, M. S. 1983. The prehistoric roadway network in the San Juan Basin. In

Remote sensing in cultural resources management: The San Juan Basin project, D. L. Drager & T. R. Lyons (eds), 117–22. Albuquerque: National Park Service.

Ollman, B. 1976. *Alienation*. Cambridge: Cambridge University Press.

Parsons, E. C. 1939. *Pueblo Indian religion*. Chicago: University of Chicago Press.

Peckham, B. A. 1981. Pueblo IV murals at Mound 7. In *Contributions to Gran Quivira archaeology*, A. C. Hayes (ed.), 15–38. National Park Service Publications in Archeology no. 17, Washington, D.C.

Pepper, G. H. 1920. *Pueblo Bonito*. Anthropological Papers of the American Museum of Natural History no. 27, New York.

Pippin, L. C. 1979. *The prehistory and paleoecology of the Guadalupe ruin, Sandoval County, New Mexico*. Unpublished PhD dissertation, Department of Anthropology, Washington State University, Pullman.

Plog, F. 1983. Political and economic alliances on the Colorado plateau A.D. 400 to 1450. *Advances in World Archaeology* **2**, 289–330.

Plog, F., S. Upham & P. C. Weigand 1982. A perspective on Mogollon–Mesoamerican interaction. In *Mogollon archaeology: Proceedings of the 1980 Conference*, P. H. Beckett (ed.) 227–38. Ramona: Acoma Books.

Polanyi, K. 1957. *Trade and markets in the early empires*. Chicago: Chicago University Press.

Powers, R. P., W. B. Gillespie & S. H. Lekson 1983. *The outlier survey*. Reports of the Chaco Center no. 3. National Parks Service, Albuquerque.

Ravesloot, J. C., J. S. Dean & M. S. Foster 1986. A new perspective on the Casas Grandes tree-ring dates. Paper presented at the Mogollon Conference, Tucson, Oct. 16–17.

Renfrew, C. 1975. Trade as action at a distance: questions of integration and communication. In *Ancient civilization and trade*, J. Sabloff & C. C. Lamberg-Karlovsky (eds), 3–59. Albuquerque: University of New Mexico Press.

Rohn, A. H. 1971. *Mug House, Mesa Verde National Park, Colorado*. National Park Service Publications in Archeology no. 7D, Washington, D.C.

Sahlins, M. D. 1972. *Stone Age economics*. Chicago: Aldine–Atherton.

Schaafsma, P. 1965. Kiva murals from Pueblo de Encierro (LA70). *El Palacio* **72**, 6–16.

Schaafsma, P. 1980. *Indian rock art of the Southwest*. Albuquerque: University of New Mexico Press.

Schaafsma, P. & C. F. Schaafsma 1974. Evidence for the origins of the Pueblo katchina cult as suggested by Southwestern rock art. *American Antiquity* **39**, 535–45.

Schneider, H. K. 1974. *Economic man*. New York: Free Press.

Schroeder, A. H. 1966. Pattern diffusion from Mexico into the Southwest after A.D. 600. *American Antiquity* **31**, 18–24.

Seddon, D. (ed.) 1974. *Relations of production: Marxist approaches to the study of economic anthropology*. London: Frank Cass.

Smith, W. 1952. *Kiva mural decorations at Awatovi and Kawaika-a, with a survey of other wall paintings in the Pueblo Southwest*. Papers of the Peabody Museum of American Archaeology and Ethnology no. 37, Harvard University, Cambridge, Mass.

Strathern, A. J. 1971. *The rope of Moka*. Cambridge: Cambridge University Press.

Tainter, J. A. & D. A. Gillio 1980. *Cultural resources overview: Mt. Taylor area, New Mexico*. Albuquerque: USDA Forest Service.

Terray, E. 1975. Classes and class consciousness in the Abron kingdom of Gyaman. In *Marxist analyses and social anthropology*, M. Bloch (ed.), 85–135. London: Malaby Press.

Upham, S. 1982. *Politics and power*. New York: Academic Press.

Vivian, R. G. & T. W. Mathews 1965. *Kin Kletso: a Pueblo III community in Chaco Canyon, New Mexico*. Southwestern Monuments Association Technical Series no. 5, Globe.

Vivian, R. G. 1974. Conservation and diversion: water-control systems in the Anasazi Southwest. In *Irrigation's impact on society*, T. E. Downing & M. Gibson (eds), 95–112. Anthropological Papers of the University of Arizona no. 25, Tucson.

Wallace, A. 1956. Revitalization movements. *American Anthropologist* **58**, 264–81.

Wallerstein, I. 1974. *The modern world-system I*. New York: Academic Press.

Wallerstein, I. 1978. Civilization and modes of production. *Theory and Society* **5**, 1–10.

Wallerstein, I. 1980. *The modern world-system II*. New York: Academic Press.

Weaver, D. E. 1978. *Prehistoric population dynamics and environmental exploitation in the Manuelito Canyon district, northwestern New Mexico*. Unpublished PhD dissertation, Department of Anthropology, Arizona State University, Tempe.

Weaver, M. P. 1972. *The Aztecs, Maya and their predecessors*. New York: Academic Press.

Weigand, P. C., G. Harbottle & E. V. Sayre 1977. Turquoise sources and source analysis: Mesoamerica and the southwestern U.S.A. In *Exchange systems in prehistory*, T. K. Earle & J. E. Ericson (eds), 15–34. New York: Academic Press.

Wetherington, R. K. 1968. *Excavations at Pot Creek pueblo*. Fort Burgwin Research Center no. 6, Taos.

Whitecotton, J. W. & R. A. Pailes 1986. New World precolumbian world systems. In *Ripples in the Chichimec Sea: new considerations of Southwestern–Mesoamerican interactions*, F. J. Mathien & R. H. McGuire (eds), 183–204. Carbondale: Southern Illinois University Press.

Wilcox, D. R. 1986. A historical analysis of the problem of Southwestern–Mesoamerican connections. In *Ripples in the Chichimec Sea: new considerations of Southwestern–Mesoamerican interactions*, F. J. Mathien & R. H. McGuire (eds), 9–44. Carbondale: Southern Illinois University Press.

Wilcox, D. R. & L. O. Shenk 1977. *The architecture of the Casa Grande and its interpretation*. Arizona State Museum Archaeological Series no. 115, Tucson.

Wolf, E. R. 1981. The mills of inequality: a marxian approach. In *Social inequality: comparative and developmental approaches*, G. D. Berreman (ed.), 41–58. New York: Academic Press.

Wolf, E. R. 1982. *Europe and the people without history*. Berkeley: University of California Press.

Worsley, P. 1957. *The trumpet shall sound*. London: MacGibbon and Kee.

Zubrow, E. 1971. Carrying capacity and dynamic equilibrium in the prehistoric Southwest. *American Antiquity* **36**, 127–38.

3 *Explaining the Iroquois: tribalization on a prehistoric periphery*

DENA F. DINCAUZE and
ROBERT J. HASENSTAB

> Given the complexity and particularity of economic, social, and ideological interaction, any analysis must be historically contextualized. Tension, and the resolution of tension within a given society, cannot be understood except in terms of its specific historical trajectory. [S]ome element of Wallerstein's 'World System' has to be incorporated in the analysis (Bender 1985, pp. 53–4).

The cultural uniqueness of the Iroquoian-speaking peoples of northeastern North America was obvious at contact, and its explanation has remained a focus of Iroquoianist research through the current century, with many different hypotheses proffered. We present here a preliminary version of an historical–contextual explanation of that uniqueness, which posits the Iroquois as part of a socio-economic system larger than has been considered previously by Iroquoianist scholars.

The problem and some suggested explanations

Although the Iroquois are presented in introductory texts and survey volumes as the quintessential exemplars of northeastern North American native cultures, Iroquoianist scholars at least since Parker (1916) have been burdened to explain the uniqueness of the Iroquois, whom they perceived as exotic elements in the greater Northeast, where hunters and gatherers and small homestead farmers otherwise dominated. Both lifeways and language set the Iroquois apart.

Most of the Iroquoian-speaking peoples of the Northeast were sedentary to semi-sedentary maize horticulturalists living in nucleated, palisaded villages or towns. Their social organization was based on extended family and lineage coresidence in longhouses, with wider linkages through clans that had political as well as social functions. Iroquoian religion contains ritual elements that correspond with the religions of sedentary farmers in the

Figure 3.1 Location map of eastern North America. The northern Iroquoian-speaking homeland is generalized for the late prehistoric period, within a region dominated by Algonquian-speaking populations. The languages to the west and south of Iroquoia are poorly known for the period.

continental interior as well as others that echo those of their hunter-gatherer neighbours (Fenton 1940). They were involved heavily in raiding warfare (Fenton 1978, Tuck 1978). The bellicosity culminated in the 17th-century fur trade wars, in which the 'League' Iroquois south of Lake Ontario destroyed the Iroquoians to the west of them.

The Algonquian-speaking northern neighbours of the Iroquois were essentially hunter-gatherers who raised little maize or other cultigens and who did not live in nucleated, semi-permanent settlements. To the east and south were Algonquian-speaking farmers who were more mobile and less

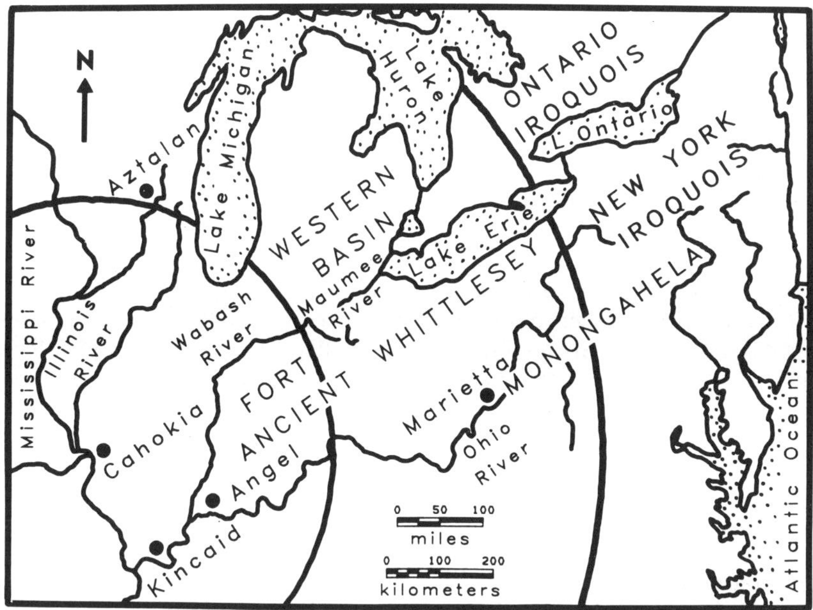

Figure 3.2 The upper Mississippi and Great Lakes drainage basins during the late prehistoric period. The locations of key archaeological sites and cultures as discussed in the text are shown with the major rivers. The Ontario and New York Iroquois cultures occupied either side of the lower Great Lakes Basin, and together comprised the northern Iroquoian-speaking peoples of Canada and the United States, respectively. Average canoe-travel times to Cahokia are indicated by concentric arcs, the inner representing 15–20 days' travel and the outer 30–40 days' travel (from Little 1987).

socially integrated than the Iroquois. To the south and west were farming peoples whose material culture, at least, resembled aspects of the culture of the Iroquois, whose languages were mostly Eastern Siouan (Fig. 3.1), and who were rapidly removed from the stage of history before the 17th century (Trigger 1978a, pp. 802–4).

The 'remarkable concordances' (Fenton 1940, p. 199) of Iroquoian culture over the span of territory they occupied in what is now southern Ontario province of Canada, western New York state, and extreme northeastern Ohio (Fig. 3.2) have been acknowledged by scholars since Morgan, among them archaeologists studying prehistoric 'Iroquoia'. Those widespread similarities have helped to define a cohesive realm of Iroquoianist scholarship during this century, and the dominant problem was early defined as the need to explain Iroquoian uniqueness.

Explanations

Early in the 20th century a migration hypothesis became widely accepted because of its parsimony in accounting for the presence of exotic traits in the

Northeast, including the Iroquoian languages. Parker (1916) elaborated the migration hypothesis into its classic form. In Parker's scenario, the Iroquois brought their horticultural subsistence base and village life from an ancestral home near the mouth of the Ohio River (confluence with the Mississippi).

By mid-century, opposition to the Iroquoian migration hypothesis was mounting, as migration hypotheses in general lost favour in North America. MacNeish's (1952) demonstration of ceramic continuities through several centuries in many areas of Iroquoia was eventually accepted as a refutation (Ritchie 1961). If there were no late prehistoric discontinuities in the culture history of the region, then a migratory origin of the Iroquois was considered disproved. As researchers tested MacNeish's ceramic continuities, and established others in house forms and successive village relocations (Wright 1966, Tuck 1971, Ritchie & Funk 1973, Pendergast 1975), the *in situ* hypothesis became the reigning explanation of Iroquoian culture history: development in place. However, neither migration from elsewhere nor development in place actually explains why a particular culture has the characteristics it displays; explanation must be sought in different spheres of understanding.

Understanding of the special character of Iroquoian culture has recently been sought in environmental or social factors, and explanations proliferate. An important contender for lead hypothesis, appearing in many versions, sees population growth, social complexity, village nucleation, and intensifying warfare as responses to maize horticulture in benign environments (e.g. Gibbon 1972, Noble 1975b). The appearance of maize and other semi-tropical cultigens in the Northeast is known to coincide roughly with the climatic amelioration centred around ad 1000, and it is argued that the cultigens diffused because people wanted them and the climate had warmed to the point that the plants could be grown in the region. Horticulture thus becomes a historic given, and it was argued that social development proceeded apace as cultigens, which can be multiplied to meet increasing need and which can be stored as well as or better than most wild foods, relieved some of the environmental pressures restricting population density. With increased sedentism, populations can grow to the extent that they can protect their stores from competitors and can acquire the resources of land and labour to provide for themselves. With growing population, and larger stores, sedentary village life becomes both an amenity and a necessity. The development of coresidential lineages out of extended families can be expected when labour must be mobilized to till soil and harvest crops. In sedentary communities, social pressures against fission will necessitate the development of some hierarchical mechanisms of social control, thus the clans and the confederacies.

However, this ecological-social argument cannot explain the uniqueness of the Iroquois, since knowledge of and access to maize and other cultigens spread throughout the Northeast to the apparent environmental limits within a few centuries. The issue of why the farming Algonquian speakers failed to converge culturally with the Iroquois, or vice versa, remains as unexplained as ever.

The Iroquois strategy of intensification seems fraught with risk for several reasons (see Hayden 1978). Dependence upon a limited number of non-indigenous plant foods near their climatic limits places the communities at risk from climatic and biological disasters (droughts, frosts, fires, blights, pests, etc.). Established villages and extensive stores are vulnerable to attack by human enemies as well as by non-human competitors such as rodents and insects. Population nucleation creates crowding stress and increased conflicts, while the possibility of social fissioning diminishes with the amount of labour invested in facilities. The Algonquian farmers, on the other hand, developed in a different direction, maintaining a mixed economy, seasonal mobility, and lower population densities. Thereby they diverged less from their older cultural patterns of subsistence and society than did the Iroquois. How are we to understand the contrast?

Seeing Iroquoian warfare as central to the uniqueness of the culture, Wright (1966) and Hayden (1978) have separately offered hypotheses based on the need for defence to explain many other aspects of Iroquoian culture. The need for civil defence is seen as explaining the palisaded villages. Other aspects of Iroquoian culture, such as matriclans, can also be related functionally to intensifying warfare (Divale 1984). The threat that initiated the need for defence is either unspecified or located in the early historic period, when trade competition developed along the St. Lawrence River and its tributaries (Hayden 1978). The chronology of several of the traits related to the defence hypothesis fails to support these arguments very well; palisaded villages occur before ad 1000 in Ontario, inter-group and interpersonal hostility becomes a salient aspect of the archaeological record by ad 1400 (Tuck 1971, Pearce 1984), and the origin of clans cannot yet be related to either of the other traits (Whallon 1968).

Recently, Ramsden (1978) and Hayden (1978) have proposed control of trade and commodity flows in the Great Lakes Basin as the source of Iroquoian strength and the explanation for their social cohesiveness. Ramsden elaborated an argument explaining how key elements of Iroquoian culture could have developed in response to the economic and social pressures engendered by successful monopolies on the transport of furs and other commodities to European traders in the Saint Lawrence Valley. Hayden (1978), noting that many of the traits implicated appear in the archaeological record prior to the 16th century, proposed some prehistoric trade monopolies as crucial factors in the formation of Iroquoian culture, but does not specify the time or the direction of this earlier trade.

Being convinced by the series of functionalist arguments summarized above that there are only a few key features that need explanation, we now set about explaining the historical or processual causes of selected features of Iroquoian culture. These may be defined as the complex of Iroquoian tribalization, intensive maize horticulture, and warfare (Hasenstab 1985) or, alternatively, the anomalous degree of social integration displayed by the Iroquois, whose society lacked any marked social stratification (D.F.D.). Believing that *historical* factors have played a larger rôle in shaping Iroquoian culture than it is currently fashionable to suggest, we call attention to the larger, regional, social and economic arenas in which Iroquoian culture may have been shaped (Fig. 3.2).

Cahokia: core and periphery

At the confluence of the Mississippi and Missouri rivers, not far above the confluence of the Ohio, the site of Cahokia sits in the American Bottom, commanding the major water routes from north and west, and within easy reach from the south and east. The largest prehistoric site in America north of Mexico, it was at the height of its size and influence between ad 900 and 1300. It is here that we look to see what forces might have impinged upon the proto-Iroquoian peoples and helped to define their cultural development in such particular ways. The phenomenon that was prehistoric Cahokia was in the right place at the right time to play such a defining rôle (Fig. 3.2; Table 3.1). One has only to be open to the possibility that the influence of an expanding chiefdom or city-state which was also a religious centre and trade nexus could have been felt 950 km to the northeast, to begin some productive speculations about processes at the interface between complex societies and village farmers.

The literature on Cahokia is contentious, revealing argument about almost every aspect of interpretation of its size and complexity. There is no consensus on whether it represented a city (e.g. Fowler 1974), although estimates of the resident population at its height range from 10 000 to 38 000

Table 3.1 Comparative chronologies at American Bottom and in the Northeast, AD 900–1500. Data compiled from various sources (see text). Note that separate columns may have different entities labelled.

Year (AD)	Cahokia area periods	Cahokia site phases	Northeast Periphery sites → E	Greater Iroquoia phase
1500				
1400	Oneota		Marietta	Chance
		Sand Prairie		
1300	Mississipian			Middleport, Oak Hill
			Kincaid, Angel	
		Moorehead		
1200				
		Stirling Lohmann	Aztalan	Glen Meyer, Owasco
1000				
	Emergent			
900	Mississipian			

within its 1336 ha (Fowler 1974, pp. 6, 25). Despite the scale of its public works, there is only argument about the possibility of its having been a state (O'Brien 1972, Gibbon 1974, Harn 1975, Iseminger 1980). There is no agreement about its representing an advanced chiefdom (Steponaitis 1978). It is hard to deny that the rich and complex interments in Mound 72, which include retainer sacrifice on a large scale, represent a hierarchy of social statuses; at least three, and probably four, levels of ranking are indicated by the differences in burial treatment. Data are inadequate to test whether the four-level site hierarchy posited by Fowler (1974, pp. 27, 32) existed at one time. There are, however, in the site scales and monumental architecture of the area, a number of suggestive parallels to Late Formative site hierarchies in Mesoamerica (cf. Wright 1977, p. 384).

The scale of the monumental earthworks is truly impressive. Monks Mound is the largest earthen structure north of Mexico; it covers roughly 6 ha of ground and rises to 30 m in height (Fowler 1974, pp. 6, 7). It is the largest of a complex of over 100 mounds, of smaller size and many shapes, that stood on the American Bottom near the present cities of St. Louis and East St. Louis. The core of the site, in its waning years, was enclosed by a bastioned palisade that required 15 000 trees to build, and was rebuilt four times between ad 1150 and 1300 (Iseminger 1982, p. 11).

The subsistence base was a horticultural economy founded upon domesticates such as maize and squash raised in gardens distributed among individual farmsteads around the American Bottom (Fowler 1974, pp. 3, 33–4, Bareis & Porter 1984, p. 185). Agricultural-scale production has not been well demonstrated, and some researchers insist that small growers in the environs of the major site were self-sufficient and not producing for a city (Bareis & Porter 1984, pp. 185–6). Wild foods and minor domesticates such as goosefoot, maygrass, knotweed, sunflower and nuts supplemented the vegetable diet. Beans are not well attested in the American Bottom, so that animal protein must have been important for nutrition; local meat sources included deer, birds (especially waterfowl), and fish (Bareis & Porter 1984, p. 185). The self-sufficiency of the Cahokia area in food has been called into question on several counts, most impressive among those being the poor nutritional state of some of its satellite populations (Goodman *et al.* 1985, Harn 1986, pp. 34–5).

The population aggregation was surpassed by no other known archaeological complex of its time north of Mexico. The site appears to have drawn population from surrounding areas, and perhaps from farther away as well. That there were expensive people to spare at the site is evidenced by the elaborate retainer sacrifices accompanying the young male buried in Mound 72, one of the smaller and earlier mounds at the site (Fowler 1974). The nature and quantity of imperishable objects found at Cahokia, and echoed in related sites along the rivers to the north, south, and east, indicate that Cahokia was also a nexus of commodity trade, attracting many kinds of raw materials and producing some specialty artefacts in large numbers (Parmalee 1958, O'Brien 1972, Prentice 1983, Yerkes 1983). Raw materials were drawn from the Gulf and Atlantic coasts and widely from within the midcontinental region. Spindle whorls imply cloth production, at a scale not yet estimated. It seems possible to infer that, like most early cities, the Cahokia area was a population and energy sink, drawing people and foodstuffs from a larger region.

Whatever its status of political organization, Cahokia functioned for a few centuries as the centre of a large political-economic network, by mechanisms unknown but probably functionally similar to tribute. In the language of world systems theory, Cahokia had many of the attributes of a core, although it certainly did not represent a capitalist or mercantile state (Hopkins & Wallerstein 1977, Wolf 1982). For the argument developed here, it is unnecessary to place the Cahokia phenomenon into any rigid taxonomic or evolutionary framework, and it is probably helpful not to do so (Gamble 1986).

During the centuries in which it dominated the continental interior, Cahokia stood at the apex of a ranked series of smaller settlements spread out along the alluvial plains of the main rivers (Fowler 1974). These sites ranged in size from major mound–plaza centres, surrounded at some time by extensive palisades, to smaller centres with a few mounds and a plaza, hamlets with or without palisades but lacking plazas and mounds, and individual farmsteads. In the north-east quarter, the sites tend to be smaller as distance from Cahokia increases. They are related to Cahokia by the site form and included structures, by artefactual similarities sometimes amounting to identity (special ceramics, stone hoes, beads, rarer items), and by ceremonial items and the rituals that those imply. The earliest of the distant mound–plaza centres was established far to the north at Aztalan (Fig. 3.2), early in the developmental period of Cahokia. Other major sites were later established on the Ohio, progressively farther east and upstream from the Mississippian confluence. Major sites for which some data are published include the Kincaid site on the Black Bottom of the Ohio (Muller 1978), with mounds, a plaza, and a bastioned stockade; Kincaid was founded sometime around ad 1200 and lasted about two centuries. Farther upriver on the Ohio is the Angel site, poorly dated but thought to be the northeasternmost site founded during the duration of Cahokia.

As Cahokia weakened as a centre, after ad 1300, the Ohio Valley sites flourished but appear to have dominated support areas much smaller than that of Cahokia (Fowler 1974). These sites, and others located in the modern states of Illinois, Indiana, Ohio, and Kentucky, may have been founded initially as ‘gateway’ sites for Cahokia’s commodity procurement network (see Hirth 1984); situated as they were at the confluences of major streams, they could have controlled river traffic. The Fort Ancient centres along the upper Ohio River contain foreign lithic and ceramic materials suggestive of involvement in commodities trade (Clay 1976, Essenpreiss 1978); a rôle as bulk-breaking facilities in the transport of commodities can be supported by archaeological data (Clay 1976, Baker 1984). They seem not to have dominated very large settlement spaces around them, but nevertheless to have maintained élite persons and perhaps ceremonial functions that would originally have reflected the Cahokian source of both social ranking and the ceremonies that supported and validated it. The pattern of increasing site size downriver toward Cahokia is supportive of this interpretation. These secondary or peripheral centres gradually impinged upon Iroquoia after ad 1300, perhaps from a power base at Marietta near the divide between the Lake Erie/Ohio Valley drainages (Fig. 3.2; Essenpreis 1978, pp. 162–3).

We are proposing that the Ohio Valley sites (like others along other major river valleys, cf. Gibbon 1974) constituted a 'periphery' for Cahokia, and that they functioned, initially at least, to funnel commodities and other valuables towards the centre. The system may be thought of as a pump, drawing energy (foodstuffs and captives), possibly additional population, commodities (hides, furs, shells, and minerals), and probably information into the heartland from a large region around it. The heartland, in turn, sent out manufactured goods (hoes, beads, possibly cloth, other precious items), ceremonial information (probably related to calendrical rites and scheduling), and some degree of political control. The presence of 'dependency élites' in the initial stages of these peripheral sites remains to be demonstrated, but it is strongly implied by the world systems model (Wallerstein 1974, Schneider 1977, Paynter 1982).

The expanding periphery appears to have superseded the centre sometime after ad 1300. At Cahokia, the century of the Sand Prairie phase was a time of stasis and then of retraction. It has been noted that this period of contraction coincided with an episode of climatic cooling (Baerreis & Bryson 1965) that may have stressed the agricultural base of the economy, reducing the influence of the élites as their ability to 'guarantee' good crops and to predict the turn of the seasons diminished. Among other processes potentially relevant to the end of Cahokia could have been the evolution of 'development' élites at the distant sites; these may have decided to risk insubordination, retain the benefits of the exchange networks nearer to home, and become leaders of settlements that were centres in their own right (Paynter 1982). Their ability to do so would have depended upon Cahokia's power being attenuated either by distance or by weakness developing within Cahokia itself, so that insubordination could not be effectively quenched. We are a long way from being able to identify the independent variables in this system, but the reasons for suspecting a systemic breakdown seem good enough in theory to allow us to proceed to examine the implications for Iroquoia.

Iroquoia as margin

Iroquoia was never part of the Cahokia periphery; societies there remained always outside of direct involvement in the expansion of the Mississippian socio-economic system. The absence of exotic goods in the archaeological record between ad 1200 and 1400 is strong testimony to the absence of élites, and to a buffered involvement, if any, in the exchange network at that time. However, Iroquoia was among those regions affected by events in the midcontinent. It received the Mississippian cultigens and, probably with them, some of the Mississippian ceremonials that supported the hoe horticulture. People within the area later to be Iroquoia adopted Mississippian ceramic technologies to the extent of creating thin-walled and smooth-surfaced globular pots that derive from ceramic traditions alien to the northeastern woodlands. Hunting weapons reflected stylistic norms characteristic of the Ohio Valley Mississippian periphery (small triangular 'Madison' points). Although house construction in Iroquoia was typically northeastern in style, with longhouses developing from oval wigwams (Tuck 1971), there are enough wall-trench structures to imply familiarity with Mississippian domestic architecture (Kapches 1980).

The systemic relationships among nucleated villages, maize horticulture, fortifications and warfare or raiding, and lineage and clan organization have been briefly alluded to above. These relationships, which are so important in defining the uniqueness of the Iroquois in the Northeast, are repeatedly observed both within and just beyond the Mississippian social periphery. This cluster of traits extends beyond the Cahokian sphere in all directions – up the Missouri River to the west, up the Mississippi and Illinois rivers and their tributaries to the north, and up the Ohio and its tributaries to the east and south-east (e.g. Gibbon 1972, Harn 1978, 1986). To the south and south-west, the cluster may precede in time the rise of Cahokia (Nassaney 1984). The trait cluster is at the foundation of all the hypotheses proposed to explain the emergence of the Iroquois in the Northeast, and we accept it as a historical given. Only the initiating variable and the emphasis given to the other variables differ from one model or scenario to another.

Developmental scenarios

We propose that the proto-Iroquoian peoples had a number of possible options available to them as they faced the encroachment of the Mississippian socio-economic system. We present some of them here in the form of scenarios that will be analysed and tentatively tested. As marginal peoples they could have become suppliers for peripheral middlemen, contributing to the flow of materials and people heading toward the heartland. They could, on the other hand, have declined to participate in the network, and might have succeeded if they were able to defend themselves from outside pressures either by withdrawal or by militancy. They could have done all of these things at different times.

Our first scenario begins with the proto-Iroquois under pressure to provide food or other valuables (hides or furs, minerals, shells, captives) to the core sites farther south-west, with the initial destinations likely to be one of the gateway communities along the Ohio or its tributaries. We can postulate that they may have given in and provided, or agreed to provide, the materials demanded. Capitulation or involvement of this sort would probably have entailed intensification of maize horticulture, in order to provide a surplus for export, or goods to exchange with more marginal groups for hides or minerals. Alternatively, if the men were engaged in resource extraction activities at a new level of intensity, maize horticulture might have substituted for foodstuffs no longer provided by males to the home communities. Nucleation of settlements, horticultural intensification, and matriclans might be expected to result from such an involvement in external exchange. The society might have seen itself benefiting from calendrical ceremonialism and some stabilization of food supplies as a consequence of involvement with the Mississippian system at its margins, even in the absence of effective force to ensure that involvement.

A second scenario accounts for Iroquoian militancy. If the initial efforts at intensification of horticulture proved inadequate to supply needs, the Iroquois might have attempted to shift the burden of producing exchange goods onto their neighbours to the north and east. In this scenario it would be postulated that the mode of doing so would have been related to that described by Sahlins (1962) as the expansion of segmentary lineages. The communities develop a warrior ethic, and undertake raids on communities outside of their own kin networks. They capture goods and people, and pass those on towards the cores. To do this effectively, they would need to safeguard their rear by firm alliances with those identified as kin. Clan organization would help here, and if Divale (1984) is correct about the efficient organization of clans in support of warriors regularly away from home, those would be matriclans. The fortification of the home villages would be a prudent course for the kin of absent warriors, as would nucleation into settlements larger than those of their victims. Large storage facilities would be granaries for the people at home as well as for the warriors away.

A third, defensive, scenario posits that, under coercion to become involved in the exchange networks of their neighbours to the south, marginal people might have refused to participate. Given that they were already involved in maize horticulture, they might nucleate settlements, fortify the villages with palisades, and bring their food stores within the villages and houses, all classic preparations for siege. The nucleation of villages formerly separate would require some special accommodative arrangements for marriage networks, land use, and dispute resolution, and we would not be surprised to find that extended families defined lineages to comprise the core of each house, and perhaps even of a small village. Subsistence farmers might tend toward matrilineages, as they have in other times and places. The extra labour invested in village facilities and fortifications would further raise the cost of moving, and tend to support extended residency at favourable places. Under such circumstances, wild foods and other resources would be depleted, and there would be internal systemic pressures for intensification of horticulture, and the raising of cultigens to the status of food staples. If the first-stage precautions proved inadequate to keep the Mississippians from the door, the next step could have been to expand alliances by discovering or defining kin networks that would link villages; clans have been a favoured solution to such problems. Inter-village clans historically provided the Iroquois with a sound basis for fielding larger groups of warriors, whether bent on defence or offence.

We see, according to these scenarios, that whether the proto-Iroquois participated or refused to participate in the encroaching Mississippian socio-economic system, their options tended to converge upon a social organization, economic base, and readiness for warfare that closely resemble those of the Iroquois of the early historic period. The responses are essentially those available to village horticulturalists at the edge of an expanding world system (cf. Hayden 1978, Ramsden 1978). Our argument here converges upon Fried's model of tribalization (1975); most of the crucial traits are characteristic of marginal tribes, with or without militancy.

Testing the scenarios against data

Given that the three scenarios posit both involvement in, and avoidance of, the greater Mississippian exchange networks on the part of the proto-Iroquois, it becomes necessary to go to the archaeological record to learn which options those people might have exercised. Although involvement and avoidance appear to be mutually exclusive responses, they might well have been exercised serially, as conditions changed. Different strategic decisions would have led, of course, to different historical trajectories, even though the outcomes in term of culture content and form would have contained many of the same elements, and could have been very similar.

Chronology of events and processes in midcontinent

The first requirement for a test of an explanatory model is the demonstration that causes precede effects. The spread of horticulture, which established some commonality of economy and probably of ceremony throughout the large region extending from Cahokia to Iroquoia and well beyond, appears to have been contemporary with the initial Mississippian settlements on the American Bottom and the establishment of the site at Cahokia (the Emergent Mississippian period of Bareis & Porter (1984), lasting from ad 800 to *c.* ad 1000). Maize was being grown in Ontario by ad 900 (Noble 1975a, Stothers 1977, pp. 115–18), and in central New York state by ad 1070 (Ritchie & Funk 1973, p. 186). We distinguish subsequent events, which are the subject of this paper, from the expansion of horticulture, which forms a background to them.

By the end of the Emergent Mississippian period, sites closely related to Cahokia included Aztalan and the early stages of the Kincaid and Angel sites (Fig. 3.2) in the Ohio River valley. The latter sites were not originally defended by palisades. Palisaded villages had been established elsewhere, beyond the inner circle, in Iowa (McKusick 1973, p. 10) and in the Western

Basin area of Lake Erie (Stothers 1975). To the east, sites of the Whittlesey culture of northern Ohio and of the Chautauqua phase of extreme western New York state were palisaded by ad 1000 (Schock 1974, p. 156, Brose 1976). Some early Glen Meyer villages of southern Ontario were palisaded in the 10th century (Noble 1975a).

The Stirling (ad 1050–1150) and Moorehead (ad 1150–1250) phases of the American Bottom represent the climax of Cahokia's culture and influence (Bareis & Porter 1984, p. 12). Monks Mound was constructed in these centuries, the palisade was erected around it and the core of the site, and the areal extent of the site reached its maximum. The large sites of Aztalan, Kincaid, and Angel flourished in these centuries, surrounded by defensive works of impressive size (see various chapters in Trigger 1978b). It is these large sites, with important mound groups, large plazas, and resident élites, that we interpret as being the significant periphery for the Cahokia core.

Farther away, on the margins, evidence of political or economic pressure can be seen in the changing settlement patterns. In the Western Basin area, settlement tended to move northward, away from the travel corridor of the Wabash-Maumee rivers (Stothers 1975). Glen Meyer populations north of Lake Erie withdrew from the Thames river into the uplands (Williamson 1985). Farther east, Owasco (proto-Iroquoian) communities similarly withdrew from major river valleys to upland sites, and settlements were increasingly palisaded (Tuck 1978), as were the Monongahela sites southwest of them (George 1974).

After ad 1250, Cahokia lost size, population, and power, and by *c.* ad 1400 the immediate area was abandoned. With the exception of Aztalan, which ended shortly after ad 1300 (Gibbon 1972), the major centres of the periphery continued to prosper during the period of Cahokia's decline. Along the Ohio and its tributaries, new sites proliferated in the Cairo lowlands at the confluence with the Mississippi (Chapman 1980). Kincaid built a palisaded enclosure (Muller 1978). The Angel site upstream echoed the development, but at a smaller scale, and at the confluence of the Wabash and Ohio rivers, the Caborn–Welborn site complex emerged later in the 14th century (Green & Munson 1978). Fort Ancient centres in the upper Ohio Valley became larger (average size doubled after ad 1300) and more militantly protected (Graybill 1981), whereas mound construction had ceased by ad 1250 (Graybill 1984). The Marietta site, still farther upstream on the Ohio, emerged as an important centre (Essenpreis 1978).

The decline of Cahokia and of Aztalan has been explained in terms of a deteriorating climate that could have exerted considerable subsistence stress upon farmers supplying the centres. However likely some subsistence stress from this factor may seem, it does not readily account for the contrasting prosperity of the Mississippian sites along the Ohio River, some of them farther north than Cahokia and its major satellites. Other site areas suffered diminution or abandonment at this time, but the circumstances do not clearly implicate climatic stress. The Western Basin area was abandoned, the inhabitants possibly moving north to the Lake St. Clair area; an intrusion of

Upper Mississippian culture up the Maumee river toward the Western basin is observable at this same time (Stothers 1975). Within southern Ontario there was a shift of occupied areas to the eastward (Pearce 1984). Sometime after ad 1300, the Monongahela area was also deserted, to remain uninhabited until the westward spread of Euro-American settlers (George 1980) in the 18th century. What we see, then, is the collapse of the Cahokia heartland, expansion and strengthening of the Ohio Valley centres, and a withdrawal of peoples on the margin of the latter developments.

Events and processes in Iroquoia

Our first scenario posits involvement of the proto-Iroquoian societies in exchange networks reaching deep into the midcontinent toward Cahokia. Evidence exists to indicate that they were involved in exchange with the Ohio and Wabash valley sites. Ceramic wares of Fort Ancient affiliation occur on sites in Ontario and southwestern New York state. Ohio cherts and *Busycon* shell beads also occur in greater Iroquoia before ad 1400. The location of early proto-Iroquoian sites on or near major canoe portages at the watershed of the Great Lakes and Ohio drainages is also indicative. Some of these sites (e.g. Westfield and Oakfield) contain large numbers of storage pits, exotic materials, and other attributes indicative of a rôle in commodities transport (Arndt 1985, Hasenstab 1985, p. 20, Lafferty 1986, cf. Latta 1980).

An assumption of physical difficulties in establishing and maintaining exchange networks over these great distances seems to have militated against serious consideration of such connections by archaeologists. However, no great geographical or technical constraints in fact apply to this case. Whether by canoe on the waters or by foot along the valleys, the rivers gave direct access to the continental interior and the North Atlantic and Middle Atlantic coasts. The Iroquois were ideally situated to play the rôle of middlemen, which they did with consummate skill during the initial centuries of European contact. Could they have had centuries of practice?

In a study of canoe travel in central North America, Little (1987) has calculated average travel times for a canoe-load of cargo moving downstream from Iroquoia toward Cahokia by several different routes. The average travel time by canoe varied according to distance, stream rank, and the amount of upstream travel involved. The concentric circles of Figure 3.2 show the major access zones involved in this argument, with times for each calculated from the outer edges. Down-the-line exchange of dried foodstuffs, moved from point to point along a chain of settlements, was possible. The distances are even more feasible for expensive lightweight goods or captives, travelling either by canoe or foot. If the secondary centres along the Ohio River periphery were directly mobilizing and transporting people and goods toward Cahokia, as is more than likely, no burden of direct travel would have been imposed on the proto-Iroquoians.

The Fort Ancient centres along the Ohio River would have been in good positions to take over the trade and attempt to expand it in their own interests as Cahokia's power waned; successful co-option of the trade on their parts could have contributed significantly to Cahokia's downfall.

Throughout Iroquoia during the 14th century ad, inter-community violence intensified. In Ontario villages increased in size, and longhouses were closely packed within impressive palisades (Noble 1975b). Multiple palisade lines appear, and some stockade ditches reached formidable proportions (Pearce 1984). As far east as central New York state, sites of the Oak Hill horizon were stockaded and situated on remote hilltops (Ritchie & Funk 1973, p. 168). Evidence of violent death and ritualized cannibalism appear in the archaeological record at this time (Tuck 1971). Climatic deterioriation has been implicated to explain these events and processes, the postulated mechanism again being subsistence stress and related competitive warfare. Violence, apparently widespread in Iroquoia, was nevertheless not confined to that area; village burnings are reported from the same century in the Illinois and Ohio valleys to the south-west, where climatic stress was probably less severe (cf. Graybill 1984, p. 46).

In this troubled period, Iroquoian ceramics crystallized into local styles which continued to evolve in place into the historic period, indicative of some isolation from societies outside of Iroquoia to the south and west. There is a notable absence of exotic materials and manufactured items at this time (Hasenstab 1984, p. 28), which reinforces the appearance of isolation from neighbouring regions. It is possible to see some of these processes as special cases of the withdrawal from the Mississippian periphery that was expressed by physical removal of populations from the Western Basin and Monongahela areas. In any case, the exchange relationships that had previously involved Iroquoia with the Mississippian periphery seem to have broken down by this time. To the extent that Iroquoian peoples depended upon such relationships to acquire critical commodities, or to support an elaborating social system, substitutes for them would have been sought, and might have been sought to the north and east, where Iroquoian impingement begins to be observed as exotic ceramics in the archaeological record.

Synthesis

On the basis of the archaeological and historical data referenced above, we propose that changes in the social, economic, and political orientations of prehistoric Iroquoia were partly, and significantly, responses to events and processes occurring among Middle and Upper Mississippian societies, centred first at Cahokia. The assumption of the costs and risks of horticultural and social intensification is explained, therefore, as a response to external pressures, and not entirely as a response to internal growth.

In the years between ad 1000 and *c.* ad 1300, Cahokia was expanding its influence aggressively throughout the midcontinent, in order to supply itself with the goods and people it needed to maintain the growth of a society approaching the complexity of a city-state. It established colonies or dependencies at distances, which served to accumulate and forward the valuables needed at the centre, and to spread, through proselytizing or threat of force, the influence of the centre. In these early years, by extension up the Ohio and other rivers originating near the Great Lakes, pressure was exerted on marginal societies by the secondary centres on the Cahokia periphery. The proto-Iroquois were among the marginal peoples affected. Initially they engaged in exchange, sending commodities downriver, receiving some precious items and probably calendrical knowledge and ceremonies helpful for raising exogenous crops. Involvement in such exchange networks would have reinforced any internal development toward intensification of maize horticulture, enlargement of storage capacity, nucleation of villages, and incipient clans. While the peripheral centres were still small, the distance to Cahokia would have insulated the proto-Iroquois from direct military threat, and they might well have benefited from the connections to the south.

Gradually, as power shifted from Cahokia to the secondary centres along the Ohio, the pressure on the Iroquois probably intensified sufficiently to shift the cost–benefit balance away from co-operation towards avoidance. By *c.* ad 1400, then, the proto-Iroquois were strongly on the defensive, nucleated into fortified villages, withdrawn from trade networks that brought them southern goods, and on the alert to repulse threats of military force from that direction. Without the trade networks as buffers for subsistence needs, pressures on local resources would increase, and local raiding and feuding might well have intensified. The nucleation of once separate villages would require some special accommodative arrangements for marriage networks, land use, and dispute resolution, and we are not surprised to find longhouses as expressions of extended families or even lineages. If purely defensive strategies were inadequate to control the threats from either the distant former trade partners or nearer rivals, the next step could have been to expand alliances by discovering or defining kin networks (clans) that would link villages, facilitating the formation of larger groups of warriors, whether bent on defence or offence.

After ad 1500 the Iroquois began to reach out to consolidate trade relationships with their non-Iroquoian neighbours, trading to the north for the furs and meat no longer abundant in their own lands (Gramly 1977), and to the east for shell beads (Ceci 1986). Other commodities were, no doubt, involved. When the European traders arrived, the Iroquois already had the contacts necessary to establish themselves as middlemen – peripheral communities to the Europeans' distant core. These processes, which contributed to the historic definition of the Iroquois, would have been familiar to them from prior experience with, and involvement in, the Mississippian expansion.

Conclusions

Our model implies a west-to-east, time-transgressive, process of 'Iroquoianization' of the Woodland farming societies that inhabited the upper

Ohio Valley and eastern Great Lakes basins. The chronology available to us does not refute that expectation, as we see the critical variables of village nucleation and palisades appearing in southern Ontario and northern Ohio before they reached New York. There is also more evidence of trade contact with the Ohio and Mississippi valleys in the Erie Basin than there is farther east. Fort Ancient ceramics, Ohio cherts, *Busycon* beads, and wall-trench house construction are more frequent in the western part of Iroquoia than in the east.

Thus, we see that the Iroquois may owe much of their uniqueness among their neighbours to political geography and a particular set of historical processes in the Midwest prior to European contact. Their location at the edge of an expanding complex society, their situation in respect to the major northeastern river systems, and their particular responses to the problems and opportunities of these circumstances were important elements in the development of Iroquoian culture and ethos. The northeastern Algonquians did not participate in those processes, and so were different when they entered the historic record. Their non-participation was defined by social and physical geography as much as by subsistence base, ethnicity, religion, or value systems, and in turn their historic and prehistoric rôles in the regional socio-political systems helped to define their own values.

The tribalization process of Fried (1975) is seen as having prehistoric beginnings, related to the rise of a native complex society. More was involved than the availability of maize–beans–squash horticulture, and we need not invoke any archaeologically invisible or inaccessible mental traits to explain the rise of tribalization among the Iroquois. '"[A]utonomous" explanations become meaningless among networked communities' (Clarke 1973, p. 13). We can subsume the tribalization process among these people under the larger class of historically documented cases in which it occurred at the margins of expanding state societies.

Our examination of a non-capitalist 'world system' has revealed some archaeological aspects that may have relevance to core–periphery systems elsewhere, and to studies of the formation of tribes. Defining the mid-continental region in the last prehistoric half-millennium as a world system, we find a complex, hierarchical society at the core, less complex but still hierarchically organized societies in the periphery, and egalitarian (or at least unranked) societies at the margin. It is useful to note that there were 'internal' marginal societies also – egalitarian societies occupying territory around and between the Mississippian centres of the periphery. The peripheral control centres, containing evidence for élites, were fortified. Many of the internal marginal societies seem to have managed without fortifications; their relationships with the élite centres may be revealed in that fact. In the margins beyond the territorial control of the periphery, the nucleated villages, not obviously élite centres, were fortified, some quite early. It is clear that among these societies there existed differential perceptions of threat and jeopardy. These archaeological observations have implications for social, economic and political organizations that we leave to others to test. The pattern may be unique to the Cahokia sphere, or may be shown to characterize other early complex societies in the Americas or elsewhere.

Acknowledgements

Our goal in this presentation is not to convince: since we lack critical data we are not fully convinced ourselves. Rather, we hope to motivate relevant research, either through presenting some problems from a theoretically-informed perspective, or by infuriating our colleagues into refuting that approach. The chapter relies heavily on synthetic references in order to keep the citations list to a manageable size. For background information and extended discussions that have shaped our thinking, we are deeply indebted to Robert Paynter, George Armelagos, Patricia O'Brien, Elizabeth Little, Brenda Baker, Michael Nassaney, Skyler Arndt, David Lacy, Robin Greenberg, and James Bradley. Bruce Trigger's comments on an earlier version of this work are greatly appreciated. We also thank all the scholars cited, and beg their tolerance of any unintended distortions of their material. Their turn follows.

References

Arndt, S. J. 1985. Archaeological interpretation: two ways to look at the Westfield site. Ms on file, Department of Anthropology, University of Massachusetts, Amherst.

Baerreis, D. A. & R. Bryson 1965. Climatic episodes and the dating of the Mississippian cultures. *Wisconsin Archeologist* **46**, 203–20.

Baker, B. J. 1984. Mississippian core–periphery relations and the development of gateway communities in the Fort Ancient tradition of southern Ohio. Ms on file, Department of Anthropology, University of Massachusetts, Amherst.

Bareis, C. J. & J. W. Porter (eds) 1984. *American Bottom archaeology*. Chicago: University of Illinois Press.

Bender, B. 1985. Emergent tribal formations in the American midcontinent. *American Antiquity* **50**, 52–62.

Brose, D. S. 1976. An initial summary of the late prehistoric period in northeastern Ohio. In *The late prehistory of the Lake Erie drainage basin*, D. S. Brose (ed.), 25–47. Cleveland: Museum of Natural History.

Ceci, L. 1986. Shell bead exchange patterns in New York. Paper presented at the 51st Annual Meeting of the Society for American Archaeology, New Orleans.

Chapman, C. H. 1980. *The archaeology of Missouri II*. Columbia: University of Missouri Press.

Clarke, D. L. 1973. Archaeology: the loss of innocence. *Antiquity* **47**, 6–18.

Clay, R. B. 1976. Tactics, strategy, and operations: the Mississippian system responds to its environment. *Mid-continental Journal of Archaeology* **1**, 137–62.

Divale, W. 1984. *Matrilocal residence in pre-literate society*. Ann Arbor: UMI Research Press.

Essenpreis, P. S. 1978. Fort Ancient settlement: differential response at a Mississippian–Lake Woodland interface. In *Mississippian settlement patterns*, B. D. Smith (ed.), 141–68. New York: Academic Press.

Fenton, W. N. 1940. Problems arising from the northeastern position of the Iroquois. *Smithsonian Miscellaneous Collections* **100**, 159–251.

Fenton, W. N. 1978. Northern Iroquoian culture patterns. In *Handbook of North American Indians*. Vol. 15, *Northeast*, B. G. Trigger (ed.), 296–321. Washington: Smithsonian Institution.

Fowler, M. L. 1974. *Cahokia: ancient capital of the Midwest*. Addison–Wesley Module in Anthropology 48. Reading, Mass.: Addison–Wesley.

Fried, M. 1975. *The notion of tribe*. Menlo Park: Cummings.

Gamble, C. 1986. Hunter-gatherers and the origin of states. In *States in history*, J. A. Hall (ed.), 22–47. Oxford: Basil Blackwell.

George, R. L. 1974. Monongahela settlement patterns and the Ryan site. *Pennsylvania Archaeologist* **44**, 1–22.

George, R. L. 1980. Notes on the possible cultural affiliation of Monongahela. *Pennsylvania Archaeologist* **50**, 45–50.

Gibbon, G. 1972. Cultural dynamics and the development of the Oneota life-way in Wisconsin. *American Antiquity* **37**, 166–85.

Gibbon, G. 1974. A model of Mississippian development and its implications for the Red Wing area. In *Aspects of Upper Great Lakes anthropology*, E. Johnson (ed.), 129–37. St Paul: Minnesota Historical Society.

Goodman, A. H., J. Lallo, G. J. Armelagos & J. C. Rose 1985. Health changes at Dickson Mounds, Illinois (A.D. 950–1300). In *Paleopathology at the origins of agriculture*, M. N. Cohen & G. J. Armelagos (eds), 271–305. Orlando: Academic Press.

Gramly, R. M. 1977. Deerskins and hunting territories: competition for a scarce resource of the northeastern Woodlands. *American Antiquity* **42**, 601–5.

Graybill, J. R. 1981. *The eastern periphery of Fort Ancient (A.D. 1050–1650): a diachronic approach to settlement variability*. PhD dissertation, Department of Anthropology, University of Washington. Ann Arbor: University Microfilms.

Graybill, J. R. 1984. The eastern periphery of Fort Ancient. *Pennsylvania Archaeologist* **54**, 40–50.

Green, T. J. & C. A. Munson 1978. Mississippian settlement patterns in southwestern Indiana. In *Mississippian settlement patterns*, B. D. Smith (ed.), 293–330. New York: Academic Press.

Harn, A. D. 1975. Cahokia and the Mississippian emergence in the Spoon River area of Illinois. *Illinois Academy of Science Transactions* **68**, 414–34.

Harn, A. D. 1978. Mississippian settlement patterns in the central Illinois River Valley. In *Mississippian settlement patterns*, B. D. Smith (ed.), 233–68. New York: Academic Press.

Harn, A. D. 1986. The Eveland site: inroad to Spoon River Mississippian society. Paper presented at the 51st Annual Meeting of the Society for American Archaeology, New Orleans.

Hasenstab, R. J. 1984. A core–periphery model for Mississippian–Iroquoian interaction during the late prehistoric period in North America. Ms on file, Department of Anthropology, University of Massachusetts, Amherst.

Hasenstab, R. J. 1985. *Pits, palisades, and longhouses: an hypothesis for the development of agriculture, warfare, and tribalization among the Iroquois of New York state*. Dissertation prospectus, Department of Anthropology, University of Massachusetts, Amherst.

Hayden, B. 1978. Bigger is better?: factors determining Ontario Iroquois site sizes. *Canadian Journal of Archaeology* **2**, 107–16.

Hirth, K. G. 1984. Catchment analysis and formative settlement in the Valley of Mexico. *American Anthropologist* **86**, 136–42.

Hopkins, R. & I. Wallerstein 1977. Patterns of development of the modern world-systems. *Review* **1**, 111–45.

Iseminger, W. R. 1980. Cahokia: a Mississippian metropolis. *Historic Illinois* **2**(6), 1–4.

Iseminger, W. R. 1982. Stockade excavations provide clues to Indian city's prehistory. *Historic Illinois* **5**(1), 10–15.

Kapches, M. 1980. Wall trenches on Iroquoian sites. *Archaeology of Eastern North America* **8**, 98–105.

Lafferty, R. H., III 1986. A review of ethnohistoric and archeological evidence of riverine canoe facilities of the eastern United States. Paper presented at the 51st Annual Meeting of the Society for American Archaeology, New Orleans.

Latta, M. A. 1980. Controlling the heights: the Iroquoian occupations of the Albion Pass region. *Archaeology of Eastern North America* **8**, 71–7.

Little, E. A. 1987. Inland waterways in the Northeast. *Mid-continental Journal of Archaeology* **12**, 55–76.,

MacNeish, R. S. 1952. *Iroquois pottery types, a technique for the study of Iroquois prehistory*. Ottawa: National Museum of Canada Bulletin 124.

McKusick, M. 1973. *The Grant Oneota village*. Office of the State Archaeologist of Iowa, Report no. 4. Iowa City: University of Iowa.

Muller, J. 1978. The Kincaid system: Mississippian settlement in the environs of a large site. In *Mississippian settlement patterns*, B. D. Smith (ed.), 269–92. New York: Academic Press.

Nassaney, M. S. 1984. *Late prehistoric site configuration in the Southeast: designing a sampling strategy for the Toltec Mounds site*. Unpublished Master's thesis, Department of Anthropology, University of Arkansas, Fayetteville.

Noble, W. C. 1975a. Van Besien (AfHd–2): a study in Glen Meyer development. *Ontario Archaeology* **24**, 3–95.

Noble, W. C. 1975b. Corn, and the development of village life in southern Ontario. *Ontario Archaeology* **25**, 37–46.

O'Brien, P. J. 1972. Urbanism, Cahokia, and Middle Mississippian. *Archaeology* **25**, 188–97.

Parker, A. C. 1916. The origin of the Iroquois as suggested by their archaeology. *American Anthropologist* **18**, 479–507.

Parmalee, P. W. 1958. Marine shells of Illinois Indian sites. *Nautilus* **71**, 132–9.

Paynter, R. 1982. Social complexity in peripheries: problems and models. In *Archaeological approaches to the study of complexity*, S. E. van der Leeuw (ed.), 118–41. Amsterdam: Universiteit van Amsterdam.

Pearce, R. J. 1984. *Mapping Middleport: a case study in societal archaeology*. PhD dissertation, McGill University. Ann Arbor: University Microfilms.

Pendergast, J. F. 1975. An in-situ hypothesis to explain the origin of the St. Lawrence Iroquois. *Ontario Archaeology* **25**, 47–55.

Prentice, G. 1983. Cottage industries: concepts and implications. *Mid-continental Journal of Archaeology* **8**, 17–48.

Ramsden, P. 1978. An hypothesis concerning the effects of early European trade among some Ontario Iroquois. *Canadian Journal of Archaeology* **2**, 101–6.

Ritchie, W. A. 1961. Iroquois archaeology and settlement patterns. In *Symposium on Cherokee and Iroquois culture*, W. N. Fenton (ed.), 25–38. Washington: Smithsonian Institution, Bureau of American Ethnology, Bulletin 180.

Ritchie, W. A. & R. E. Funk 1973. *Aboriginal settlement patterns in the Northeast*. Albany: New York State Museum and Science Service, Memoir 20.

Sahlins, M. D. 1962. The segmentary lineage: an organization of predatory expansion. *American Anthropologist* **63**, 322–45.

Schneider, J. 1977. Was there a pre-capitalist world-system? *Peasant Studies* **6**, 20–9.

Schock, J. M. 1974. *The Chautauqua phase and other Late Woodland sites in southwestern New York*. PhD dissertation, State University of New York, Buffalo. Ann Arbor: University Microfilms.

Steponaitis, V. P. 1978. Location theory and complex chiefdoms: a Mississippian example. In *Mississippian settlement patterns*, B. D. Smith (ed.), 417–54. New York: Academic Press.

Stothers, D. M. 1975. The emergence and development of the Younge and Ontario Iroquois traditions. *Ontario Archaeology* **25**, 21–30.

Stothers, D. M. 1977. *The Princess Point complex*. Archaeological Survey of Canada Paper 58, Mercury Series. Ottawa: National Museum of Man.

Trigger, B. G. 1978a. Cultural unity and diversity. In *Handbook of North American Indians*. Vol. 15, *Northeast*, B. G. Trigger (ed.), 798–804. Washington: Smithsonian Institution.

Trigger, B. G. (ed.) 1978b. *Handbook of North American Indians*. Vol. 15, *Northeast*. Washington: Smithsonian Institution.

Tuck, J. A. 1971. *Onondaga Iroquois prehistory: a study in settlement archaeology*. Syracuse: Syracuse University Press.

Tuck, J. A. 1978. Northern Iroquoian prehistory. In *Handbook of North American Indians*. Vol. 15, *Northeast*, B. G. Trigger (ed.), 322–33. Washington: Smithsonian Institution.

Wallerstein, I. 1974. *The modern world-system I*. New York: Academic Press.

Whallon, R. 1968. Investigations of late prehistoric social organization in New York State. In *New perspectives in archaeology*, S. R. Binford & L. R. Binford (eds), 223–44. Chicago: Aldine.

Williamson, R. 1985. *Glen Meyer: people in transition*. Unpublished PhD dissertation, Department of Anthropology, McGill University, Montreal.

Wolf, E. R. 1982. *Europe and the people without history*. Berkeley: University of California Press.

Wright, H. T. 1977. Recent research on the origin of the state. *Annual Review of Anthropology* **6**, 379–97.

Wright, J. V. 1966. *The Ontario Iroquois tradition*. Ottawa: National Museum of Canada, Bulletin 210.

Yerkes, R. W. 1983. Microwear, microdrills, and Mississippian craft specialization. *American Antiquity* **48**, 499–518.

4 *Divergent trajectories in central Italy 1200–500 BC*

SIMON STODDART

Introduction

The terms core, semi-periphery and periphery have been taken up by archaeologists, with a certain lack of criticism, from the concepts of political economy applied to the recent historical world. The dangers of transferring models based on capitalist economies to the study of pre-capitalist socio-political formations are self-evident. However, it should be recalled that although Wallerstein primarily directed the term world economy towards a modern world system, he explicitly mentioned the existence of world economies that pre-dated the political and economic structure of the modern world (Wallerstein 1974, p. 16). Generalized processes allied to the core–periphery phenomenon may be detectable in pre-capitalist contexts, even if they are somewhat different in form (cf. Paynter 1981, p. 238). Nevertheless, the use of the terms core and periphery in a formative phase of socio-political development, prior to the politically unified, imperial world systems that Wallerstein specifically noted, remains a dangerous step.

Beyond this fundamental problem, the terms core and periphery are often loosely applied to describe zones of high and low development set in a putative relationship one to another. This simple dichotomy conceals a complexity that must be further explored. The core–periphery concept is, in fact, inextricably attached to an economic relationship that contrasts zones of accumulation of surplus and zones of extraction (Wallerstein 1979, Paynter 1981) coupled with respective trends towards variety and specialization on the one hand and monoculture on the other (Wallerstein 1974, p. 102). This strongly contrasting zonation of modern cores and peripheries is not necessarily strictly reproduced even in modern world economies. Cores and peripheries are not likely to be distributed in a simple or even manner across space, nor to be stable in their long-term development. The form that the core–periphery structure takes is often an 'unequal development in a multi-layered format of layers' structured across space (Wallerstein 1974, p. 86). Cores and peripheries do not remain stable with respect to one another, but may exchange rôles over long historical trajectories. Simple dichotomies are equally implausible in the context of formative economic and political processes prior to the development of capitalist world economies.

A major problem with the study of any system is closure. In the case of the core–periphery concept, there are real problems in defining the scale of the world system, or, expressed differently, the boundary where a peripheral area becomes an area external to the world system under study. Wallerstein (1974, p. 17), following Braudel, defined the boundaries in terms of the distance that could be covered in a time period of 40 to 60 days; this distance varied according to the technology of the developing world economy. The problem of scale is, however, equally important at a local level in terms of defining the local economic and political components that formed the larger entities in the core and periphery. The very nature of the concept of

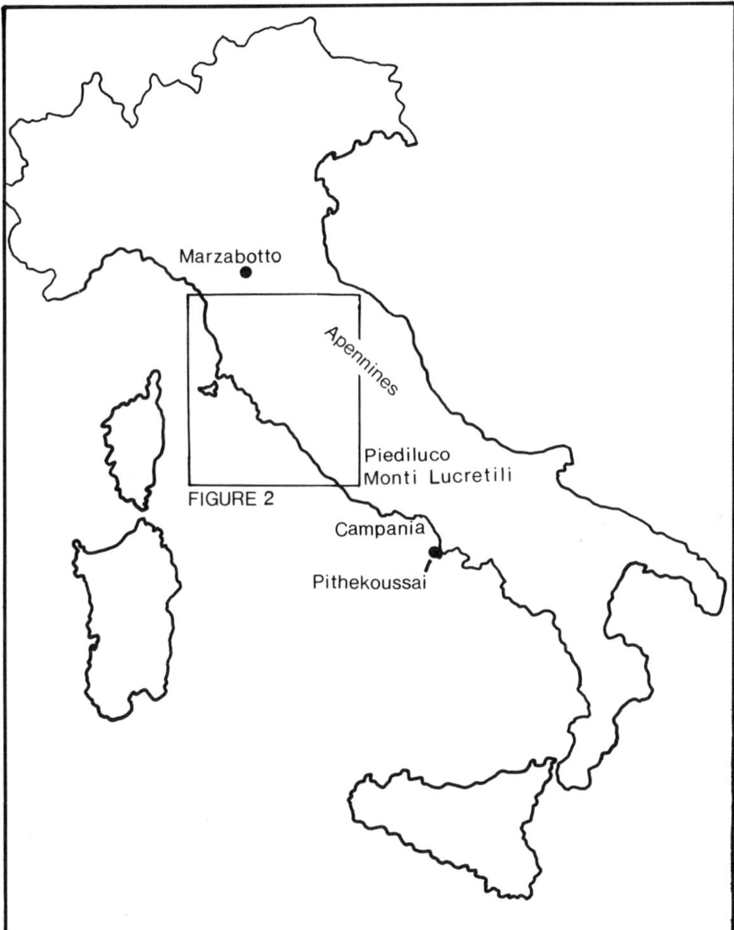

Figure 4.1 General map of Italy showing the location of the area discussed in the text.

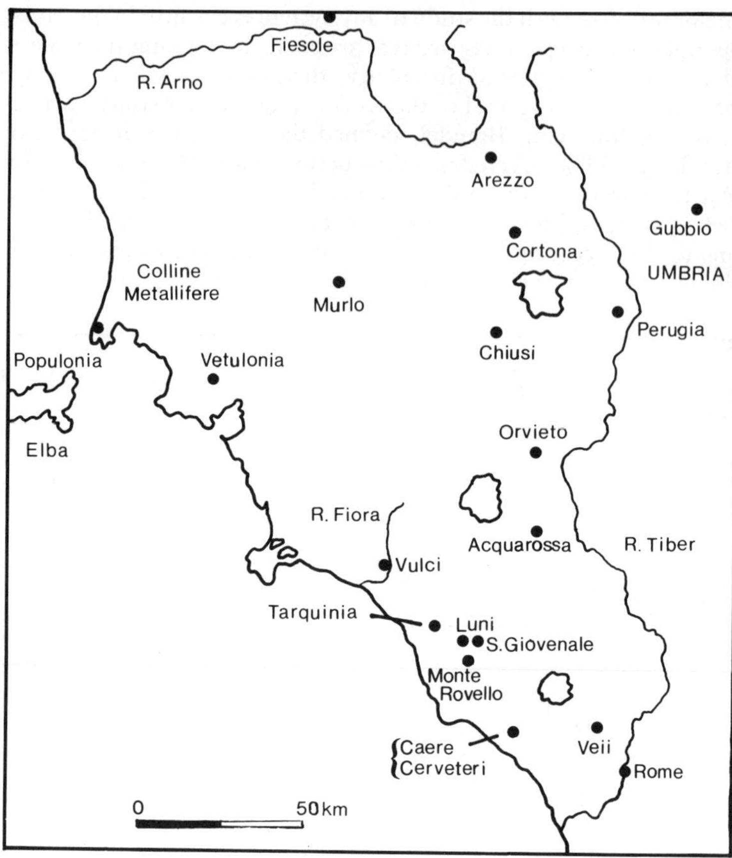

Figure 4.2 Map of Etruria and surrounding area, showing sites mentioned in the text.

core–periphery suggests that these would have varied in coherence and size according to their structural rôle in the wider political economy. In the context of a pre-capitalist world system, the scale of reference would again have been different.

The context of archaeological research highlights rather than diminishes these problems, even though at a methodological level the variables of interest to a political economist are generally accessible to the archaeologist. Archaeologists have tended to emphasize the external relationships of general areas without closely examining the internal complexities. The scale and boundaries of the system components as well as of the encompassing system are difficult to calculate. Nevertheless, the materialist basis of the world system can be measured readily by developed archaeological research. Settlement orientated studies, particularly at an extra-regional scale, based on a foundation of rigorously collected regional data and over a long time range, potentially provide a good measure of political development. Stylistic studies, potentially indicative of another dimension of core and periphery, however, tend to be relatively unintegrated with more explicitly materialistic approaches. Nevertheless, as suggested by Paynter (1981), it is only through a collection of studies exploring the strength and weakness of this type of approach that any regularities in the development of precapitalist political economies will be revealed.

This chapter examines the area of Etruria (Figs 4.1 and 4.2), in the light of the problems already raised. The development of Etruria has been classically viewed as primarily a relationship to more developed societies. Much research has been preoccupied with the origins of the Etruscans, has been mystified by the supposedly taxing nature of the language, and has concentrated on external relationships. The conception of Etruria as a periphery in some research is evident in two themes of study: the resources that the supposedly higher civilizations of the east must have extracted from Etruria and the measurement of the artistic achievements of the Etruscans on the periphery against those of the Greeks and Phoenicians in the core areas.

Views of Etruria as a periphery in archaeological research

The view of Etruria as a periphery is derived from a simplistic reading of culture history. The major social and cultural transformation of society that occurred from the 9th century BC might at first sight be most easily explained in terms of the response of a periphery to the impact of a core area. Art-historically, the transformation of Etruscan society seemed pervaded by eastern influences. Economically, it seemed only logical that Etruria was a land rich in resources ripe for exploitation by more developed political organizations. Politically, the development of Etruria appeared to be a natural consequence of economic subordination.

The notion of the peripheral status of Etruria has been gradually moderated over time. The most extreme position was that taken by the classical authors, headed by Herodotus, and by more recent scholars who accepted the views presented by the classical authors without rigorous questioning. From this point of view Etruria was so peripheral to main developments that the migration or provenance of a formed people was the only solution: Etruria was an unoccupied zone to be exploited by colonists. This general model varied over time (Pallottino 1961, 1975, pp. 64–81). Different dates for the movement of the Etruscans were suggested. Different numbers of participants were envisaged. Different sources of the migrations were traced. Different cultural admixtures were posited. The large-scale migrations considered in early theories were generally scaled down over time to analogies to Norman conquests. In general, the mythological charters of legitimization formulated by the early Etruscan state, and taken up initially by the majority of classical authors as a historical truth, were confused with archaeological reality.

Under the influence of Pallottino (1961) and Altheim (1950), the issue of origin by derivation or migration was replaced by the more processual concept of formation (Hus 1961). This reassessment may have abandoned the more extreme views of Etruria as a political vacuum incorporated within an eastern orbit, but it has still left considerable room for the importance of the East in Etruscan development. Pallottino himself states (1961, p. 6) that, although he has rejected the arrival of a people, he does not deny the importance of the contacts and relationships with the East.

The traditional fields of Etruscan research encouraged the emphasis on an eastern origin: exotic imports into funerary contexts, and the non-Indo-European language. More modern research on settlements (both by excavation and survey) and subsistence is likely to give a more balanced picture suggesting, if not continuity, essentially continuous development from the Bronze Age. Under the influence of this development, more recent research has been able to concentrate on the independent nature of Etruscan society and the relative importance of contacts with the rest of the Mediterranean.

The modern view of Etruria with respect to the rest of the Mediterranean is, therefore, relatively varied. There is a residual group of scholars who continue to give weight to the replacement of population. This approach survives most strongly in Swedish writings, although the peripheral nature of Etruria can vary between the arrival of a new ethnic group at Caere (Pohl 1972) and the intense cultural influence of orientalization on Protovillanovan stock at San Giovenale (Olinder & Pohl 1981, pp. 77–81, 83–4, Pohl 1984, pp. 91–6). Another view which continues to relegate Etruria to a position of relatively extreme peripherality is that presented by the supporters of 'banalizzazione' (Camporeale 1975). Etruria is considered to be the uncomprehending receptor of pure Greek artistic themes, by implication in return for the extractive opportunities offered to the core powers.

Generally, however, the subtlety of the development of Etruria is being established. Many scholars are concentrating on the measurement of the fluctuation of contact with the Mediterranean world in relationship to social process. Scholars generally stress the predominance of a local development, but allow a considerable rôle for eastern contact. There is now a healthy tendency towards seeing the origin of Villanovan centres and Etruscans as long-term in time but not in space (Colonna 1977, p. 193): in other words the development of the socio-political complexity is to be sought in the latest Bronze Age, not in the mass movement of people or in major external influence. This investigation of Mediterranean contact is not restricted to the 1st millennium BC. For instance, according to di Gennaro (1986, p. 130), the beginning of the Bronze Age cycle of development began with the onset of contacts with the Aegean world in the Mycenaean period. D'Agostino (1985, p. 43), while emphasizing the continuity from the Late Bronze Age and Villanovan, stresses that he does not exclude the possibility of new cultural arrivals and contacts from outside, including a powerful contact with east central Europe during the Villanovan. Nevertheless, he makes the important point that, although the increasing imports in the course of the 8th century BC are not unconnected with the changes in central Italian society, the eastern contacts would not have had an impact if central Italian society had not already been politically developed. Cristofani and Zevi (1985, p. 121) see Greek colonization as altering the political balance in central Italy, favouring the development of the coastal Etruscan centres in contrast to the Latial centres. In spite of the clear changes in the view of the Etruscans, the relationship between Etruscans and the East is still considered asymmetrical in terms of economic development.

An important factor behind this asymmetrical view is linked to the possibilities of metal extraction from Etruria. Statements of the importance of metals abound. 'The Colline metallifere of Tuscany, together with the island of Elba, are rich in metals – especially iron – that may reasonably be supposed to have focused the attention of the outside world on Etruria' (Ridgway 1981, p. 17). Ridgway (1967, p. 318) suggested and later developed (1984, pp. 156–9) the idea that the large quantity of Greek finds at Veii and the lack of finds in northern Etruria, combined with the sourcing of metal ores at Pithekoussai, demonstrated an intermediary rôle between southern Etruscan centres and centres close to metal sources further north. The claim of Ridgway is that the Greeks offered high poetic culture in exchange for metals. An important point to emphasize is that the extraction of these metals was not carried out directly by a core civilization, but was implemented through politically developed intermediaries within Etruria itself.

The development of Etruria

The problem to be tackled remains the transformation, within a few centuries, of a relatively stable socio-economic organization in the Bronze Age into the state-organized society of the Archaic period. In the context of the present discussion of the applicability of the concept of core and periphery, the socio-political transformation will be explored by identifying changes in settlement, levels of extraction and the degree of contact with the rest of the Mediterranean.

The Bronze Age background

It is now increasingly accepted that, although it is methodologically incorrect to seek the ethnic origins of the Etruscans in prehistory, the social and economic processes that culminated in the Etruscan state should be traced from the 2nd millennium BC. That millennium appears to have been a phase of socio-economic stability (Barker 1981, pp. 218–19). However, stable systems can conceal an increasing pressure towards change. The stimulus for that change is not readily to be found externally. The intensity and duration of the direct contact of central Italy with the Mycenaean world was not great, if it can be measured accurately in terms of the few Mycenaean finds from Luni, Monte Rovello and San Giovenale. Central Italy appears to have been at the end of a Mycenaean exchange network (Marazzi & Tusa 1976) which shows little solid evidence for the extraction of ore (or indeed any other kind of resource). The principal areas suitable for metal extraction in the Colline Metallifere do not appear to be associated with increased economic activity, but rather to lie somewhat on the fringe during the Middle Bronze Age.

It is now increasingly evident that, whereas there was a sharp break between settlement occupation in the Middle Bronze Age and preceding periods, there is clear evidence for settlement continuity from the Middle Bronze Age into the later periods of the Bronze Age (Bietti Sestieri 1985, Peroni & di Gennaro 1986). Barker (1981, p. 155) has suggested a three-stage development of infilling of the landscape that extends even further back into the Neolithic: a first stage of Neolithic inland settlements and lowland temporary camps; a second stage of lowland and upland settlements using alternative seasonal pastures and a third stage with seemingly peripheral settlements on the edge of preferred areas of habitation. The second stage was in fact a major break in development represented by the onset of the Middle Bronze Age. The third stage has subsequently been shown to be not merely an infilling of upland areas but part of a much more widespread socio-political process which was a particular feature of the Final Bronze Age.

The Final Bronze Age (c. 1200–900 BC)

The economy of the latest Bronze Age shows evidence for intensification along diverse lines. Different strategies of extraction can be detected, but there is no evidence that this represented a structurally peripheral relationship to the Mediterranean world. The extraction of ores from the Elba–Colline Metallifere region has been suggested frequently as the underlying structural relationship with the rest of the Mediterranean world, but the evidence for an increase in the extraction of metal resources postdates the cessation of clear-cut evidence of contact with the Mycenaean world.

The extraction of resources from particular ecological zones probably formed the basis for the development of distinctive regional settlement systems, but there is no evidence for the extraction of resources from one area to the exclusive benefit of another. Present evidence does suggest, however, that the areas of south Etruria later involved in the settlement transformation of the 9th century BC were most intensively occupied during this period. In south Etruria, 70% of known sites of this period are in broadly similar defensive positions, particularly the tufa outcrop (di Gennaro 1986, Peroni and di Gennaro 1986). Although research has been biased towards this topographical location, the present distribution of settlement suggests a relatively packed and competitive political landscape compared with areas outside south Etruria. Outside south Etruria, coastal sand dunes, colluvial flanks, caves, lacustrine margins and high mountains were occupied according to the local context. In some areas of central Italy, the late Bronze Age was already marked by localized population aggregation, but this was principally for economic reasons: the centralized control of upland and lowland resources. The overall impression is of a non-hierarchically organized settlement arranged in different configurations and densities, according to the increasingly specialized mode of production for individual areas. This specialization did not, however, denote an economic dependence of one area on another in the structural sense denoted by a core–periphery relationship. There is no evidence for the extraction or mobilization of resources in an area of dependency to favour an external area.

During the Final Bronze Age, there was an important network of interaction in the peninsula of Italy that had as great an impact in the upland mountain basins of the Apennines as on the more coastally-placed sites. Recent work on different classes of material culture (Peroni 1980) has distinguished many local variations, but the level of stylistic interaction in the peninsula remains high. This existence of an extensive, principally metallurgical, *koine* suggests that the relationship with the rest of the Mediterranean was not one-sided. Common processes of metallurgical development were in progress.

The Villanovan transformation

The transformation of the settlement system in the Villanovan period has been frequently subsumed under the term of synoecism. This term has been employed by some authors as a generic term for population aggregation in the central as well as eastern Mediterranean during this general time period (Holloway 1985). The cause of this transformation, however, remains for most authors an open question, even if its consequences for subsequent socio-political development are considered undeniably important (Ridgway 1981, p. 15). The uncertainty about the cause of these marked cultural and organizational changes is not unconnected with the lack of a ready solution in terms of Mediterranean interaction. The transformation was during a low point in trade networks with the Mediterranean as a whole (Rittatore Vonwiller 1977, p. 111). Conversely, the disappearance of the preceding interaction system cannot be seen as a cause: its intensity, with respect to Etruria, was not sufficiently great. Holloway has laid some emphasis on the political leadership that was involved in the context of Bronze Age Sicily, but for the case of the Villanovan he suggests a less politically directed transformation. Colonna feels that it is not possible to distinguish whether forced or peaceful synoecism was involved (Colonna 1977, p. 196).

The 9th century BC is a key period for the understanding of the subsequent development of Etruria. Although some signs of concentrated population are known from the latest periods of the Bronze Age, it was the formation of the Villanovan centres that marked a major shift towards settlement nucleation. The abrupt nature of the transformation can, however, now be somewhat downplayed. It has been known for some time that some isolated Late Bronze Age burials and sporadic finds have been discovered in almost all the Villanovan centres (Veii, Cerveteri, Vetulonia and Populonia). More recent work has demonstrated that at least limited parts of the later Villanovan centres were previously occupied in the Final Bronze Age: Tarquinia (Bonghi Jovino 1986); Orvieto (di Gennaro 1986, pp. 21–2); Veii (di Gennaro 1986, pp. 103–4). This raises the interesting possibility that state formation was not an abrupt political discontinuity, but a development out of the preceding political landscape. Certain Late Bronze Age sites were continuously occupied into the Iron Age. These same Late Bronze Age sites may have become the political focus of the aggregation of population in the 9th century BC, mobilizing population from a wider catchment area, until incorporation within one settlement unit took place. The early Villanovan was most probably the culmination of a long-term economic process involving the organization of production, with political consequences and implications (see Bietti Sestieri 1981) that only came about later. The nature of this settlement continuity requires further research from excavation and field survey to understand the relationship of Late Bronze Age and Iron Age occupation. The recent discovery of some Late Bronze Age material under Villanovan occupation layers could still be coincidental, and not indicative of any form of socio-political continuity. Furthermore, recent survey of Villanovan settlements has suggested that they may have formed as integrated communities from the beginning rather than as separate, but inter-related, component communities (Guaitoli 1981).

Despite the remaining controversies, it is clear that the Villanovan transformation marked a break in the cultural and socio-political uniformity of central Italy. On the one hand regional diversity is visible even within the Villanovan cultural area itself (Peroni 1969). On the other hand, areas of central Italy that had equal participation in the economic processes of the Late Bronze Age were not at this stage transformed by the same change in settlement organization. Etruria between the Tiber and the Fiora underwent the major settlement changes. By contrast, some areas such as the Piediluco and Monte Lucretili seem to have lost population in the 9th and 8th centuries BC. Other areas such as the region around Chiusi appear to have undergone settlement nucleation, but of a less concentrated 'primate' nature. Further areas such as Gubbio appear to have been relatively unaffected by contemporary processes in south Etruria. The foundations for sharply differing political trajectories were laid. The causes are to be found in the internal economic and socio-political restructuring of the landscape, not in the response of a collective periphery to the external Mediterranean world.

Renewed contact with the East

This transformed political landscape underwent a second, more gradual, internal political development during the 8th century BC. In the 9th century BC there is no sign of differential access to wealth within the Villanovan communities, either in the few settlement excavations themselves (Linington *et al.* 1978) or in the cemeteries. However, in the 8th century BC, the first funerary evidence for social ranking does seem to coincide with the presence of oriental imports. The power centres in the new political landscape appear to have exploited the opportunity presented by exotic forms from the eastern Mediterranean.

These new and exotic stylistic forms became the medium for representing political status and consolidating political change. The objects involved were, at least initially, low in number, circulating only amongst a restricted sector of the community, in the same way as literacy was almost certainly restricted, when introduced at the end of the 8th century BC. In this model, the importance of the extraction of metal resources from Elba and the Colline Metallifere is reduced; although there is some evidence of the smelting of Elban ore on Pithekoussai (Ridgway 1984, p. 108), the most probable source of the early Greek pottery imports, metal extraction is not granted a causative rôle in socio-political development. According to this model, the orientalizing trade networks were participated in by societies of a relatively comparable level of social development. The equal participation of these different cultural communities is shown by the confusion over the source of the art styles and particularly by the objects themselves; even the early 'Greek' finds at Quattro Fontanili, so important for the chronology of the period, are the subject of intense debate about manufacture and date (Toms 1986, pp. 73–7).

Starting in the same period, there are corresponding changes in the organization of settlement. In contrast to the 9th century BC, population was less confined to the 'primate' centres (Peroni and di Gennaro 1986, p. 197, Fig. 4). Some of the new centres were clearly politically dependent on those primate centres. Other settlements were, however, of sufficient size and so placed spatially as to suggest a certain political independence. This decentralization of the landscape appears to have continued into the 7th century and has been noted in the territories of Vetulonia (Curri 1977, Cucini 1985), Veii (Potter 1979), Chiusi (Bianchi Bandinelli 1925) and Vulci (Colonna 1977, pp. 197–8) in different forms. On the one hand, there is a degree of dispersal of population into the political territories of the primate centres. On the other hand, some centres, intermediate in size and spatial position, developed with a degree of political independence. The political authority of centres such as Murlo or Acquarossa appears to have been accompanied by the development of distinctive art styles. Independent evidence for the decentralization of political authority is provided by the dispersal of inscriptions outside the primate centres during this same time period.

The archaic city-state

Good statistics now exist that show the degree of contact, measured in fine pottery and amphorae, of Etruria with the Greek world in the 6th and 5th centuries BC. As a working model, the major coastal polities seem to have administered luxury trade, at first directly and then through the coastal emporia. Under the same administrative control, some of these products passed to lesser settlements arranged spatially in a distant ring around the primate centres. Inland Etruria and Umbria, although having less access to such goods, do not appear to have been subject to the same political administration of trade; there is a less marked disparity in access to luxury goods between smaller and larger settlements.

The coastal trade networks of Etruria appear to have had some effect on the development of settlement, but one that cannot be described as peripheralization, given the strength of the pre-existing local authority. On the coast, trade was administered from the politically dominant centres that were derived historically from the transformation of the political landscape in the Villanovan period. These primate centres dominated directly their immediate hinterland where, with the exception of the coastal emporia, nucleated settlements were virtually excluded. The majority of the subsidiary centres were located at some distance from the primate centre, concentrated on the margins of the political territory. Even those more distant subsidiary centres were restricted in size to a maximum of one tenth of the size of the major centre. The settlement structure of some inland territories, most notably that of Chiusi, was based on a much more dispersed settlement organization. The impact of the external trade networks, however, appears to have been restricted to the foundation of ritually sanctioned emporia by the highly centralized political authorities of the coastal area. The development of subsidiary settlements on the periphery of the territories of the coastal primate centres was as much related to the maintenance of political control from the disproportionately large primate centres.

A probably related development is the formation of a core–periphery structure internal to Etruria and Umbria during this period. In sharp contrast to the centralized political authority of the coast, north-east Etruria presents a pattern of relative decentralization and retarded socio-political development. Fiesole, Arezzo, Cortona and Chiusi did not dominate their local territories to the same extent as did the centres of south Etruria. Chiusi, in particular, although itself relatively rapid in its socio-political development, seems to have had a much more gently graded hierarchical structure. This pattern is confirmed independently by the distribution of inscriptions which were consistently less concentrated in the primate centres of north-east Etruria. Other important differences are visible in the organization of ritual. Prior to the 5th century BC, ritual practice in north-east Etruria was less formalised than in south Etruria; the deposition of bronze figurines was preferred to the temple decorated with terracottas. Beyond these more decentralized political zones, there were also frontier zones involved in political expansion, particularly in the fifth century BC. The political territories of Perugia to the east, Marzabotto to the north and Campania to the south developed at this stage. The iconographic evidence of the Sperandio sarcophagus from the 'frontier' area of Perugia suggests that part of the process was extractive through superior political, particularly military, force. It is, therefore, highly probable that Etruria had its own internalized periphery, but Etruria itself cannot be reduced to this status with respect to the rest of the Mediterranean.

Conclusion

This chapter concludes that the socio-political development of central Italy, which reached a visible climax in the Archaic Etruscan city-states, must be envisaged primarily as a long-term economic transformation already in progress by the Final Bronze Age and most probably extending back into the Middle Bronze Age. The political re-formulation of the 9th century BC was a product of the inability of the pre-existing political structures to absorb these changes, and at present appears to have been centred on the more densely occupied areas of the Late Bronze Age landscape. In the succeeding centuries, the new political order exploited the renewed contacts with the Mediterranean to provide exotic symbols of political dominance. The intense trading contacts of the 6th and 5th centuries BC had some effect on the political landscape of Etruria, but the political strength of Etruria was such by this stage that this was by no means the response of a periphery. Etruria was already beginning to exploit her own periphery; expansion took place on the fringes of the Etruscan cultural area. The manipulation of inscriptions is one of the best-preserved indicators of the relationship between an innovation ultimately derived from initial contact with the Greeks and its subsequent reworking in the Etruscan world. These inscriptions register the oscillations of authority in the Etruscan political landscape without indicating a peripheral relationship to the Mediterranean world.

References

Altheim, F. 1950. *Der Ursprung der Etrusker*. Baden Baden: Verlag für Kunst und Wissenschaft.

Barker, G. 1981. *Landscape and society. Prehistoric central Italy*. London: Academic Press.

Bianchi Bandinelli, R. 1925. Clusium: ricerche archeologiche e topografiche su Chiusi e il suo territorio in età etrusca. *Monumenti Antichi* **30**, 210–578.

Bietti Sestieri, A. M. 1981. Produzione e scambio nell'Italia protostorica. Alcune ipotesi sul ruolo dell'industria metallurgica nell'Etruria mineraria alla fine dell'età del bronzo. In *L'Etruria Mineraria*. Atti del XII convegno di Studi Etruschi e Italici. Firenze–Populonia–Piombino, 16–20 giugno, 1979, 223–64. Florence: Olschki.

Bietti Sestieri, A. M. 1985. La cultura di villaggio. In *Civiltà degli Etruschi*, M. Cristofani (ed.), 27–30. Milan: Electa.

Bonghi Jovino, M. 1986. Gli scavi della università degli studi di Milano (Campagne

1982–1985) sul Pian della Cività. L'orizzonte protovillanoviano. In *Gi Etruschi di Tarquinia*, M. Bonghi Jovino (ed.), 83–6. Modena: Panini.

Camporeale, G. 1975. Review of I. Krauskopf, *Der thebanischen Sagenkreis und andere griechischen Sagen in der etruschischen Kunst* (Mainz: Von Zabern). *Studi Etruschi* **43**, 357–65.

Colonna, G. 1977. La presenza di Vulci nelle valli del Fiora e dell'Albegna prima del IV secolo a.C. In *La Civiltà arcaica di Vulci e la sua espansione*. Atti del X convegno di Studi Etruschi e Italici, 189–213. Florence: Olschki.

Cristofani, M. & F. Zevi, 1985. L'espansione politica. In *Civiltà degli Etruschi*, M. Cristofani (ed.), 121–8. Milan: Electa.

Cucini, C. 1985. Topografia del territorio delle valli del Pecora e dell'Alma. In *Scarlino I. Storia e territorio* (Ricerche di Archeologia Alto Medievale e Medievale), R. Francovich (ed.), 147–320. Florence: All'Insegna del Giglio.

Curri, C. 1977. Relazioni fra un centro costiero di Vetulonia e il territorio di Vulci. In *La Civiltà arcaica di Vulci e la sua espansione*. Atti del X Convegno di Studi Etruschi e Italici, 259–76. Florence: Olschki.

d'Agostino, B. 1985. La formazione dei centri urbani. In *Civiltà degli Etruschi*, M. Cristofani (ed.), 43–7. Milan: Electa.

di Gennaro, F. 1986. *Forme di insediamento tra Tevere e Fiora dal Bronzo Finale al Principio dell'età del ferro*. Biblioteca di Studi Etruschi 14. Florence: Olschki.

Guaitoli, M. 1981. Notizie preliminari su recenti ricognizioni svolte in seminari dell'Istituto. *Quaderni dell'Istituto di Topografia antica dell'Università di Roma* **9**, 79–87.

Holloway, R. 1985. Synoicism in Bronze Age Sicily. In *Papers in Italian Archaeology IV. The Cambridge Conference. Part iii: Patterns in Protohistory*, C. A. T. Malone & S. K. F. Stoddart (eds), 389–98. British Archaeological Reports International Series 245, Oxford.

Hus, A. 1961. *The Etruscans*. London: Evergreen Books.

Linington, R. E., F. Delpino & M. Pallottino 1978. Alle origini di Tarquinia: scoperta di un abitato Villanoviano sui Monterozzi. *Studi Etruschi* **46**, 3–24.

Marazzi, M. & S. Tusa 1976. Interrelazioni dei centri siciliani e peninsulari durante la penetrazione micenea. *Sicilia Archeologica* **9**, 49–90.

Olinder, B. & I. Pohl 1981. *S. Giovenale. The semi-subterranean building in area B*. Acta Instituti Romani Regni Sueciae 4^0, 26 (2) (4), Stockholm.

Pallottino, M. 1961. Nuovi studi sul problema delle origini etrusche. Bilancio critico. *Studi Etruschi* **29**, 3–30.

Pallottino, M. 1975. *The Etruscans*. London: Allen Lane.

Paynter, R. 1981. *Models of spatial inequality. Settlement patterns in historical archeology*. New York: Academic Press.

Peroni, R. 1969. Per uno studio dell'economia di scambio in Italia nel quadro dell'ambiente culturale dei secoli intorno al mille a.C. *Parola del Passato* **24**, 134–60.

Peroni, R. 1980. Per una definizione critica dei facies locali: nuovi strumenti metodologici. In *Il Bronzo Finale*, R. Peroni (ed.), 9–12. Bari: De Donato.

Peroni, R. & F. di Gennaro 1986. Aspetti regionali dello sviluppo dell'insediamento protostorico nell'Italia centro-meridionale alla luce dei dati archeologici e ambientali. *Dialoghi di Archeologia* **2**, 193–200.

Pohl, I. 1972. *The Iron Age necropolis of Sorbo at Cerveteri*. Acta Instituti Romani Regni Sueciae 4^0, 32, Stockholm.

Pohl, I. 1984. Riassunto generale: risultati e problemi. In *San Giovenale. Materiale e Problemi. Atti del Simposio all'Istituto Svedese di Studi Classici a Roma. 6 Aprile 1983*,

S. Forsberg and B. F. Thomasson (eds), 91–6. Acta Instituti Romani Regni Sueciae 4^{0}, 41, Stockholm.

Potter, T. W. 1979. *The changing landscape of south Etruria*. London: Elek.

Ridgway, D. 1967. Coppe cicladiche da Veio. *Studi Etruschi* **35**, 311–21.

Ridgway, D. 1981. *The Etruscans*. University of Edinburgh, Department of Archaeology, Occasional Paper 6.

Ridgway, D. 1984. *L'Alba di Magna Grecia*. Milan: Longanesi.

Rittatore Vonwiller, F. 1977. Preistoria e Protostoria della Valle del Fiume Fiora. In *La Civiltà arcaica di Vulci e la sua espansione*. Atti del X Convegno di Studi Etruschi ed Italici, 99–113. Florence: Olschki.

Toms, J. 1986. The relative chronology of the Villanovan cemetery of Quattro Fontanili at Veii. *Annali. Archeologia e Storia Antica* **8**, 41–97.

Wallerstein, I. 1974. *The modern world-system*, vol. 1. New York: Academic Press.

Wallerstein, I. 1979. *The capitalist world economy*. Cambridge: Cambridge University Press.

5 *Greeks and natives in south-east Italy: approaches to the archaeological evidence*

RUTH D. WHITEHOUSE and JOHN B. WILKINS

Introduction

Recent years have seen much work on the relationship between Greeks and the populations of southern Italy that were *in situ* before the Greeks arrived.[1] While much of this work is interesting, the majority continues to be characterized by two tendencies that we regard as unhelpful. First, there is the uncritical acceptance of the writings of Greek and Roman authors and a corresponding inclination to interpret the archaeological record in traditional historical terms, in line with the ancient authors. We have written about this elsewhere, so will not pursue it further here (Whitehouse & Wilkins 1985). Equally invidious is the strongly pro-Greek prejudice of most scholars, which leads them to regard all things Greek as inherently superior. It follows that Greekness is seen as something that other societies will acquire through simple exposure – like measles (but nicer!). These attitudes are apparent in the vocabulary used to describe the process: scholars write of the 'hellenization' of southern Italy, rather than employing terms such as 'urbanization' or 'civilization'. However, hellenization is a weak concept, lacking in analytical power, since it is evident that not all aspects of Hellenic culture are equally likely to have been adopted by the native south Italians, or at the same rate. The concept of hellenization may have some use in a restricted context, for a study of pottery styles or architecture, for instance. As a tool for examining profound changes in the organization of society it bypasses the relevant issues.

In this chapter we accept that profound changes in native society *did* occur after the arrival of the Greek settlers. We must emphasize, however, that we do not believe that these changes occurred as the direct result of some inherent or factually documented cultural superiority of the Greeks. On the contrary it is plausible to assume that the Greeks themselves were not fully urbanized at the time of their arrival, and were themselves subject to the general Mediterranean transition towards full urbanization during the first few centuries of their Italian settlement. For the native inland peoples, the case appears rather to be that these general Mediterranean moves towards urbanization were *mediated* through the Greek settlers on their southern and

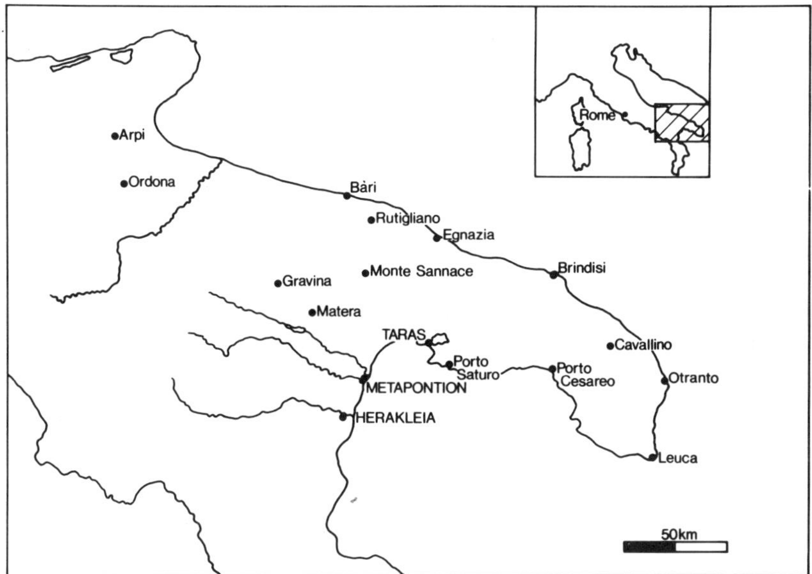

Figure 5.1 Map of south-east Italy showing the most important sites mentioned in the text.

western coasts. Our approach to the issue here is through an examination of the archaeological evidence. It is not intended as a comprehensive account, but rather as a preliminary attempt to cast off the shackles of the pseudo-historical approach and to employ models appropriate to the examination of archaeological data. The area of the study is limited to south-east Italy, defined as the region of Puglia and the eastern part of the region of Basilicata (Fig. 5.1).

We shall discuss in turn (a) the evidence, (b) the Greek cities, (c) the relationship between Greeks and natives, and (d) changes in the native communities.

The evidence

The quality of the archaeological evidence available for analysis is uneven and often very poor.

Settlements

Many native settlements are known, but few have been excavated or surveyed on any considerable scale. Many of them underlie sites of later periods and are more or less inaccessible. Because of the restricted scale of excavations, little is known about the layout or the buildings of these settlements. In many cases the existence of a native settlement is inferred from the discovery of cemeteries, but the settlement site itself has not been located.

Burials

Very large numbers of tombs of the 8th–3rd centuries BC are known in south-east Italy and between them they have produced vast numbers of pottery vessels, as well as many artefacts of metal and other materials. Unfortunately, the combination of large-scale tomb-robbing, in both ancient and modern times, and poor recording by earlier generations of archaeologists, means that we rarely have even small groups of tombs, let alone whole cemeteries, where the tomb structure, human remains and grave goods all survived and were adequately recorded. Detailed analyses of individual cemeteries are therefore precluded, although it is possible to identify general trends in development.

Data from aerial photographs

The application of aerial photography to the archaeology of south-east Italy began with the work of John Bradford at the end of the last war (Bradford 1957) and has been continued by Italian archaeologists ever since. In south-east Italy the technique has proved particularly useful in the Tavoliere plain, where not only the well-known Neolithic ditched sites, but also settlements of Iron Age and Roman date show up as crop marks. Aerial photography has also brought to light the system of land boundaries in the territory of the Greek city of Metapontion, modern Metaponto (Schmiedt & Chevallier 1969, Adamesteanu & Vatin 1976). Large areas of south-east Italy, however, are given over to the cultivation of olives and other trees, and in these areas aerial photography is of little use.

Data from field survey

Modern field survey, which can provide important information about the past exploitation of whole landscapes, has not been applied widely in south-east Italy and not very often to the Iron Age or classical periods. Surveys in the Tavoliere (Cassano & Manfredini 1983), the Ofanto Valley (Cipolloni Sampò 1980), the Murge between Gravina and Matera, and in the Brindisino have concentrated on earlier periods, especially the Neolithic (references in Whitehouse 1981b). Two surveys which *are* of relevance to the present study are those conducted in the territory of Metaponto (Uggeri 1969, Chevallier 1971, Carter 1981) and between Gravina and Venosa (Vinson 1973, and forthcoming).

The Greek cities

In the area that concerns us there were only two major Greek cities: Taras and Metapontion, both situated on the Ionian Gulf. There were no Greek cities on the Adriatic coast of southern Italy, although it is possible that there may have been Greek communities existing within some native settlements, such as Brindisi and perhaps Otranto.

From an archaeological point of view Taras and Metapontion present a marked contrast. Taras lies directly under the modern town of Taranto and there has been continuous occupation of the site from the prehistoric period to the present day. As a result there are very few surviving Greek remains, and reconstruction of the plan of the ancient town is dependent on judicious exploitation of urban redevelopment and on chance finds. The situation of Metapontion could hardly be more different, since as a result of geological and climatic factors and especially the incidence of malaria, the area was more or less uninhabited from the late Roman period until after World War II. A comprehensive programme of aerial photography, field survey and excavation carried out since 1966 under the guiding hand of Dinu Adamesteanu (1979), former Soprintendente archeologico for Basilicata, has produced a wealth of information about the layout and buildings of the city itself and also about the land divisions of its territory (*chora*).

Taras

According to classical writers Taras was founded in 706–705 BC by dispossessed illegitimate sons (*Partheniai*) of Spartan women and helot men. (The helots were a subject class in Spartan society.) Archaeology seems to give support to the date, since the earliest material yet found in the city dates to the late 8th century BC. It also appears to support the account (Strabo VI, 278–9) that the establishment of Taras was preceded by an earlier settlement at Satyrion. This site has been identified at Porto Saturo, south of Taranto, where excavations have yielded Greek material dating from *c.* 750 BC onwards (Lo Porto 1964). The first settlement of Taras, perhaps provided with defensive walls from an early stage, lies under the present Città Vecchia, while its cemeteries are situated to the east under the Borgo Nuovo. Evidence of at least two arterial roads has been found and it is likely that the orthogonal plan that characterizes the present street system goes back to the 6th century BC. In the 5th century BC the city expanded into the former cemetery area and new defences were built, with a length of some 10 km. The city flourished until the 3rd century BC, falling to the Romans in 272 BC, after which it never regained its former status.

As the classical authors describe it, Taras was a city rich in buildings and sculpture, but of all the architectural splendour nothing survives but a few columns and fragmentary foundations underlying later buildings in the Città Vecchia. However, a range of statues, bronzes and fine pottery found in

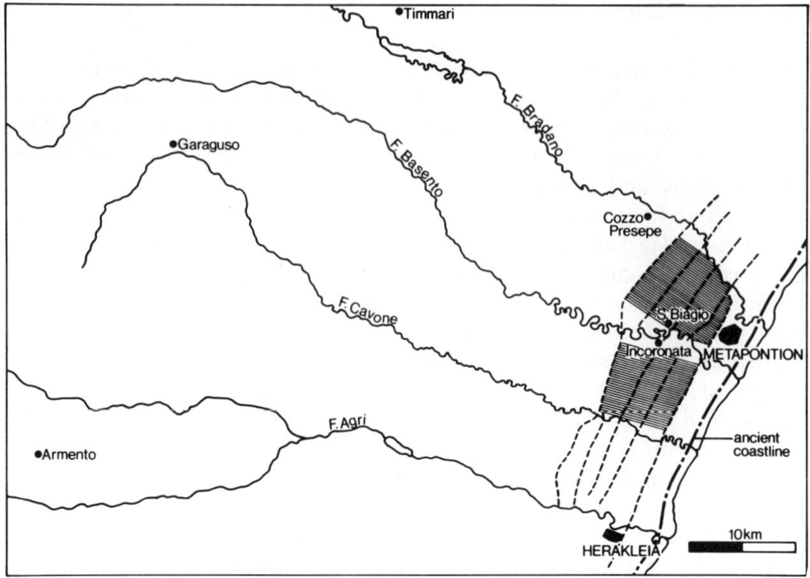

Figure 5.2 Map showing the territory and hinterland of Metapontion.

Taranto and now in the National Museum provides some indication of the artistic wealth of the ancient city.

Metapontion

The city of Metapontion was situated some 40 km southwest of Taras, further round the Ionian Gulf. According to tradition it was founded by men from Achaia and Troizen in central Greece in 773 BC, but in this case the archaeological evidence does not support the traditional foundation date. In fact the city on the sea shore was not established before about 650 BC, although as at Taras there is evidence of Greek material in the area from the mid 8th century BC onwards: the site of Incoronata, some 9 km inland on the west side of the Basento river, has produced both native pottery and Athenian and Corinthian wares dated *c.* 750–650 BC. Excavations in the city of Metapontion have uncovered parts of the city walls (probably first built in the 6th century BC) and many public buildings, including several temples, the agora, and the theatre. There was an industrial area in a central part of the city where a series of kilns has been excavated which produced, *inter alia*, Red-figure pottery of the later 5th century BC. The city flourished in the 6th and 5th centuries BC, but declined from the 4th century BC onwards, suffering attacks, according to the traditional historical record, from Lucanians, Romans and eventually Carthaginians (in the Punic Wars of the late 3rd century BC).

The most exciting aspect of the work at Metaponto has been the discovery of the land divisions of the city's *chora* (Fig. 5.2). It was found that anomalies on aerial photographs corresponded to regularly spaced depressions in the ground distinguishable by lusher vegetation and assumed to be ancient land divisions (possibly also serving for land drainage, at least in a later phase of use). The pattern consists of long parallel strips, stretching 12–14 km inland from the city wall and crossed by transverse boundaries delimiting individual lots. There were two areas of such land divisions: an eastern area between the Bradano and Basento rivers containing 39 strips of land, and a western area, slightly smaller in size and perhaps also slightly later in date, between the Basento and the Cavone rivers. The total surface area covered is *c.* 13 000 ha and probably represents the entire territory of Metapontion, since the area east of the Bradano was almost certainly Tarentine territory, while the area west of the Cavone belonged to the neighbouring Greek city (Siris at an early stage, later Herakleia). Field survey has discovered some 400 sites in the territory of Metapontion, mostly identified as isolated farmhouses. Many of these were constructed in the 6th century BC and it seems likely that the system of land division was laid out in that century, perhaps in the first half. Around 600 BC the native settlement at Cozzo Presepe, situated to the west of the Bradano river some 15 km inland, was violently destroyed and replaced by a heavily fortified Greek stronghold. It seems likely that it became a Metapontine outpost guarding the farmsteads and should therefore be associated with the laying out of the land divisions. It may also be taken to mark the north-east corner of Metapontine territory.

Greek territorial control

As we have seen, Metapontion seems to have controlled a territory of some 13 000 ha extending no more than 14 or 15 km inland. We have no comparable information from aerial photography or field survey about the territory of Taras, but we can make some calculations about its maximum extent from the distribution of known native settlements in the area; we may safely assume that native settlements of any size would not have been allowed to flourish within the *chora* of Taras itself. On this basis we may deduce that Taras controlled an area with a radius of only 10–12 km around the city itself, and a strip of land extending along the coast to the west as far as the Bradano river (and the territory of Metapontion), and inland no more than *c.* 15 km (Fig. 5.2). The maximum area that could have been under Tarantine control was about six times the size of the territory of Metapontion.

The point that should be emphasized is the small amount of land that was under direct Greek control, extending no more than 15 km from the Mediterranean coast – a situation that may well have been true of the other Greek cities of Magna Graecia also. Plato's image (*Phaedo* 109B) of the Greeks as frogs around a puddle seems appropriate indeed! Beyond the 15 km line native settlements continued to flourish, apparently free of direct

Table 5.1 Archaeological expectations for two hypotheses

Evidence	Greek control	Coexistence
Greek settlements	Outlying settlements or at least forts in native territory	None outside *chorai* of Greek cities
Greek-style defences and architecture		
nature	Indistinguishable from those of Greek cities	No more than generic similarity to those of Greek cities
distribution	Uneven distribution: some sites more Greek than others	Even distribution within given radius of Greek area on sites of equal status; decline with distance from Greek area
date	Early occurrence on some sites in strategic positions throughout territory	Generally later; date becomes later with distance from Greek area
Greek artefacts		
nature	Domestic as well as prestige goods on some sites; also coins	Emphasis on prestige goods and transport amphorae
context	Domestic as well as funerary and ritual	Mostly funerary and ritual
association	Some 'pure' Greek contexts	Always associated with local products
distribution	Uneven distribution: some sites with much more Greek material than others	Even distribution within given radius of Greek area on sites of equal status; decline with distance from Greek area
date	Early occurrence on some sites throughout territory	Date becomes later with distance from Greek area

Greek control, though certainly in contact with the Greek cities. It is the *nature* and especially the *effects* of these contacts that concern us in the pages that follow.

The relationship between Greeks and natives

The main theoretical alternatives would seem to be:

(a) Political or military control of the natives by the Greeks. This would require a significant Greek presence in the area, either on separate sites or within native settlements. One would expect either a system of separate forts or well-fortified native settlements in which the Greek administrators and service personnel could be housed.

(b) Coexistence between Greeks and natives. For coexistence to work, it would have had to be generally peaceful, although there could well have been episodes of hostility or actual warfare. Peaceful coexistence would have been articulated by mechanisms such as trade or exchange relations and marriage alliances, as well as diplomatic contacts and possibly formally negotiated treaties.

In order to choose between the two hypotheses, we may list the archaeological expectations for each case. Some of these expectations, chosen for the likelihood of recognition in the archaeological record in this particular case, are tabulated here (Table 5.1).

Greek settlements

Outside the *chorai* of Metapontion and Taras no 'pure' Greek settlement or fort sites have been found.

Greek-style architecture and fortifications

Throughout inland Calabria, Basilicata and Apulia native settlements acquired fortifications which were in a general sense of Greek type. How these should be interpreted depends on three main factors: their nature, their distribution and their date. As far as their nature is concerned, they do not seem to be unequivocally Greek. Morel (1983, p. 127) has written: '. . . many of these fortifications are *grosso modo* of Greek type, but with variations or errors in planning which prevent their being considered completely Greek'. This would suggest that they were built by natives copying Greek prototypes. Their distribution is very widespread within inland southern Italy, but the information on chronology is so poor that we cannot establish whether the distribution represents a chronological palimpsest or a uniform pattern established more or less at one time. On very few sites are the defences well dated: at both Botromagno (Gravina) and Monte Sannace (Gioia del Colle) they were apparently built in the 4th century BC, while on some of the sites to the west of the area under immediate consideration they were built either in the 5th century (Satrianum) or in the 4th (Serra di Vaglio) (Scarfi 1962, Holloway 1970, Greco 1980). There is no clear evidence of the appearance of Greek-type defences earlier than the 5th century BC on any site.

Little is known about the buildings within the native settlements before the 4th century BC. The presence of Greek-type decorative elements, such as terracotta antefixes, from the 6th century onwards, is sometimes taken to indicate the existence of buildings of Greek type, specifically temples or other public buildings. However, no such buildings have yet been found on any native site, and their presence cannot be assumed on the basis of the architectural terracottas alone. In fact these terracottas may have been traded as elements in their own right, along with other kiln products such as pottery vessels and votive figurines; they may have been attached to buildings of non-Greek type or indeed used for some other purpose altogether. That they did not necessarily come off buildings of Greek type is indicated by their occurrence on sites in the Tavoliere plain of northern Apulia where very few imported Greek objects occur, and which remained relatively unaffected by Greek culture throughout the whole period under discussion. Where buildings have been excavated in the native settlements they appear, like the fortifications, similar in a general way to Greek buildings without showing any very close parallels. Few good examples are known before the 4th century BC.

The most Greek-looking features to appear in inland southern Italy are the sanctuaries. Recent work has brought to light a series of sanctuaries of Greek type both in southern Apulia (provinces of Lecce, Taranto and Brindisi) (Fig. 5.1) and in Basilicata, to the west of our area (Fig. 5.2). To date none have been found further north in central or northern Apulia. The south Apulian examples occur at Leuca (Grotta della Porcinara), Porto Cesareo (Scala di Furno), Oria, Rocavecchia and Egnazia; the earliest are those at Leuca and Porto Cesareo, dating to the 7th century BC (Adamesteanu 1979). The sanctuaries in Basilicata occur at Timmari, Garaguso, Serra di Vaglio, Rossano di Vaglio and Serra Lustrante di Armento (Dilthey 1980, Lattanzi 1980). Most were in use from the 6th century BC, although the monumental sanctuary at Rossano di Vaglio was built only in the 4th century. Most of these sanctuaries are not within settlements but outside them, often associated with water sources. Most of them have no monumental structure, or slight structural traces only, and are known from votive deposits containing pottery vessels (both Greek and native), figurines, and sometimes coins and other metal objects. Only in the later examples, such as Rossano di Vaglio, do we find actual buildings. These rural sanctuaries are very similar to those found in the *chorai* of the Greek cities themselves. The Metaponto survey found such sanctuaries at Incoronata, S. Biagio, Pizzica, S. Angelo Vecchio and S. Angelo Grieco, with dates from the 7th to the 5th centuries BC (Carter 1981, Dilthey 1980). Only the latest example, S. Angelo Grieco, produced any monumental structural remains. In the area of Taranto we know of two sanctuaries at Torre Saturo (Satyrion): one on the acropolis and another associated with a spring on the southern slope.

Greek artefacts

NATURE

The Greek artefacts found in the native area fall predominantly into the class of prestige goods, mostly fine pottery, including Corinthian and Attic imports (Figs 5.3 & 5.4). Many are vessels associated with wine drinking: the drinking vessels known as 'Ionian cups' are the commonest, but jugs of various kinds (*oinochoai* and *olpai*) and mixing and storage vessels such as *krateres*, *stamnoi* and *hydriai* also occur. Small vessels for unguents – *aryballoi*, *alabastra* and *lekythoi* – occur too. Transport amphorae, used for wine and olive oil, are also found, but as these normally occur in fragmentary form on

Figure 5.3 Early 5th-century BC Attic Red-figure *krater* from a tomb on Botromagno, Gravina. Height=41 cm.

A settlement sites rather than complete in tombs, they are less likely to be recognized. Votive figurines are found, usually in the sanctuary sites. As well as pottery, bronzes occur: Corinthian-style helmets and other armour; gold and silver objects, such as jewelry, are known from a few rich tombs like those at Rutigliano. Coins occur rarely before the 4th century BC; when they do, they occur mainly as stray finds, although a few hoards are known. They are too few for them to have been in general circulation. Greek-type household wares do not normally occur before the 5th century BC and do not become common until the 4th, by which time they were being made in many centres throughout southern Italy.

Figure 5.4 Early 5th-century BC Attic Red-figure *lekythos* from a tomb on Botromagno, Gravina. Height=17.5 cm.

CONTEXT

Numerically, most of the Greek imports have been found in tombs, although the sanctuary sites have produced disproportionately large quantities of Greek goods in relation to their number. By contrast, relatively little

Greek material is found in domestic deposits on settlement sites. Morel (1983, p. 129), has made this point in connection with Garaguso, where three different types of context have been excavated. The highest proportion of Greek pots occurs in the votive deposits (where native pots are rare, though not entirely absent); the tombs produce both Greek and native pots, while the settlement produces very little Greek pottery and native wares predominate. This pattern is probably a general one throughout southern Italy. Incidentally, it serves well to illustrate the problematic nature of the concept of 'hellenization' discussed above, for the sanctuary at Garaguso is more hellenized than the cemetery, which is itself more hellenized than the settlement – and yet probably all three (and almost certainly the settlement and the cemetery) were used by the same people.

ASSOCIATION

Greek artefacts are invariably associated with native products on all sites outside the *chorai* of the Greek cities; there are no 'pure' Greek sites, though at Garaguso the sanctuary site produced only tiny quantities of local material. Elsewhere the mix is more evenly balanced or is weighted strongly in favour of the local products.

DISTRIBUTION AND DATE

The unevenness of data recovery makes it difficult to assess the distribution of Greek goods in south-east Italy. In general, however, there seems to be a pattern of greatest quantity and earliest date in areas nearest to the Greek colonies, with a reduction in quantity and lowering of date with distance from them. Native sites in southern Apulia have produced Greek pottery of 7th-century BC date (Leuca, Brindisi), or even 8th-century (i.e. 'pre-colonial') date (Otranto, Porto Cesareo, Cavallino) (Adamesteanu 1979, Istituto di Archeologia 1978, 1979a, 1979b). In the area of central Apulia and eastern Basilicata, the imports began in the late 7th century BC and became common in the 6th. (Central Apulian sites include Ruvo, Rutigliano, Noicattaro, Valenzano, Conversano, Gioia del Colle (Monte Sannace), Altamura, and Gravina (Botromagno) (Adamesteanu 1979); sites in eastern Basilicata include Pisticci, Montescaglioso, Miglionico, Ferrandina, Garaguso, Timmari, Matera and Monte Irsi (Soprintendenza 1971, 1976, Lo Porto 1973).) Further north still, in northern Apulia, the first imports belong to the later 6th century BC and are very much sparser in distribution than further south. (Sites where they have been found include Canosa, Ascoli, Lavello, Arpi, Ordona, Salapia, Guadone and Cupola (Mazzei 1985).)

Reference to Table 5.1 indicates that in almost all respects the data fit the 'coexistence' model better than the 'Greek control' model. This point is emphasized if we compare the evidence with that for the period of the Roman Republic from the late 4th century BC onwards. The Romans undoubtedly *did* exercise political and military control over southern Italy and at that time we find evidence of most of the features listed in column 2 of

Table 5.1, which are notably lacking in the earlier period. For example the Romans established settlements within the area they brought under their control (Lucera, founded 314 BC, Venosa, founded 291 BC) and these were in every respect like Roman towns elsewhere in Italy. Therefore we feel justified in accepting the coexistence model for the earlier period. The one aspect of the evidence which seems somewhat anomalous is the occurrence of sanctuaries of Greek type, with predominantly Greek goods in their votive deposits, in the native area. However, small rural sanctuaries cannot easily be seen as instruments of political control and we tentatively propose a different interpretation, compatible with the 'coexistence' model, below.

Trade or exchange

If the Greeks did not exercise political or military control over the native inhabitants, then relationships between them (documented by the evidence just discussed) must be subsumed under the general heading of trade or exchange. Can we say anything about the nature of this exchange, either from the available data or from anthropological theory? Very little specific work has been done on this topic and we can only make a few general and preliminary remarks here.

(1) It is unlikely to have taken the form of true 'commercial' trade, based on the price-fixing market, motivated by the desire for profits and controlled by market forces. The market economy was not really developed in the Greek world before the 5th or 4th century BC, and was certainly not in existence in the native communities before this date.

(2) Ethnographic analogy would suggest that the most likely type of exchange was a prestige-goods system, organized by the local élites and motivated by status considerations rather than the profit motive. The overwhelming predominance of prestige goods among the Greek imports, including those associated with wine-drinking – very probably a status activity in these societies – supports this interpretation. Possible parallels can be found in Southeast Asia, among communities such as the Iban, the Land Dayak and the Lamet who live in hinterlands engaged in exchange with more sophisticated cultural centres (all discussed in Sahlins 1972, pp. 224–6). Sahlins writes:

> From the perspective of the advanced center, they are backwaters serving as secondary sources of rice and other goods. From the hinterlands view, the critical aspect of the intercultural relation is that the subsistence staple, rice, is exported for cash, iron tools and prestige goods, many of the last quite expensive.

The prestige goods, exotic items such as Chinese pottery and brass gongs, are used as ceremonial display items and in marriage prestations.

(3) This analogy may also offer some suggestions about the nature of the goods traded in exchange for the Greek products. South-east Italy lacks

useful raw materials such as metals or other minerals, and the only items available for exchange would probably have had to come out of the domestic economy – either actual subsistence goods or secondary products forming part of the same economy, such as textiles, skins, goods made of bone etc. It is possible that, as in Southeast Asia, one of the main commodities traded was the subsistence staple: in this case, wheat. However, Metapontion at least was situated in very good agricultural land and was famous for its cereal production; the ear of wheat found on almost all Metapontine coins symbolizes this agricultural prosperity, which was also enjoyed by other Greek cities around the Ionian Gulf, such as Sybaris. It therefore seems unlikely that Metapontion would have needed to import additional grain, though Taras may have been in a slightly less favourable position. The most likely import, still within the sphere of the domestic economy, is perhaps woollen textiles. At a slightly later period, under the Romans, Apulia was famous for its wool production and large numbers of sheep were kept, transhuming from lowland winter pastures to the mountains in summer. It is unlikely that the Greek cities themselves could have produced very much wool, since it would have been impossible to keep large flocks of sheep all the year round within their small, exclusively lowland, territories and, if we are right about the area under their direct control, they would not have had access to the upland summer pastures which were essential for the support of large flocks. The native settlements of this period all produce very large numbers of pottery loomweights – they are among the commonest finds on excavations – suggesting production of textiles (presumably wool since we have no evidence of any suitable plant being grown) above the level required by domestic consumption alone.

(4) Finally we might speculate about the way in which the exchange took place and also where it took place. In well developed prestige-goods exchange systems, one usually finds trading partnerships between leaders of the different communities, and special trading places, known to historians as emporia (although anthropologists sometimes refer to them as ports-of-trade or gateway communities). Special trading sites of this sort are administered by the native élite, but are inhabited and frequented mostly by alien merchants. They are usually located in places apart from the normal residential settlements, and special conditions prevail which make them neutral ground for the two trading parties, where their personal safety and fair conditions for trading are guaranteed. In the south-east Italian instance, it is unlikely that either trade partnerships or emporia existed in developed form, particularly at an early stage, but we might expect them to appear in some embryo or prototype form.

We suggest tentatively that the sanctuary sites of Greek type associated with native settlements might be considered proto-emporia of this kind. A similar view has been expressed by Morel in connection with some of the 'pre-colonial' sites such as Incoronata.

> In every case these are centres of 'redistribution' in the sense that the Greeks (or others) did not dare or could not or would not penetrate to

> any extent into native territory and thus brought their products to these points where the natives – at least according to the most probable conjecture – came for them and then traded them further among their own people (Morel 1983, p. 149).

The sanctuary sites, with their religious associations, and situated outside the settlements themselves, might provide an appropriate environment for trade of this sort. On many of these sites the votive goods include products from a variety of different sources, which is what one might expect on a specialized trading site. The locations of some of the sanctuaries would also fit such an interpretation: they are situated within reasonable distance of the Greek cities on natural routes penetrating into native territory. Examples include Timmari, *c.* 40 km inland from Metaponto, close to the Bradano river, and Garaguso, *c.* 40 km from Metaponto, between the Basento and the Cavone rivers; Armento is in a similar position in relation to Herakleia, i.e. *c.* 40 km inland, close to the Agri river. In the case of Taranto, Oria is *c.* 35 km to the east, Porto Cesareo *c.* 60 km south-east, Egnazia *c.* 50 km north; both Porto Cesareo and Egnazia are on the coast (of the Ionian Gulf in the former case, the Adriatic in the latter) and could represent coastal emporia for sea-borne rather than overland trade. As far as the inland sites are concerned, it is possible that the Greek traders penetrated 50–60 km from their home cities but no further. Beyond a radius of this sort Greek goods would have been passed on as items of exchange between different native settlements.

Changes in the native communities

In the centuries that followed the settlement of Greeks in southern Italy, considerable changes occurred in the organization of the native communities. These changes were both complex and far-reaching and they deserve detailed examination through carefully designed research projects. No such research has yet been undertaken, however, and we shall restrict ourselves here to a few comments on three aspects of the changes involved: (a) urbanization, (b) social differentiation, and (c) ethnicity and political organization.

Urbanization

The criteria we can use to assess the degree of urbanization present include: (a) the absolute size of sites; (b) the existence of urban features such as fortifications, public buildings, and street systems; (c) evidence for the rôle of a site as a 'central place' within a system of sites in a region. Unfortunately the scarcity of good quality data from excavations and the general lack of field survey make it difficult to assess any of these aspects. However, we do have some data for two areas of south-east Italy, which suggest rather different settlement patterns. The first area is the Tavoliere plain; the second is the area between Gravina and Venosa where Vinson (1973) carried out his survey. Outside these two areas we have very little evidence for overall settlement pattern, although individual sites have been excavated in some cases.

In the Tavoliere we have evidence of sites of the Early Iron Age both along the coast, where they have Bronze Age antecedents, and in the interior, where Bronze Age occupation was apparently lacking. We know little about the sites of the 10th to 8th centuries BC except that they existed, though remains of post-built rectangular huts with apsidal ends have been excavated at Salpi (Salapia 1: Tinè Bertocchi 1975). In the 7th or 6th centuries BC several sites may have been equipped with defences, although only at Arpi have the defences actually been dated, to the 7th century BC. The defences were not stone walls of Greek type but earthworks, comprising a ditch and internal bank, with, at Arpi, traces of a wall on top, with stone footings, possibly surmounted by mudbrick. At Arpi the defences enclosed a semi-circular area, with the straight side protected by the Celone river; the enclosed area measures a huge 1000 ha (10 sq km), with a 13 km perimeter. Unfortunately we know nothing about the internal layout or buildings at Arpi and, although it is tempting to label such a site 'urban' on the basis of size alone, there are alternative explanations. Both Tinè Bertocchi (1975, p. 274) and De Juliis (1975, p. 287) assume that the defences enclosed areas of agricultural land and cemeteries as well as dwellings, and that they might have served to house the entire population of the territory in times of threat. It is certainly the case that tombs have been found within the defences. Arpi is not the only huge defended site on the Tavoliere: Tiati, in the far north-west, occupies two hills divided by a deep valley, the whole enclosed by defences 11 km long. Unfortunately very little is known about Tiati; even the plan is known only from aerial photographs. Other major sites are known at Ordona, Ascoli Satriano, Salpi, Cupola, Orsara and, just south of the Tavoliere, at Canosa. Clearly the construction of these vast defended enclosures represents a new form of territorial exploitation, but not necessarily a characteristically urban form. We badly need information on what was inside these enclosures.

In the Gravina area we find a different pattern. Some of the 10th–8th-century BC settlements, of the period before the arrival of the Greeks, covered large areas, but show no obviously urban features. At Botromagno (Gravina), for instance, material of this date has been excavated or collected from the surface over a large area of the hilltop and the slope down to the river gorge, covering perhaps 100 ha in all. However, at present we do not know what this spread means: it could be a group of small settlements separated by open spaces. Even if it was all occupied, there is no indication of overall urban organization, such as planned layout or defences. It should be said here that the type of location chosen for settlement in this area was normally a high, steep hill protected by natural ravines and gullies, where the need for artificial defences would have been less pressing than in the almost flat Tavoliere plain.

From the 7th century BC on, contemporary with the Greek settlement of the coast, four sites in Vinson's survey (1973) reached a size which he feels justifies the term 'town'. He provides no detailed information on size, but Botromagno, at 100 ha, was the largest of them. There may have been three other settlements of this status underlying later towns, making seven in all. However, as in the Tavoliere, we lack any indication of urban buildings, defences, or street systems, until a late stage. As we have seen, Botromagno was equipped with Greek-type stone defences in the 4th century BC (as was Monte Sannace, further east) (Scarfi 1962). By this stage Botromagno, like Monte Sannace, seems to have been generally urban in character, with densely built-up areas laid out along streets, though no unequivocal public buildings have been found. Vinson's survey found that around the end of the 5th or the beginning of the 4th century BC many (20 out of 33) smaller village sites were abandoned and, though many new sites were established in the centuries that followed, these were generally smaller in size and may represent single farms rather than villages or hamlets. We may tentatively interpret this pattern as follows. A tendency towards the growth of a few large centres can be seen from at least the 7th century BC onwards, if not earlier, but it is not accompanied by notably urban formal features. The late 5th–4th centuries BC saw a phase of full urbanization, with marked development of the towns themselves, accompanied by abandonment of many villages in the countryside. In their place single family farms were established, presumably dependent on the main towns – a pattern similar to that found in the territory of Metapontion, and possibly characteristic of the Greek cities in general.

In view of the paucity of the data, it would be premature to frame any hypothesis connecting the urbanization of the native communities with exchange with the Greek settlements. One thing is clear, however, and that is that the influence of the Greek communities did not rapidly give rise to urbanization of the hinterland. The Greek settlements themselves apparently achieved urban status only in the 6th century BC, while the native communities do not appear really urban for another two centuries.

Social differentiation

In the absence of good settlement excavations, the evidence for social differentiation comes almost exclusively from burials. Even here the evidence is not good: in our area we have no complete cemeteries, or even parts of cemeteries, which have both escaped robbing and been excavated and recorded in modern scientific fashion. For the present we have to content ourselves with documenting general trends in the burial evidence.

There are clear distinctions in the grave goods provided with burials even in the 9th and 8th centuries BC, before the arrival of the Greeks. Whereas some burials are equipped with only one or two pots, others have abundant bronze and iron goods: these include weapons such as spearheads, and ornaments such as fibulae, pendants and earrings (e.g. Lo Porto 1969). However, there is no distinction in form between the richer and the poorer tombs – most are small slab cists under stone cairns – and they occur in the same cemeteries. In the late 7th and 6th centuries BC the distinction between rich and poor burials becomes much more marked. The rich burials contain many Greek goods, both pottery and bronzes, and occasionally precious metals as well. The imported vessels include Corinthian and Attic vases of very high quality. Characteristically the imported goods reflect two status areas: wine-drinking (pottery cups, jugs, storage and mixing vessels) and warfare (bronze helmets, greaves and other armour, iron spearheads). These rich tombs often contain very large quantities of material, including many pots of local geometric wares as well as imported vessels (for examples see Lo Porto 1973). At this stage rich burials are sometimes in tombs of distinctive form and sometimes found in locations apart from the main cemeteries. The rich early 6th-century tomb at Armento is a case in point (Adamesteanu 1972). At Botromagno rich tombs were sometimes placed within the settlement, while poorer burials were situated in cemeteries outside. Four tombs, falling within the period *c.* 530–470 BC, were found in the recent excavations at Botromagno in one small area of the settlement: all had been robbed in antiquity, but the fragmentary remains of the grave goods indicate that three at least were originally rich, equipped with abundant imported Attic and Metapontine pottery (Figs 5.3 & 5.4), as well as fine wares of local type and imported bronzes (interim reports in Whitehouse 1979, 1980, 1981a, 1982, 1983, 1984). Rich burials continue in the 4th century BC, but the goods were now predominantly of local manufacture, since Greek-type wares were being produced in many south Italian centres by this stage. Pottery dominates the grave goods in 4th-century tombs and frequently large numbers of vessels are found, up to 50 being not unusual. The tombs themselves are more impressive than previously, being rock-cut chamber tombs with monumental entrances, equipped with jambs, lintels, thresholds and blocking slabs of local limestone.

Rich burials occur commonly in southern and central Apulia and in Basilicata, but are rare in northern Apulia, where before the 4th century BC most graves contain only pottery vessels of local type and bronze ornaments such as fibulae; Greek imports are rare.

In general it seems clear that an increase in social differentiation in the native communities followed the arrival of the Greeks. Since Greek goods figure so prominently in the rich graves, it seems reasonable to assume that there was a direct association between the importation of Greek goods and the increasing differentiation. Models to explain the connection are not hard to find. It has been suggested in several different contexts that the availability of prestige goods imported from outside provides a means for some individuals to increase their wealth and status by the acquisition of these desirable luxury goods. It has been suggested, for instance, for the 6th-century BC Hallstatt communities of west-central Europe who gained access to goods of both Greek and Etruscan manufacture (Wells 1980, 1985). Another case where a similar interpretation is proposed is the 1st-century BC–1st-century AD communities of south-east England, which acquired luxury goods from the Romans (Haselgrove 1982). A number of assumptions are made in these cases. One is that the trade would have been in the hands of relatively few individuals, usually community heads, who wielded authority locally and were the centres of redistributive economic systems (chiefs, in a word) and would therefore be in a position to concentrate the surplus products of the whole community for exchange with the outside world. A second assumption often made is that the goods exchanged for the luxury imports would have included raw materials such as metals or other minerals, which would have required mining or quarrying, and perhaps also products such as furs or hides which would have required specialist skills to acquire. Exchange based on such products would have required considerable centralized organization to administer and it is often suggested that the need to exploit such resources to exchange for prestige goods encouraged the growth of urban communities and complex political organization.

However, the example of the Iban, the Land Dayak and the Lamet, quoted above, shows that there are other possibilities. In these cases the products exchanged for the prestige imports are not raw materials but the subsistence staple, rice, and other products of the domestic economy. Thus they are goods produced by the household (in the domestic mode of production) and there is no special requirement for centralized organization or concentration of either labour or products; each household could trade for itself. Sahlins (1972, p. 225) lists the consequences for the economy and polity of the hinterland communities as follows:

> (1) Different households, by virtue of variations in ratio and number of effective producers, amass different amounts of the subsistence-export staple. The productive differences range between surfeit above and deficit below family consumption requirements. These differences, however, are not liquidated by sharing in favor of need. Instead (2) the intensity of sharing within the village or tribe is low, and (3) the principal reciprocal relation between households is a closely calculated balanced exchange of labour service . . . (4) Even household commensality may be rather rigidly supervised, subjected to accounting of each person's rice dole in the interest of developing an exchange reserve . . . (5) Restricted sharing of staples, demanded by articulation with the siphoning market, finds its social complement in an atomization and fragmentation of community structure. Lineages, or like systems of extensive and corporate solidary relations, are incompatible with the external drain on household staples and the corresponding posture of self-interest required *vis-à-vis* other households. Large local descent groups are absent or inconsequential. Instead, the solidary relations are of the small family itself . . . (6) Prestige apparently hinges upon obtaining exotic items – Chinese pottery, brass gongs etc – from the outside in exchange for rice or work. Prestige does not, obviously cannot, rest on generous assistance to one's fellows in the manner of a tribal big-man. The exotic goods figure internally as ceremonial display

items and in marriage prestations – thus insofar as status is linked to them it is principally as possession and ability to make payments, again not through giving them away.

In such a system the importation of prestige goods leads to increasing differences in wealth and status between individuals, but *not* to increasing centralization or associated traits such as increasing nucleation of settlement. Indeed, there is a tendency to fragmentation of the social structure, rather than increased coherence. We suggest tentatively that the situation in south-east Italy after the arrival of the Greeks is closer to this model than to that proposed for central Europe at the same period or south-east England in the late pre-Roman period. It would fit the suggestion made earlier that the main exported products were woollen textiles, produced by individual households, as well as the lack of clear evidence for urbanization before the 4th century BC.

Ethnicity and political organization

In almost all works on the subject of this chapter by other authors the native inhabitants of southern Italy are referred to by a series of 'tribal' names attributed to them by Greek and Roman authors (the names relevant to our area are Enotrians and Iapygians, the latter subdivided into Daunians, Peucetians and Messapians). We have been careful to avoid this practice, for a number of reasons. Firstly, the literary references are ambiguous and sometimes contradictory. For instance, the Peucetians figure as allies of the Iapygians on a Tarentine dedication at Delphi of the early 5th century (described by Pausanias X.13.10), whereas other authors (e.g. Polybius III.88 and Strabo VI, 279) regard the Peucetians as a subdivision of the Iapygians, along with the Daunians and the Messapians. A more crucial criticism relates to the attitudes of the ancient writers and their expectations about the world of the 'barbarians' living outside their own Greek world. We have dealt with this issue elsewhere (Whitehouse & Wilkins 1985) and concluded that it was natural for the Greek and Roman writers to conceptualize the world around them in terms of 'peoples' to whom they could attribute names, but that there was no a priori reason to deduce from this that the pre-Greek occupants of southern Italy actually thought of themselves as one people or a number of peoples.

If we leave aside the literary sources, we can turn to anthropological and archaeological theory to help us examine the material evidence. In our earlier work we referred to important articles about the nature of 'tribes' and 'peoples' by Fried (1968) and Renfrew (1978). We concluded from our discussion of these works that the concept of 'peoples' has no meaning in the context of organizationally simple societies and that we should expect it to appear only with at least relatively complex political organization, perhaps at the level of the state.

In his article Fried (1968, p. 15) argued that the development of more complex societies, with a clear ethnic self-awareness, occurs through contact with more highly organized societies, as in the classic colonial situation. Here we shall attempt to establish whether this model fits the situation in south-east Italy in the 7th–4th centuries BC. To do this we must look for archaeological evidence for two separate (but perhaps interconnected) social phenomena: (a) the emergence of ethnic self-awareness, and (b) the development of complex political organization.

ETHNIC SELF-AWARENESS

Ian Hodder (1979) has addressed this issue in an important article in which he suggests that differences in material culture may be used to emphasize group identities, especially in times of economic and social stress. He argues, in connection with ethnographic field work carried out in the Baringo district of western Kenya, that 'the material culture differences between tribes can only be understood if material culture is seen as a language, expressing within-group cohesion in competition over scarce resources' (1979, p. 447). The inhabitants of south-east Italy may have been in a position of economic and social stress as a result of changes induced by contact with the Greek settlements; indeed they might have been in competition over scarce resources – the resources in question being the prestige goods produced by the Greeks. If this was the case, we might expect to find more material culture distinctions appearing in the period after the arrival of the Greeks, created by the 'need to stress overtly clear, unambiguous identities' (Hodder 1979, p. 447). In fact we do find some evidence for such distinctions in the archaeological record. In pottery styles, for instance, the 9th and 8th centuries BC are characterized by a rather uniform geometric painted ware, called Iapygian Geometric, which occurs throughout Apulia and widely in Basilicata, as far west as the Campanian and Calabrian borders. In the 7th–6th centuries we find the emergence of distinctive regional styles, each with characteristic forms and decoration; they are usually given the traditional 'ethnic' labels, i.e. Daunian in northern Apulia, Peucetian in central Apulia, and Messapian in southern Apulia; a fourth style (Enotrian) can also be defined, if more tentatively, in Basilicata (De la Genière 1979). At least a few other artefact types also seem to be specific to particular culture areas. In the 'Daunian' region we find remarkable stone funerary stelae, dated to the later 7th and 6th centuries BC. Some fibulae types may be specific too: the double-bow type, often made of silver, of the 6th–5th centuries BC seems to have been a 'Peucetian' form. Much more work needs to be done on this subject, but we may tentatively conclude that the 7th–6th centuries saw the emergence of ethnic group identities (four within our area) out of the undifferentiated culture of the First Iron Age. These can *perhaps* be correlated with the peoples described by the classical writers, though the problems of ambiguity and contradiction in these sources remain.

COMPLEX POLITICAL ORGANIZATION

Complex political organization is most easily recognized archaeologically in spatial terms, since it is reflected in a hierarchical settlement pattern, with large central places surrounded by smaller dependent settlements, either of more or less uniform size or in 'tiers' of different sizes. Unfortuantely, as we have seen in the discussion of urbanization, we have very little data to assess this. However, two features are of some interest in this context: (a) the enclosure of large areas of land by earthworks in northern Apulia (Daunia), and (b) the tendency towards the emergence of a few large centres from the 7th century BC onwards in the area of the Gravina survey (and probably elsewhere in both Apulia and Basilicata). The 'Daunian' phenomenon cannot really be described as nucleation of settlement, since it is unlikely that the enclosures were densely built-up inside, but it does suggest territorial claims on land on behalf of the whole community of a type not seen at an earlier date. It can perhaps be compared to the large earthworks constructed at Colchester and other locations in south-east England in the period before the Roman conquest. It may indicate a time when settlements were being called upon to serve urban *functions* (e.g. protection of citizens from outside attack, administrative centres, centres of craft production) before they have really acquired urban *form*. The pattern in the Gravina area may reflect the slow development of an increasingly centralized pattern, although on present evidence it would be difficult to show that the smaller centres were dependent on the larger ones before the 4th century BC, when we see the emergence of a pattern characterized by a few large 'town-sized' settlements surrounded by numerous small 'farm-sized' sites. Tentatively we may conclude that society did develop towards a more complex political form after the arrival of the Greeks, but only at a slow pace. We would hesitate to suggest that full state organization was in existence before the 4th, or at earliest the 5th, century BC.

Conclusion

We have looked briefly at both the *nature* of the contact between Greeks and natives in south-east Italy and at some of the possible *effects* of this contact. Obviously there are many aspects of the subject that we have not touched on; in particular craft specialization, internal trade or exchange, and trade with areas other than the Greek cities would all repay attention. However, we offer this chapter as a contribution towards a specifically archaeological approach to this subject, in the belief that such an approach has a profitable future ahead of it. We have tried to demonstrate that an analysis of the development in south-east Italy in terms of a centre–periphery model can give important insights into the precise forms of social and economic relations through which the native communities were brought into contact with the Greeks, and we have highlighted the specific importance of prestige goods for the transformation of native economies and social organization.

Note

1 There exists no satisfactory term to describe such local peoples. 'Local' is imprecise; 'indigenous' is inappropriate, because of its implication of permanent habitation since the beginning of time; while 'native' carries romantic or colonial overtones. As the least evil we choose 'native' here.

References

Adamesteanu, D. 1972. Una tomba arcaica di Armento. *Atti e Memorie della Società Magna Grecia* **11–12** (1970–1), 83–92.

Adamesteanu, D. 1979. La colonizzazione greca in Puglia. In *La Puglia dal Paleolitico al Tardoromano*, D. Adamesteanu, F. Biancofiore, G. Cremonesi, F. D'Andria, A. Geniola & A. Palma di Cesnola, 193–269. Milan: Electa.

Adamesteanu, D. & C. Vatin, 1976. L'arrière-pays de Metaponte. *Compte Rendu de l'Académie des Inscriptions*, 110–23.

Bradford, J. S. P. 1957. *Ancient landscapes*. London: Bell.

Carter, J. C. 1981. Rural settlement at Metaponto. In *Archaeology and Italian society*, G. Barker & R. Hodges (eds), 167–78. British Archaeological Reports International Series 102, Oxford.

Cassano, S. M. & A. Manfredini 1983. *Studi sul neolitico del Tavoliere della Puglia*. British Archaeological Reports International Series 160, Oxford.

Chevallier, R. 1971. Mission archéologique de la faculté des lettres de Tours à Metaponte. *Revue Archéologique* **2**, 309–26.

Cipolloni Sampò, M. 1980. Le comunità neolitiche della Valle dell'Ofanto: proposta di lettura di un'analisi territoriale. In *Attività archeologica in Basilicata 1964–1977. Studi in onore di Dinu Adamesteanu*, E. Lattanzi (ed.), 283–311. Matera: Meta.

de La Genière, J. 1979. The Iron Age in southern Italy. In *Italy before the Romans*, D. Ridgway & F. Ridgway (eds), 59–93. London and New York: Academic Press.

De Juliis, E. M. 1975. Caratteri della civiltà daunia dal VI secolo aC all'arrivo dei Romani. In *Civiltà preistoriche e protostoriche della Daunia*, S. Tinè (ed.), 286–97. Florence: Parenti.

Dilthey, H. 1980. Sorgenti acque luoghi sacri in Basilicata. In *Attività archeologica in Basilicata 1964–1977. Studi in onore di Dinu Adamesteanu*, E. Lattanzi (ed.), 539–60. Matera: Meta.

Fried, M. H. 1968. On the concepts of 'tribe' and 'tribal society'. In *Essays on the problem of the tribe*, J. Helm (ed.), 3–20. Washington: University of Washington Press.

Greco, G. 1980. Le fasi cronologiche dell'abitato di Serra di Vaglio. In *Attività archeologica in Basilicata 1964–1977. Studi in onore di Dinu Adamesteanu*, E. Lattanzi (ed.), 367–404. Matera: Meta.

Haselgrove, C. 1982. Wealth, prestige and power: the dynamics of political centralisation in south-east England. In *Ranking, resource and exchange*, C. Renfrew & S. Shennan (eds), 79–88. Cambridge: Cambridge University Press.

Hodder, I. 1979. Economic and social stress and material culture patterning. *American Antiquity* **44**, 446–54.

Holloway, R. R. 1970. *Satrianum*. Providence: Brown University.

Istituto di Archeologia e Storia antica dell'Università di Lecce, 1978. *Leuca*. Lecce: University of Lecce.

Istituto di Archeologia e Storia antica dell'Università di Lecce, 1979a. *Salento arcaico*. Lecce: University of Lecce.

Istituto di Archeologia e Storia antica dell'Università di Lecce, 1979b. *Cavallino*. Lecce: University of Lecce.

Lattanzi, E. 1980. L'insediamento indigeno sul pianoro di Timmari (Matera). In *Attività archeologica in Basilicata 1964–1977. Studi in onore di Dinu Adamesteanu*, E. Lattanzi (ed.), 239–82. Matera: Meta.

Lo Porto, F. G. 1964. Satyrion (Taranto). Scavi e ricerche nel luogo del più antico insediamento laconico in Puglia. *Notizie degli scavi di antichità* **18**, 177–279.

Lo Porto, F. G. 1969. Metaponto. Tombe a tumulo dell'età del ferro scoperte nel suo entroterra. *Notizie degli scavi di antichità* **23**, 121–70.

Lo Porto, F. G. 1973. Civiltà indigena e penetrazione greca nella Lucania orientale. *Monumenti Antichi*, serie miscellanea **1–3**, 149–250.

Mazzei, M. 1985. Importazioni ceramiche e influssi culturali in Daunia nel VI e V sec. aC. In *Papers in Italian archaeology IV. Part iii: Patterns in protohistory*, C. Malone & S. Stoddart (eds), 263–79. British Archaeological Reports International Series 246, Oxford.

Morel, J.-P. 1983. Greek colonization in Italy and the West (problems of evidence and interpretation). In *Crossroads of the Mediterranean*, T. Hackens, N. D. Holloway & R. R. Holloway (eds), 123–61. Louvain: Catholic University of Louvain.

Renfrew, C. 1978. Space, time and polity. In *The evolution of social systems*, J. Friedman and M. J. Rowlands (eds), 89–112. London: Duckworth.

Sahlins, M. 1972. *Stone Age economics*. London: Tavistock.

Scarfi, B. M. 1962. Gioia del Colle (Bari) – L'abitato peucetico di Monte Sannace. *Notizie degli scavi di antichità* **16**, 1–283.

Schmiedt, G. & Chevallier, R. 1969. *Metaponto e Caulonia*. Milan: l'Universo.

Soprintendenza alle Antichità della Basilicata, Potenza, 1971. *Popoli Anellenici in Basilicata*. Naples: La Buona Stampa.

Soprintendenza Archeologica della Basilicata, 1976. *Il Museo Nazionale Ridola di Matera*. Matera: Meta.

Tinè Bertocchi, F. 1975. Formazione della civiltà daunia dal X al VI secolo aC. In *Civiltà preistoriche e protostoriche della Daunia*, S. Tinè (ed.), 271–85. Florence: Parenti.

Uggeri, G. 1969. Κλῆροι arcaici e bonifica classica nella χώρα di Metaponto. *Parola del Passato* **118**, 51–71.

Vinson, S. P. 1973. Ancient roads between Venosa and Gravina. *Papers of the British School at Rome* **40**, 58–90.

Vinson, S. P. forthcoming. *Ancient roads between Venosa and Gravina: Conclusions*. Unpublished ms.

Wells, P. S. 1980. *Culture contact and culture change: early Iron Age Central Europe and the Mediterranean world*. Cambridge: Cambridge University Press.

Wells, P. S. 1985. Italy and Central Europe: material culture, ritual and communication in the Iron Age. In *Papers in Italian Archaeology IV. Part iii: Patterns in protohistory*, C. Malone & S. Stoddart (eds), 255–62. British Archaeological Reports International Series 245, Oxford.

Whitehouse, R. D. 1979. Botromagno, Gravina in Puglia (Bari province). *Lancaster in Italy*, 1–4. Lancaster: University of Lancaster.

Whitehouse, R. D. 1980. Botromagno, Gravina in Puglia (Bari province). *Lancaster in Italy*, 16–21. Lancaster: University of Lancaster.

Whitehouse, R. D. 1981a. Botromagno, Gravina in Puglia (Bari province). *Lancaster in Italy and North Africa*, 20–5. Lancaster: University of Lancaster.

Whitehouse, R. D. 1981b. Prehistoric settlement patterns in southeast Italy. In *Archaeology and Italian Society*, G. Barker & R. Hodges (eds), 157–65. British Archaeological Reports International Series 102, Oxford.

Whitehouse, R: D. 1982. Botromagno, Gravina in Puglia (Bari province). *Lancaster in Italy*, 12–17. Lancaster: University of Lancaster.

Whitehouse, R. D. 1983. Botromagno, Gravina in Puglia (Bari province). *Lancaster in Italy*, 23–9. Lancaster: University of Lancaster.

Whitehouse, R. D. 1984. Botromagno, Gravina in Puglia (Bari province). *Lancaster in Italy*, 26–33. Lancaster: University of Lancaster.

Whitehouse, R. D. & J. B. Wilkins 1985. Magna Graecia before the Greeks: towards a reconciliation of the evidence. In *Papers in Italian Archaeology IV. Part iii: Patterns in protohistory*, C. Malone & S. Stoddart (eds), 89–109. British Archaeological Reports International Series 245, Oxford.

6 *Greeks, Etruscans, and thirsty barbarians: Early Iron Age interaction in the Rhône Basin of France*

MICHAEL DIETLER

Although an explicitly formulated, testable centre–periphery model has evident heuristic value in many contexts, the uncritical application of such concepts can actually hinder the recognition of important socio-economic processes in the archaeological record. Precisely because the model is useful in explaining the development of secondary 'centres' in peripheral areas, there is a risk that attention may be focused on apparent centres (and their immediate peripheries), and that areas which do not fit neatly into a presumed dendritic network of dependent relations may be ignored. Significant developments in areas which did not respond to external trade contacts by forming recognizable cores of political centralization (by no means a universal response to such contacts: Gray & Birmingham 1970) may thus be overlooked or misunderstood, even though they may form an important component of the larger system under consideration.

I would argue that an implicit, rather nebulous form of a centre–periphery concept has long dominated the perception of relations between the Mediterranean world and the 'barbarians' of western and central Europe in the Early Iron Age (Fig. 6.1). Such an orientation is obvious both in the enduring focus of research in southern France on the process of 'hellenization' and in the numerous studies of Mediterranean trade and the rise of the central Hallstatt chiefdom sites (*Fürstensitze*) of eastern France and south-west Germany. I would further argue that an excessive emphasis in much of this research on the direct influence of the 'primary centre' of the Mediterranean colonial civilizations upon secondary centres in the indigenous 'periphery', and a corresponding neglect of the structural relations linking the indigenous socio-economic systems, has hampered the conceptualization of the complexities of trade relations and associated socio-cultural processes in the area. Specifically, I believe that, in contrast to the common assumption of direct Mediterranean trade penetrating Hallstatt Europe,[1] there is a plausible case to be made for the potentially crucial rôle of the Early Iron Age inhabitants of the lower Rhône Basin in articulating and perhaps even initiating long-distance trade contacts.

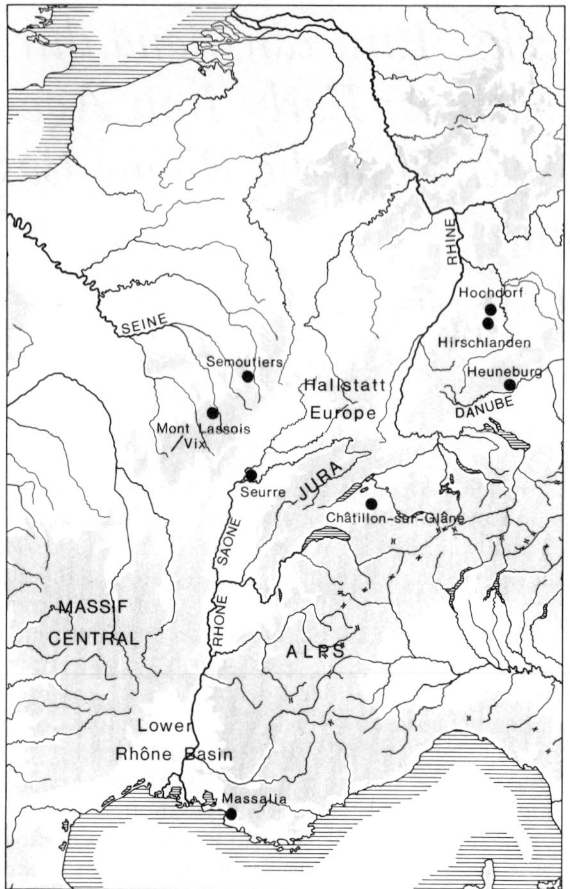

Figure 6.1 Sites and regions referred to in the text.

This chapter offers a caveat against overly rigid expectations of the socio-economic structures and processes subsumed under the centre–periphery dichotomy. As such, it does not attempt to formulate or analytically examine a precise model, but rather to address in a speculative way the question of the mechanism of long-distance trade in the Early Iron Age Rhône Basin.[2] The question is not a trivial one, because, as comparative analysis of African responses to early international trade suggests, the primary determinants of the various forms such responses may take are not the goods received from outside or even the structure of the external trading partner, but rather the internal articulation of the areas involved and the institutional and technological organization of the zones linking the indigenous sector to the external market (Austen 1978, p. 16).

A glance at the most recent of a voluminous literature on the subject (e.g. Frankenstein & Rowlands 1978, Wells 1980, 1984, Kimmig 1983, Spindler 1983, Brun 1987) would seem to indicate that there is little doubt about the existence of trade between the Mediterranean civilizations and Hallstatt Europe, or that such trade was of sufficient magnitude to foster dependent relations of a centre–periphery nature. Indeed, the situation has even been characterized as a 'trade explosion' (Collis 1984). However, it must be admitted that this interpretation rests more on the quality of the Mediterranean imports found in Hallstatt contexts than on their quantity. In comparison with the number of imported items found in the same region from a later, more securely recognizable trade network (Tchernia 1983, Fitzpatrick 1985), or even those found in southern France from the same Early Iron Age time period (Benoit 1965, Py 1971, Jully 1982), the quantity appears remarkably limited.

In addition to the Attic pottery and Massaliot amphorae found on a handful of Hallstatt settlements, however, a small number of extraordinary Greek and Etruscan bronze vessels (along with jewelry, carved ivory, silk cloth, and other items) have been recovered from a series of tumulus burials (the so called *Fürstengräber*) already richly elaborated with indigenous 'prestige' elements. It is largely the unusual character of objects such as the 1.64 m high bronze *krater* from the Vix tumulus in Burgundy (Joffroy 1954) or the 500-litre bronze cauldron with cast-bronze lions from a tumulus near Hochdorf in Baden-Württemberg (Biel 1982) – objects of a class which in the Greek world were largely confined to special rôles as religious dedications or political gifts – which has prompted the interpretation of their use as alliance-fostering offerings between Greeks and barbarians (Fischer 1973). The exotic luxury items in the tumuli are thus seen as the highly visible symbols of a trade which is archaeologically considerably less visible.

The route by which these items reached Hallstatt Europe from the Mediterranean is now subject to less disagreement than formerly (see Hatt 1958). Although the passage of some types of objects (especially small bronzes) over the Alpine passes is recognized (Pauli 1971, Boucher 1976), the major Mediterranean imports are generally thought to have arrived in Hallstatt contexts by passage up the Rhône valley from the Phocaean colony of Massalia (modern Marseilles) (e.g. Villard 1960, p. 132, Clavel-Lévêque 1977, p. 21, Wells 1980, Spindler 1983; still *contra*: Joffroy 1980). A few very recent discoveries in the middle Rhône area (e.g. at Lyon: Bellon *et al.* 1986), for long a problematic void in the distribution maps documenting this trade route, certainly enhance the plausibility of this hypothesis. However, the simple identification of the route by which these objects were transported is not sufficient to justify the assumption of a direct relationship between Massalia and Hallstatt Europe, as will be discussed later.

That this presumed trade had important social and economic consequences in Hallstatt Europe has for long been surmised, and has, in a sense, even served implicitly to verify the existence of the trade. The seductive implications of the presence of impressive Mediterranean imports in a context which is widely regarded as one of dramatically increasing social stratification have been frequently discussed (e.g. Zürn 1970, Kimmig & Gersbach 1971, Frankenstein & Rowlands 1978, Wells 1980). The fact that most of the key settlements linked to the wealthy burials were newly founded at strategic positions along possible trade routes (Härke 1979, p. 136) is equally suggestive. However, the marked social differentiation suggested by the late Hallstatt burial data represents only an intensification of a process which began centuries earlier (Champion 1982). Furthermore, even the most rigorously formulated model yet proposed for the mechanism by which trade links with the Mediterranean stimulated political developments among Hallstatt 'chiefdoms' (Frankenstein & Rowlands 1978) ultimately lacks the evidence to verify the dependent quality of such ties. The model convincingly demonstrates how redistribution of prestige items may have been used by Hallstatt chiefs to consolidate and expand political power, but the burial data used to test the model seem to show that the principal objects used in this redistribution network were indigenously produced rather than imported from the Mediterranean. Objects of the latter type are, in fact, hardly redistributed at all, but are largely confined to, and concentrated in, a small number of graves representing the highest level of the proposed political structure (Frankenstein & Rowlands 1978, pp. 84, 100) (with the exception of coral, which is found mostly as inclusions in indigenous metalwork: Champion 1976). Moreover, many of these objects show evidence of curation before their eventual burial, which further argues against the idea of a healthy flow of such imports sustaining Hallstatt redistributive institutions (Bintliff 1981, p. 167). If the articulation of the regional political structure of southwestern Germany had become so dependent upon redistribution of Mediterranean prestige goods that a shift in the supply due to turmoil in the Mediterranean could provoke a political crisis (Frankenstein & Rowlands 1978, p. 108), then one might reasonably expect to see more evidence of their redistribution. Of course, imported items passed down to lower levels in the hierarchy may have been of a more perishable nature (such as cloth) or may have been consumed as part of the institutions of redistributive hospitality rather than buried (hence the wine amphorae and wine-service pottery found on settlements). If, on the other hand, the objects recovered are a representative sample of the Mediterranean goods actually imported, then these were most probably rare 'luxury goods' (in the sense of Appadurai 1986, p. 38) which would have been more important for their diacritical symbolic function in defining élite consumption than as tokens in networks of redistribution (Dietler 1988). In any case, it seems prudent for the moment to allow at least a little scepticism about the magnitude of Mediterranean influence in Hallstatt Europe.

The idea that Massaliot Greeks were responsible for initiating and conducting trade with Hallstatt chiefdoms enjoys wide acceptance in the archaeological literature (e.g. Villard 1960, Benoit 1965, Wells 1980, Spindler 1983) although the evidence for this assumption is less than clear. While Massalia's interest in exploiting the resources of southern France (Benoit

1965, pp. 191–213), and probably the Spanish metal trade (Benoit 1965, p. 31), seems credible and well attested, the suggestion that the colony was founded near the mouth of the Rhône river with the intention of exploiting this route to the interior of Gaul (Benoit 1958, p. 16, Boardman 1980, p. 162) is more problematic. The location may be fortuitous, as it was also the best natural harbour along the South French coast and the site was apparently not occupied by natives (Villard 1960, p. 76). Alternatively, it may simply have been access to the Rhône delta and the peoples surrounding it that made the location attractive. Significantly, although evidence is widespread for almost immediate contact with virtually the entire South French littoral zone (Benoit 1965, Py 1971), it was at least two generations after the founding of Massalia (in about 600 BC) before there was any major penetration of Mediterranean imports further north than the lower Rhône Basin. Also, the pattern of colonial stations founded later by Massalia (see Benoit 1965, pp. 99–134, Clavel-Lévêque 1977, pp. 79–84) appears to resemble much more closely a dendritic network geared towards the exploitation of an extended coastal hinterland, such as that established in 'medieval' East Africa (Austen 1978, p. 13), than one directed towards an inland trade route.

Although other interpretations are possible,[3] the pattern of Etruscan trade in southern France, which predates and overlaps with that of Massalia, seems to show an even greater lack of interest in penetrating the Rhône corridor (Py 1982, p. 108). Etruscan amphorae, *bucchero nero* pottery, and, to a lesser extent, boss-rimmed bronze bowls are widely represented along the South French littoral zone and in the lower Rhône Basin, but fail to penetrate much beyond this area (Lagrand 1979, Morel 1981, Bouloumié & Lagrand 1977). A vastly smaller number of Etruscan bronze vessels, mostly of post-6th century BC date, found in contexts ranging further north have a distinct distribution and are thought to be connected with a later, separate sphere of trade relations (Morel 1981, pp. 495–500).

The difficulties facing Mediterranean traders attempting to undertake direct trade with west-central Europe have been somewhat overlooked in the archaeological literature (e.g. Spindler 1983, pp. 316–21). Although products from this area could have been shipped down the Saône and Rhône rivers to Massalia without great difficulty, the journey northward would almost certainly have had to have been overland, and for distances well in excess of 500 km. The Rhône is a swift river plagued by the ferocious north wind, the Mistral. The formidable problems of up-river navigation were obvious to Greek and Roman authors who, until the 1st century BC, treated the Rhône more as a defensive barrier than a trade route (Saint-Denis 1981). As in Roman times, haulage would have been the only feasible means of up-river transport, and there is good reason to doubt that, given the originally swampy nature of the valley floor, the necessary riverside tracks would have been established in this early period (Piggott 1977, p. 144). Indeed, overland travellers would probably have been forced to avoid the valley itself in favour of the higher ground to the east (Chapotat 1981).

Greeks and Etruscans lacked the superiority in weaponry which enabled Arab traders to push caravan routes safely into the interior of Africa (Gray & Birmingham 1970, p. 13). Overland travel for them would have been possible only by making arrangements for safe passage, and probably for food supplies, with all the indigenous peoples through whose territory they passed. This would have been no simple feat, as there is little evidence to suggest the existence of any large-scale indigenous centralized political authority in southeastern France at this time which could have guaranteed safe passage over long distances, and the attacks on traders by Alpine natives and frequent hostility of Massalia's neighbours, which are a common theme in later classical references (e.g. Justin XLIII, 4–5, Avienus V, 701, see also Barruol 1975, pp. 102–5, Villard 1960, p. 33), are unlikely to have been uniquely a feature of later periods. Examples of similar situations in Africa demonstrate that such trade expeditions could be very costly, as a caravan might be forced to yield up to 20–25% of its goods in tribute in a few days' journey (Roberts 1970, p. 70, note 6).

The incentives for Mediterranean traders to be willing to face such costs and difficulties would have had to have been considerable, yet it is not entirely clear what these might have been. The most likely alternatives would be either some rare material unobtainable elsewhere because of a restricted natural distribution, or some goods which, although available elsewhere, were restricted by the limited distribution of societies with an adequate capacity for production, or accumulation, for export.

Of the first type, tin from Cornwall and Brittany is the most frequently suggested material (e.g. Villard 1960, pp. 142–61, Kimmig 1974). However, there are a number of reasons for thinking that it did not, in fact, provide an incentive for trade in the Early Iron Age. Firstly, the earliest and largest part of the Mediterranean imports in Hallstatt contexts appears to the east of the Rhône–Saône corridor, rather than towards the western tin sources. Furthermore, the evidence from England for the Late Hallstatt period suggests a minimal exploitation of Cornish metal ores, incompatible with a major export trade (Northover 1984, p. 131). There is little evidence to suggest much contact between Mont Lassois (the settlement most often linked to the supposed tin trade, see Joffroy 1960, pp. 144–6, Villard 1960, p. 141) and England or Brittany, and excavations at Mont Lassois have failed to produce any sign of tin ingots (Piggott 1977).

Moreover, it is difficult to imagine how the Greeks or Etruscans would have come to see the Rhône valley as a route to tin supplies in the first place. In Britain at least, alloying of copper with tin was carried out at or near primary production centres (Northover 1982, p. 50), and in north-west Europe as a whole the large-scale transport of tin in ingot form for the manufacture of bronze at sites removed from copper deposits does not appear to have occurred before Roman times[4] (Northover 1984, p. 132). There is certainly little reason to believe that ingot tin was ever imported into the Provençal hinterland of Massalia in the Late Bronze Age or Early Iron Age, as the area does not then appear even to have had an independent bronze industry, but to have relied primarily on the importation of finished bronze objects from a variety of sources (Lagrand 1976, p. 457, Arcelin 1976, p. 668).

Although gold (Joffroy 1954), iron (Pittioni 1966), and various animal, agricultural, and forest products (Wells 1980, pp. 67–70) have also been suggested, with the exception of tin there are few such materials which are not available in areas more readily accessible to Massalia than west-central Europe (see Ramin 1963, Benoit 1965, pp. 191–213). The much greater quantities of Mediterranean imports found in South French contexts, as well as the rapid development of specialist indigenous ceramic industries (Lagrand 1963, Arcelin-Pradelle 1984, Py 1971), would also seem to indicate that the indigenous societies of the area were organizationally competent to produce a variety of products for trade at an early date. Slaves, however, remain perhaps the best candidate for a possible item of export from west-central Europe (Finley 1959), as the type of centralized, ranked political structure posited as characteristic of Hallstatt chiefdoms (Frankenstein & Rowlands 1978) would have been particularly well adapted to the predatory exploitation of this type of trade. Unfortunately, archaeological evidence for slavery, insofar as this is possible, is not available until several centuries later (e.g. Daubigney & Guillaumet 1985), and the only textual evidence (e.g. Diodorus Siculus V, 26, 2–3, Strabo IV, 5, 2) also dates from this much later period when the significantly greater Roman demand for slaves must be taken into account.[5]

The objections raised against the likelihood of direct Mediterranean trade in west-central Europe do not, however, apply to the trade relations of the indigenous inhabitants of the lower Rhône basin. This area was always poor in metal resources and, as mentioned earlier, relied predominantly on the importation of finished bronze objects from a variety of other areas in both the Late Bronze Age and the Early Iron Age. A network of exchange links over long distances to secure metal goods was thus of long standing in the area, although it was probably on the periphery of the main currents of metal exchange which traversed western and central Europe.

With the beginnings of Etruscan trading interests in southern France in the 7th century BC, and especially after the founding of the Greek settlement of Massalia at the beginning of the 6th century BC, there must have occurred a stimulation of the indigenous economy which involved both the surplus production of a variety of products for trade (Benoit 1965 191–213, Py 1971, pp. 129–48) and the fairly rapid development of specialized ceramic industries using adopted Mediterranean techniques but serving indigenous demand (Arcelin-Pradelle 1984, Lagrand 1963, Py 1971). By the second quarter of the 6th century BC at the latest, wheel-made grey monochrome pottery (*céramique grise*, also known as *céramique phocéenne*) was being produced well in the interior of the lower Rhône Basin (Arcelin-Pradelle 1984), and this was soon complemented by indigenous production of a wheel-made ware with painted decoration (known as *pseudo-ionienne*: see Lagrand 1963), clearly indicating that the mechanisms were already in place at an early date for the fairly large-scale production and distribution of specialist native products.

It is curious that only rarely has the idea of an important rôle for indigenous peoples in the diffusion of Greek products to the deep interior been taken seriously (Morel 1975, p. 880, 1983a, p. 567) because, as Massaliot trade expanded in the lower Rhône area, some of these peoples would have found themselves in an excellent position to exploit both old and new trading contacts. This could have been either by using established trade relationships to act as middlemen in pushing Greek trading interests (e.g. for slaves) further up the Rhône valley, or by simply using Mediterranean imports obtained in exchange for local products to improve their own position in the traditional exchange networks for metal (and perhaps other goods). In the latter case, one need not take any account of Mediterranean interests in explaining the distribution of Mediterranean imports in Hallstatt Europe. For example, while Pittioni's (1966) suggestion that the wealth of Mont Lassois may be related to the exploitation for trade of Lorraine iron ore is not very convincing if the ultimate destination is assumed to be Massalia, it is considerably more plausible if one accepts that the iron may have been sought by the inhabitants of the lower Rhône area, who lacked both metal resources and Massalia's access to sea-borne trade. In this case, as well, the apparent breakdown of the Rhône corridor trade to Hallstatt Europe in the early 5th century BC need not be related to disruptive movements in the latter area (Villard 1960, p. 139), nor to political conflict among the Mediterranean powers (Frankenstein & Rowlands 1978, p. 108). Rather, it may simply have been the result of the indigenous economy of southeastern France being drawn more completely towards Massalia for its exchange needs, and consequently abandoning some traditional northern channels (which is not to deny that this may have had serious consequences for Hallstatt Europe).

It is noteworthy that sherds of both *céramique grise* and *pseudo-ionienne* pottery have been found at several settlements north of the Rhône valley in association with Mediterranean imports, and that some of the fragments of the former found at Châtillon-sur-Glâne in Switzerland and at Bragny-sur-Saône in Burgundy have been identified as belonging to production groups originating in indigenous territory in the lower Rhône Basin (Schwab 1982, Feugère & Guillot 1986). The recurrent association of this pottery (which is most unlikely to have been transported north by Greek merchants) with Mediterranean imports in Hallstatt Europe, although suggestive, does not prove that the two arrived by the same means. Meagre as this evidence is, however, it is no weaker than the evidence often advanced to suggest a direct Mediterranean presence in the north (e.g. Wells 1977, p. 192). For example, Rolley (1982) has convincingly refuted the necessity to believe that the Vix *krater* was reassembled in Burgundy by Greek craftsmen.[6] Likewise, the curious spacing of the bastions of the unusual Greek-type mud-brick wall at the Heuneburg settlement in Baden-Württemberg (Kimmig 1968, pp. 51, 55–6) belies an understanding of their function by the builders and therefore argues against direct Greek involvement in the project. Finally, we know too little about native traditions of sculpture in wood or other perishable materials to assume that the stone statue from a tumulus near Hirschlanden in Baden-Württemberg must be modelled on the Greek *kouros* or other Mediterranean prototype.[7]

The Early Iron Age archaeological evidence in the lower Rhône Basin offers little indication of a tendency towards increasing political centralization or marked ranking of a type that might be interpreted as the development of 'secondary centres'. But this contrast with Hallstatt Europe should in no way inhibit the conceptualization of a significant degree of economic stimulation or a major rôle in regional trade. The African ethnohistorical literature offers many examples of peoples who developed dynamic trading complexes under the catalyst of external contact with little or no tendency towards increasing political centralization, of which the Kamba (Lamphear 1970, Cummings 1976) and Nyamwezi (Roberts 1970) are notable examples.

The differing nature and pattern of Mediterranean imports found in Hallstatt Europe and the lower Rhône area may, in this sense, be seen to reflect the different mechanisms articulating the regional economies of the two areas. The ostentatious concentration of spectacular luxury items in a few Hallstatt tombs clustered around settlements with presumed central economic and political functions corresponds well with the type of economy in which external trade is controlled and manipulated by a political élite (Frankenstein & Rowlands 1978). Trade with such societies might require the furnishing of both minor exotic items (useful as diacritical symbolic markers) destined to be internally redistributed, and the prestation of particularly impressive prestige items appropriate to the status of the chiefs sought as trading partners. In the lower Rhône area, the imports are at the same time less spectacular and vastly more numerous, and they are spread over a wider variety of settlements and a few relatively unostentatious tombs. This pattern would seem to correspond to a more generalized participation in trade and a political structure without restricted access to trade opportunities. Given an atmosphere of more egalitarian competition functioning in the absence of centralized political control of trade, the very ostentatious imports necessary to form trade linkages in the Hallstatt area would be unnecessary and inappropriate to the south.

In this context, the fact that the vast majority of Mediterranean imports (both Greek and Etruscan) in the lower Rhône Basin are wine amphorae (Etruscan and Massaliot) and wine-service ceramics (Etruscan *kantharoi*, Attic cups, Ionian cups, etc.) may have a significance quite different from the often discussed 'hellenization' of the population. Morel (1981, p. 484) has suggested, on the basis of comparison with contemporary imports at Carthage and Tharros, that, at least for the Etruscan trade, this pattern probably reflects consumer demand rather than what was offered by the supplier. I would further agree with Morel (1983b, pp. 131–3) that the reasons for this prodigious barbarian thirst lay not in passive emulation of

Greek customs, and suggest that it had rather to do with the function of these items in the local political economy. Given the fact that labour is rarely a marketable commodity in traditional societies (Bohannan & Dalton 1962), drinking ceremonies and feasts can be an important means of mobilizing labour in societies lacking coercive political authority (Dietler 1988). To cite but two examples from eastern Africa, the pre-colonial iron production supplying several thousand square kilometres of Luo and Samia territory (politically acephalous societies) functioned entirely on the basis of beer feasts used by wealthy men to generate ore-gathering projects (Dietler 1986), and the vast network of Kamba trade supplying the coastal trading ports of the Kenyan coast owed much of its development to the innovative use of the traditional *mwethya* institution (a work-party feast) to organize communal action for trade expeditions (Cummings 1976, pp. 92–3). It is possible that Mediterranean wine, as a prestigious augmentation to traditional feasting institutions, may have served a similar rôle in the development of the indigenous economy of the lower Rhône Basin (see Dietler 1988).

In conclusion, it will be apparent that the preceding discussion relies largely on suggestive arguments about the relative plausibility of alternative explanations rather than on a rigorous analysis of formal models. This is in keeping with the modest intentions of this chapter, which were not to suggest that the data currently available refute the hypothesis of direct Mediterranean trade in Hallstatt Europe, but merely to indicate, in the spirit of 'devil's advocate', that an equally plausible hypothesis can be advanced to accommodate these data which does not invoke Mediterranean interests or presence in west-central Europe. Doubtless, other reasonable hypotheses are possible as well. A detailed study of the archaeological data bearing on the structural relations of *all* the regional socio-economic systems in question and the mechanisms articulating them is the only viable means of sorting out the probable from the plausible among these hypotheses, and arriving at some understanding of the complex nature of the influence of Mediterranean civilizations in the area. The simple dichotomization of intricate patterns of interaction into relations of dominant 'centres' and dependent 'peripheries' will be of little heuristic value if it obscures other important socio-economic relations and processes. In this case, as in others, the usefulness and relevance of the centre–periphery concept will depend upon the subtlety of its application and, most critically, on the attention paid to the structural articulation of the 'peripheries'.

Acknowledgements

I owe a debt of gratitude to many persons in France, England, and the U.S.A., but most particularly to Dr Pierre Dupont (Lyon), Dr Charles Lagrand (Marseilles), Prof Jean-Paul Morel (Aix-en-Provence), and Prof Ruth Tringham (Berkeley). Obviously, none of these scholars is in any way to blame for shortcomings of this chapter. Herzlichen Dank also to Ingrid Herbich for artwork, inspiration, and Übersetzung.

Notes

1 For convenience, the term 'Hallstatt Europe' is used somewhat idiosyncratically here to designate an area of west-central Europe encompassing parts of eastern France, southern Germany, and Switzerland occupied during the Early Iron Age by societies sharing certain similarities in material culture which have led them to be traditionally lumped under the designation 'West Hallstatt Culture'. Despite internal differences, the material culture of these societies as a whole is distinctively different from those societies of the lower Rhône valley and the South French littoral in general.

2 The subject will be given more systematic treatment in the PhD thesis being prepared by the author for the University of California, Berkeley.

3 For example, Bouloumié (1981) hypothesizes that Etruscan wine may have been transported further north in perishable containers rather than in the ceramic amphorae found in southern France.

4 A small tin ingot has been recovered from a tumulus of Hallstatt C date at Semoutiers (Haute-Marne) in northeastern France (Bouillerot 1913, cited in Freidin 1982, p. 20). However, this remains a very rare find (see Colls *et al.* 1975, p. 83) and it is not clear that this was intended for use in bronze metallurgy; pottery was sometimes decorated with tin inlays, although this technique was not common in this area.

5 Moreover, according to Daubigney's (1983) interpretation of the texts, they actually argue against a significant development of external trade in slaves before late in the La Tène period.

6 The well-known engraved symbols on the *krater* were probably an assembly code linking the work of different sections of a workshop. The code is far too complex to be a viable key for reassembly by Greek merchants. Furthermore, the small cast-bronze figures, which are the main object of the code, are the least likely elements to be disassembled for transport (Rolley 1982).

7 In fact, the Heuneburg wall exemplifies a pattern noted by Morel (1983b, p. 127) for many fortifications on inland Italian sites. These are of general Greek appearance, but with mistakes or odd variations in their layout which demonstrate that they are of native rather than Greek construction.

8 Compare, for example, the very similar treatment rendered in the roughly contemporary fragment of a wooden statue recently found in the Saône river at Seurre (Bonnamour 1985, p. 28, Fig. 1). My thanks to Louis Bonnamour for showing me this object before it was published.

References

Appadurai, A. 1986. Introduction: commodities and the politics of value. In *The social life of things: commodities in cultural perspective*, A. Appadurai (ed.), 3–63. Cambridge: Cambridge University Press.

Arcelin, P. 1976. Les civilisations de l'Age du Fer en Provence. In *La Préhistoire française*, J. Guilaine (ed.), Vol. 2, 657–75. Paris: C.N.R.S.

Arcelin-Pradelle, C. 1984. *La céramique grise monochrome en Provence*. Supplément 10 of the Revue Archéologique de Narbonnaise. Paris: Boccard.

Austen, R. A. 1978. African commerce without Europeans: the development impact of international trade in the pre-modern era. *Kenya Historical Review* **6**, 1–21.

Barruol, G. 1975. *Les peuples préromains du sud-est de la Gaule.* Supplément 1 of the Revue Archéologique de Narbonnaise. Paris: Boccard.
Bellon, C., J. Burnouf & J.-M. Martin 1986. Premiers résultats des fouilles sur le site protohistorique de Gorge-de-Loup (Vaise, Lyon, Rhône). *Revue Archéologique de l'Est et du Centre-Est* **37**, 247–51.
Benoit, F. 1958. Observations sur les routes du commerce gréco-étrusque. In *Actes du Colloque sur les Influences Helléniques en Gaule, Dijon 1957*, 15–21. Dijon: Université de Dijon.
Benoit, F. 1965. *Recherches sur l'hellénisation du Midi de la Gaule.* Aix-en-Provence: Annales de la Faculté des Lettres, 43.
Biel, J. 1982. Ein Fürstengrabhügel der späten Hallstattzeit bei Eberdingen-Hochdorf, Kr. Ludwigsburg (Baden-Württemberg). Vorbericht. *Germania* **60**, 61–84.
Boardman, J. 1980. *The Greeks overseas*, revised edn. London: Thames & Hudson.
Bohannan, P. & G. Dalton 1962. Introduction. In *Markets in Africa*, P. Bohannan & G. Dalton (eds), 1–26. Evanston, Ill.: Northwestern University Press.
Bonnamour, L. 1985. Les sites de la Saône aux Ages du Fer: problématique. In *Les Ages du Fer dans la vallée de la Saône (VIIe–Ier siècles avant notre ère)*, L. Bonnamour, A. Duval & J.-P. Guillaumet (eds), 25–31. Supplément 6 of the Revue Archéologique de l'Est et du Centre-Est. Paris: C.N.R.S.
Boucher, S. 1976. *Recherches sur les bronzes figurés de Gaule préromaine et romaine.* Paris: Boccard.
Bouillerot, P. 1913. Sépultures de Semoutiers (Haute-Marne) (Epoques de Hallstatt et de La Tène I). In *La Collection Millon: Antiquités préhistoriques et gallo-romaines*, J. Déchelette (ed.), 87–100. Paris: Geuthner.
Bouloumié, B. 1981. Le vin étrusque et la première hellénisation du Midi de la Gaule. *Revue Archéologique de l'Est et du Centre-Est* **32**, 75–81.
Bouloumié, B. & C. Lagrand 1977. Les bassins à rebord perlé et autres bassins de Provence. *Revue Archéologique de Narbonnaise* **10**, 1–31.
Brun, P. 1987. *Princes et princesses de la Celtique: le premier âge du fer (850–450 av. J.-C.).* Paris: Editions Errance.
Champion, S. T. 1976. Coral in Europe: commerce and Celtic ornament. In *Celtic art in ancient Europe: five protohistoric centuries*, P.-M. Duval & C. F. C. Hawkes (eds), 29–40. London: Seminar Press.
Champion, T. 1982. Fortification, ranking and subsistence. In *Ranking, resource and exchange*, C. Renfrew & S. Shennan (eds), 61–6. Cambridge: Cambridge University Press.
Chapotat, G. 1981. La voie protohistorique sud de la Croisée de Vienne, essai de reconstitution de son tracé jusqu'à Marseille. *Revue Archéologique de l'Est et du Centre-Est* **32**, 83–91.
Clavel-Lévêque, M. 1977. *Marseille grecque: la dynamique d'un impérialisme marchand.* Marseille: Jeanne Laffitte.
Collis, J. 1984. *The European Iron Age.* London: Batsford.
Colls, D., C. Domergue, F. Laubenheimer & B. Liou 1975. Les lingots d'étain de l'épave Port-Vendres II. *Gallia* **33**, 82–6.
Cummings, R. J. 1976. The early development of Akamba local trade history, *c.* 1780–1820. *Kenya Historical Review* **4**, 85–110.
Daubigney, A. 1983. Relations marchandes méditerranéennes et procès des rapports de dépendance (*magu-* et ambactes) en Gaule protohistorique. In *Modes de contacts et processus de transformation dans les sociétés anciennes*, 659–83. Actes du colloque de Cortone (24–30 mai 1981). Collection de l'Ecole Française de Rome, 67, Rome.

Daubigney, A. & J.-P. Guillaumet 1985. L'entrave de Glanon (Côte-d'Or): les Eduens et l'esclavage. In *Les Ages du Fer dans la vallée de la Saône (VIIe–Ier siècles avant notre ère)*, L. Bonnamour, A. Duval & J.-P. Guillaumet (eds), 171–7. Supplément 6 of the Revue Archéologique de l'Est et du Centre-Est. Paris: C.N.R.S.

Dietler, M. D. 1986. Women, wealth, and the origin of markets in Alego: an ethnohistorical study in western Kenya. Paper presented at Conference in Honor of J. Desmond Clark, Berkeley, April 1986.

Dietler, M. D. 1988. Driven by drink: the social uses of imported wine and implications for economic and political change in French Iron Age societies. Paper presented at the 53rd Annual Meeting of the Society for American Archaeology, Phoenix, Arizona, April 1988.

Feugère, M. & A. Guillot 1986. Les fouilles de Bragny, 1: les petits objets dans leur contexte du Hallstatt final. *Revue Archéologique de l'Est et du Centre-Est* **37**, 159–221.

Finley, M. I. 1959. Was Greek civilization based on slave labour? *Historia* **8**, 145–64.

Fischer, F. 1973. ΚΕΙΜΗΛΙΑ: Bemerkungen zur kulturgeschichtlichen Interpretation des sogenannten Südimports in der späten Hallstatt- und frühen Latènekultur des westlichen Mitteleuropa. *Germania* **51**, 436–59.

Fitzpatrick, A. 1985. The distribution of Dressel 1 amphorae in north-west Europe. *Oxford Journal of Archaeology* **4**, 305–40.

Frankenstein, S. & M. J. Rowlands 1978. The internal structure and regional context of Early Iron Age society in southwestern Germany. *Bulletin of the Institute of Archaeology, London* **15**, 73–112.

Freidin, N. 1982. *The Early Iron Age in the Paris Basin, Hallstatt C and D*. British Archaeological Reports International Series, 131, Oxford.

Gray, R. & D. Birmingham 1970. Some economic and political consequences of trade in Central and Eastern Africa in the pre-colonial period. In *Pre-colonial African trade*, R. Gray & D. Birmingham (eds), 1–23. London: Oxford University Press.

Härke, H. 1979. *Settlement types and patterns in the West Hallstatt Province*. British Archaeological Reports International Series, 57, Oxford.

Hatt, J.-J. 1958. Les Celtes et la Mediterranée. *Rhodania* 1958, 15–22.

Joffroy, R. 1954. *Le trésor de Vix (Côte-d'Or)*. Paris: Presses Universitaires de France.

Joffroy, R. 1960. *L'oppidum de Vix et la civilisation hallstattienne finale dans l'Est de la France*. Paris: Les Belles Lettres.

Joffroy, R. 1980. Die Handelswege in Gallien in der frühen Eisenzeit im lichte der letzten Entdeckungen. In *Die Hallstattkultur, Symposium Steyr 1980* 417–19. Linz: Oberöstereichische Landesverlag.

Jully, J.-J. 1982. *Céramiques grecques ou de type grec et autres céramiques en Languedoc mediterranéen, Rousillon et Catalogne, VIIe–IVe s. avant notre ère et leur contexte socio-culturel*. Annales Littéraires de l'Université de Besançon, 275. Paris: Les Belles Lettres.

Kimmig, W. 1968. *Die Heuneburg an der oberen Donau*. Stuttgart: Konrad Theiss.

Kimmig, W. 1974. Zum Fragment eines Este-Gefässes von der Heuneburg an der oberen Donau. *Hamburger Beiträge zur Archäologie* **4**, 33–96.

Kimmig, W. 1983. Die griechische Kolonisation im westlichen Mittelmeergebeit und ihre Wirkung auf die Landschaften des westlichen Mitteleuropa. *Jahrbuch des Römisch-Germanischen Zentralmuseums Mainz* **30**, 5–78.

Kimmig, W. & E. Gersbach 1971. Die Grabungen auf der Heuneburg 1966–1969. *Germania* **49**, 21–91.

Lagrand, C. 1963. La céramique 'pseudo-ionienne' dans la vallée du Rhône. *Cahiers Rhodaniens* **10**, 37–82.

Lagrand, C. 1976. Les civilisations de l'Age du Bronze en Provence. In *La préhistoire française*, J. Guilaine (ed.), Vol. 2, 452–8. Paris: C.N.R.S.

Lagrand, C. 1979. La repartition du bucchero nero dans la vallée du Rhône et en Provence-Côte-d'Azur. In *Actes de la Table-Ronde sur le bucchero nero étrusque et sa diffusion en Gaule méridionale, Aix-en-Provence, 21–23 mai 1975*, 124–34. Brussels: Latomus.

Lamphear, J. 1970. The Kamba and the northern Mrima coast. In *Pre-colonial African trade*, R. Gray & D. Birmingham (eds), 75–101. London: Oxford University Press.

Morel, J.-P. 1975. L'expansion phocéenne en Occident: dix ans de recherches (1966–1975). *Bulletin de Correspondance Hellénique* **99**, 853–96.

Morel, J.-P. 1981. Le commerce étrusque en France, en Espagne et en Afrique. In *L'Etruria Mineraria: Atti del XII Convegno di Studi Etruschi e Italici, Firenze 1979*, 463–508. Florence: Olschki.

Morel, J.-P. 1983a. Les relations économiques dans l'Occident grec. In *Modes de contacts et processus de transformation dans les sociétés anciennes*, 549–76. Actes du colloque de Cortone (24–30 mai 1981). Collection de l'Ecole Française de Rome, 67, Rome.

Morel, J.-P. 1983b. Greek colonization in Italy and in the West: problems of evidence and interpretation. In *Crossroads of the Mediterranean*, T. Hackens, N. D. Holloway & R. R. Holloway (eds), 123–61. Louvain-la-Neuve: Publications d'Histoire de l'Art et d'Archéologie de l'Université Catholique de Louvain 38.

Northover, P. 1982. The exploration of long-distance movement of bronze in Bronze and Early Iron Age Europe. *Bulletin of the Institute of Archaeology, London University* **19**, 45–72.

Northover, P. 1984. Iron Age bronze metallurgy in central southern England. In *Aspects of the Iron Age in central southern England*, B. Cunliffe & D. Miles (eds), 126–45. Oxford: Oxford University Committee for Archaeology.

Pauli, L. 1971. *Die Golasecca-Kultur und Mitteleuropa: ein Beitrag zur Geschichte des Handels über die Alpen*. Hamburger Beiträge zur Archäologie 1(1). Hamburg: Helmut Buske.

Piggott, S. 1977. A glance at Cornish tin. In *Ancient Europe and the Mediterranean*, V. Markotic (ed.), 141–5. Warminster: Aris & Phillips.

Pittioni, R. 1966. Grächwil und Vix handelsgeschichtlich gesehen. In *Helvetia Antiqua: Festschrift Emil Vogt*, 123–8. Zurich: Conzett & Huber.

Py, M. 1971. La céramique grecque de Vaunage (Gard) et sa signification. *Cahiers Ligures de Préhistoire et d'Archéologie* **30**, 5–154.

Py, M. 1982. Civilisation indigène et urbanisation durant la protohistoire en Languedoc-Roussillon. *KTEMA: Civilisations de l'Orient, de la Grèce et de Rome Antiques* **7**, 101–19.

Ramin, J. 1974. L'espace économique en Gaule: les documents historiques concernant les mines. In *Mélanges offerts à Roger Dion*, R. Chevallier (ed.), 417–37. Paris: Picard.

Roberts, A. 1970. Nyamwezi trade. In *Pre-colonial African trade*, R. Gray & D. Birmingham (eds), 39–74. London: Oxford University Press.

Rolley, C. 1982. *Les vases de bronze de l'archaïsme recent en Grande Grèce*. Naples: Centre Jean Bérard.

Saint-Denis, E. de 1981. Le Rhône vu par les Grecs et les Latins de l'Antiquité: sujet d'actualité. *Latomus* **40**(3), 545–70.

Schwab, H. 1982. Pseudophokäische und Phokäische Keramik in Châtillon-sur-Glâne. *Archäologisches Korrespondenzblatt* **12**, 363–72.

Spindler, K. 1983. *Die frühen Kelten*. Stuttgart: Reclam.

Tchernia, A. 1983. Italian wine in Gaul at the end of the Republic. In *Trade in the ancient economy*, P. Garnsey, K. Hopkins & C. R. Whittaker (eds), 87–104. London: Chatto & Windus.

Villard, F. 1960. *La céramique grecque de Marseille (VI–IV s.). Essai d'histoire économique*. Bibliothèque des Ecoles françaises d'Athènes et de Rome, 195. Paris: Boccard.

Wells, P. 1977. Late Hallstatt interactions with the Mediterranean: one suggestion. In *Ancient Europe and the Mediterranean*, V. Markotic (ed.), 189–96. Warminster: Aris & Phillips.

Wells, P. 1980. *Culture contact and culture change: Early Iron Age Central Europe and the Mediterranean*. Cambridge: Cambridge University Press.

Wells, P. S. 1984. *Farms, villages and cities: commerce and urban origins in late prehistoric Europe*. Ithaca, NY: Cornell University Press.

Zürn, H. 1970. *Hallstattforschungen in Nordwürttemberg*. Stuttgart: Staatliches Amt für Denkmalpflege.

7 *The impact of the Roman amphora trade on pre-Roman Britain*

DAVID F. WILLIAMS

Introduction

The vast majority of traded commodities in the ancient world, many of which were undoubtedly perishables, rarely leave traces behind for the archaeologist or historian interested in the trade routes and commerce of antiquity. However, certain prized traded goods such as wine, olive-oil and fish products were often transported long distances in large pottery container jars – amphorae – which were tightly sealed and sturdily built to stand up to the buffeting of the long sea and land journey. These types of vessel were used over a long period of time in the Mediterranean and outlying areas and broken sherds of amphorae are commonly found on a variety of sites during the Greco-Roman and Byzantine eras. A detailed study of such amphorae can frequently provide valuable evidence of economic activity not easily available from most other classes of pottery. These large two-handled jars were specifically intended as containers for the bulk carrying of certain goods. Unlike the majority of other pottery types it was the contents that were prized rather than the vessel itself. An appreciation of the goods carried in amphorae and their origin can often furnish us with information on the ancient economy, the trade routes employed at particular times, and the relative importance of the centres of exportation and importation. In addition, it may throw some light on the lifestyle of the people who chose to import the best Italian wine or acquired a taste for high quality Spanish fish sauces.

Despite the fact that amphorae were produced in large quantities and were quite likely to be broken up and discarded on receipt of their contents, as the large sherd mound of Monte Testaccio just outside ancient Rome testifies, there is nevertheless a high degree of standardization within each category of form. The numerous producing centres situated around the Roman world appear to have had their own particular amphorae shapes, perhaps for easy recognition of the contents present, although similar forms were often made in different areas. This can make attribution to source areas difficult. However, through an appreciation of the many different fabrics involved, largely due to recent petrological work and to some extent chemical analyses, it is possible confidently to allocate many amphora types to the exporting centres involved in this trade (Peacock & Williams 1986). Moreover, perhaps of equal importance is the fact that formless bodysherds can now often be attributed to particular types where distinctive fabrics are involved.

These last two points are especially relevant for Late Iron Age studies in southern Britain. In recent years a detailed examination of the forms and fabrics of Roman amphorae found in pre-Roman Britain has considerably advanced our understanding of the trade contacts, chronology, and to some extent the political events of the British La Tène III period of the 1st century BC and the early 1st century AD (Peacock 1971, 1984, Williams 1981, 1986). Over the past few years an attempt has been made by the writer to collect quantitative data on amphorae from archaeological excavations so that general trends and patterns can be recognized. In some cases this has involved the counting and weighing of every amphora sherd from particular sites. Amphorae are never very plentiful in Britain, unlike the Mediterranean homeland where they tend to be commonplace, and much research effort has been directed towards the identification of the forms to which undiagnostic bodysherds belong. This chapter reviews the amphora imports to Iron Age Britain and the implications of this trade, at a time when the country lay outside of the direct political control of the Roman Empire.

Roman amphorae in Late Iron Age Britain

The Dressel 1 amphora form (1A and 1B varieties) is the most important amphora type found in Late Iron Age Britain (Fig. 7.1(1 & 2)). It was widely distributed in western Europe and was undoubtedly one of the more important amphora forms of the Roman world (Tchernia 1983, Fitzpatrick 1985, Peacock & Williams 1986). *Tituli picti* suggest that the normal contents carried were wine (Zevi 1966, Beltrán 1970), although on occasion other commodities have been found in vessels from shipwrecks, including *spondylus* shells, resin and hazelnuts (see Sealey 1985). The Dressel 1A variety with a characteristic short triangular rim was made primarily in the Campanian, Latin and Etrurian districts of Italy (Peacock 1971, 1977). Production of Dressel 1A has also been claimed in southern France (Sabir *et al.* 1983), though if this is substantiated it can only have been on a very small scale compared to the Italian industry. Dressel 1A was produced in Italy from about 130 BC (Tchernia 1983) until around the middle of the 1st century BC (Lamboglia 1955, Peacock 1971). There are similarities of rim profiles with the earlier Greco-Italic types (cf. Peacock & Williams 1986), but, as Peacock (1984) suggests, it is unlikely that the latter types were ever exported to northern Europe in any quantity. It is probably best therefore to regard these triangular-shaped rim sherds from British Iron Age sites as belonging to the Dressel 1A form rather than the Greco-Italic.

Two Dressel 1A amphorae have recently been found north of the Thames

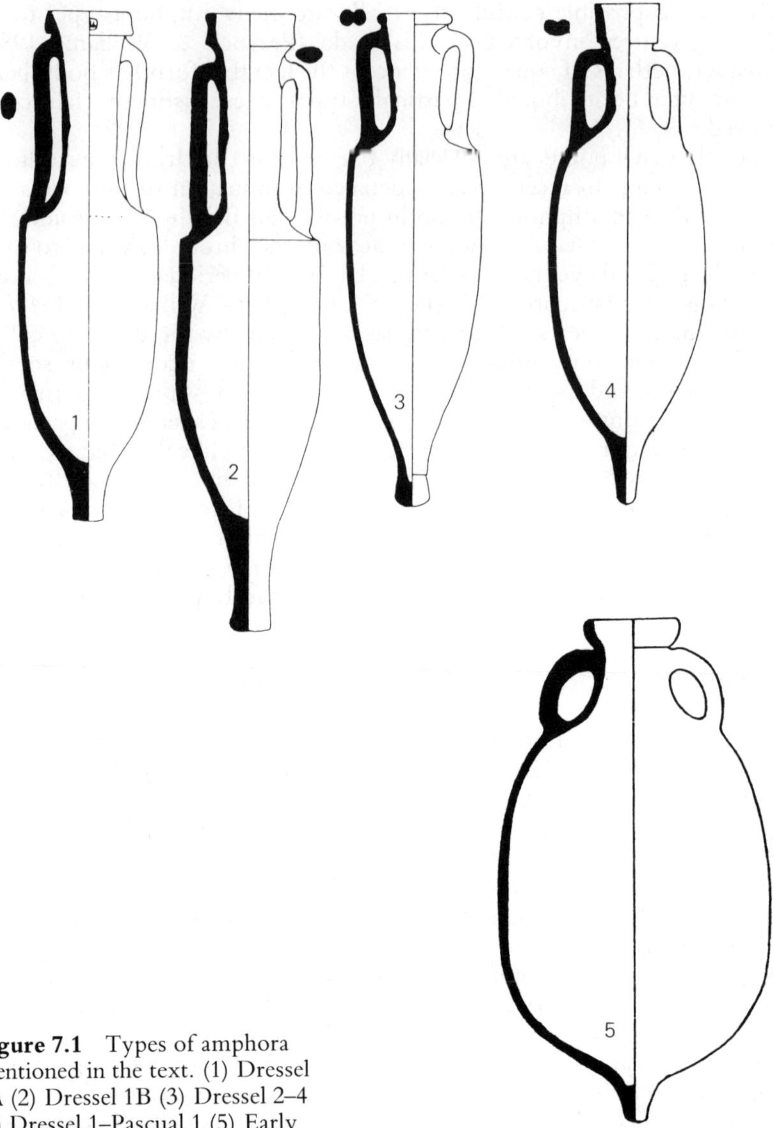

Figure 7.1 Types of amphora mentioned in the text. (1) Dressel 1A (2) Dressel 1B (3) Dressel 2–4 (4) Dressel 1–Pascual 1 (5) Early Dressel 20 (Oberaden 83).

at Gatesbury Track and Baldock, although the distribution of the finds is predominantly south of the Thames with the largest number, probably some thirty-odd vessels, coming from the coastal site of Hengistbury Head in Dorset. This relatively large group of amphorae from Hengistbury Head, a possible trading station, could represent either a trickle of imports over some eighty-odd years, or a more concentrated trade within a much shorter period. At present it is difficult to say which is more likely to have been the case.

The slightly larger Dressel 1B amphora with a thick, near vertical collar-rim also carried wine and was made in the same parts of Italy as the earlier Dressel 1A type. Both types share a common range of fabrics, making it difficult to assign bodysherds to one or the other form. Dressel 1B appears to have been made from about shortly after the first quarter of the 1st century BC till the last decade of the century (Peacock 1971, 1977, Sealey 1985). The last consular dates mentioned on this form are those of 13 BC (Zevi 1966). Significantly, no Dressel 1 forms were found amongst the 360 amphorae buried in a ditch at La Longarina, Ostia, dated to *c.* AD 5 (Hesnard 1980). It is probable then that no new wine was racked into Dressel 1B types later than about 10 BC (see Sealey 1985 for a fuller discussion of the terminal date for Dressel 1B). There are some finds of Dressel 1B south of the Thames, but the majority are concentrated in the south-east of the country, more especially the Hertfordshire–Essex region, and should be mainly after Caesar's invasion in date.

It is tempting to see these Dressel 1B wine containers as representing the tangible benefits of an alliance between Caesar and local British tribes of this region (Peacock 1971); the comparative lack of finds of Dressel 1B in southern Britain could then be regarded as the result of the support given by the local southern tribes to the Veneti across the Channel in their abortive uprising against the Romans in 56 BC. The trade in amphorae which had previously been directed to southern Britain was now redirected to East Anglia. However, it may be too simplistic to assume that this neat correlation results from the ending of the trade in amphorae with southern Britain (Peacock 1984). Furthermore, it is not clear whether we are to visualize this trade as being carried on directly by Roman merchants from the Mediterranean via the Atlantic coast or the Rhône–Rhine waterway, or through the Gaulish tribes across the Channel, where finds of Dressel 1 have greatly increased in recent years (Tchernia 1983, Galliou 1984). What is clear, however, is that at this time Britain was very much on the periphery of the Italian wine trade to north-west Europe. The numbers of Dressel 1 amphorae recorded from Britain (Peacock 1971) are few indeed when compared to the hundreds and sometimes thousands of such vessels that occur on some Gaulish sites (Tchernia 1983).

The earliest appearance of new amphora forms in eastern Britain is probably at the Lexden tumulus near Colchester, dated shortly after 15 BC, where 11, possibly 13, Dressel 2–4 vessels (Fig. 7.1(3)) were found buried with some six Dressel 1B (Williams 1986). A Rhodian-style handle was also reported (Peacock 1971), but this now seems less likely and this form is more characteristic of post-Conquest contexts (Williams 1986).

The Dressel 2–4 form with a simple rounded rim and long bifid handles formed from two rods is the direct successor on Italian kiln sites to Dressel 1B and occurs in a similar range of fabrics, dating from the latter part of the

1st century BC to the mid-second century AD (Zevi 1966). It is now clear that production in Italy may have started earlier than originally thought, perhaps in the 30s or 50s BC (see Sealey 1985). However, this form was produced outside Italy in considerable quantity, mostly but by no means exclusively in the western Mediterranean region. The more important western non-Italian production areas include Catalonia and Baetica in Spain (Tchernia & Zevi 1972, Beltrán 1977, Pascual 1977) and southern and central France (Zevi 1966, Tchernia & Villa 1977, A. Ferdière pers. comm.). As with Dressel 1, *tituli picti* suggest that the main content carried was wine, although on occasion other commodities such as dates, fish sauce and even olive-oil could be transported in these vessels (Zevi 1966, Sealey 1985, Peacock & Williams 1986).

At Lexden in eastern England there is nothing in the fabrics of the Dressel 2–4 vessels to suggest a non-Italian origin, which is also true of the earlier Dressel 1 amphorae which arrived in Britain (Williams 1986). However, the situation regarding amphora supplies to the south of Britain appears to be somewhat different, with regard to both forms and origin. At Hengistbury Head recent excavations by Cunliffe (1987) have turned up very little in the way of Dressel 2–4. Instead, during the latter years of the 1st century BC and the early years of the 1st century AD wine reaching the site seems to have arrived not from Italy but in the Catalan amphora form Dressel 1–Pascual 1 from Spain (Fig. 7.1(4)). Exactly the same situation can be seen at the nearby coastal site of Cleaval Point, where only three Dressel 2–4 sherds were recovered against nearly 270 sherds of Dressel 1–Pascual 1 (Williams 1986). The latter amphora type is characteristic of the Catalonian region of Spain, particularly the Barcelona area, and probably carried wine as its principal content (Pascual 1962, 1977). It was made from the late Republican period until at least AD 79, when examples are found at Pompeii (Tchernia 1971). The majority of dateable finds from northwestern Europe, however, are generally Augustan in date (Deniaux 1980, Williams 1981, Galliou 1984). At Cleaval Point Dressel 1–Pascual 1 amphorae were associated with Tiberian imitation Gallo-Belgic forms, together with pottery from the Aquitaine region of western France which could be early Augustan in date (pers. comm. J. Timby). It is possible that supplies of this amphora came from northern Spain via the Narbonensis–Garonne waterway route and then around the coast of Brittany. The use of this route would also more easily explain the presence at Cleaval Point of early Augustan pottery from Aquitaine.

The most common amphora type imported into Roman Britain is Dressel 20 (Fig. 7.1(5)) and sherds of this amphora are a common feature on many sites from the Conquest to at least the latter part of the 3rd century AD, when their numbers show a decline from a peak in the second half of the 2nd century AD (Williams & Peacock 1983). However, recent research has made it clear that this form was already present in some numbers during the Late Iron Age as well (Williams & Peacock 1983). Dressel 20 amphorae were made along the banks of the River Guadalquivir and its tributaries between

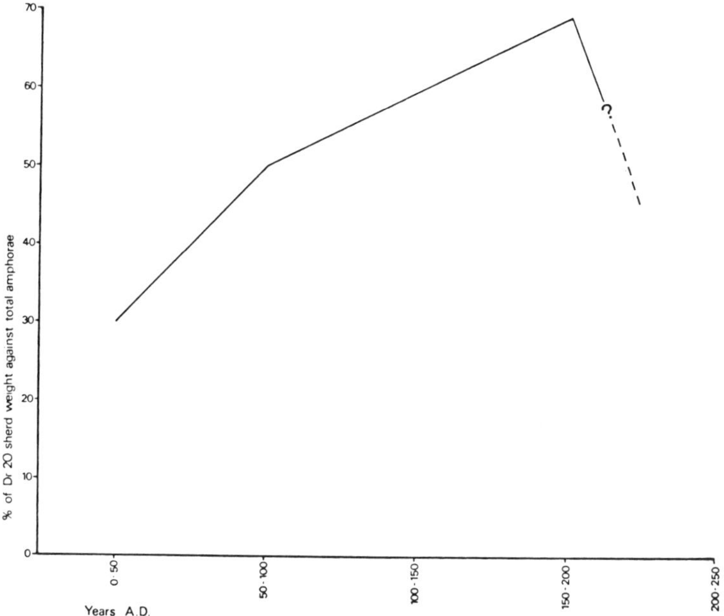

Figure 7.2 Graph showing percentage of finds of Dressel 20 against other amphora types, from 33 British sites.

Seville and Cordoba in the southern Spanish province of Baetica, where they were used for the transportation of olive-oil (Bonsor 1931, Ponsich 1974, 1979). This type of amphora has a wide date-range, from the Augustan prototype (Oberaden 83) with a fairly upright rim, a short spike, and less of a squat bulbous body than the later form, to the well-known globular shape which, with some typological variation, was in use up to the late 3rd century AD. Rim-forms of the earlier Oberaden 83 type are known from pre-Roman levels at Prae Wood and at Gatesbury Track, so that importation of Baetican olive-oil into Britain may well have begun from as early as the last decade of the 1st century BC (Williams & Peacock 1983).

Figure 7.2 presents in a graphical form the percentage of finds of Dressel 20 against other amphora types from some 33 British sites (for full details of the sites involved see Williams & Peacock 1983). The graph is subjective to some extent because of the problem of rubbish survival, but nevertheless has been put together from detailed information. It shows a fairly rapid increase in olive-oil imports during the 1st century AD, followed by a slight levelling off up to the later 2nd century, after which there is a rapid decline. It is significant that this graph shows an almost identical trend to Pascual's (1980, Fig. 4) quantitative examination of the proportion of Dressel 20 amphorae present on Mediterranean shipwrecks. This suggests that the supply mechanisms for amphorae to Britain before the conquest were similar to those of the Mediterranean world, despite the different routes taken. However, the really significant point that emerges from all this is that the Roman conquest of Britain is *not* shown in the graph. This would imply that the Late Iron Age British tribes were supplied with Spanish olive-oil (for cooking and lighting) as though they were *already* part of the Roman Empire. In other words there is no indication at this time that the tribal communities of southern Britain were receiving different cargoes of Baetican olive-oil than other parts of the Roman world, although Britain remained independent until she became a province of the Empire with the first stage of conquest in AD 43.

Conclusion

The southern tribes of Late Iron Age Britain may have started to receive supplies of Italian wine in amphorae as early as the second half of the 2nd century BC. This might have started off in a very small way with a trickle of infrequent supplies, for this trade or exchange appears to have been slight compared with the numbers of similar wine amphorae found in Gaul at this time. At the beginning of this trade there seems to have been a broad chronological division between the south of the country where Dressel 1A are more commonly found and the eastern counties north of the Thames where finds of Dressel 1B are more normal. This regional trade division is also reflected later around the turn of the 1st century BC at Hengistbury Head and Cleaval Point on the south coast where Dressel 1–Pascual 1 from Catalonia is found in some numbers while Italian Dressel 2–4, fairly common at this time north of the Thames, is comparatively rare. However, shortly after this date the normal container for Baetican olive-oil, Dressel 20, probably started arriving, together with some Spanish Dressel 7–11 fish sauce amphorae, and as far as one can tell was fairly evenly distributed both north and south of the Thames. The quantitative figures for Dressel 20 on a variety of sites clearly show that before the Roman conquest supplies of Spanish olive-oil were arriving in Britain as though the country (or at least the southern part of it) was already part of the Empire.

Acknowledgements

Many of the amphora identifications were undertaken as part of the English Heritage Ceramic Petrology Programme. I should like to thank the following for kindly providing information and material for study: Barry Cunliffe, Jennifer Foster, David Peacock, Peter Woodward and the Colchester & Essex Museum.

References

Beltrán Lloris, M. 1970. *Las anforas Romanas en España*. Zaragoza: Fernando el Católico.

Beltrán Lloris, M. 1977. Problemas de la morfología y del concepto historico–geografico qui recubre la noción tipo. *Collection de l'École Française de Rome* **32**, 97–132.

Bonsor, G. E. 1931. *The archaeological expedition along the Guadalquivir, 1889–1901*. New York: Hispanic Society of America.

Cunliffe, B. W. 1987. *Hengistbury Head, Dorset*. Oxford: Oxford University Committee for Archaeology.

Deniaux, E. 1980. *Recherches sur les amphores de Basse-Normandie*. Caen: Cahier des Annales de Normandie.

Fitzpatrick, A. 1985. The distribution of Dressel 1 amphorae in north-west Europe. *Oxford Journal of Archaeology* **4**, 305–40.

Galliou, P. 1984. Days of wine and roses? Early Armorica and the Atlantic wine trade. In *Cross-Channel trade between Gaul and Britain in the pre-Roman Iron Age*, S. Macready & F. H. Thompson (eds), 24–36. Society of Antiquaries Occasional Paper 4, London.

Hesnard, A. 1980. Un dépôt augustéen d'amphores à La Longarina, Ostie. In *The seaborne commerce of ancient Rome*, J. H. D'Arms & E. C. Kopff (eds), 141–56. Memoirs of the American Academy in Rome 36.

Lamboglia, N. 1955. Sulla cronologia delle anfore romane de età republicana. *Rivista Studi Liguri* **21**, 252–60.

Pascual Guasch, R. 1962. Centros de producción y diffusion geographica de un tipo anfore. *VIIe Congresso Nacional de Arqueologia*, 334–45. Zaragoza: Universidad de Zaragoza.

Pascual Guasch, R. 1977. Las anforas de la Layetania. *Collection de L'Ecole Française de Rome* **32**, 47–96.

Pascual Guasch, R. 1980. La evolución de las exportaciones betica durante el Imperio. In *Producción y comercio del aceite en la antiguedad*, J. M. Blazquez (ed.), 233–42. Madrid: Universidad Complutense de Madrid.

Peacock, D. P. S. 1971. Roman amphorae in pre-Roman Britain. In *The Iron Age and its hill-forts*, M. Jesson & D. Hill (eds), 169–88. Southampton: University of Southampton.

Peacock, D. P. S. 1977. Recent discoveries of Roman amphorae kilns in Italy. *Antiquaries Journal* **57**, 262–9.

Peacock, D. P. S. 1984. Amphorae in Iron Age Britain: a reassessment. In *Cross-Channel trade between Gaul and Britain in the pre-Roman Iron Age*, S. Macready & F. H. Thompson (eds), 37–42. Society of Antiquaries Occasional Paper 4, London.

Peacock, D. P. S. & D. F. Williams 1986. *Amphorae and the Roman economy*. London: Longman.

Ponsich, M. 1974. *Implantation rurale antique sur le Bas-Guadalquivir*. Madrid: Casa de Velázquez.

Ponsich, M. 1979. *Implantation rurale antique sur le Bas-Guadalquivir*. Paris: Casa de Velázquez.

Sabir, A., F. Laubenheimer, J. Leblanc & F. Widemann 1983. Production d'amphores vinaires républicaines en Gaule du sud. *Documents d'Archéologie Meridionale* **6**, 109–13.

Sealey, P. 1985. *Amphorae from the 1970 excavations at Colchester Sheepen*. British Archaeological Reports British Series 142, Oxford.

Tchernia, A. 1971. Les amphores vinaires de Tarraconaise et leur exportation au début de l'empire. *Archivo Español de Arqueologia* **44**, 38–85.

Tchernia, A. 1983. Italian wine in Gaul at the end of the Republic. In *Trade in the ancient economy*, P. Garnsey, K. Hopkins & C. R. Whittaker (eds), 87–104. London: Chatto & Windus.

Tchernia, A. & J. P. Villa 1977. Note sur le matériel recueilli dans la fouille d'un atelier d'amphores à Velaux (Bouches-du-Rhône). *Collection de L'École Française de Rome* **32**, 231–9.

Tchernia, A. & F. Zevi 1972. Amphores vinaires de Campanie et de Tarraconaise à Ostie. *Collection de L'École Française de Rome* **10**, 35–67.

Williams, D. F. 1981. The Roman amphorae trade with Late Iron Age Britain. In *Production and distribution: a ceramic viewpoint*, H. Howard & E. Morris (eds), 123–32. British Archaeological Reports International Series 120, Oxford.

Williams, D. F. 1986. Report on the amphorae. In J. Foster, *The Lexden Tumulus*, 124–32. British Archaeological Reports British Series, 156, Oxford.

Williams, D. F. 1987. The amphorae. In *Romano-British industries in Purbeck*, N. Sunter & P. Woodward (eds), 79–81. Dorset Natural History and Archaeological Society Monograph 6, Dorchester.

Williams, D. F. & D. P. S. Peacock 1983. The importation of olive-oil into Roman Britain. In *Producción y comercio de aceite en la antiguedad. II Congresso*, J. Blazquez & J. Remesal (eds), 263–80. Madrid: Universidad Complutense de Madrid.

Zevi, F. 1966. Appunti sulle anfore romane. *Archaeologia Classica* **18**, 207–47.

8 *Interactions between the nomadic cultures of central Asia and China in the Middle Ages*

SLAWOJ SZYNKIEWICZ

Notions of centre and periphery as used in archaeology and anthropology, irrespective of how they are technically understood, are often value-laden, since they tend to rank cultures according to their level of technological advancement or general development. Such is the common approach in the West, including that of a useful Soviet review of the subject (Pershits & Khazanov 1978). It is no wonder then that an even stronger relativism should be characteristic of the naturally ethnocentric approach of those particular cultures whose conceptualization of their contacts with their neighbours is based on the opposition 'we versus them'. A classic example is China with her self-centred world-view.

In the process of acquiring new territories, the realm of China has been concentrically adding new peripheries to its original centre, where the Yang-shao civilization formed the basis of the entity which later became the Chinese ethnos. Thus an inner periphery was created, consisting of groups of alien ethnic affinity or with unlike economies. With the gradual acculturation of those close peripheral circles, the inner periphery became ever more extensive, up to the limits of the ever-growing state territory. Beyond, there existed an outer periphery, segments of which changed their status to become parts of the inner periphery, with at least partial loss of independence.

In the case of peripheral peoples who were also agricultural or prepared to adopt agriculture, the change of status was facilitated by a basic difference between them and the society of the centre. Those absorbed were simply organized and less complex than the absorbing Chinese society. The latter's complexity acted as if it were an inviting vacuum; in this case the complexity consumed the simpleness. The process continued until societies of the outer periphery became absorbed, or so far developed their own adequately complex institutions as to lose interest in the advantages of participation in an organized alien polity, and instead fostered ambitions of forming polities of their own. At that point a new pattern of borders or march-lands emerged; one in which both parties claimed that the intermediate zone was part of its own inner periphery.

That was also the time when Chinese civilization and politics began to develop a distinct attitude of closedness. Partial responsibility for that lies in relations of conflict with the outer world. This attitude did not prevent territorial expansion towards the central Asian steppes, whose inhabitants in their turn considered China a periphery to their own economic and political centre. In this region the process of absorbtion was seriously hampered by the basic difference between the respective economies.

The foregoing is a most simplified piece of history, picking up just selected trends deemed to be of great consequence. The transitive character of frontiers in the northern regions, which allowed the extension of economic activities and political control in both directions, has been well established by Lattimore (1940).

The diffusionist legacy in our thinking, especially pronounced in orientalist writing, would attach the notion of a 'centre' to great societies and cultures, that is cases where a high complexity of culture correlates with a similar complexity of society. Much hesitation would, however, follow if one applied the term 'centre' to the nomadic culture of the east Asian steppes, since, notwithstanding its attainments, it was not correlated with a fixed social substrate with permanently developed social institutions. Nevertheless, any political organization emerging from that substrate would consider itself a centre and let itself be known as such to its neighbours, often including China itself. Thus we should agree that 'centre' is a relative concept asserted by a culture in consequence of its prevailing world-view and system of values. It is then a claimed value on the level of social practice.

Any objectivization of the concept is precarious, since it is not properly defined. If complexity of culture were a defining component, we would not be able to measure it. On the other hand, we can measure the intensity of cultural borrowings and the results of acculturation, but it is rather dubious whether this can be made an index of the attribute of being a 'centre'; the more so as China would show varying indices in relation to her various neighbours. Besides, there is a notable contrast between the minimal disposition of Chinese culture to assimilate alien cultures (recorded as a feature of long duration) and its great effectiveness in the adaptation of those cultures to Chinese political and economic organization (Pershits & Khazanov 1978, pp. 112–18).

A stereotyped view would reduce centre–periphery relations to a one-sided flow of cultural values and artefacts from a developed region to an underdeveloped one, and would treat partners in the process solely as emitting or receiving agencies. The great renown won by Chinese culture seems to exemplify without question such a stereotype, if China is regarded as a centre. It could then easily be accepted that China was a patron and a source of innovation for her neighbours of dissimilar cultures. It is often overlooked, however, that in the Shang and Zhou (Chou) dynasties at the turn of the 2nd millennium BC the dissimilarity was not so distinctly pronounced, and hence relations were more balanced. In later times too the situation was not clear in this respect.

With the growing advancement of agricultural and pastoral economies, the respective societies became more differentiated. This included a difference in complexity of social organization. Chinese society consisted of various groups composing a vertical stratification and a horizontal network, mutually interdependent and controlled with varying intensity by combined means of political, social and economic dependence. The interests of a particular group were liable to suppression by a central authority without endangering the interests of the whole society, provided that it was functioning normally. Even the removal of some groups or the disruption of society would not necessarily destroy the organization of the remaining part.

The opposite was the case with nomadic societies, which were much simpler in their organization. Intra-tribal institutions and authority were derived from kinship principles, while inter-tribal ones were based on political and military dependence. Both combined into a horizontal network of comparable units. Political structures emerged often as purposeful organizations and could be easily split and transformed, depending on the capabilities of the individual leaders and on external pressures. As a rule, nomadic polities were established in conditions of prolonged contact with sedentary societies for the purposes of securing compatibility with the latters' complexity, hence their aim was to regulate the contacts. If these polities acquired a degree of permanence, the political organization of the nomads would become stabilized over a period, thus achieving some complexity of social structure and of authority. These were, however, still transitory unless a state combined both nomadic and agricultural populations (Khazanov 1984, pp. 228).

The history of contacts between the Chinese and the nomadic pastoralists has been divided by Eberhard (1965, pp. 119–34) into three stages: (a) neighbourly relations, (b) Chinese rule over some nomads, (c) nomadic rule over China. These stages cannot be precisely fixed in time, and particular circumstances changed independently of this general progression. As a classification of contacts, however, the suggestion is still valid.

Eberhard's neighbourly relations cover the early period of east Asian medieval history, traditionally extending from the 2nd century BC to about the 3rd century AD. They included political relationships based on 'brotherhood', as well as military clashes, and attempts at increasing each side's influence. Contacts during the period from the Zhou (Chou) dynasty until the erection of defensive walls including the Great Wall were probably not very different from those of ancient times.

The nomadic contribution to the building of Chinese statehood, ethnicity and nation has been recognized but not adequately studied. Quasi-nomadic elements of old Chinese culture are inferred rather than established, since even a vague method of diachronic analogy has not been developed in this case, while written sources remain unreliable for a critical historian.

At the end of the 2nd millennium BC a two-way diffusion of artefacts from southern Siberia and from further west to China is reported (Watson

1971, p. 51). The go-betweens were then semi-nomads since at that time a full pastoral nomadism had probably not yet developed. These intermediary peoples also left some imprint on Chinese culture, as evidenced by chariots, some types of swords and knives, and in ritual as well.

It is known that the steppes of east central Asia yielded agricultural produce from neolithic times until the last millennium BC, and exceptionally even later. The reasons for the discontinuation of agriculture are uncertain; most probably, however, they were of internal origin pertaining to ecological circumstances. Thus Eberhard's interpretation (1965, pp. 113, 120), that the pastoral peoples gave up agriculture when they got interested in robbing Chinese peasants of their produce, seems very doubtful. It would appear that they ceased cultivation because they were in want of foodstuffs and decided to acquire them by a new, uncertain, and politically dangerous strategy. The first conflicts of this sort on the Chinese border are recorded with certainty in the 2nd century BC, although they could well have a longer tradition.

Few accounts of relations between nomadic and sedentary populations overlook the use of force, or raids for booty. This is a predictable chapter of most writing on nomads, as opposed to works on settled peoples. The literature, including that of specialist anthropology, is full of accounts and instances of the pillage-oriented economy of the nomads. Little care has been taken to verify such cases in order to exclude biased interpretations arising from an unconscious prejudice against strange nomads by authors rooted in sedentary cultures.

An important attempt at re-evaluation of this archetype of nomadic behaviour in their contacts with the sedentary Chinese has been undertaken by Lattimore (1940). He has described the nomadic turbulence in frontier areas as a reaction to Chinese pressure exercised through expanding agricultural settlement and the tax-collecting vocation of regional officials. Subsequently some authors have begun to correlate raids by pastoralists with the changing conditions of their external trade (Khazanov 1984, p. 202). The theory has been most positively formulated by Zlatkin (1974, p. 141). In his opinion, raids by the nomads on their agricultural peripheries constituted a primitive form of normal trade, and when trade had been established, raids occurred as a substitute for broken trade relations. The following analysis draws on the second part of Zlatkin's theory, not excluding, however, the possibility that other conditions may also have been responsible for some of the cases under consideration.

Raids are certainly part of the nomadic way of life, although we have to be careful to distinguish between unprovoked ones, intended simply for plunder, and those which are punitive expeditions of some kind. The former are a simple auxiliary to the pastoral economy. The latter exert power and thus belong, not to the sphere of economic practice, but to the sphere of administrative means (the concept of administration, however, has to be related to a particular cultural specificity). Of course, both may bring gain to those who carry them out, but analogous results do not necessarily imply a similarity of purpose.

It is possible to suggest a correlation between the two types of raids and the level of social complexity. Robbery raids seem to be characteristic of simple, usually small, groups of pastoral societies, lacking a central authority with an established hierarchy of leaders and complexity of aims. Their system of values and political ambitions do not favour constant relations with agricultural neighbours nor any responsible planning for the benefit of the whole group in the present or future.

Notwithstanding raids, almost all nomads are eager to trade with agriculturalists in order to supplement their simple diet and limited range of handicrafts. Moreover, the concept of the sedentary economy as complementary to that of the nomads has long been part and parcel of their world-view. Central Asiatic nomads, as opposed to their western counterparts, have not been able, however, to dictate the terms and conditions of the trade since their main partners in that part of the world were militarily strong and politically bold. Efforts to continue the trade and to set favourable terms have been an essential feature in relations between the pastoral and agricultural peoples for centuries.

Trade contacts between China and her northern steppe neighbours were probably established in the 6th century BC, and some of this trade was surprisingly not on a simple barter basis, as evidenced by coin finds (Watson 1972, p. 143). Written sources refer only to barter exchange, conducted at selected points on the border where, according to mutual agreement, fairs were held annually or even more frequently. The first report of the existence of such fairs relates to the year 129 BC (Bichurin 1950, p. 63).

Chinese exports included cereals, tea, sugar, spirits, silk and cotton cloth, metals, luxury goods for display of wealth and status, pottery, and paper. Among imports the dominant items were animals (notably horses), husbandry produce (hides, white felt, wool), salt, antlers and sometimes slaves.

The partners in this exchange usually displayed varying interests as to their essential goals. The pastoral populations wanted goods necessary for their existence, mostly consumable ones. Capital investment was provided inside their own economy, although some technical investment in weapons was required from outside. The sedentary populations were theoretically independent of nomadic produce, though this was a political theory rather than a practical reality. These two contradictory attitudes, of explicit interest and of manifest disinterest, have defined the mutual relations of the east Asian peoples in question.

This allowed the Chinese to aim at regulating the trade according to their wishes. Applying political pressure to the nomads by denying them rights to trade with sedentary societies was not an infrequent ploy throughout central Asia on the part of the rulers of agricultural states (Khazanov 1984, pp. 206–7). The motives behind such an attitude were sometimes as simple as prejudice, but particular considerations concerning the possible rise in the power of the nomads with the help of imported strategic goods were also involved. The Tanguts even restricted access to such strategic items as dishes for the Mongols shortly before their country was totally subdued by Chinggis-khan (Khazanov 1984, p. 207).

Periodically providing, and then refusing, goods in exchange as a stratagem in relations with the nomads is said to have been invented by Chia I, a Chinese expert on the nomadic Hsiung-nu of the 2nd century BC (Eberhard 1965, p. 121). This trick was continued until modern times.

Trading with the nomads was synonymous with political control in official Chinese thinking. A chronicle *Ming Shi*, describing a system of purchasing horses from the Tibetans in the 15th century, concludes in this way: 'and thus Tai-Zu administered the Fans', i.e. the Tibetans. Another chronicle explains the aims of exchange: 'not only that China is short of good horses . . . but also that the Fan barbarians living in frontier areas are thus getting attracted [to China]' (quoted from Martynov 1970, pp. 82, 84).

Foreign trade was a state monopoly in China and any private entrepreneur could face the death penalty (Kychanov 1968, p. 95). Refusal of barter might have been detrimental to the local Chinese of the frontier provinces, but not to the state as a whole. The Chinese state was interested in few items from outside, its only constant need being for horses for the army. Since the northern neighbours and the Tibetans to the west were horse exporters all eager to sell, there was practically no danger of severing this strategic import link.

Trade restrictions as a means of foreign policy were practised towards the neighbouring states of the Tanguts and, to a lesser extent, the Kitans. Their dual economy provided much agricultural produce for internal markets but some imports were necessary. Besides, raw materials for handicrafts were needed, as well as luxury goods. Their relatively developed economy produced a surplus which had to be traded abroad, and the Chinese market was the most promising. At the same time it was the most difficult because, being under government control, it had to follow central policy. Frontier fairs were therefore often closed at will, and it was always the Chinese who acted in this way, even contrary to the interests of the Chinese in the region (Kychanov 1968, pp. 92–9). Except for some local troubles, mainly over cultivated frontier lands, no wars between the two states broke out solely for reasons of trade. The determining factor here was the centralized authority of the Tanguts and Kitans, which restrained their own citizens and their ambitions.

Such a restraint was weak or absent in fully nomadic societies organized on tribal principles. This was true for at least 18 centuries, starting from a peace treaty with the Hsiung-nu at the beginning of the 2nd century BC and closing with the Mongol expeditions led by Altan-khan, who demanded fairness in trade. Annoying pressure exerted by the Chinese who were the stronger party at barter fairs was resisted by the nomads seeking their own advantage here.

Reactions to the Chinese manipulation of trade are indicated by a report in a Chinese chronicle that Tanguts, arriving at a closed fair-place, shouted at the guards in anger: 'unless you let us barter whenever we come, we will start killing again' (Kychanov 1968, p. 95n). This should serve as a motto for any research on the relations with the nomads of eastern Asia.

An early form of acquiring merchandise from China by nomad societies was a 'tribute' given to their leaders by the Chinese court. The 'tribute' is an imprecise term for ceremonial gifts presented reciprocally, although those bestowed by the Chinese side often exceeded the balance. Already the peace treaty with the Hsiung-nu had established that the Chinese would provide the Hsiung-nu leader with some wine, 50 000 sacks of rice, and 10 000 pieces of silk annually. It was reaffirmed in AD 50 after a long period of not infrequently interrupted practice (Bichurin 1950, pp. 76, 119). The Chinese contribution to the welfare of the northern states increased greatly with time, and some ten centuries later the Kitan emperor received as much as 300 000 pieces of silk per year in addition to an amount of silver (Tashkin 1979, pp. 283, 290).

Distribution of these 'tribute' goods was certainly unequal, and limited only to groups important to the continued exercise of the khan's power. The amount of goods acquired was obviously too small to apportion an adequate share to each family, but there was enough of them for selected recipients among close associates and allies from more distant tribes. Ordinary members of the tribe were still in need of imported goods and on occasion conducted petty raids on the march-lands. The Hsiung-nu leaders constrained them, but at the same time tolerated them (Bichurin 1950, pp. 110–11). It seems that irregular border fairs allowing for barter, a new institution at that time, were not sufficient to meet the nomads' various demands.

The tribute system of procuring gains was rather free of conflict, though it depended on the changing nature of political relationships. The reason why cessation of tribute alone did not provoke the use of force lay in its content: luxury goods prevailed over those of practical use.

Nomadic leaders understood that in order to consolidate their power they would have to draw on a more stable resource than tribute. The pastoral economy did not provide them with this opportunity, since even the exchange of surplus produce was not extensive nor directed for consumption. Subsidising a state organization, in particular a complex one after the Chinese model, was an expensive business. A ruler had to rely on internal income for that purpose, and only a diversified economy could support such ambitions. For this reason nomadic aristocracy tended to build a state which would include some agricultural peripheries. This policy, however, though well conceived, was not well carried out.

A great number of local dynasties organized by Turkic, Mongol and Tibetan leaders on China's periphery in the first millennium were short-lived and of limited territorial extent. Their most important feature was the underlying model of a state organized by the nomads: a combination of two types of economy, modes of occupying space and interacting cultures. Such a diversified state, approaching the nomadic ideal of economic autonomy, could not last for long in territories with a tradition of Chinese statehood, since the latter tended to revert to its uniform character. The reason behind this reversion was the difficulty which the predominantly Chinese officials faced in administering the state structure combining the two varying forms of social organization: tribal among the nomads and communal among the agricultural villagers.

To summarize this review of relations between the pastoral nomadic and the sedentary agricultural systems of east Asia, it seems essential to abandon the commonly-held view which sees them simply in terms of invasion and resistance. They are rather relationships of exchange, combined with policies of conflict, which preceded relations based on force. It seems unwarranted to regard the nomads either as just destructive or as a destabilizing agent in the regions they occupied. They were rather an active factor in intercultural contacts and communication, and a dynamic one. The underlying motive was that the nomads were handicapped in the division of labour, and hence the outside world was complementary to theirs. It was also inherent in this position of the nomads as structurally related to sedentary societies that they could in certain circumstances be transformed from suppliers of products of their pastoral economy into a major military threat to the agricultural 'centre', with the potential for political domination from the periphery.

References

Bichurin, N. Y. 1950. *Sobranie svedeniy o narodakh obitavshikh v Sredney Azii v drevnie vremena*, Vol. 1. Moscow–Leningrad: Izd. Akademii Nauk SSSR.

Eberhard, W. 1965. *Conquerors and rulers. Social forces in medieval China*. 2nd edn. Leiden: Brill.

Khazanov, A. M. 1984. *Nomads and the outside world*. Cambridge: Cambridge University Press.

Kychanov, E. I. 1968. *Ocherk istorii tangustkogo gosudarstva*. Moscow: Nauk.

Lattimore, O. 1940. *Inner Asian frontiers of China*. New York: American Geographical Society.

Martynov, A. S. 1970. K probleme obmena na fan'skoy periferii pri dinastii Min. In *Istorya, kul'tura, yazyki narodov Vostoka*, Y. A. Petrosyan (ed.), 80–7. Moscow: Nauka.

Pershits, A. I. and A. M. Khazanov (eds) 1978. *Pervobytnaya periferiya klassovykh obshchestv do nachala velikikh geograficheskikh otkrytiy*. Moscow: Nauk.

Tashkin, V. S. 1979. *Ye Long-li. Istoriya gosudarstva kidaney (Qidan guo zhi)*. Moscow: Nauka.

Watson, W. 1971. *Cultural frontiers in ancient east Asia*. Edinburgh: Edinburgh University Press.

Watson, W. 1972. The Chinese contribution to eastern nomad culture in the pre-Han and early Han periods. *World Archaeology* **4**, 139–49.

Zlatkin, I. Y. 1974. Torgovlya kak factor vneshnepoliticheskikh i ekonomicheskikh svyazey kochevykh narodov Mongolii v drevnosti i srednie veka. In *Rol' kochevykh narodov v civilizacii Central'noy Azii*. Ulan Bator: Akademiya Nauk MNR.

9 *Diffusion and cultural evolution in Iron Age Serbia*

FREDERICK A. WINTER and
H. ARTHUR BANKOFF

During the mid-first millennium BC, the range of settlement localities in Serbia (Fig. 9.1) was expanded to include sites immediately adjacent to the area's larger rivers. Previously, during the Bronze Age, sites had been more often set back from the major waterways and positioned on the upper terraces of the river valleys. This locational shift was accompanied by the appearance of new artefact types, primarily luxury or élite goods recovered from burials, which show morphological influence from classical Mediterranean cultures. By the end of the 1st millennium BC, classical technological innovations such as the potter's wheel had been firmly established throughout the area. This terminal phase of the pre-Roman Iron Age in Serbia is characterized by an increasing use of metals as well as expanded faunal and floral assemblages.

These developments in material culture and settlement locational decisions may be explained in terms of a model that views change as the result of an interaction between foreign innovations and the internal evolution of the local society. The process began with the introduction of iron metallurgy into the Balkans in the first half of the 1st millennium BC. The area in and around Serbia is rich in the raw ores needed for the production of this metal, a situation which is in sharp contrast to that of Greece where, by classical times, although industrialization had become quite advanced, the necessary metal resources were almost entirely lacking. The desire or need on the part of classical Greek society to acquire the raw materials necessary to its economy brought Mediterranean populations, goods, and ideas into Serbia for the first time. Foreign influences altered the cultural systems operative during the Bronze Age, as first 'international' trade and then military considerations focused the attention of the local populace on the world outside the immediate region. The end result was the development of large-scale tribal or primitive state societies in the Balkans. Further local evolution was cut short by another foreign factor, the advance of the Roman Empire. For Serbia, this was marked by the incorporation of the province of Moesia in *c.* AD 6.

The general European economic trends for this period have been discussed in a number of recent synthetic works (e.g. Champion *et al.* 1984, Collis 1984, Wells 1980, 1984) which describe an increase in Greek mercantile activity in

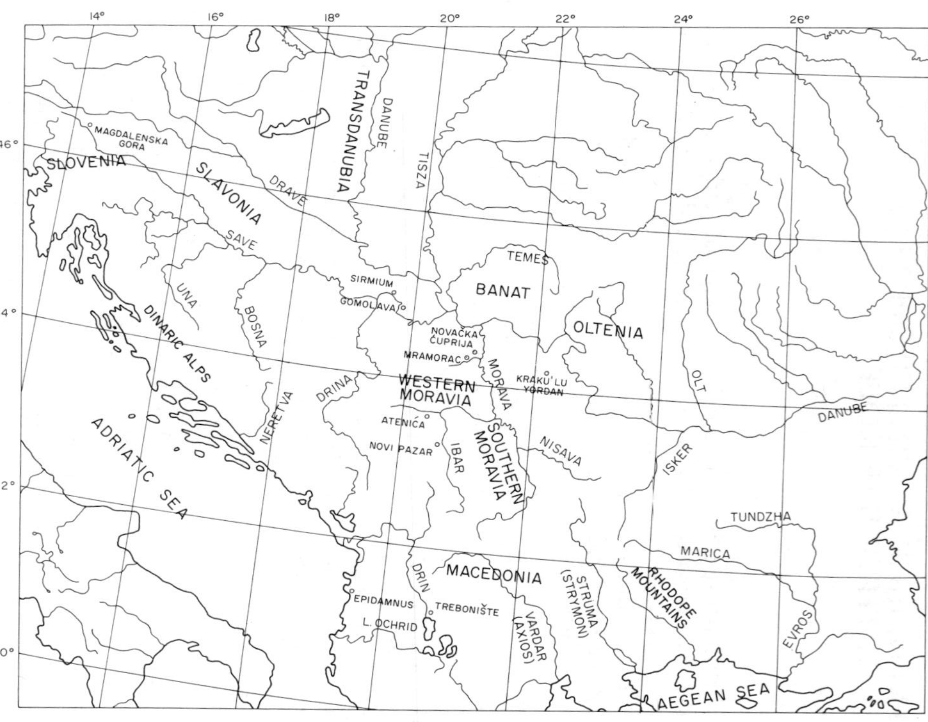

Figure 9.1 Serbia and surrounding regions showing sites mentioned in the text.

west-central Europe beginning in *c*. 600 BC. This western trade ended abruptly about a century later when Greek traders, possibly in response to the hostility of west Mediterranean Carthage (Ahl 1982, p. 397), redirected their attentions further east, to the north Adriatic with its central and eastern European connections, and to the Black Sea. In the west, trade did not intensify again until the later 3rd and 2nd centuries BC with the advent of Roman commercial activity in Europe following the Second Punic War. Urban development in western Europe, which took place during this period of renewed contact with the Mediterranean, was viewed by Collis (1976) as a result of late La Tène increases in trade, the growth of iron production (and manufacturing), and the appearance of a coinage-using economy. The social correlates of these economic and technological developments have been outlined briefly in his more recent work (Collis 1982). Similarly, Alexander (1972, p. 847) identified four factors as characterizing later prehistoric European urbanism: (1) increased trade and commerce; (2) association with tribal systems; (3) communal enterprise, particularly apparent in the construction of fortifications; and (4) industrialization, especially in the fields of metallurgy, glasswork, and enamelling. In particular, Alexander (1972, p. 845) noted that the contribution of craft specialization as a factor in European urbanization may have been overemphasized. In contrast, Crumley (1974, esp. pp. 75–7) suggested that industrialization was the central development in the cultural changes that took place in late La Tène western Europe. She saw cultural change in Gaul as proceeding from a foreign demand for European trade goods. This demand led to a period of primitive industrialization which resulted in the growth of 'an autonomous middle class, made up initially of artisans, but soon joined by merchants and bureaucrats'. Within this new social structure, achieved status (derived from occupation, wealth, personal exploits and accomplishments) would have gained increasingly in importance at the expense of ascribed (on the basis of birth or lineage) status criteria.

Within Serbia and the broader middle Danube region, Mediterranean merchants would have been attracted by the availability of raw materials (predominantly metal ores, but also agricultural products and perhaps slaves). The failure of extractive industries such as mining to stimulate industrial growth and its concomitant social correlates may easily be documented from examples in recent 19th- and 20th-century imperialism. Regarding industrialization, the classical and hellenistic Greeks' lack of interest in Balkan manufactured goods is reflected by the extreme paucity of Balkan goods in Greek archaeological contexts and by the total absence of southeastern European and La Tène Celtic influence on the classical and hellenistic assemblages of Greece (Winter 1976), a situation markedly different from that found in western Mediterranean Italy. Thus, primitive industrialization within the Balkans would have developed in response to a market demand that was purely local and was considerably less intense than the pressures supporting industry in the West. Radical change and sudden cultural shifts of the type seen in the explosive growth of the large western European La Tène industrial centres and oppida did not occur in the East.

Although occasional Greek imports appear in Serbia in the 8th to early 6th centuries BC (Parović-Pešikan 1985), it is not until late in the 6th century that evidence for Mediterranean trade begins to appear on a regular basis. This trade is reflected in the imported luxury goods that appear in burials such as those at Magdalenska Gora to the north-west and at Novi Pazar (Figs 9.2–5) and Trebenište to the south-west (Filow 1927, Mano-Zisi & Popović 1969, Popović 1975, Vasić 1977, pp. 31–53, Hencken 1978, Palavestra 1984). The presence of these goods in the valley of the Western Morava in central Serbia is demonstrated by the contents of two princely burial mounds from Atenica near Čačak (Vasić 1977, p. 25, Palavestra 1984, pp. 35–46). The character of the foreign imports, which include vessels made of bronze and precious metals, fibulae and other types of jewelry, and horse trappings, and their differential distribution among the burials within the cemeteries, suggest that these goods were being used as status markers in a stratified society that later literary sources indicate was organized along tribal lines (see Vasić 1972).

In dealing with the contemporary high-status burials of central and western Europe, Wells (1977, pp. 192ff) suggested that Mediterranean luxury goods served as gift-offerings designed to establish treaty relationships between the European élites who controlled access to raw materials and foreign merchants who were providing for the demands of the Greek market. There is no reason why similar practices could not have been followed further east. Various routes were available to bring the imported goods from the Mediterranean world into Serbia. The north Adriatic route would have been stimulated by the establishment of the Greek trading colony at Spina in Italy and the shift in Greek trade away from Massilia (modern Marseilles) and toward the Adriatic in the early 5th century BC (see Wells 1979). There is evidence also for a southern Adriatic route, proceeding from Epidamnus to Lake Ochrid and thence inland (Boardman 1971), while overland routes from Macedonia (e.g. via the Axios/Vardar–Morava Valley link) were also possible.

In addition, oriental influences were present in the adjacent lower Danube regions during the mid-first millennium BC. Darius's campaign along the Danube in 513–512 BC, which was followed by 30 years of Achaemenid occupation before the subsequent withdrawal of the Persians under Xerxes in 480–479 BC, introduced oriental goods to Thrace and the lower Danube, leaving the seeds of a local industry that had strong eastern and especially Anatolian connections. Powell (1971) has suggested that this metal industry continued to function during the hellenistic era, producing, among other works, the famous Gundestrup cauldron. Finally, it is necessary to take into account the evidence for Thraco-Cimmerian and later Scythian influence in areas as far west as Slovenia (Vasić 1977, pp. 16ff, Hencken 1978, p. 6).

To assess the impact of these foreign influences on the prehistoric cultures of Serbia, it is necessary to consider them within the context of the local socially-stratified society. It may generally be assumed that in a stratified society where access to status and status-marking goods is not severely

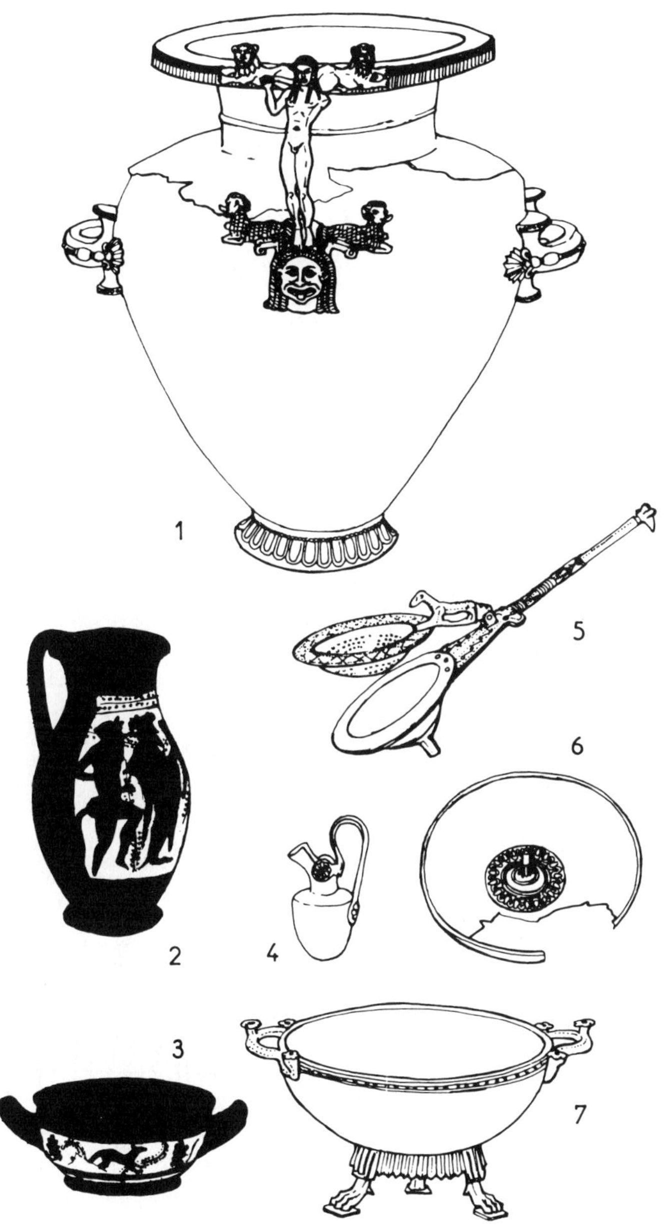

Figure 9.2 Novi Pazar: 1, 4–7 bronze; 2–3 clay. Scale 1/4 (after Vasić 1977).

Figure 9.3 Novi Pazar: amber. Scale 1/1 (after Vasić 1977).

Figure 9.4 Novi Pazar: 1–11 gold; 12 glass. Scale: 1, 3–7, 12: 1/3; 2, 8–11: 1/2.

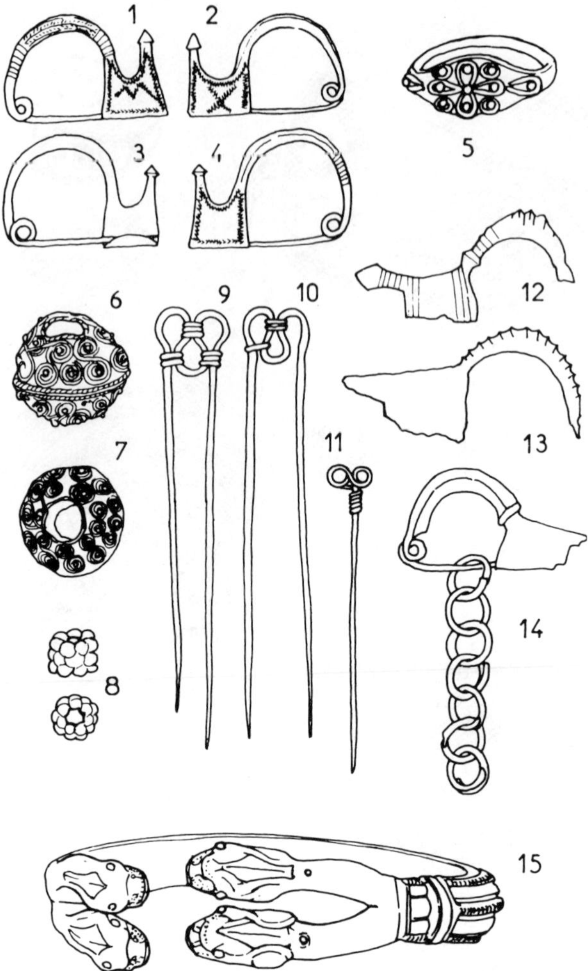

Figure 9.5 Novi Pazar: 1–2, 5–8, 11 gold; 3–4, 9–10, 15 silver; 12–14 bronze. Scale: 1–4, 12–14: 3/4; 5–11, 15: 8/9.

restricted or controlled, and where the possibility for upward social mobility either within or across class lines exists, the reliance of a culture on status markers will result in an intensified demand for the markers and the status that they both symbolize and provide. Such increased demand may be met in two ways: either by increasing the production of established status markers or by introducing new markers. These new markers may consist of entirely new goods or may be more readily available imitations of the established markers.

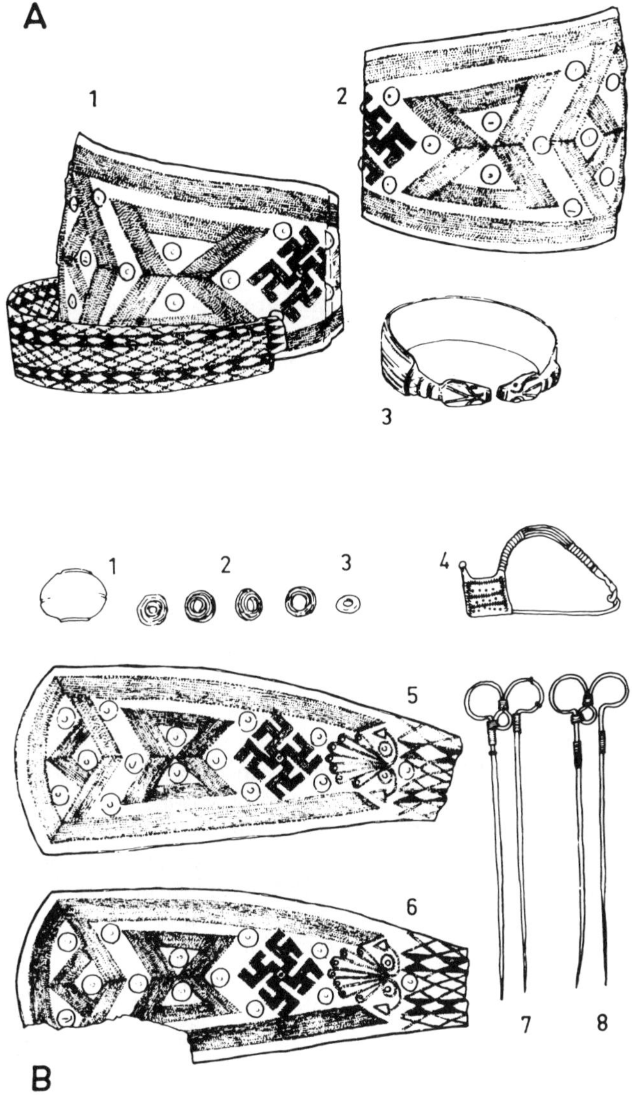

Figure 9.6 Mramorac (A) and Umčari (B): A 1–2, B 2, 4–8 silver; A 3 gold; B 1 bronze; B 3 glass. Scale: A 1–2, B 5–6: 1/4; A 3, B 2–4, 7–8: 1/2; B 1: 1/3.

Both of these alternatives were utilized by the people of Iron Age Serbia. The introduction of foreign élite goods resulted not only in the intensification and expansion of foreign trade in such goods, but also in the production of locally made status markers, such as the silver belts and related metalware with embossed decoration found primarily in the valley of the lower Morava (Vasić 1972, pp. 122–8) (Fig. 9.6). Archaeologically, this process should reveal itself not only in the obvious manner of increasing the quantity of foreign and local status indicators, but also in the development of a growing homogeneity in the region's artefactual assemblage. This would come about as the local and foreign status markers spread through the region, initially moving independently of, but eventually having an impact on, the locally-evolved regional styles.

Concomitant with the intensification of importation and local production would be a 'trickle effect' as lower-status individuals devalued goods symbolic of higher status by obtaining them, thereby forcing high-status individuals to seek alternative high-status goods (Fallers 1966, p. 403). The end result of this 'trickle effect' would be an increase in competition for status goods throughout the society (Crumley 1974, p. 80), a further intensification in foreign trade, and an intensification in local production and inter-market communication. This helps explain the preference for new Iron Age sites on the larger rivers, as well as the suggestions of local metal-working (in the form of slags from iron smelting) found at Iron Age sites in Serbia.

The military gear that often accompanies the foreign and locally produced status markers in the graves of the Iron Age, and which itself would have served as a status indicator, suggests another manifestation of this limited-availability, high-demand market. Competition for access to the new and relatively scarce status goods would lead both to military conflict and to the establishment of convenient political alliances. Some of these would be short-term, others of longer duration as stronger leaders asserted themselves and maintained political sway over greater numbers of their peers (see Carneiro 1981). Such military competition would manifest itself archaeologically in a shift to settlement sites which were easily defensible and which lent themselves to use as military strongholds (see Stojić 1986). Foreign military incursions would also support this preference for strategic settlement sites, while also encouraging the local populace to band together on a supra-regional level in order to oppose the invaders. Thus, when Alexander the Great campaigned in the Balkans in 335 BC, the Triballi (the tribe controlling the lower Morava Valley) mustered a defensive army that was large enough to sustain 3000 casualties in a single battle and still remain a military force worthy of consideration in Alexander's plans (Arrian I.i–ii). Even allowing for an inflated 'body count', the numbers of dead suggest that Alexander met a force considerably larger than a limited regional military élite.

Not long after Alexander's campaign, central European Celts invaded and settled in Serbia. The Celts had already established themselves along the Adriatic by the third quarter of the 4th century BC (Arrian I.v). In 279 BC, a large-scale Celtic migratory invasion of Greece passed down the Morava Valley on its way south to meet disastrous defeat at the sanctuary of Apollo at Delphi. After the defeat at Delphi, some of the Celtic refugees retreated back into Serbia. Archaeologically, the introduction of these Celtic military forces would have tended to reinforce existing trends giving preference to prominent strategic settlement sites. Evidence from sites in the region suggests that, with the exception of weapon types, the old status markers continued to be used (Todorović 1974, p. 235). Some Celtic technological innovations would have filtered down to the local peasantry (e.g. the potter's wheel, although this particular piece of technology may have been introduced to Serbia directly from the Greek world without Celtic involvement), but in general the period of Celtic domination would have resulted in little immediate change in the region's archaeological assemblage or in its subsistence and mercantile patterns. Innovations that were introduced by the newcomers would have been subject to the same stabilizing pressures inherent in the local conservative agrarian society as those that affected the locally-evolved patterns. The status system that had been developed internally in response to economic contacts with the Mediterranean world had become a factor that held the region back from entering the 'modern' world.

It remained for the Romans to introduce extensive and rapid change into the economy and social life of Serbia. As was the case elsewhere, the Romans used pre-existing status differences to establish relations with a tribal élite, through which they made rapid inroads towards 'romanization' and conquest (see Luttwack 1976). The Moesian tribe of Serbia was incorporated into the province of Macedonia in 29 BC following the successful campaign of M. Crassus (Dio Cassius 51.21.1). The separate province of Moesia was constituted in *c.* AD 6; the province was organized in a more definite form during the reign of Tiberius (Appian III.30).

It is possible to use the analysis of the finds from the excavations at Novačka Ćuprija South, in the lower Morava valley, to get a glimpse of the changes under the Romans (Bankoff & Winter 1982). With the establishment of Roman rule Roman mass-produced goods entered the area and the general standard of living rose. The four bronze fibulae from the La Tène and Roman settlement at Novačka Ćuprija South, in addition to one late La Tène fibula and a bronze pin from Novačka Ćuprija Central, are the only 'luxury' goods found at Novačka Ćuprija, a locality that had been occupied since the Eneolithic, or indeed at any of the Iron Age and earlier sites surveyed by the Morava Valley project. The expansion of trade and foreign influence during Roman times is particularly evident in the pottery found at Novačka Ćuprija South. Imported *terra sigillata* accounts for 2% of the total analysed pottery from the site. If that figure seems low, it can also be noted that oxidized fired pottery, virtually non-existent during the Bronze Age and pre-Roman Iron Age, now accounts for 13% of the ceramics. It is most likely that this reflects the impact of Roman red wares on the local ceramic industry.

It is probable that, in order to take fullest advantage of the expanded economic horizons, villages and hamlets would have been encouraged to develop in areas formerly occupied only by scattered farmsteads. At Novačka Ćuprija, occupation during the Roman period was focused almost exclusively on the southern portion of the site. It is clear that the surface scatter of sherds is considerably denser on this southern locality than elsewhere on the site. It is probable that this reflects an increased intensity of settlement, as well as other possible factors. The introduction of oats (*Avena* sp.), possibly as fodder, and horsebeans (*Vicia faba*) into the floral assemblage at this time may also be an indication of changes in the agrarian way of life. With the incorporation of the region into the Roman economic world, regional heterogeneity further declined. The finest ceramic table-ware now consisted of Roman *terra sigillata*, distributed throughout the empire, rather than a locally made luxury ware. 'Local' fine wheel-made grey wares found in the Morava Valley share shapes and fabrics with pottery found at least as far away as Sirmium and Gomolava along the Sava (Parović-Pešikan 1971, p. 35) and sites in the Djerdap.

The pattern of foreign interaction suggested by the finds from early Roman Imperial Novačka Ćuprija South stands in sharp contrast to the pattern observed at the later Imperial site of Kraku'lu Yordan in eastern Serbia (Bartel *et al.* 1979). There, the excavators found only limited evidence for direct Roman interaction at a 4th-century AD iron production site. The finds at Kraku'lu Yordan were almost exclusively local in terms of material, and only one of the 6252 sherds from the 1976 excavations was identifiable as a Roman import. The volume of iron production at the site did not seem to go beyond local needs, and the production technology was again such as to suggest a purely local industry. The observed differences in Roman influence from those seen at Novačka Ćuprija South may result from differing diachronic patterns of interaction with the Roman economic world (1st century BC to 2nd century AD at Novačka Ćuprija, as opposed to 4th century AD at Kraku'lu Yordan). It may also be due to other factors such as site proximity to road systems or accessibility. Certainly, the iron-mining district of Kraku'lu Yordan would seem to have had more to attract the Romans than a small outlying farming village such as Novačka Ćuprija South, especially if Kraku'lu Yordan were an iron-smelting site as the excavators suggest.

In summary, foreign mercantile activity and the consumption of foreign goods by the local autochthonous élite may be seen as the primary factor initiating social change in the Early Iron Age Balkans. Beginning as an attempt to secure the scarce resources accruing to the suppliers of raw materials to the classical markets, economic and political centralization led to an increasing demand for foreign status-marking goods and their local equivalents, thus further drawing the region into the Mediterranean orbit. The development which followed the initiation of foreign trade contacts led to (or accelerated an already existing trend towards) the evolution of historically attested large-scale tribal states. The failure of the societies of Serbia and, more generally, southeastern Europe to follow the trajectory of the states to the west, which led to primitive industrialization, the growth of an autonomous middle class, and a social structure that stressed achievement rather than ascription, may be sought in the primacy of extractive industries in the Balkans. The reliance on extraction rather than production led to the concentration of wealth and power in a small élite who controlled the contacts with those buying the raw material and supplying the luxury goods. Finally, the Roman conquest, motivated by the presence of raw materials and extractive industries, as well as by a need to secure the Empire's borders, terminated this internal evolution, incorporating Serbia and its environs into the Roman political state and mass-market.

Acknowledgements

Research for this chapter was supported by funds provided by the Professional Staff Congress – City University of New York Faculty Research Awards Program. Participation in the World Archaeological Congress was partially funded by a travel stipend from Brooklyn College of the City University of New York.

References

Ahl, F. M. 1982. Amber, Avallon, and Apollo's singing swan. *American Journal of Philology* 103, 373–412.

Alexander, J. 1972. The beginnings of urban life in Europe. In *Man, settlement and urbanism*, P. J. Ucko, R. Tringham & G. W. Dimbleby (eds), 843–50. London: Duckworth.

Bankoff, H. A. & F. A. Winter 1982. The Morava Valley project in Yugoslavia: preliminary report, 1977–1980. *Journal of Field Archaeology* **9**, 149–64.

Bartel, B., V. Kondić & M. Werner 1979. Excavations at Kraku'lu Yordan, northeast Serbia. *Journal of Field Archaeology* **8**, 127–49.

Boardman, J. 1971. A southern view of Situla art. In *The European community in later prehistory*, J. Boardman, M. A. Brown & T. G. E. Powell (eds), 121–40. London: Routledge and Kegan Paul.

Carneiro, R. 1981. The chiefdom: precursor of the state. In *The transition to statehood in the New World*, G. Jones and R. Kautz (eds), 37–79. Cambridge: Cambridge University Press.

Champion, T., C. Gamble, S. Shennan & A. Whittle 1984. *Prehistoric Europe*. London: Academic Press.

Collis, J. 1976. Town and market in Iron Age Europe. In *Oppida: the beginnings of urbanisation in barbarian Europe*, B. Cunliffe & T. Rowley (eds), 3–23. British Archaeological Reports Supplementary Series 11, Oxford.

Collis, J. 1982. Gradual growth and sudden change – urbanisation in temperate Europe. In *Ranking, resource and exchange*, C. Renfrew & S. Shennan (eds), 73–8. Cambridge: Cambridge University Press.

Collis, J. 1984. *The European Iron Age*. London: Batsford.

Crumley, C. 1974. *Celtic social structure: the generation of archaeologically testable hypotheses from literary evidence*. Museum of Anthropology, University of Michigan Anthropological Papers 54, Ann Arbor.

Fallers, L. A. 1966. A note on the trickle effect. In *Status, class and power*, R. Bendix & M. Lipset (eds), 402–5. New York: Free Press.

Filow, B. 1927. *Die archaische Nekropole von Trebenischte*. Berlin: de Gruyter.

Hencken, H. 1978. *Mecklenberg collection, Pt. II: The Iron Age cemetery of Magdalenska*

Gora in Slovenia. Bulletin 32: American School of Prehistoric Research. Harvard: Peabody Museum.

Luttwack, E. 1976. *The grand strategy of the Roman Empire*. Baltimore: Johns Hopkins University Press.

Mano-Zisi, D. & Lj. B. Popović 1969. *Novi Pazar*. Belgrade: National Museum.

Palavestra, A. 1984. *Princely tombs during the Early Iron Age in the central Balkans*. Belgrade: Serbian Academy of Sciences and Arts, Institute for Balkan Studies.

Parović-Pešikan, M. 1971. Excavations of a Late Roman villa at Sirmium. In *Sirmium II*, V. Popović & E. Ochsenschlager (eds), 15–44. Belgrade: Archaeological Institute of Belgrade, Denison University, City University of New York.

Parović-Pešikan, M. 1985. Neki novi aspekti širenja ejgejske i grčke kulture na centralni balkan. *Starinar* **36**, 19–46.

Popović, L. 1975. *Archaic Greek culture in the middle Balkans*. Belgrade: National Museum.

Powell, T. G. E. 1971. From Urartu to Gundestrup: The agency of Thracian metal-work. In *The European community in later prehistory*, J. Boardman, M. A. Brown & T. G. E. Powell (eds), 181–210. London: Routledge and Kegan Paul.

Stojić, M. 1986. *Gvozdeno doba u basenu Velike Morave*. Belgrade: University of Belgrade.

Todorović, J. 1974. *Skordisci*. Belgrade: Institut za izučavanje istorije Vojvodine.

Vasić, R. 1972. Notes on the Autariatae and Triballi. *Balcanica* **3**, 118–33.

Vasić, R. 1977. *The chronology of the Early Iron Age in Serbia*. British Archaeological Reports Supplementary Series 31, Oxford.

Wells, P. S. 1977. Late Hallstatt interactions with the Mediterranean. In *Ancient Europe and the Mediterranean*, V. Markotic (ed.), 189–96. Warminster: Aris & Phillips.

Wells, P. S. 1979. West Central Europe and the Mediterranean. *Expedition* **21**, 18–24.

Wells, P. S. 1980. *Culture contact and culture change*. Cambridge: Cambridge University Press.

Wells, P. S. 1984. *Farms, villages and cities*. Ithaca: Cornell University Press.

Winter, F. A. 1976. Celts in the art of the hellenistic East. Paper delivered at the 78th General Meeting of the Archaeological Institute of America.

10 *Acculturation and ethnicity in Roman Moesia Superior*

BRAD BARTEL

Introduction

A welcome trend in archeology over the last decade has been the development of fieldwork approaches for both theory generation and cross-cultural comparison related to an archaeology of colonialism. A comparable set of research questions has also been developed for the study of imperialism, but there has been a lag in their application to archaeological data sets. In a series of articles (Bartel 1980, 1985, Bartel *et al.* forthcoming) my colleagues and I have attempted to establish a number of research design priorities for this type of study. My own field research concerning the nature and degree of Roman colonialism in the province of Moesia Superior (what is now northeastern Serbia, Yugoslavia) is a logical extension of these concerns.

An evaluation of recent and historical examples of colonialism and imperialism strongly indicates three distinct strategies for political and economic control of native populations. This matrix of six possible outcomes (Fig. 10.1), all to varying degrees archaeologically detectable, rests as a methodological tool whose applicability is relative to our ability to detect both ethnicity and acculturation in the archaeological record.

I will first present some thoughts about the closeness of fit between the social anthropological and archaeological perspectives on ethnicity and acculturation. These will be followed by a synthetic treatment of the colonial situation in Moesia Superior as known through ethnohistory and recent archaeological excavation. The theoretical model discussed herein represents how we have examined the archaeological record for Moesia Superior. This research is still in its first phase; that of examining the synchronic relationships among natives and Romans, with later projects looking at the region prior to and after Roman colonialism.

Archaeological detection of ethnic groups

Any investigation of colonialism must begin with detection of identification markers for the indigenous group; either the whole society or a 'part society' such as an ethnic group. The ethnographic work of Barth (1969) and his associates stimulated new approaches in the social study of ethnicity. Barth's

STRATEGIES	POLICIES: COLONIALISM (settlers)	POLICIES: IMPERIALISM
ERADICATION-RESETTLEMENT	abrupt culture change	regional 'empty cell'
ACCULTURATION	slow indigenous culture change	slow indigenous culture change
EQUILIBRIUM	settlement enclaves	indigenous cultural maintenance

Figure 10.1 A matrix of probable behavioural outcomes in situations of power domination.

emphasis was on the social and physical boundaries among groups which are maintained through time to encourage the stability of one's own ethnic identification and to secure predictable avenues of economic exchange with the other ethnic groups sharing those boundaries. By emphasizing boundaries and integration along the landscape, rather than social traits developed through the enculturation process, Barth felt a more dynamic understanding could be realized. In his model, ethnicity becomes a product of integration rather than of isolation.

Since Barth's model was published, the emphasis has shifted to a balanced research perspective incorporating an analysis of both content and boundary behaviours among groups (Lyman & Douglass 1973, Keyes 1981, Royce 1982). This perspective is often coupled to a psychological understanding of ethnicity as awareness of identity, with any change in membership being a change in psychological characteristics of the individual (Mannoni 1956, Doornbus 1972, DeVos & Romanucci-Ross 1975).

There has been an increasing interest in detecting ethnicity from the archaeological record, especially with regard to urban situations (Millon 1974). Most present investigators follow the lead of Barth. For example, Kamp and Yoffee's (1981) research into the detection of ethnic groups coexisting in Bronze Age western Asia shows a major advancement in understanding the dangers and potentials of this form of analysis. They present a research strategy involving a number of critical sets of data. One must first examine diagnostic behaviour used by the ethnic groups to symbolize identity. Two forms of information are involved. The first involves the overt signals having material correlates, such as jewelry or clothing used as signals of ethnic awareness to other ethnic groups within the same territory with whom long-term relations occur. The second diagnostic feature within this data set is the rule of endogamy which tends to occur with high frequency, and should be seen in genetic clustering of skeletal material when measured intra-societally, and also against other genetic data sets within the same urban settlement or across the immediate landscape.

The second set of information pertains to the enculturation process. Each ethnic group should exhibit a specific polythetic range of artefact types through time. Some degree of individual stylistic preference causing material variation should be expected, and if one ethnic group is widely distributed across diverse ecozones, a greater polythetic range will exist.

The third set of information is related to Barth's hypothesis that ethnic identity maintenance fosters a given economic advantage. The archaeological record is evaluated to acquire data about specific occupational rôles which are exclusively played by members of a given ethnic group when compared to others with whom they interact.

The approach of Kamp and Yoffee or of McGuire (1982) amounts to a new orientation, acknowledging that scale differences exist when one analyses an ethnic group versus a whole society. It represents a reasonable multivariate approach based upon a perspective gained from the ethnographic practice of analysing both ethnic content and cross-ethnic integration.

Ethnoarchaeological approaches to ethnicity

There are a number of recent ethnoarchaeological researches of ethnicity which validate the modern archaeological approaches (Okely 1979, Phillipson 1979, Spencer 1979, Kramer 1985). Of greatest importance is the work of Hodder (1977, 1978, 1979, 1982).

Hodder's analyses of tribes coexisting in one region of Kenya emphasizes the spatial range of household inventories, articles of self-adornment, and settlement configuration. Aside from his findings concerning gender differences in social contact among different groups, the most important finding relative to ethnicity was that those material objects overtly identified with a specific group tend to cluster within that group's territory. Although the strongest clustering was with tribal identity, this tends to confirm from an ethnoarchaeological perspective Barth's hypothesis that ethnic identity continues in spite of intense social and economic contacts. However, Hodder was unable to confirm the same strong clustering for ethnic groups.

Ethnological theories of acculturation

Throughout the last half century, the observation and interpretation of culture contact resulting in acculturation has been an important part of ethnology. Programmatic statements of how such research should be conducted began to appear during the 1930s (Redfield *et al.* 1936, Herskovits 1938, Linton 1940).

Most of the early ethnographic studies stressed unilineal directions for culture change, while modern studies have emphasized reciprocal changes, even between societies widely disparate in terms of scale, technology and ecological adaptation (Beidelman 1982). It is felt by modern researchers that if any two societies come into continuous contact with sufficient social intensity at many levels of interaction, extensive changes will occur in both.

A theme pervading all ethnological acculturation research is that such a process is dynamic and diachronic, and that rates of change may differ for different societies under the same colonial system of dominance, or even for groups of individuals from one specific society.

Ianni's (1958) programmatic research strategy for an ethnological understanding of acculturation has equal merit for archaeology. A diachronic perspective is strongly advocated, whereby the pre-contact society is first evaluated and understood in terms of its material culture and values, and the nature and degree of its contact with other societies. There follows an analysis of subsequent changes in lifestyle brought about by long-term contact with another group, and finally of further changes when the society is no longer exposed to that culture.

Most important from the point of view of either an ethnological or an archaeological model of acculturation is exactly which variables are to be selected as critical tests for change. Testing for acculturation by cultural anthropologists has always consisted of examining the possession of a series of indigenous cultural traits. Some are material and closely associated with normative rules of behaviour instilled through the enculturation process (food preparation, consumption, disposal, material symbols of self-identification).

Probably the most significant theoretical orientation for archaeologists studying acculturation, in colonial situations or otherwise, comes from the work of Gillin and Raimy (1940) and Spiro (1955). These researchers proposed that external and observable features measuring acculturation (material culture) are often accepted by indigenous peoples without major changes in value-orientation and personality. What this means to the archaeologist attempting to analyse acculturation is that one can measure change in material culture without feeling it necessary to discover patterns expressive of changes in value-orientation, most of which are not visible in the archaeological record.

Archaeological orientations towards acculturation

When compared to ethnographic research on acculturation, modern archaeological orientations lack sophistication. Few general statements exist in archaeology as to how one detects acculturation, with researchers assuming total acculturation by an indigenous society or ethnic group to a technologically superior one.

D. L. Clarke (1968) presents one of the few detailed archaeological discussions of acculturation. His systems and cybernetic approach views culture as always open to the reception of new information. A given culture may come under the influence of saturated diffusion, a 'cumulative integration of new elements with a resulting inevitable system transmutation' (Clarke 1968, p. 106). The degree and rate of loss of cultural identity is judged relative to the critical mass of the group, or to the variables of population size, density, and settlement dispersion pattern.

In the years since Clarke's statement, a number of archaeologists have analysed acculturation through a small range of material traits. Most use diachronic changes in cuisine (food preparation, consumption, disposal) as key variables (Gibbon 1972, Greenwood 1980). Others have used ideological variables related to mortuary practice or economic transactions (Ray 1978, Wells 1980). All these studies indicate that the archaeologist must remain flexible in the selection of material traits.

The archaeology of colonialism: a case study

During the last ten years a group of Yugoslav and American archaeologists have designed research through survey and excavation to understand the colonial situation in the Roman province of Meosia Superior during the 4th century AD (Fig. 10.2). This newly devised programme of investigation combines existing ethnohistoric material with archaeology relative to theoretical concerns expressed above and in greater detail elsewhere (Bartel 1985). This is the first time in Yugoslavian archaeology that such a synthetic treatment of this political problem has occurred.

This new research design for classical archaeology greatly alters the existing survey and excavation models in Yugoslavia. The shift is towards a diachronic understanding of the native populations, with the determination of which artefacts and assemblages represent self-identification markers, and how such markers may change with colonialism. Within any region of Moesia Superior the entire area must be surveyed for a constellation of patterns which may show ethnic choices. Even after a decade of this research programme, only a preliminary perspective can be offered in relation to ethnic self-identification and whether groups changed with external political control.

Moesia Superior represents an interesting test case for colonial control. Superficially, its location on the northern border of the Roman Empire combined with its great natural wealth in metal resources would orientate a researcher to believe that the Roman administration would have needed to exercise firm control over the province in order to ensure an uninterrupted supply of minerals. Stability of mineral extraction could have been combined with a political solution whereby the native populations would have been pacified to the greatest extent possible. These were the intuitive propositions we had prior to full archaeological investigation.

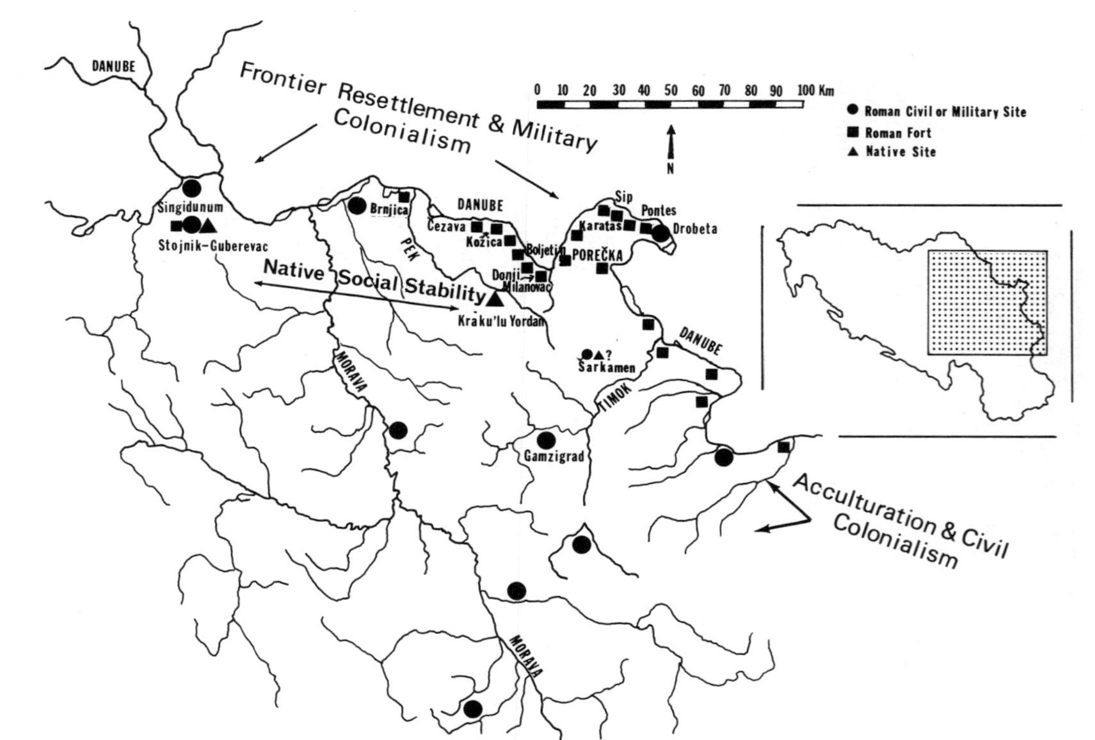

Figure 10.2 The portion of Moesia Superior discussed in the text. Only sites mentioned in the text are labelled.

Almost all of the original propositions generated during the early 1970s were found to be incorrect: excavation progressively revealed a different set of patterns in this colonial control. As stated previously (Bartel 1980), Roman control within the province took on a threefold strategy: (1) a strong colonial military presence along the northern frontier formed by the River Danube, (2) a complex strategy of colonial enclaves or weak imperialism through metallurgical production and distribution within the interior of the province, and (3) large administrative centres with a high degree of acculturation along the southern borders. In the five years since that article was published new excavation has strengthened this model.

The northern frontier zone

The Danubian northern boundary of Moesia Superior appears to have been a critical pathway for economic transportation of the provincial resources, especially metals, to the Adriatic. The southern tributaries of the Danube which flows through the province and adjacent regions, the Morava, Pek, Timok, and Porečka, were the most suitable manner of delivering resources to the Danube. Overland routes were non-existent for bulky commodities, owing to the mountainous terrain. More is known about Roman sites in the Danubian region than in the other two zones due to extensive salvage operations during the last two decades prior to the construction of hydroelectric facilities in the Iron Gorge area between Yugoslavia and Rumania.

The archaeological and historical evidence strongly indicates a Roman strategy of making this frontier boundary a secure Roman-only zone. From the time of Tiberius onward, legions were stationed on the Danube to protect against incursions by such groups as the Dacians and Sarmatians. This area of the Danube valley where the river cuts through the Carpathian mountains represents difficult terrain for both surveillance and east–west movement of troops. Any invading groups have advantages in this irregular terrain, which makes for ease of concealment and an ability to gain access to the interior through the valleys of the Danubian tributaries.

The Romans clearly understood the balance of advantages and disadvantages of this Danubian frontier zone. Beginning around AD 30 a road was constructed, approximately 130 km long, paralleling and in places overhanging the river. The road relieved the military dependence on the Danube, since the river was sometimes blocked with ice during the winter. There soon followed a series of strategically placed garrison posts. Excavation points to a starting date in the first three decades of the 1st century AD for these military installations.

Some direct archaeological evidence exists indicating removal of native populations from the Danube. At the fort site of Boljetin a combined Roman fort and cemetery was excavated (Zotović 1969). The cemetery is similar to that found at the site of Singidunum (modern Belgrade), with cremation in *pozzo* tombs. The cemetery at Boljetin, like that at Singidunum, cuts into an Iron Age habitation site dated to the 1st century AD. The settlements appear to have been deliberately cleared of artefactual or organic materials.

Archaeological survey and excavation have revealed a dense packing of military installations ranging from large garrisons to watchtowers along this northern boundary. Along with these forts such as Sip, Pontes, Drobeta, Čezava, Donji Milanovac, Karatas and Pojejena, the post-Trajanic period saw large-scale maintenance of the waterway through barge canals, dredging and road upgrades (Kondić 1974, pp. 41–53, Gudea & Bozu 1979, p. 184).

Thus it appears that the alignment of fortifications along the Danube was organized with a number of economic and social goals in mind. The geographic location coincided with the natural routing of rivers that also ran adjacent to sites of major metallurgical processing within the interior. Secondly, the Danube was in large part a frontier zone, with sometimes hostile groups across the river. So that the area could be secured, indigenous populations (Moesi, Pincenses) seem to have been resettled. Survey and excavation does not indicate that there were native settlements within the Danube corridor during most of the 3rd and 4th centuries AD. The Roman presence was functionally and symbolically reinforced by large barrier walls with towers built across the outlets of the Danubian tributaries (Petrović 1980, p. 759).

These tower and wall combinations are known from the sites of Brnjica, Kozica, and at the mouth of the Porečka river. The one at Porečka covered a distance of 450 m and was approximately 1.9 m in thickness. It remains unclear what the function of these fortifications was. The most common explanation is that they served to secure the ore resources transported by river from the interior to the Danube.

The provincial interior

Although the first evidence for Roman interest in the mineral resources of the region date to the latter part of the 1st century AD, the 4th century appears to include the greatest number of established metallurgical extraction and processing sites. Such sites include Kraku'lu Yordan in the upper Pek valley (Bartel *et al.* 1979) and the Stojnik military and civilian complex within the Mount Kosmaj district. It is within the interior of the province that we have the complex interaction between native and colonist, resulting in different social outcomes seen in the archaeological record.

Prior to Roman penetration of the interior, ethnohistorical and archaeological evidence indicates the coexistence of a number of different Illyrian-speaking groups. Recent archaeological excavation and survey indicates a surprising flexibility of control for these native populations.

In the upper Pek valley, roughly the area from the modern settlements of Šena in the north-west to Železnik in the south-east, survey indicates a general lack of true Roman settlements, roads, or military installations. The fragmentary information provided by recent survey and excavation indicates one unusual metallurgical complex known by the modern name of Kraku'lu

Yordan. The only other indication of 4th-century AD Roman activity comes from frequent finds of bricks stamped by the Legion Seventh Claudia around the modern village of Voluja (Riznić 1888, p. 33, M. Garašanin & D. Garašanin 1951, pp. 142–3), and late 19th-century visitors' reports of the remains of a Roman fort at Šena, protecting access from the north and the Danube to the series of mining complexes at Kučajna, Nerešnica, and Brodica. Thus with all of the rich metallurgical resources throughout the Pek valley, no indications exist of a Roman presence.

The site of Kraku'lu Yordan is reported in detail elsewhere (Bartel *et al.* 1979, forthcoming), but some additional comments may be made. The hilltop metallurgical complex was the site of processing activities involving iron smelting, bronze casting, and possibly gold refining. The ceramic assemblage is totally local, as are the stone and metal artefact assemblages. We have suggested a native construction, use and distribution for the site, with some sort of franchise arrangement with the Roman populations north on the Danube. Specific Pincenses ethnic markers were recovered, including fibulas, belt buckles and finger rings.

Another interior site in the process of excavation with greater potential for furthering our understanding of the social relationship between Roman and native is the Stojnik fortress near Mount Kosmaj. The site appears to have been a long-term base of operations for a mounted cohort (Dušanič 1977, p. 237). Excavations conducted at the beginning of this century at this site place it among the larger military installations in the province (200 to 250 m on a side). By comparison, all of the excavated sites along the Danube are significantly smaller. What is known about the interior architecture at Stojnik indicates a more established military presence than in the Pek valley. The original excavations exposed a large storehouse, most likely a granary (Vulić 1911, p. 288). The fort complex was also provided with heated buildings, bath structures and the usual grouping of barracks.

Of special interest for understanding social interaction is the excavation of the adjacent civilian settlement at Stojnik. Trial excavation presently underway indicates intensive lead smelting activity during the first phase of occupation. One of the most significant discoveries during the 1985 and 1986 field seasons was the large religious complex built over the area of lead smelting. A large circular structure surrounded by rectangular rooms with mosaic was excavated. The architecture and artefactual information from this complex of buildings suggests some amalgamation of function, probably of a religious nature. The results of excavation conducted during 1983–86 are still preliminary, but the range of artefacts found suggests that an opportunity will exist for testing for social identification and interaction. For example, the preliminary faunal analysis from three field seasons at Stojnik indicates a difference in species selection and age of butchering at Stojnik versus Kraku'lu Yordan. Cattle dominate at Stojnik, *ovicaprid* at Kraku'lu Yordan; subadults at Stojnik, adults at Kraku'lu Yordan (C. A. Schwartz pers. comm.).

The emerging artefactual pattern from the Stojnik civilian settlement and a necropolis of the same date a few kilometres away near the modern village of Guberevac, when combined with the information from the civilian settlement, suggests an enclave model of interaction. During the 1986 field season a number of cremation burials were excavated along with grave goods suggestive of native beliefs. Thus it is probable that although the native population was living in close proximity to the Roman fortress during the 3rd century AD, there were low levels of social interaction between the two groups.

The interior zone of Moesia Superior may have been extensively controlled through enclaves. The rationale for enclave control through minimal exposure to native populations is usually in terms of the desire for stabilized economic transactions and decreased civil administration; what amounts to a low-profile strategy. This approach allows for the most efficient control and exploitation of locations believed important (coastlines, waterways, natural resource sites), while indigenous populations are limited in cultural exposure and retain their native values. Where empires controlled vast tracts of land, as the Romans or British did, this was the only feasible approach to acquiring resources and pacifying large populations.

What is being suggested is that the indigenous Illyrian-speaking populations of Moesia Superior possessed a long tradition of metallurgy and existed in locations unsuited for large-scale agriculture or any other activity but metallurgy. For the most part they offered no social trouble to the Roman administration, and thus the Romans developed an economic relationship with them based upon metallurgical processing. In some localities, such as Kraku'lu Yordan, Roman presence was sporadic. Towards the west, in an area just south of the Danube, such as Kosmaj, a true enclave approach was established.

The southern zone

Still another social situation appears to have existed within the southern portion of Moesia Superior during the late Empire. This is characterized by the existence of a local road network, mining localities, and sites with labour-intensive architecture. The best known of these sites is the 3rd- to 4th-century locality known today as Gamzigrad. The stone walls of the site are massive, and the exterior dimensions of a late phase (early 4th century AD) are 200 by 240 m. The walls encompass numerous interior features, including one which may be for metallurgical activities (Srejović 1983, pp. 100–2, Fig. 71).

A similar site, built on a smaller scale, is located on the northern edge of the metal-rich region around the modern city of Bor. This site of Šarkamen, with internal dimensions of 90 by 90 m, dates to the early 4th century AD (Janković 1980, pp. 87, 92). No extensive excavation has taken place at the site, but the building techniques used for the walls, and the metal-processing debris at the site and adjacent to it, indicate it may be another metallurgical site combining actual metallurgical processing with an administrative function.

The southern extremities of the province appear to be characterized by still a third political strategy. Unlike the pure military situation on the Danube, the southern region has a strong Roman civilian flavour with some military sites and good Roman road networks. A tentative model for understanding the southern zone is that political control was so secure and long-lasting through a combination of metallurgy, agriculture and communication with other provinces to the south and east that native populations may have had a great tendency towards acculturation; certainly more so than in the previous two regions of the province. This southern zone has yet to be tested through an excavation strategy developed explicitly to confirm this interpretation.

Conclusion

The last ten years of research on Roman–native interaction within Moesia Superior has generated a model of colonialism characterized by administrative flexibility by the colonial power. In the region with the most important economic status, indigenous populations were resettled away from the Danube and junctures of its tributaries, and replaced with military installations. Since the region immediately south of the Danube is not suitable for large-scale agriculture, the native populations were either administratively left alone, or allowed to reside close to Roman settlements. In these enclave situations, acculturation levels appear to have been low. Finally, the southern limits of the province contained a strong administrative and military Roman presence, and the degree of acculturation by the native populations may have been high.

The validity of these conclusions will be tested by new excavation and survey at the Stojnik site, along with new excavation programmes for the periods before and after Roman intervention.

Acknowledgements

The research at the site of Kraku'lu Yordan was supported by a grant from the National Science Foundation (BNS 76–10174). The project was under the direction of Bartel, Kondić, and Werner. The research at the Stojnik-Kosmaj sites is supported by grants from the United States Department of State/Smithsonian Institution Foreign Currency Program and the Center for Field Research. The project is under the direction of Kondić and Werner, with the author serving as research consultant.

References

Bartel, B. 1980. Colonialism and cultural responses: problems related to Roman provincial analysis. *World Archaeology* **12**, 11–26.

Bartel, B. 1985. Comparative historical archaeology and archaeological theory. In *Comparative studies in the archaeology of colonialism*, S. L. Dyson (ed.), 8–37. British Archaeological Reports International Series 233, Oxford.

Bartel, B., V. Kondić, & M. R. Werner 1979. Excavations at Kraku'lu Yordan, northeast Serbia: preliminary report, 1973–76 seasons. *Journal of Field Archaeology* **6**, 127–49.

Bartel, B., V. Kondić, & M. R. Werner forthcoming. *Roman and native in Moesia Superior*. British Archaeological Reports International Series, Oxford.

Barth, F. (ed.) 1969. *Ethnic groups and boundaries*. Boston: Little, Brown.

Beidelman, T. O. 1982. *Colonial evangelism: a socio-historical study of an east African mission at the grassroots*. Bloomington: Indiana University Press.

Clarke, D. L. 1968. *Analytical archaeology*. London: Methuen.

DeVos, G. & L. Romanucci-Ross (eds) 1975. *Ethnic identity: cultural continuities and change*. Palo Alto: Mayfield.

Doornbus, M. 1972. Some conceptual problems concerning ethnicity in integration analysis. *Civilizations* **22**, 263–84.

Dušanić, S. 1977. Mounted cohorts in Moesia Superior. In *Limes Akten den XI Internationalen Limeskongresses*, J. Fitz (ed.), 237–47. Budapest: Akademiai Kiado.

Garašanin, M. & D. Garašanin 1951. *Arheoloska Nalaziste u Srbiji*. Belgrade: Arheološki Institut.

Gibbon, G. E. 1972. Cultural dynamics and the development of the Oneota life-way in Wisconsin. *American Antiquity* **37**, 166–85.

Gillin, J. & V. Raimy 1940. Acculturation and personality. *American Sociological Review* **5**, 371–80.

Greenwood, R. A. 1980. The Chinese on main street. In *Archaeological perspectives on ethnicity in America*, R. L. Schuyler (ed.), 113–23. Farmingdale: Baywood.

Gudea, N. & O. Bozu 1979. Report preliminar asupra sapaturilor arheologice executate la castrul Roman de la Pojejena in Anii 1977–1978. *Banatica* **8**, 181–5.

Herskovits, M. J. 1938. *Acculturation: the study of culture contact*. New York: J. J. Augustin.

Hodder, I. 1977. Distribution of material culture in the Baringo district, western Kenya. *Man* **12**, 239–69.

Hodder, I. 1978. Social organization and human interaction: the development of some tentative hypotheses in terms of material culture. In *The spatial organization of culture*, I. Hodder (ed.), 199–269. London: Duckworth.

Hodder, I. 1979. Economic and social stress and material culture patterning. *American Antiquity* **44**, 446–54.

Hodder, I. 1982. *Symbols in action: ethnoarchaeological studies of material culture*. Cambridge: Cambridge University Press.

Ianni, F. A. 1958. Time and place as variables in acculturation research. *American Anthropologist* **60**, 39–46.

Janković, D. 1980. Istraživanje spomenika u Vrelu, Šarkamen. *Starinar* **31**, 87–93.

Kamp, K. A. & N. Yoffee 1981. Ethnicity in ancient western Asia during the early second millennium B.C.: archaeological assessments and ethnoarchaeological perspectives. *Bulletin of the American School for Oriental Research* **237**, 85–104.

Keyes, C. F. (ed.) 1981. *Ethnic change*. Seattle: University of Washington Press.

Kondić, V. 1974. Ergebnisse der neuen Forschungen auf dem obermoesischen Donaulimes. In *Actes du IXe Congrès International d'Etudes sur les Frontières Romaines*, D. M. Pippidi (ed.), 39–54. Bucharest: Editura Academiei.

Kramer, C. 1985. Ceramic ethnoarchaeology. In *Annual Review of Anthropology*, B. J. Siegal, A. R. Beals & S. A. Tyler (eds), 77–102. Palo Alto: Annual Reviews.

Linton, R. 1940. *Acculturation in seven American Indian tribes*. New York: Appleton Century.

Lyman, S. M. & W. A. Douglass 1973. Ethnicity: strategies of collective and individual impression management. *Social Research* **40**, 344–65.

McGuire, R. H. 1982. The study of ethnicity in historical archaeology. *Journal of Anthropological Archaeology* **1**, 159–78.

Mannoni, D. 1956. *Prospero and Caliban: the psychology of colonization* (translated by P. Powesland). London: Methuen.

Millon, R. 1974. The study of urbanism at Teotihuacan, Mexico. In *Mesoamerican archaeology: new approaches*, N. Hammond (ed.), 335–63. Austin: University of Texas Press.

Okely, J. 1979. An anthropological contribution to the history and archaeology of an ethnic group. In *Space, hierarchy and society*, B. C. Burnham & J. Kingsbury (eds), 81–92. British Archaeological Reports International Series 59, Oxford.

Petrović, P. 1980. O snabdevanju rimskih trupa na djerdapskom limesu. *Starinar* **31**, 53–63.

Phillipson, D. W. 1979. Migration, ethnic differentiation and state formation in the Iron Age of Bantu Africa. In *Space, hierarchy and society*, B. C. Burnham & J. Kingsbury (eds), 205–14. British Archaeological Reports International Series 59, Oxford.

Ray, A. J. 1978. History and archaeology of the northern fur trade. *American antiquity* **43**, 26–34.

Redfield, R., R. Linton & M. J. Herskovits 1936. Memorandum for the study of acculturation. *American Anthropologist* **38**, 149–52.

Riznić, M. 1888. Starinski ostaci u srežu žviskom. *Starinar* **5**, 31–9, 54–62.

Royce, A. P. 1982. *Ethnic identity: strategies of diversity*. Bloomington: Indiana University Press.

Spencer, P. 1978. Three types of ethnic interaction among Masai-speaking people in east Africa. In *Space, hierarchy and society*, B. C. Burnham & J. Kingsbury (eds), 195–204. British Archaeological Reports International Series 59, Oxford.

Spiro, M. E. 1955. The acculturation of American ethnic groups. *American Anthropologist* **57**, 1240–52.

Srejović, D. 1983. *Gamzigrad: kasnoantiči carski dvorac*. Belgrade: Arheološki Institut.

Vulić, N. 1911. Izveštaj o otkopavanju rimskog kastela u Stojniku godine 1911. *Godisnjak Srpske Kraljevske Akademije (Belgrade)* **25**, 285–93.

Wells, P. S. 1980. *Culture contact and culture change: Early Iron Age central Europe and the Mediterranean world*. Cambridge: Cambridge University Press.

Zotović, L. 1969. Boljetin, Lepena kod Karaule: rimska nekropola spaljenih pokojnika. *Arheoloski Pregled* **11**, 114–18.

11 *Native American acculturation in the Spanish colonial empire: the Franciscan missions of Alta California*

PAUL FARNSWORTH

Introduction

In 1769 the Spanish occupied Alta California and began the construction of a chain of Franciscan missions which would ultimately stretch approximately 500 miles from San Diego Bay in the south, to beyond San Francisco Bay in the north (Fig. 11.1). The missions were built to convert and civilize the Native Americans who lived along the California coast. Their impact was both dramatic and devastating. Indians entering the missions were exposed both to a completely foreign culture and to diseases to which they had no resistance. Cultural change and death came hand in hand. By the time the missions were secularized in 1834, the Indians had been decimated. Those who survived had lost their traditional culture in the missions, and had to adapt to a world with ever-increasing European influences. Historical archaeologists are attempting to understand the changes which occurred in the missions, the processes involved, and the degree to which Indian culture may have survived. This chapter provides an overview of the cultural contact between the Spanish and the California Indians, and examines archaeological approaches which are being used to gain a better understanding of native American acculturation in the Franciscan missions of Alta California.

The California Indians[1]

The California Indians were hunters and gatherers, and, unlike most of the peoples in the New World, they did not practise agriculture. Their staple food was the acorn. Many species of oak flourished throughout the state, and acorns, when ground into a fine powder, leached to remove the harmful, bitter-tasting tannin, and then cooked into a mush, provided a highly nutritious food. This was supplemented by a wide variety of seeds and game. Acorns and other seeds would also be stored for those times of the year when resources became limited.

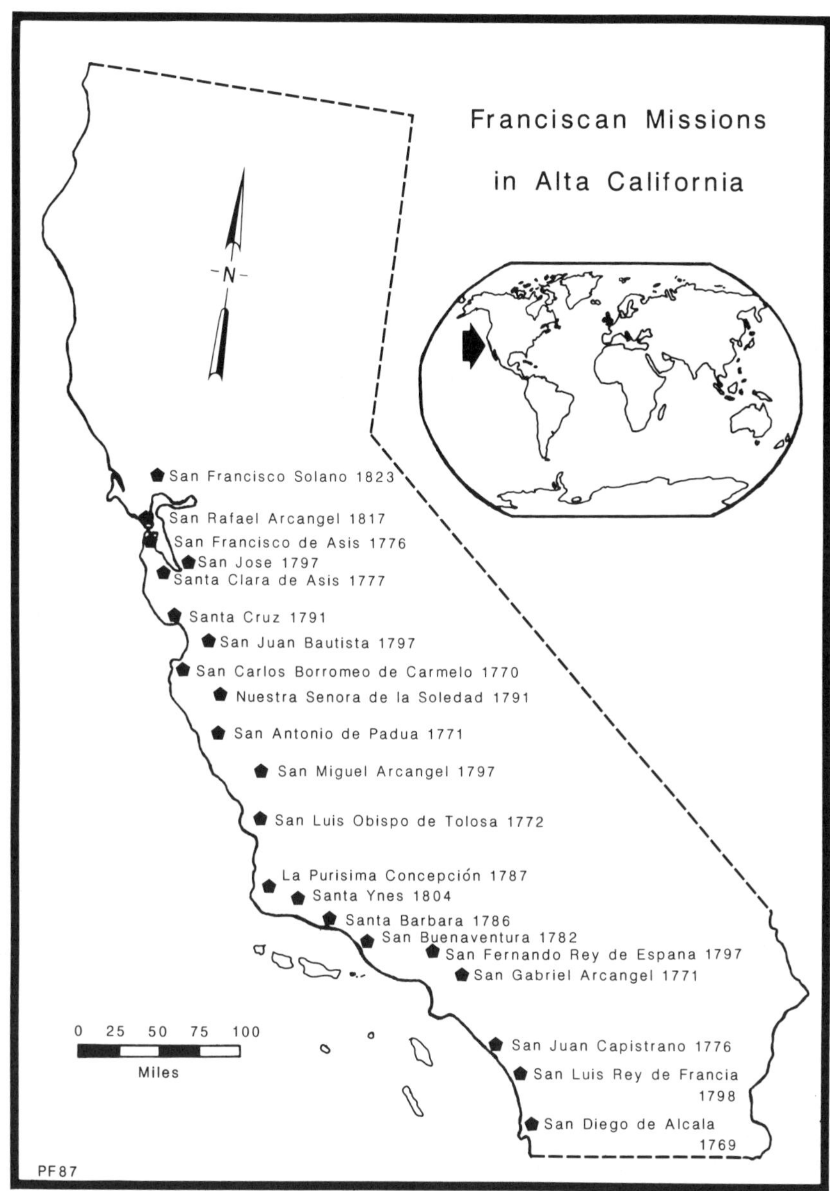

Figure 11.1 Map showing the locations and dates of founding of the Franciscan missions in Alta California.

By employing a seasonal round, the Indians were able to use a variety of ecological zones, usually returning to the same desirable locations once or twice each year. The seasonal round was usually limited to one watershed, and most California Indians never ventured more than 50 miles from their birthplace.

On the coast, the use of marine resources enabled a more settled existence to develop. Many marine resources are also seasonal, but they can be obtained from one coastal location. As a result, the largest and most permanent settlements developed along the California coast.

In inland areas, rivers, especially those that flowed all year, presented another resource zone that could supplement terrestrial resources. In Northern California, the Central Valley, and the Delta area, large populations developed because of the resources available in the rivers and marshes. In these areas, where the ocean or a major river provided a more constant supply of food, year-round settlements developed, though small groups of Indians would leave for a few weeks at a time to use other resources.

The non-sedentary nature of the California Indians' life clearly affected their material culture. They had little use for objects that could not be carried easily from place to place, or which could not be quickly replaced in the new location. For example, baskets were made that would hold anything a pot could, including water, and were even used for cooking. Baskets were much easier and lighter to carry than heavy, and comparatively fragile, pottery; only those living in Southern California made pottery, and that was a recent development.

Similarly, there was no need for a permanent dwelling that took a great deal of time and effort to construct, when in a few weeks or months it would be abandoned. A hut made of branches and brush, or of reeds, was just as serviceable and could be made in half a day.

The California Indians had no knowledge of metalworking. All their tools were manufactured from materials available in the environment. Reeds, grasses, wood, bone, antler, shell, and stone were all used to make tools. Debitage from the manufacture of stone tools is the most numerous 'artefact type', recovered at almost every archaeological site. Knives, scrapers, projectile points, mortars, and pestles were just some of the stone implements used by the Indians.

The village was the major unit of social organization. There was rarely a larger political unit than a group of two or three villages (or tribelet) and the term 'tribe', when applied to California, refers not to a political unit, but rather to a group sharing the same language and displaying a degree of cultural homogeneity.

Belief systems varied considerably from tribe to tribe, but all were shamanistic with a pantheon of sacred characters. The belief system was central to all aspects of life, and controlled every activity. The shaman, him- or herself, was regarded as extremely powerful, although every individual had some religious power of his or her own, which could be increased by certain activities. Increasing personal power enhanced status within the group.

Leadership was a separate rôle from that of the shaman, and did not bring the kind of power over others that existed in many societies. The head of the tribelet settled disputes and, in consultation with other respected elders, made decisions such as when and where to move to use fresh resources. But if enough people were dissatisfied with his decisions, a new leader would be chosen. The new leader could be any man of suitable standing in the group, and, although certain families may have retained the leadership between them, there was not usually direct inheritance of leadership from father to son.

The Spanish in Alta California[2]

California had been discovered, and the entire coast explored, by Juan Rodriguez Cabrillo in 1542. However, the colonization of California by sea proved impossible in the 16th century, with voyages hindered by wind and current directions, and violent storms. Not until 1769 did Spain take the first steps towards occupying California. This was not to be a province founded by bold conquistadores in search of gold, silver, and other untold riches, but a religious mission. Franciscan missionaries were going to convert the peaceful California Indians to the 'true faith' by drawing them into a chain of missions throughout the coastal province of California. The Indians would emerge from the missions as loyal Spanish subjects to populate the new province.

Eventually 21 missions were founded in Alta California (Fig. 11.1). The first mission was founded in 1769 in San Diego, and the second, in 1770, was in Monterey, which was to become the provincial capital. With the founding of the sixth mission in 1776, in San Francisco, the Spanish brought under control the entire section of the coast they were to occupy. Thereafter, it was a process of filling in the gaps between the earlier missions to ensure complete control of the coastal groups of California Indians.

However, although the Indians were attracted to the missions, they did not adapt well to life in them. The dramatic changes demanded of them, from hunter-gatherer to agriculturalist, from 'heathen' to strict Catholic, from one culture to a completely different one, proved to be too great. Progress was much slower than had been anticipated, and the Indians died at an alarming rate from the diseases the Spanish unwittingly brought with them. Only an influx of fresh neophytes, as the mission Indians were called, could maintain and increase the missions' population. As all the Indians in the area around each mission were drawn in, the padres looked further afield for their converts. Indians came, or were brought, from outside the Spanish province, in particular from the Central Valley of California. Nonetheless, the population of the missions never stabilized, and experienced a gradual decline.

In spite of these problems, the missions were a tremendous economic success. They rapidly became self-sufficient in most basic commodities, producing wool, leather, tallow, beef, wheat, maize, and barley. Surpluses were supplied to the military, civilians, and exported to Mexico to pay for manufactured goods that could not be produced in the province. After 1790, an illicit trade, mostly in hides and tallow, developed for manufactured goods with foreign, predominantly English, vessels. Smuggling grew steadily as supplies from Mexico became more unreliable, until the revolution in Mexico cut off California's only legal source of supplies after 1810, and Mexican independence in 1821 brought the opening of California's ports to foreign traders.

This foreign trade, both the earlier illicit and the more recently legalized, stimulated the economic aspects of the missions at the same time as their acculturative rôle was declining with the deaths of the local Indians. The missions owned vast lands in California, had a large labour force, which was regularly augmented by Indians brought from the Central Valley, and were able to produce and ship thousands of hides. The legalized hide and tallow trade was dominated by Yankee traders who exchanged manufactured goods from both England and the United States for the raw materials needed by the growing industrial nations (Hornbeck 1983, p. 56).

The changing emphasis from religious to economic goals led to direct competition with the civilian population of the province. The missions occupied most of the land in the province, and if the civilian population was going to benefit from the growing trade, it would need to gain control of the missions' land. This was achieved through secularization. Ostensibly, this was returning the land to the Indians, creating a *pueblo* (town) from the mission. However, in reality, land was transferred to the Spanish civilian population and divided into *ranchos*.

The Indians were left to fend for themselves. Some remained at the decaying missions, while others attempted to return to their former way of life, usually unsuccessfully. Most, however, were absorbed into the *ranchos*, forming the labour force on which the *ranchos* depended.

The Franciscan missions

While the details varied from mission to mission, the permanent structures were usually built around a central quadrangle, with the church forming part or all of one side. The padres' quarters were usually adjacent to the church, and the unmarried neophyte women's quarters were next to them. The remaining buildings housed guest rooms, a carpenter's shop, a granary, a weaving workshop, a kitchen, and various storerooms. The basic building material for all of these structures was adobe (sun-dried mud brick). The bricks were made close to the new construction, and required no kiln. Many roofs were thatched, but most of the major buildings, especially the central quadrangle, were roofed with terracotta tiles made at the mission itself. Walls were usually given a mud or lime plaster coating, and were sometimes whitewashed, especially externally. Water was the major hazard with this construction method, so walls were based on rock foundations to raise them above ground level, while the whitewash and plaster gave protection from rain. As long as the roof was sound, the building would last for centuries, as some indeed have.

The central courtyard was a work area, not a garden as many have today, and might have contained an olive mill and press, a wine press, threshing floors, an animal-powered mill, bread ovens, and frequently a well. Many other structures were located just outside the central quadrangle. Typically, these include Indian dormitories for the mission's neophyte population (except the unmarried women); soldiers' quarters for the small military detachment (usually around five soldiers) that was stationed at each mission; stables for both military animals and the mission's own stock; a forge; a grist mill; tanning vats; soap and tallow vats; threshing floors; tile kilns; and, perhaps, a pottery and kiln (if the mission made its own pottery).

In addition, there were many elements of the mission's complex aqueduct and irrigation system, including water reservoirs, settling tanks, a filter house, washing features, the aqueducts themselves, drainage, and irrigation ditches. Some of these aqueducts ran through the central quadrangle, while others served the industrial zone, the living quarters, the garden, the orchard, the vineyard, and the fields. The irrigation system stretched over incredible distances, and usually included one or more dams to collect and store water.

Close to the central complex was the mission's vegetable garden, orchard, and probably, vineyard. Each was protected from stray animals by either a wall or a cactus hedge, and included a house for the gardener, orchardist, or vineyardist, respectively.

Slightly further away were the fields where the mission's main crops were grown, wheat and corn being the staples. In California, irrigation is essential to the success of these crops, and this limited the areas that could be planted.

Some distance away from the central complex were the vast herds of cattle and sheep that the mission possessed. These roamed free over the mission's territory, often mixing with the herds of the adjacent missions. The Indians who tended these herds frequently could not return to the central complex at night because the distances were too great. Instead, the mission established separate *ranchos* for these Indians. If the distance was so great that it was not possible for these Indians to come to church, then the *rancho* would include its own chapel, becoming an assistant mission, or *assistencia*.

This permanent, centralized, and highly structured settlement pattern contrasted sharply with the temporary, mobile, dispersed settlement pattern of the Indians before Spanish contact. The Indians' life in the mission was also dramatically different. Instead of learning to perform all tasks necessary for life, the Indian was taught to specialize in agriculture, animal husbandry, carpentry, smithing, tanning, or tile making, etc. Women were taught the 'proper' Spanish way of cooking, weaving, and so forth. Even children experienced dramatic changes, as they, too, were expected to work in the fields, the kitchen, or anywhere else they could be useful. They were taught Spanish, the rudiments of reading and writing, and, of course, the Catholic faith. All of the neophytes were taught the basics of the Catholic faith and the Spanish language, but greater emphasis was placed on educating the children.

The mission also imposed strict Catholic morality on the Indians, and the padres suppressed any elements of the prehistoric religious belief system that manifested themselves. No attempt was made to incorporate the Indians' existing political structure into the missions, and rank and social status were determined by the padres.

The Indians who adapted well to the mission environment and learned the skills taught by the Spanish were rewarded by being made overseers, or *alcaldes*. Punishment for those who broke the mission's rules could be harsh, and was usually physical, just as it was in 18th-century Europe. It was usually carried out by the *alcaldes*, or, at the request of the padre, by the soldiers.

The congregation of once-scattered Indian populations at one location facilitated the spread among them of contagious diseases accidentally introduced by the Spanish. With European medical knowledge that had not improved greatly since the Middle Ages, the Franciscan padres were frequently in despair over the high mortality rate at the missions. The only major success was the control of smallpox by the use of variolation techniques (Little & Hoover n.d.). Diseases such as measles, pneumonia, diphtheria, typhoid, dysentery, tuberculosis, and syphilis all took a heavy toll (Cook 1976, p. 13).

Native American acculturation

Although the reasons for occupying California were economic, the means of control of the Indian population, and the method by which it might ultimately become economically productive, was through acculturation. Thus, the basic rôle of the California missions was to create a productive, Spanish peasant society from the California Indians.

Acculturation studies have been a major anthropological theme for many years, resulting in a voluminous literature on the subject. The Social Science Research Council Summer Seminar in 1953 focused on the subject of acculturation. The resulting publication (Broom *et al.* 1954, p. 974) defines acculturation as ' . . . culture change that is initiated by the conjunction of two or more autonomous cultural systems'. It is important to note that this is a two-way process, and not just one-way as is so often assumed to be the case. This publication also provides a useful framework for considering any acculturative situation. Therefore, the contact between the Spanish and the California Indians in the missions was analyzed using this anthropological model of acculturation (Broom *et al.* 1954) to define the important factors of the contact situation (Farnsworth 1987).

Four major facets of acculturation were defined in the anthropological analysis: (1) characterization of the autonomous cultural systems in contact; (2) the nature of the contact situation; (3) analysis of the conjunctive relations between the systems; and (4) the cultural processes that flow from the conjunction of the systems (Broom *et al.* 1954, p. 975). Certain aspects of each of these four facets were defined as being of major importance in the study of acculturation.

It was apparent that the documentary evidence allowed the examination of the nature of the cultural systems, the contact situation, and the conjunctive relations. However, there were many questions which could not be answered about the acculturative processes which operated between the two cultures, and the results that they produced.

Historical archaeology offers a means of answering some of these questions, and of testing the information derived from the documentary evidence. There has been relatively little historical-archaeological investigation of the processes of acculturation in North America, whether on the East Coast or in the areas that once comprised New Spain. Where research has been carried out in recent years, the situations were very different from those found in the missions of Spanish California. Therefore, these studies do not provide much useful comparative information, as major elements do not apply to California. For example, a heavy emphasis is found on the changes in Indian ceramic styles and distributions in contact-period sites. However, in California, most of the Indians did not produce ceramics prior to European contact.

Although major elements of the limited comparative database do not apply to California, some of the techniques used to analyse archaeological assemblages from the perspective of acculturation may be useful there. However, analysis has proceeded along the usual archaeological classificatory lines, with classifications based first on material, and then on form and function. Individual artefacts that are characteristically Indian, in European sites, or European, in Indian sites, have been singled out for more detailed description. In addition, new forms of artefacts that have resulted from contact have also been singled out for special description. These oddities in the archaeological assemblage have then been related to the ethnohistoric literature to illustrate the changes which occurred. The bulk of the assemblage, which is not extraordinary, has merely been described with some comments about how the rest of the culture remained unaffected.

One classification system has been designed specifically for the study of acculturation and material culture. This was produced by Quimby and Spoehr (1951) for the analysis of museum collections. This system had seven groups, the first four being for artefacts new to the area, and the second three groups for prehistoric forms modified by contact. Using this typology,

Quimby and Spoehr (1951, pp. 146–7) surveyed the collections of the Chicago Natural History Museum.

Quimby (1960, p. 416) later suggested that this typology can be used for elements that are lost from the culture, as well as new elements that are added to it. In addition, he discussed how, by comparing the cultural traits from a culture at one time-period with those from the same culture at a subsequent time-period, a rate of cultural change could be calculated in terms of the number of cultural traits gained or lost per unit of time. Thus, a quantification of both the rate of change and the amount of change between two periods would be obtained.

Although neither Quimby & Spoehr (1951) nor Quimby (1960) were applied to archaeological assemblages, they present approaches that could have considerable utility in archaeological analysis of contact situations. Hoover and Costello (1985, pp. 118–19) have used the typology of Quimby & Spoehr (1951) as a framework for some of their conclusions about acculturation in the Indian dormitory at Mission San Antonio de Padua (Fig. 11.1). However, much of their discussion draws upon evidence from the California missions as a whole, and the discussion is again based on unusual, illustrative artefacts.

A different approach was adopted by Deetz (1963, p. 186), who in his analysis of materials from Mission La Purisima Concepción (Fig. 11.1) compared them with the assemblage from an Indian midden site in the area, which dated from the Spanish period. By comparing the numbers of artefacts in each class, defined in terms of material such as chipped stone, shell beads, steatite, iron, copper, and earthenware, he was able to show that at the mission there was greater acculturation occurring in male than in female activities. He also discusses the dramatic replacement of traditionally-used materials by European materials at the mission.

It may also be useful to analyse assemblages from the California missions in terms of the functional approach used by Di Peso (1974) in his analysis of artefacts recovered from Mission San Antonio de Casas Grandes (Chihuahua, Northern Mexico). The entire assemblage was divided into seven functional categories: personal adornment; builders' tools and hardware; weavers' tools; socio-religious goods; food preparation and serving; horse culture; and warfare and hunting (Di Peso 1974, p. 916). The contribution of artefacts from each of the two cultures (the Spanish donor and the Indian recipient) in each category was then calculated, both as a percentage of the total number of artefacts from that culture in the assemblage, and as a percentage of the artefacts in that category (Di Peso 1974, pp. 916–19).

Using this analysis, Di Peso was able to illustrate the nature of Spanish control from the artefact assemblage, and show important differences in the contribution of each cultural group to the entire assemblage. Unfortunately, Di Peso only examined his entire assemblage, and did not carry out this analysis on the assemblages from just the Indian dwellings or just the padres' quarters, which could have revealed significant differences. In addition, there is an implicit assumption throughout his analysis that only Indians used traditional Indian artefacts, and vice versa. Finally, this analytical system has no place for the artefacts that are not directly from either cultural system. These are the artefacts which Quimby and Spoehr (1951) so carefully classified. Di Peso (1974) solved this problem by including them with whichever culture he believed used the modified form at the mission. Di Peso's acculturation model is Spanish donor to Indian recipient, thus excluding any Indian-to-Spanish cultural transmission. Hence, there cannot have been any Spanish cultural change, and this invariably meant including these artefacts with the Indian assemblage.

In spite of the problems with the application of Di Peso's analysis, the approach showed considerable promise. Unfortunately, Di Peso used categories which were too site-specific for use on sites in other contexts, in particular for use in California.

What is required is a method of analysis that divides artefact assemblages into functional groups, so that changes within them can be studied, and yet provides a method for putting the assemblages back together to enable comparisons to be made between assemblages. The basis of such an analytical system already exists in the literature of historical archaeology, although it was not designed for the purpose of studying acculturation. This is the method of artefact pattern analysis first published by South (1977). This analytical tool deals with entire assemblages and functional groups within them. In addition, the functional groups are divided into artefact classes, which provide an analytical level suitable for studying acculturation within each group (Table 11.1).

There are a few minor differences between the list in Table 11.1 and that first proposed by South. Some of these changes have also been made by other researchers (Garrow 1981, Armstrong 1983, Deagan 1983). The result is a flexible system that can be adapted to a wide range of archaeological situations.

Artefact group analysis

Table 11.2 shows the pattern from the Indian neophytes' barracks at Mission San Antonio de Padua, which dates from approximately 1810, and was excavated by Hoover and Costello (1985). Table 11.2 also shows the pattern from the Indian neophytes' barracks at Mission La Purisima Concepción, which dates from the 1820s, and was excavated by Deetz (1963). The patterns from the neophytes at Mission La Purisima and Mission San Antonio are similar. The principal differences are more clothing-related artefacts, and fewer activities artefacts at La Purisima. Both share low percentages in the other groups, including the architectural group, which is due to the use of adobe construction.

Table 11.2 also shows the assemblage from a higher-status room at Mission San Antonio excavated by Hoover and Costello (1985). There is very little difference between this higher-status and the neophytes' assemblages. The principal difference is in the clothing group. An assemblage

Table 11.1 Groups and classes used in artefact pattern analysis.

Kitchen Group	*Personal Group*
Imported ceramics	Coins
Locally-made earthenwares	Keys
Wine bottles	Personal items
Case bottles	
Pharmaceutical bottles	*Tobacco Pipe Group*
Unidentified bottles	Tobacco pipes
Glassware	Stub-stemmed pipes
Tumblers	
Unidentified glass	*Activities Group*
Tableware	Construction tools
Kitchenwares	Farm tools
	Toys
Architectural Group	Fishing gear
Window glass	Storage items
Nails	Stable & barn
Spikes	Miscellaneous hardware
Construction hardware	Military objects
Door-lock parts	Lithic manufacture
	Used flakes
Furniture Group	Flaked-stone tools
Furniture hardware	Heat-glazed rocks
	Fire-cracked rocks
Arms Group	Industrial waste products
Musket balls, shot, & sprue	Tile wasters
Gunflints	Power objects
Gun parts & bullet moulds	Other activities
Other arms	
Clothing Group	
Buckles	
Thimbles	
Buttons	
Scissors	
Straight pins & needles	
Hook & eye fasteners	
Bale seals	
Shell, bone, & stone beads	
Glass beads	

from the European/*mestizo* rooms at La Purisima, also excavated by Deetz (1963) (Table 11.2), is dramatically different from the other assemblages. There is a significant increase in kitchen and activity group artefacts, and a big decrease in the clothing group.

The similarity between both the neophytes' assemblages and the higher-status assemblage from San Antonio suggests that chronological, functional,

Table 11.2 Analysis of five assemblages from California mission excavations, showing the percentage of artefacts in each group.

Artefact group	San Antonio neophytes	La Purisima neophytes	San Antonio higher-status	La Purisima European/ *mestizo*	La Soledad kitchen
Kitchen	38.7	36.7	36.1	50.0	59.0
Architectural	2.6	4.4	4.9	9.0	5.7
Furniture	0.0	0.0	0.0	0.0	0.0
Arms	2.6	1.1	0.0	0.0	0.0
Clothing	27.7	40.0	32.8	7.0	11.0
Personal	1.3	1.1	0.0	2.0	0.5
Tobacco pipe	0.0	0.0	0.0	0.0	0.0
Activities	27.1	16.7	26.2	32.0	23.8
Total	100.0%	100.0%	100.0%	100.0%	100.0%

economic, or status factors are not responsible for the big difference between these and the assemblage from the European/*mestizo* rooms at La Purisima, leaving cultural differences as the most likely explanation. The occupant of the higher-status room at San Antonio was almost certainly an Indian and the occupant of the La Purisima rooms was either a *mestizo* or more likely a European. Hence, an increased emphasis on the kitchen group may be a feature of European rather than Indian assemblages.

The kitchen at Mission Nuestra Señora de la Soledad (Fig. 11.1) excavated by the author in 1984, and dating to the end of the first decade of the 19th century (Table 11.2), is quite different from the neophytes' or higher-status assemblages from Mission San Antonio de Padua. It most resembles the European/*mestizo* assemblage from La Purisima, but the documentary evidence reveals that the kitchen workers were Indians. As would be expected, the assemblage has an even higher percentage of kitchen group artefacts, and a lower percentage in the activities group. This is due to the functional differences between the origins of this and the other assemblages.

Analysis of the assemblages from Missions La Purisima Concepción and San Antonio de Padua revealed considerable similarity in assemblages from identical functional areas and cultures, but from different times, locations, and even social status. In addition, this analysis showed that when the cultural affiliation was different, the assemblage also differed, as long as the functional origin did not change. However, this level of analysis is principally sensitive to functional change, as shown by the kitchen at Mission Soledad, and secondarily to cultural origin. It does not appear to be sufficiently sensitive to cultural changes to enable them to be reliably distinguished from the effects of other variables.

Table 11.3 Analysis of the kitchen group in five assemblages from California mission excavations, showing the percentage of artefacts in each class.

Artefact group	San Antonio neophytes	La Purisima neophytes	San Antonio higher-status	La Purisima European/ *mestizo*	La Soledad kitchen
Imported ceramics	10.3	16.7	23.0	15.0	32.9
Locally-made earthenwares	13.5	0.0	3.3	1.0	0.5
Wine bottles	0.0	0.0	0.0	0.0	7.6
Case bottles	0.0	0.0	0.0	0.0	0.0
Pharmaceutical bottles	0.0	0.0	0.0	0.0	0.0
Unidentified bottles	5.8	1.1	1.6	6.0	1.0
Glassware	0.0	1.1	0.0	0.0	1.0
Tumblers	0.0	0.0	0.0	0.0	0.0
Unidentified glass	1.9	10.0	1.6	9.0	0.0
Tableware	2.6	0.0	1.6	1.0	0.0
Kitchenwares	4.5	7.8	4.9	18.0	16.2
*Total**	38.6%	36.7%	36.0%	50.0%	59.2%

*Differences between these totals and those in the artefact group analysis are due to the effects of rounding the figures off to one decimal place.

Artefact class analysis

The preceding analysis does not reflect significant changes that occurred within each functional group. Therefore, it would appear to be critical to analyse each of the different artefact classes in each functional group and compare them between assemblages, to reveal the differences due mainly to acculturation as well as other factors. However, for the California mission assemblages, only the kitchen, clothing, and activities groups consistently contained sufficient numbers of artefacts to make this a viable proposition.

THE KITCHEN GROUP

The kitchen group forms the majority of most of the assemblages discussed here. Table 11.3 shows the kitchen group artefact classes from the neophytes at Missions San Antonio de Padua and La Purisima Concepción. It is apparent that the similarity between the total percentages masks considerable differences within the functional group. The neophytes at Mission San Antonio had much greater access to locally-made earthenwares, while it appears that the Indians at La Purisima had greater access to, or preferred to use, imported goods, as the percentage of imported ceramics and glass is higher. This may suggest greater acculturation, but the higher percentage of traditional kitchenwares argues against this. It is more likely that this reflects the greater availability of imported goods in the 1820s, and greater wealth of Mission La Purisima at that time.

It was also possible to compare female acculturation in the kitchen group for these assemblages. Both had similar percentages of kitchen group artefacts, but the San Antonio assemblage contained under 5% traditional Indian kitchen group items, compared to approximately 8% at La Purisima. This indicates less female acculturation at La Purisima.

The higher-status room at Mission San Antonio (Table 11.3) also contained a similar total percentage of kitchen group artefacts. There is a much higher percentage of imported ceramics and fewer locally-made earthenwares in comparison to the adjacent neophytes' rooms. The percentage of glass artefacts is lower, while the percentage of kitchenwares is about the same. Thus, it appears that higher status is reflected in greater quantities of imported ceramics, perhaps as a reflection of greater access to imported goods. However, the decrease in glass contradicts the predicted trend. The continuity of kitchenwares may reflect the racial origin of this individual, who is believed to have been an Indian.

The European/*mestizo* room at Mission La Purisima (Table 11.3) is not as strikingly different from the neophytes' rooms at the same mission as would be predicted. There is a slight decrease in imported ceramics, compensated for by a small percentage of locally-made earthenwares, and more glass. However, the major change is a doubling in the percentage of kitchenwares, much of this being due to the use of traditional Indian artefacts. This may be a reflection of the cultural background of this higher-status individual, who is clearly different from the higher-status individual at Mission San Antonio, but still uses many traditional Indian items for food preparation.

Two explanations are possible. The first is that this individual is a *mestizo*, not a European, for the greatest element of cultural conservatism is in food preparation techniques. The second possibility is that these rooms were occupied by a married couple, not just one individual, a European or *mestizo* man and his Indian wife. This was not an uncommon situation, as many Mexican soldiers and servants who came to California took Indian wives. Thus, in food preparation, a female activity, Indian artefacts were used, but in serving and consumption, imported items of a European nature were used.

The assemblage from the kitchen at Mission Soledad (Table 11.3) conforms to the pattern which would be predicted. The percentage of imported ceramics is higher than for any of the assemblages at Missions San Antonio and La Purisima. The percentage of kitchenwares is approximately equal to that in the European or *mestizo*'s rooms at La Purisima, but considerably exceeds that of the other assemblages. The percentages of glass bottles is also higher than in any of the other assemblages, although the total percentage of glass artefacts is less than in both of the later assemblages from La Purisima. This provides further confirmation that the total percentage of glass in these

Table 11.4 Analysis of the clothing group in five assemblages from California mission excavations, showing the percentage of artefacts in each class.

Artefact group	San Antonio neophytes	La Purisima neophytes	San Antonio higher-status	La Purisima European/ *mestizo*	La Soledad kitchen
Buckles	0.0	0.0	0.0	1.0	0.0
Thimbles	0.0	0.0	0.0	0.0	0.0
Buttons	2.6	1.1	1.6	0.0	0.0
Scissors	0.6	1.1	0.0	0.0	0.0
Straight pins & needles	0.6	0.0	0.0	0.0	0.0
Hook & eye fasteners	0.0	0.0	0.0	0.0	0.0
Bale seals	0.0	0.0	0.0	0.0	0.0
Shell, bone, & stone beads	5.2	16.7	6.6	1.0	0.5
Glass beads	18.7	21.1	24.6	5.0	10.5
Total	27.7%	40.0%	32.8%	7.0%	11.0%

assemblages is directly related to its availability through foreign trade, which increases considerably in the 1820s. Overall, this analysis confirms the identification of the room, based on its architectural features, as a kitchen, and indicates that a blend of Indian and Spanish food preparation techniques were in use.

THE CLOTHING GROUP

The clothing group was dominated by the two bead classes. The combined percentage of the two bead classes represents a measure of the degree of continuity of traditional values. That is to say, the less acculturated the Indian, the more the percentage of beads, for if European values have been adopted, then beads have minimal value. However, it must also be remembered that in traditional Indian society beads were a measure of wealth and status. Thus, a high percentage of beads also indicates high status in the mission Indian community. Unfortunately, the picture is further confused by the function of the assemblage, as this affects the probability of losing beads. A storeroom has a low probability, as little time is spent in the room. Conversely, a living room has much higher probability. A room used for quiet, sedentary activities will have fewer beads than a room where physical labour is carried out.

The relative ratio of glass to shell beads is a function of their availability to the individual. Glass beads were distributed by the Spanish. Therefore, individuals who were viewed as deserving by the Spanish had access to glass beads. Conversely, those who did not enjoy Spanish favour had restricted access to them. However, the introduction of iron wire, which could be used to drill the holes in shell beads, made them easier to manufacture. Thus these individuals could make up this deficit with shell beads, if they had sufficient status in the community. Therefore, while the total percentage of beads is a measure of either Indian status or level of acculturation, the ratio of glass to shell is a measure of the degree to which an individual's status was conferred by the Spanish or the Indians.

Table 11.4 shows the clothing group artefact classes from the neophytes at Missions San Antonio and La Purisima. The total percentage of beads at San Antonio is in the region of 25%, whereas at La Purisima it is 40%, suggesting greater Indian continuity at La Purisima, at a much later date, or greater wealth and status in Indian terms. As both of these assemblages come from several different individuals' rooms, individual wealth or status is less likely to be the explanation. The ratio of glass to shell beads is also quite different. A much higher ratio of European glass beads were in use at Mission San Antonio. This indicates that the status of the Indians at San Antonio reflected Spanish ideas more than at La Purisima.

The higher-status room at Mission San Antonio (Table 11.4) contained a higher percentage of beads in comparison to the adjacent neophytes' rooms, and the ratio of glass to shell beads is also slightly higher. Thus, this higher-status individual, who was an Indian, continued to display his status by wearing more beads, a continuity of traditional Indian practice. The fact that this individual is still wearing traditional shell beads also shows continuity with Indian traditions, while the slightly higher proportion of glass beads suggests that his position was recognized to some degree by the Spanish.

The European/*mestizo* rooms at Mission La Purisima (Table 11.4) are strikingly different from the neophytes' rooms, as they contained far fewer beads. This is more acculturated, and supports a different racial origin for this assemblage. The fact that the beads which are present are almost all glass is also significant, showing that this individual's status was related to the Spanish value system.

The Soledad kitchen (Table 11.4) contains a lower total percentage of beads compared to any Indian assemblage. However, it also features a higher ratio of glass to shell beads. The lower percentage of beads suggests increased acculturation of these favoured Indians, their favoured status also being shown by the very high ratio of glass to shell beads.

THE ACTIVITIES GROUP

The activities group contains the most artefact classes of all the artefact groups, and is very diverse. This group is composed of artefacts representing traditional Indian activities and a variety of new activities introduced by the Spanish. The frequency of artefacts in any particular class is regarded as a measure of frequency of the activity represented. The functional origin of the assemblage is the most direct influence on this group, but analysis of the individual classes represented provides a measure of the range of activities taking place.

Table 11.5 Analysis of the activities group in five assemblages from California mission excavations, showing the percentage of artefacts in each class.

Artefact group	San Antonio neophytes	La Purisima neophytes	San Antonio higher-status	La Purisima European/ *mestizo*	La Soledad kitchen
Construction tools	0.0	0.0	3.3	1.0	0.0
Farm tools	0.0	0.0	0.0	2.0	0.0
Toys	1.9	0.0	0.0	0.0	1.0
Fishing gear	0.0	0.0	0.0	0.0	0.0
Storage items	1.3	1.1	0.0	0.0	0.0
Stable & barn	0.6	0.0	0.0	2.0	0.0
Misc. hardware	0.6	4.4	1.6	19.0	2.9
Military objects	0.0	0.0	0.0	0.0	0.0
Lithic manufacture	16.8	3.3	19.7	1.0	17.1
Used flakes	?	0.0	?	0.0	1.4
Flaked-stone tools	5.2	0.0	1.6	0.0	0.0
Heat-glazed rocks	0.0	0.0	0.0	0.0	0.0
Fire-cracked rocks	0.0	0.0	0.0	0.0	0.0
Industrial waste products	0.0	1.1	0.0	0.0	0.5
Tile wasters	0.0	0.0	0.0	0.0	1.0
Power objects	0.0	0.0	0.0	0.0	0.0
Other activities	0.6	6.7	0.0	7.0	0.0
Total★	27.0%	16.6%	26.2%	32.0%	23.9%

★Differences between these totals and those in the artefact group analysis are due to the effects of rounding the figures off to one decimal place.

Table 11.5 shows the activities group artefact classes for the neophytes' room at Mission San Antonio. Two related activities dominate the group, lithic manufacture and flaked-stone tools. The absence of any used flakes is due to these having been weighed and not counted in the published excavation report (Hoover & Costello 1985), and further emphasizes the importance of this traditional activity. Evidence of the manufacture of stone tools is not surprising, but that over 20% of the assemblage is devoted to it illustrates a surprising degree of continuity of traditional Indian activities.

The neophytes at La Purisima (Table 11.5) did not engage in the manufacture of stone tools to the same extent, although the other activities class, which is the largest here, is composed of lumps of steatite and asphaltum, both materials used in the manufacture of traditional objects. However, even when added to the lithic manufacture class, the total is only 10% of the assemblage. Thus, there is some degree of continuity, but there is also a higher percentage of miscellaneous hardware items that are entirely Spanish in origin.

The higher-status room at Mission San Antonio (Table 11.5), like the neophytes' rooms next to it, has over 20% of the assemblage consisting of artefacts related to lithic manufacture and flaked tools. This supports the conclusion that this individual was a higher-status Indian, and not a European. The contrast with the European/*mestizo* rooms at La Purisima (Table 11.5) is striking, for there are virtually no artefacts associated with lithic manufacture, but between 20 and 25% of the assemblage is miscellaneous hardware and European tools.

The kitchen at Mission Soledad (Table 11.5) contains just under 20% of lithic-related artefacts, comparable to the neophytes at San Antonio, in spite of the function as a kitchen. Only in terms of this percentage were the two missions similar. Thus, even in the mission kitchen, the acculturated neophytes maintained a considerable degree of continuity of traditional activities.

Summary

The analysis of the kitchen groups from the neophytes' rooms at Missions San Antonio and La Purisima suggests that the Salinan Indians at Mission San Antonio were less wealthy and had less access to imported goods than the Chumash Indians at Mission La Purisima in the following decade. Measured in traditional Indian terms in the clothing group, the Salinans also had less status, and were more influenced by Spanish values than the Chumash. The differences in wealth in these assemblages are the result of the comparative wealth of the missions, and the change in international trade patterns. However, the differences in status, and its recognition by the Spanish, may be specific to the small number of rooms sampled, and may not extend to all of the Indians at these missions.

In terms of acculturation, both missions contained a contradiction between the clothing and activities group analyses. At Mission San Antonio, the Indians appeared more acculturated in the clothing group, but less in the activities group, while the reverse was the case at La Purisima. Such differences are to be expected, and result from the different acculturative, political, and economic influences on each assemblage. The activities group is dominated by male-oriented artefacts, and this may account for its different pattern, indicating that the males at La Purisima were more acculturated than at San Antonio. Both sexes wore the beads that dominate the clothing group. Analysis of the kitchen group suggested less female acculturation at La Purisima than at San Antonio.

The analyses show that the higher-status room at Mission San Antonio was clearly an Indian assemblage. The kitchen group analysis also showed that the Indian had greater access to imported goods, while the clothing group confirmed his higher status both in Indian and, to some degree, Spanish terms. Both the clothing and the activities groups indicated that this individual was less acculturated than the European or *mestizo* at La Purisima. The analyses showed him to be less acculturated in clothing, but more in activities than the neophytes at San Antonio, but the opposite was the case when compared to the neophytes at La Purisima.

The European/*mestizo* assemblage at La Purisima was different in all aspects of the artefact pattern analysis. The only hint that this was not a completely European assemblage was in the kitchen group, where the presence of kitchenwares representing traditional Indian food preparation techniques suggested the presence of an Indian wife, or mixed racial origins.

The assemblage from the kitchen at Mission Soledad demonstrated its kitchen origin in both the analysis of the artefact groups and the kitchen group. The clothing group analysis showed high acculturation and high recognition by the Spanish. However, this was not confirmed by the activities group which contained many artefacts related to Indian activities.

Thus, the Indians in the kitchen at Mission Soledad were more acculturated than at Missions San Antonio and La Purisima. This is not surprising, considering that more favoured Indians are known to have worked in the mission kitchens. However, even here, the Indians still maintained a high percentage of artefacts related to traditional Indian activities.

Through the use of artefact pattern analysis, both on the group level and the classes within the groups, it is possible to compare assemblages from different missions to extract significant new information. This analysis takes account of many factors, the major ones being function, status, racial origin, wealth, and availability of goods. However, through careful comparisons, and by using all the contextual evidence available, it is possible to use this technique to examine the processes of both native American, and Spanish, acculturation in the Franciscan missions of Alta California.

Acknowledgements

I would like to thank Dr Merrick Posnansky for his support and advice throughout this project. The study has been greatly enhanced by advice from the following individuals: Dr C. Rainer Berger, Dr Clement W. Meighan, Dr James F. Deetz, Dr Robert L. McPherron, Dr Robert L. Hoover, and Dr Douglas V. Armstrong. I also with to express my appreciation to all the students and volunteers who have participated in the excavations at Soledad. The Catholic Diocese of Monterey and the Mission Soledad Restoration Committee both granted permission for the excavations at Mission Soledad, which form the core of this project. Funding for this research has been provided by: the University Research Expeditions Program (UREP); UCLA Summer Sessions; UCLA Graduate Division; the UCLA Friends of Archaeology; the Mission Soledad Restoration Committee; the Native Daughters of the Golden West; the UCLA Program on Mexico; the Institute of Archaeology, UCLA; the Institute of American Cultures; and the American Indian Studies Center, both at UCLA.

Notes

1 For more specific information about the California Indians, the reader is referred to Kroeber (1925), Heizer (1978), Heizer & Elsasser (1980), Chartkoff & Chartkoff (1984), and Moratto (1984).

2 The following overview draws on the work of many historians. The reader is referred to the following works for more information: Bancroft (1886), Barnes *et al.* (1981), Bolton (1917), Cook (1976), Engelhardt (1908–15), Farnsworth (1986), Hornbeck (1983), Stoddard *et al.* (1983), and Webb (1952).

References

Armstrong, D. V. 1983. *The 'Old Village' at Drax Hall plantation: an archaeological examination of an Afro-Jamaican settlement.* PhD dissertation, University of California, Los Angeles. Ann Arbor: University Microfilms.

Bancroft, H. H. 1886. *History of California.* San Francisco: The History Company.

Barnes, T. C., T. H. Naylor & C. W. Polzer 1981. *Northern New Spain: a research guide.* Tucson: University of Arizona Press.

Bolton, H. E. 1917. The mission as a frontier institution in the Spanish American colonies. *American Historical Review* **22**, 42–61

Broom, L., B. J. Siegel, E. Z. Vogt & J. B. Watson 1954. Acculturation: an exploratory formulation. *American Anthropologist* **56**, 973–1002.

Chartkoff, J. L. & K. K. Chartkoff 1984. *The archaeology of California.* Stanford: Stanford University Press.

Cook, S. F. 1976. *The conflict between the California Indian and White civilization.* Berkeley: University of California Press.

Deagan, K. 1983. *Spanish St. Augustine: the archaeology of a colonial Creole community.* New York: Academic Press.

Deetz, J. F. 1963. Archaeological investigations at La Purisima Mission. *UCLA Archaeological Survey Annual Report* **5**, 163–208.

Di Peso, C. C. 1974. *Casas Grandes* Vol. 3. Dragoon, Arizona: Amerind Foundation.

Engelhardt, Z. 1908–15. *The missions and missionaries of California.* San Francisco: James H. Barry.

Farnsworth, P. 1986. Spanish California: the final frontier. *Journal of New World Archaeology* **6** (4), 35–46.

Farnsworth, P. 1987. *The economics of acculturation in the California missions: a historical and archaeological study of Mission Nuestra Señora de la Soledad.* PhD dissertation, University of California, Los Angeles. Ann Arbor: University Microfilms.

Garrow, P. H. 1981. Investigations of Yaughan and Curriboo plantations. Paper presented at the 14th Annual Meeting of the Society for Historical Archaeology, New Orleans.

Heizer, R. F. (ed.) 1978. *Handbook of North American Indians.* Vol. 8, *California.* Washington: Smithsonian Institution.

Heizer, R. F. & A. B. Elsasser 1980. *The natural world of the California Indians.* Berkeley: University of California Press.

Hoover, R. L. & J. G. Costello 1985. *Excavations at Mission San Antonio: the first three seasons, 1976–1978.* Monograph XXVI, Institute of Archaeology, University of California, Los Angeles.

Hornbeck, D. 1983. *California patterns: a geographical and historical Atlas.* Palo Alto: Mayfield.

Kroeber, A. L. 1925. *Handbook of the Indians of California.* Bulletin 78, Bureau of American Ethnology, Smithsonian Institution, Washington (Reprinted by Dover Publications, New York, 1976).

Little, W. T. & R. L. Hoover n.d. Smallpox variolation and treatment in Spanish California. Unpublished ms on file, Department of Sociology and Anthropology, California Polytechnic State University, San Luis Obispo.

Moratto, M. J. 1984. *California archaeology*. Orlando: Academic Press.

Quimby, G. I. 1960. Rates of culture change in archaeology. *American Antiquity* **25**(3), 416–17.

Quimby, G. I. & A. Spoehr 1951. Acculturation and material culture–I. *Fieldiana: Anthropology* **3**(6), 107–47.

South, S. 1977. *Method and theory in historical archaeology*. New York: Academic Press.

Stoddard, E. R., R. L. Nostrand & J. P. West (eds) 1983. *Borderlands Sourcebook: a guide to the literature on northern Mexico and the American Southwest*. Norman: University of Oklahoma Press.

Webb, E. B. 1952. *Indian life at the old missions*. Los Angeles: W. F. Lewis. (Reprinted by University of Nebraska Press, Lincoln, 1982.)

12 *The town, the power, and the land: Denmark and Europe during the first millennium AD*

KLAVS RANDSBORG

When men shake hands with time, time crushes
Them like tumblers; little pieces of glass.
Abu al-Ala al Ma'arri (973–1057)

Once upon a time there was a Europe that took three types of society into a partnership. To the south an empire was established, only to collapse. To the north the gifts of the empire transformed simple societies into kingdoms. And finally a seigneurial relation between political power and the ownership of land emerged. From this society the configurations of the European future were to rise.

If we try to examine these connections, we can look at Denmark, as in a magnifying glass, and even the events of the furthest regions of Europe will be reflected there. We can look at Europe on a wider scale too, and Denmark will be in it (Randsborg in preparation).

Students of societies love playing games of 'now you see it, now you don't'. They also like to look at things near and things distant, and to speculate about how the fact that not everything is in the same place affects both social relationships and the development of societies. Scholars usually speak of the core–periphery model. The core is often thought, in this kind of reasoning, to have a strong impact on the periphery, at least as long as the core is a dynamic one. But in most cases we have great difficulties in establishing the causes for the effects we observe in, for instance, our archaeological data. This chapter does not pretend to have solved the problem. On the contrary. But it may still be of a little use in the debate as it is looking at the core from the periphery and not, as is usual, vice versa (Fig. 12.1).

The 1st millennium AD

During the first centuries of the 1st millennium AD the social order of the early Roman Empire culminated and dwindled. In archaeological terms this is best shown with the help of a graph that demonstrates the dramatic decline in sculpted portraits in Anatolia around AD 300 (data from İnan & Rosen-

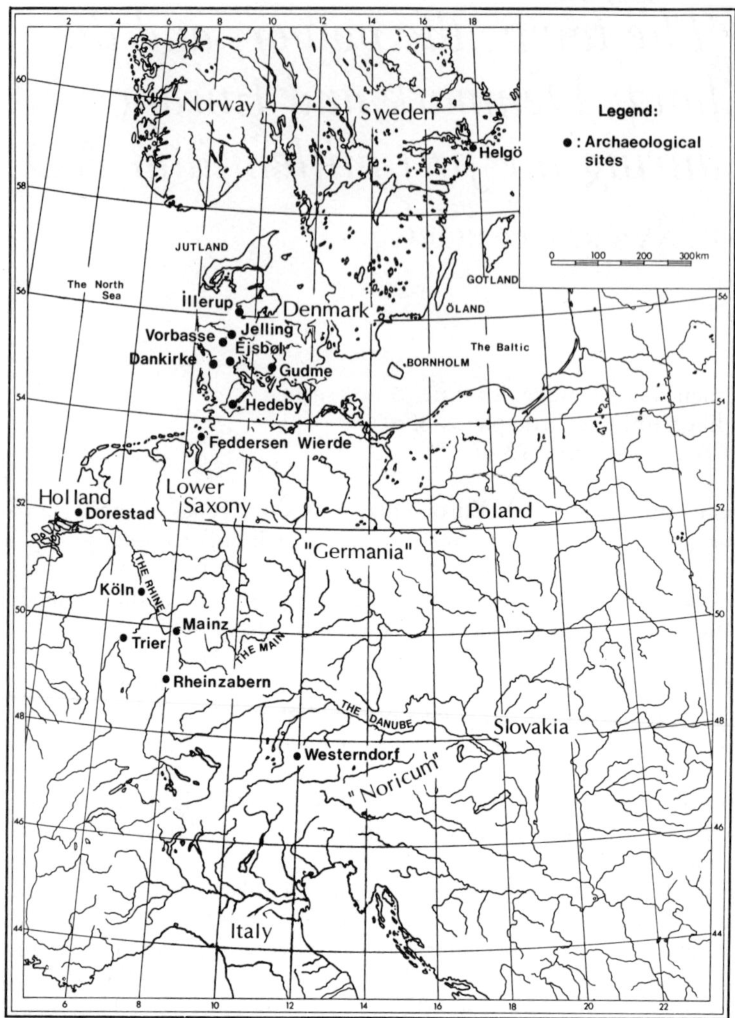

Figure 12.1 Map of Central Europe showing regions and sites mentioned.

baum 1966, Alföldi-Rosenbaum & İnan 1979) (Fig. 12.2). The portraits belonged to statues and monuments adorning the towns of the Roman Empire. A considerable proportion of the portraits represent the Emperor and his family, especially at the beginning of the Empire, when the new order had to be legitimated.

The focus of society in the early Empire was the town and its territory, or a network and hierarchy of towns, whose citizens autonomously ruled their

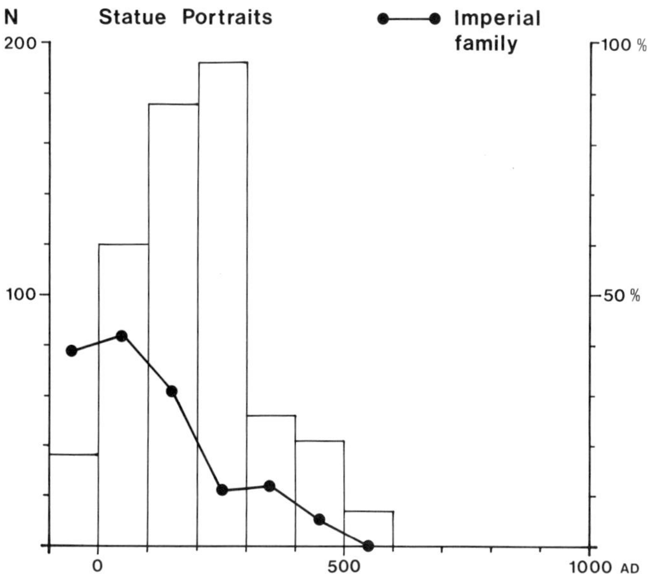

Figure 12.2 Statue portraits from Anatolia.

territories. The towns competed between themselves through the media of monumental architecture, inscriptions, adornments, works of art, etc. *Vis-à-vis* the Roman Empire, these towns were the basic administrative and fiscal units until around AD 300, when a new state apparatus, showing an interest in the single taxpayer, was established in an attempt to continue the Empire after the military and economic crisis of the 3rd century (Jones 1966, Wickham 1984).

The restored Empire was centred on the eastern provinces, while the western provinces were written off as the military pressure from outside the borders increased and the tax revenue of the state, as well as the profit of the landowners, diminished. Sometimes this process ran out of control, but on the whole what happened was a slow abandonment of the territory and a gradual loss of control over the resources of the early Empire (Goffart 1980). The late Empire, and after AD 500 the successor Byzantine Empire, saw no disparity between the interests of the state and those of the aristocracy. Only by serving the state was it possible to lay hands on the very big incomes, deriving from the considerable tax revenue, that it was still possible to extract from especially the eastern and southern provinces. But as a consequence, the towns, especially in the west, shrank, and monumental architecture almost disappeared, with the exception of the big churches, erected by the representatives of the state and, to a lesser degree, of the church itself (Ward-Perkins 1984). These monuments have an anonymous

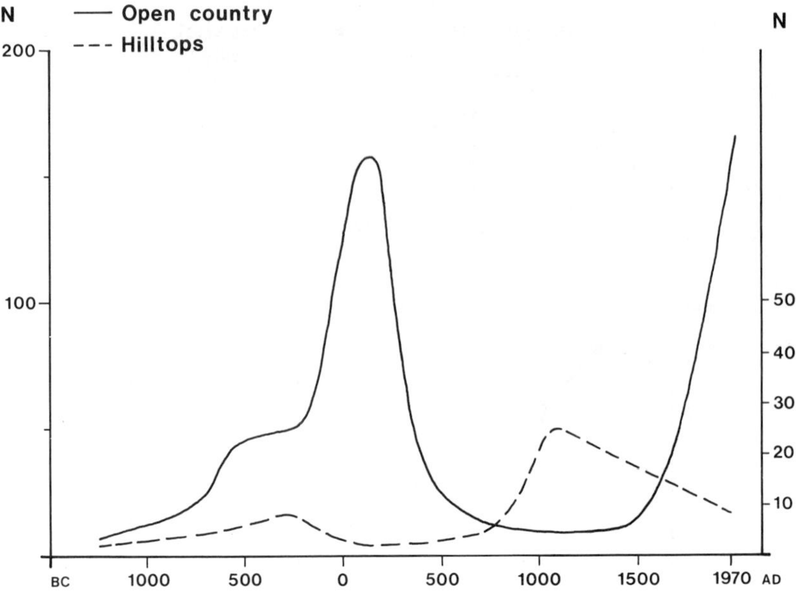

Figure 12.3 The development of settlement in the Ager Faliscus, to the north of Rome. Note the different scales used (left) for localities in the open land (mostly villas) and (right) for hill-top villages, mainly fortified.

appearance, since the power now belonged exclusively to the hierarchy of the state apparatus, and in spite of the sense of beauty of the era, they evoke memories of the monuments of Stalinist Russia.

Around AD 500 the situation in Europe and around the Mediterranean seems to have stabilized. Surplus production was generally converted into readily available funds, and the number of coins was enormous because of the tax system and also because of the payments to the civil servants of the state, to the military personnel and even to the peoples outside the borders, whose behaviour it was desirable to regulate. Trade and exchange were still flourishing, and the economy was still supra-regional in scope. For instance, fine African ceramics still flowed into Italy (Maioli 1983). But, as in other parts of the west, agriculture was degenerating even there. The densely built-up landscape of the early Empire was now succeeded by one with a few villas and scattered houses (Potter 1976, p. 214) (Fig. 12.3). The attempts by the eastern Empire during the 6th century to reconquer Italy from the Ostrogoths and Africa (Tunisia, first and foremost) from the Vandals only caused further decline. And when the Persians shortly afterwards conquered vast parts of the Byzantine Near East, the possibilities for the Byzantine state to control production and to extract a surplus from it were further reduced (see Randsborg 1988). It is true that from a military point of view the

Persians were beaten, but the Byzantine state only survived as a civilization because of one town, the heavily fortified and strategically placed Constantinople, which could be supplied easily by sea, and from many different areas. With Constantinople as a stronghold it was possible to maintain part of the south Italian and, more important, most of the Aegean territory, as well as Anatolia, a potentially rich area of whose agricultural organization, however, we know almost nothing in this period. In North Africa and in the rest of the Near East, Islamic states had assumed political and military control around AD 700, a period when the Byzantine Empire found itself in its most difficult crisis, in spite of the respect it commanded everywhere. The barbarian west had already from the beginning of the 7th century had to do without the Byzantine 'presents' bestowed by Constantinople on its subordinates (Grierson 1981, cf. Gregory of Tours V, 2). The reason was, among other things, the almost total disappearance of a money economy, which, nevertheless, did not cause the establishment of feudalism, since the tax system remained intact. During the Scandinavian Late Viking period of the 10th and 11th centuries Byzantium reconquered parts of its old territory, but even then the Empire only played a minor role *vis-à-vis* Europe, North Africa and western Asia. The only areas with which Byzantium could now enter into profitable commercial transactions were Russia and a few other places, mainly in the Balkans, where indeed we find Byzantine gold coins from the period around AD 1000 (Mosser 1935).

The Roman Empire and Germania

In western Europe the Roman Empire had already established its military frontier along the Rhine–Danube line around the beginning of the Christian era, and within a hundred years the frontier region was fully organized, with villas and towns after a Mediterranean model (Bechert 1982). Thus a clear cultural border was created across Europe, and with this a distinct disequilibrium in affluence between the areas on either side of the border. Barbarian societies in the north were already aware of such differences in prosperity and power before the arrival of the Roman legions. The border regions were particularly well supplied because of the presence of the soldiers, but the barbarian societies were not able to produce a surplus of provisions and other things of more permanent importance to the Romans (Groenman-van Waateringe 1980). Had they been able to do so, they would certainly have been incorporated into the Empire like, for example, Britannia and Dacia, in accordance with the innate impetus of empires to expand to the point where the expenditure and the receipts connected with the expansion get out of balance. The same holds true when empires 'clash', as was the case with the confrontation of the Roman and Persian Empires in the east.

This, nevertheless, does not exclude the possibility that some exchange of provisions and other products may have taken place in the border regions, if only to neutralize the frustrations of the barbarians. In fact, the written

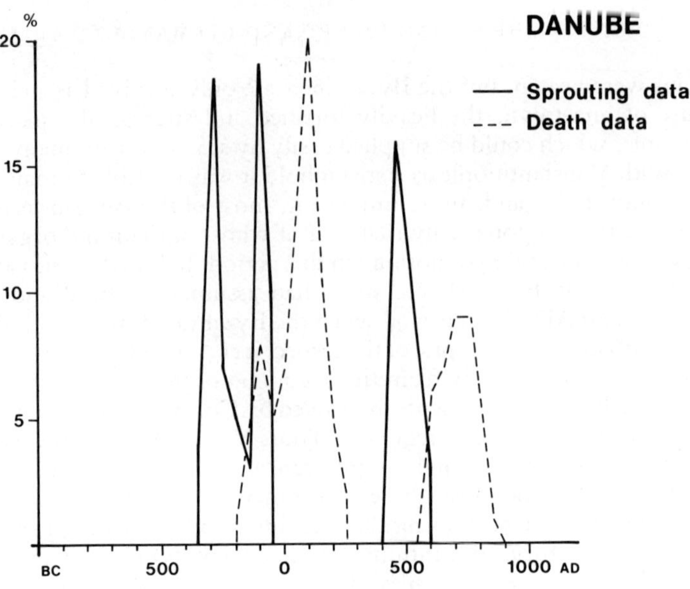

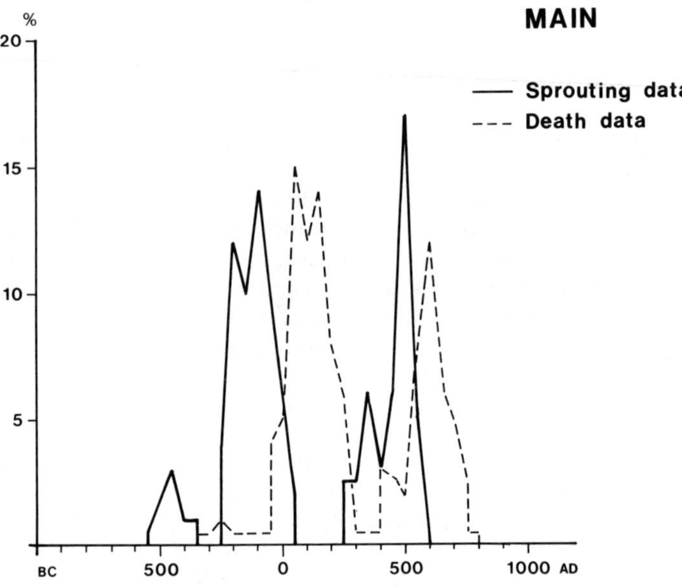

Figure 12.4 Sprouting data and death data for tree-trunks found in river deposits in the Danube and the Main. (The trees are supposedly felled by river floods caused by erosion, a side-effect of intensive agriculture in the river valleys.)

sources of the first centuries AD give several examples of border trade, though examples of restrictions and prohibitions are more numerous (Thompson 1982, pp. 3ff). In the late Roman period the prohibitions are manifestly dominant. The Empire clearly wished to link together political and material relations with neighbouring people, as is clear from the fact that Huns, Ostrogoths, Persians and others were heavily subsidized by the Empire in this very period (e.g. Jones 1966, pp. 77 *passim*). Besides the historical and archaeological sources for exchange between Romans and Germans, botanical and geological evidence gives reliable information on a parallel development of agriculture on both sides of the border. The Roman agricultural expansion in the Upper Rhine and Upper Danube areas during the first quarter of the 1st millennium AD was accompanied by drastic erosion and floods, phenomena manifested by fossilized tree-trunks in the river deposits (Becker 1982) (Fig. 12.4). Agriculture in the Upper Main area, at a fair distance outside the Limes, expanded in exactly the same period. Still more interestingly, in both the above-mentioned areas there occurred in the period after AD 400 a renewed growth of trees in the bottoms of the valleys, which is normally the primary farmland; the fifth century, of course, marks the collapse of the Roman Empire in the west. This period of regeneration was followed by a new phase of agricultural expansion with subsequent erosion and the disappearance of the growth of trees along the rivers. This final phase reflects the agricultural activities of the Merovingian era.

The archaeological picture of Roman–Germanic exchange is well known (Kunow 1983). Northern Holland lies so near the Roman Empire that regular contact must be assumed. Bronze coins, which did not represent any great value and therefore were very seldom carried over great distances, are common in the provinces of Friesland, Groeningen and Drente, especially during the 2nd century AD (van Es 1960). Along the coast there are more bronze coins than coins of silver and gold, but only 50 km inland the proportion of bronze coins falls to a quarter. In this area, culturally and socially akin to inner Germania, the Roman finds are dominated by a limited number of valuables, dinner-sets, especially for beverages, weapons and precious metal. As is also demonstrated by the Danish finds, the flow of this kind of goods increased steadily until at least the 3rd century AD (Hansen 1976).

In the coastal regions of north Holland there is also found a considerable amount of fine Roman pottery, first and foremost *terra sigillata* from the 2nd century AD (Glasbergen 1940–44). Part of this pottery was produced in French workshops and part of it in workshops in Trier. The *terra sigillata* found in the areas of Holland south of the Rhine, i.e. in the Roman Empire proper, shows the same pattern of distribution (Bloemers & Safartij 1976, Haalebos 1977, pp. 119ff, Bloemers 1978, pp. 241ff). This observation is important when we consider the imports into the Nordic zone in the Roman period, at least in the 2nd century. In the north *terra sigillata* is very rare, but when it occurs, it comes from the workshops in Rheinzabern (Upper Rhine) and its offshoot Westerndorf in the Upper Danube area

(Hansen 1982). The very rich finds of *terra sigillata* from western Slovakia and from central Poland come from the same workshops (Rutkowski 1960, Křížek 1961, 1966). In spite of Trier and Rheinzabern being situated only 150 km from each other, it is clear that their products went to very different markets in Roman Europe and, as a consequence thereof, to very different markets among the barbarians beyond (see von Bülow 1975, p. 262). This means that the communication between the north and the areas around the Middle Rhine, documented at least for the 2nd century AD, cannot normally have followed the coastal route from the Rhine estuary (or rather the first big harbour at Boulogne), via Jutland to the western Baltic, and that Denmark, in spite of its access to the ocean, must be seen in the context of the inner heartland of the Germanic world, where a more general intercourse with the Roman Empire was almost excluded. This, of course, does not imply that products from the Empire were rare; an estimation from Poland shows that 20% of the graves contain imports (Kolendo 1981). Even with a population of only a few millions we are talking about a considerable quantity of luxuries, and it is very difficult to imagine that the barbarian payments could have been of the same volume, if they were in provisions or other products. This leaves us only the trade in slaves and a few other valuables from the Nordic territories, if we want to see Roman–Germanic exchange in an economic perspective (cf. Randsborg 1984a).

We do have information on the slave-trade across the Danube as late as the 4th century AD (Thompson 1982, pp. 13ff), but over the years the trade underwent fluctuations. Maybe it was the organization of the Roman border regions that generated this kind of transaction, because as a whole slavery was in decline in the Roman Empire. It had only been of decisive economic importance in the central provinces during the early Empire. In the frontier province of Noricum (more or less present-day Austria) a fair number of inscriptions mentioning slaves and freedmen have been found (Alföldy 1974, p. 191). Freedmen dominated in the towns, while slaves were more frequent in the countryside. This kind of inscription almost disappears after the 2nd century AD, and though other inscriptions also disappear, in the general transformation of imperial society and its norms, the decline in slave inscriptions is so drastic that it can only be explained by a change in the number and in the social mobility of the slaves. Nevertheless it would be wrong to consider slavery abolished in the Roman Empire after the 2nd century AD (Dockès 1982). In periods and areas with sufficient political and military control, as for example in the 4th century, slavery continued. This is true also for the later Carolingian state and the Islamic successor states in the Middle East. In spite of the falling demand for slaves during the first millennium AD, it is very likely that the trade in slaves was an important factor in those periods which saw many imports into Denmark: the early Empire, the short period of stabilization around AD 500, and the early Islamic period at the end of the millennium.

We may also discern a feature that could have influenced the slave trade inside the Germanic societies themselves. In the settlement evidence we see how the farm after AD 200 became big, independent units that can hardly have been managed by a single family alone, but where slaves, or others, must have participated in cultivation (Hvass 1982).

Denmark in the Iron Age[1]

In Denmark and adjacent areas the quantity and chronology of Roman imports are well documented. In addition, the finds of offerings of spoils of war in the bogs suggest that there must have been clashes of interest within the northern Germanic societies. The number of weapons in the finds shows that they belonged to armies of a few hundred men, i.e. 'raiding parties' rather than larger mobilized forces. Since we do not find the defeated warriors themselves, but only their equipment, it is very likely that any survivors were taken as slaves. The first wave of bog finds (especially Illerup 2) developed and culminated simultaneously with the big phase of imports in the 2nd and at the beginning of the 3rd century AD (Ilkjær 1984). After that, bog finds seem to occur mainly in periods with few imports, i.e. the same situation as observed in the Viking Age, where periods of trade and exchange alternate with periods of raids and internal fighting (Randsborg 1981c).

To judge from the coin material, the 4th century, when the Roman Empire was re-established, and the period around AD 500 were periods of trade and exchange (Balling 1984). In the latter period the western Roman Empire was relatively stable after the establishment of the Germanic successor states, and the eastern Roman, or Byzantine, Empire was characterized by continued growth after the loss of the many unproductive western provinces. In contrast to this, we have in Denmark the bog finds from the turbulent late 3rd and perhaps early 4th century, such as Ejsbøl Nord, and the late group of *pars pro toto* offerings, where only part of the leaders' equipment went to the bottom of the lake (which would later become the bog). With these finds we have reached the 5th century, a period of breaking-up in Europe, when for instance the Goths and later the Vandals sacked Rome, an event with profound ideological repercussions, but with few economic consequences.

The cessation of the bog finds does not imply that fighting stopped altogether during the Germanic Iron Age. I am more inclined to see the late *pars pro toto* offerings as reflecting a new social order in Denmark, where valuables won in war did not necessarily have to be disposed of, but could enter the normal system of ownership. Already a little earlier, the graves seem to reflect the same development. Around AD 300 at the latest the grave goods became very poor. This does not reflect an economic recession, but rather an extension of the rights of private ownership, so that a person's private belongings could be inherited (Randsborg 1982). Returning to the settlement pattern, the 'Vorbasse village-type' of about AD 300 reflects precisely the extension of private rights and claims in a social system far more differentiated and productive than during the earlier periods of Iron Age Denmark (Hvass 1982).

When we look further at the graves from respectively the Early and the Late Roman Iron Age it is important to bear in mind that in practice only graves containing grave-goods can be chronologically determined, and among these the female graves in particular have been considered identifiable. The reason for this is that many finds are not determinable as regards sex, that weapons are not very common in the graves, and that jewelry is associated with women rather than with men. Some recently published re-analyses of the skeletal material give a more reliable picture and show an interesting difference between the Early and the Late Roman periods (data in Sellevold *et al.* 1984, pp. 213ff, cf. Randsborg 1984b). During the Early Roman period men constituted two-thirds of the osteologically sex-determined graves, while during the Late Roman period, as well as during the later Viking Age, they only made up half of the graves. Thus, it seems that during the Early Roman Iron Age men in particular received an archaeologically recognizable burial, that is one with datable grave-goods and a 'decent' bed for the body, indicating that the status and rights of men played a central rôle in the family as well as in society. And, interestingly enough, this pattern seems to go further back in time. In the Early Bronze Age, for instance, where a high proportion of the graves have been determined with regard to sex, though exclusively on the basis of the types of finds, there are twice as many male as female graves, a situation that seems to have started as early as the end of the Neolithic Funnel Beaker period.

The Late Roman and following periods differ from this pattern. In these periods women were treated with the same care as men, which of course does not necessarily reflect an actual equality of status. During the Viking period, for instance, practically no runestones were raised over women (in this respect the royal Jelling stone is an exception). I see the runestones as a kind of deeds denoting status and property (Randsborg 1980, pp. 25ff, 1981a). In general, though, the transactions in connection with the death of a magnate were of such obvious character that the raising of runestones was not required or might have been importunate and therefore undesirable. In any case, the situation is historically relatively well illustrated, among other things through the study of medieval conditions: men were the primary heirs to landed property, but the women could play an intermediary rôle when there was no adult male heir. Furthermore, these women were also daughters of other magnates, and could thus play a rôle in the hereditary transactions of their original family. The basic assumption is, of course, the existence of a patrilocal residence pattern, an assumption widely agreed on for late prehistory and the Middle Ages in the Nordic countries. This means that the increased social stratification of the Roman period caused at least those women belonging through family ties to the group of land owners to become, if not equal to the men in status, at least on the same level in questions regarding inheritance of property. We can thus conclude that the lineage family as we know it from the Middle Ages took shape not later than

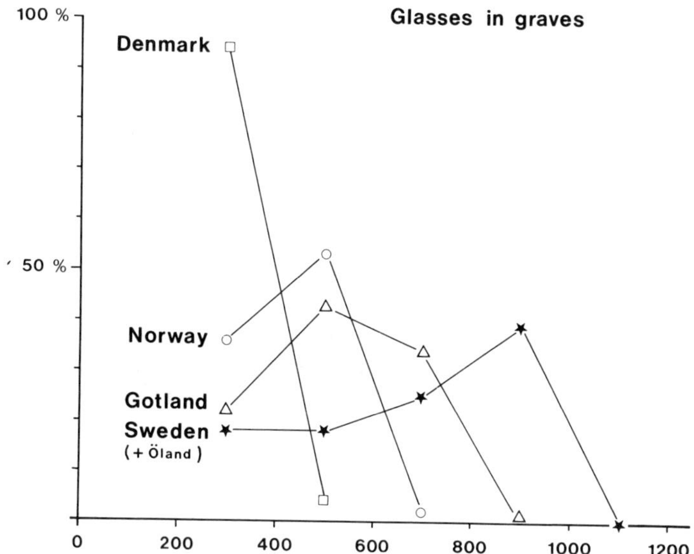

Figure 12.5 Glasses in Scandinavian graves from the Iron Age, comparing data from Denmark, Norway, Gotland, and the rest of Sweden.

the Late Roman Iron Age in association with the introduction of new agricultural systems, and that those social and productive conditions were the basis for the kingdoms, known historically from the Early Viking Age onwards in Denmark, though probably somewhat older, at least as 'passive' systems.

With these observations we have produced the framework for a type of society far more differentiated than those of the Iron Age at the time of Caesar or Tacitus, and also one which could enter regional and international economic relations with far greater strength. The poverty of the burial goods in Danish graves after about AD 300 should certainly not make us fall into the methodological trap of believing naïvely, on these grounds, that trade and exchange were poorly developed. An exotic luxury like glass vessels was indeed very common in those parts of Scandinavia which still had lavishly equipped burials in the later Iron Age (Hunter 1975) (Fig. 12.5). I should also, in this context, draw attention to the many workshops on settlements like Feddersen Wierde (Haarnagel 1979) and Vorbasse of the latest Roman Iron Age and following periods. Indeed, when very rich settlement deposits are encountered, as at Dankirke near Ribe, Gudme on Funen (Thrane 1985), or, in Sweden, at Helgø (Holmqvist 1976), it is clear from the many imports on such sites that the societies of the late Roman Iron Age and of the following Late Iron Age were not only busy creating regional economies but even ports-of-trade that would enable the incorporation of the smaller systems. This happened during a period when international conditions were not the most favourable, especially between about AD 550 and 750.

When the opportunities were right, as during the great period of expansion of trade and other contacts around AD 800, these social systems showed a remarkable energy (Randsborg 1988). During this phase it became possible to link the Near East (and indirectly even China) with Carolingian western Europe by way of the barbarian economies in Russia and Scandinavia. But these systems were also fragile, and it is hardly a coincidence that the flourishing period around AD 800 was followed, after the interruption of the international trade contacts, by unrest and plundering, in the form of the famous Viking raids (Randsborg 1981b). Earlier on in the Late Iron Age the last military bog-finds seem, as indicated above, to have been deposited during periods with relatively few imports. It is also during such periods that we have information on naval plundering raids like the Danish attacks on the Frankish realm (probably Frisia) in about AD 520 and again in AD 574 (Musset 1971, p. 116; cf. Gregory of Tours III, 3), obviously raids for slaves, or the mysterious expedition with seven ships and an armed force of 'bog-find size' (400 warriors), which 'Heruls', seemingly from Scandinavia, carried out against northernmost Spain in AD 455 and repeated four years later (Thompson 1982, pp. 180ff).

Northwestern Europe after the Roman Empire

We have seen how the Roman Empire changed Europe both inside and outside its borders. We have also seen how the Empire itself underwent changes, and how the 'aristocratic' urban culture, where extensive resources remained in the local society, was replaced by the late Roman society generated by the structural crisis of the 3rd century in the west. To meet its vast military and administrative expenses this late Roman state was forced to monopolize an extensive part of the surplus production, and this in turn brought about a tendency to give up 'unprofitable' regions, which then subsided to mere subsistence economies, and were eventually subjugated by political and military powers other than Rome. Parallel with and influenced by this Roman development, the barbarian societies changed from collectively organized or small-scale kinship-based ones to socially-stratified societies, where a person might gain individual access to use of and rights to the land. This led to the formation a powerful political/military élite. In the Roman border regions, like the Rhine provinces and northern France, as well as other places, such societies eventually took hold of both political power and vast stretches of land under the control of military leaders or 'kings'.

In the face of this development the Roman tax system eventually became ineffective (see Wickham 1984). The German armies consisted of a leader and his sworn followers, i.e. a non-professional, and therefore unpaid, retinue. The rewards for the service rendered were booty and allotment of land. These allotments of land were, at least in the Rhine areas sometime after

AD 600, considered 'private' property (Bergengruen 1958). Though the Roman tax system was still formally in force, at least in the southern parts of Gaul, as stated by Gregory of Tours at the end of the 6th century, the tax yield was low. Under the Carolingians taxation of land disappeared altogether, and the rudimentary state apparatus was now thrown back upon its own income plus sporadic collections of customs duty, etc. The estates belonging to the aristocracy and the magnates were tilled by copyholders and slaves, as they were during the late Roman period. Thus the transformation from the city-state to the so-called feudal society of the Middle Ages was completed, though the Carolingian empire was still rather primitive in a political sense and in many ways more a confederation than a state proper. The towns were undeveloped, the market system rudimentary and in the countryside many of the settlements were abandoned during the 9th century (Randsborg 1985, p. 253). Before looking specifically at the Danish reaction to this development we will first review the wider archaeological picture.

The Roman cities along the northwestern borders of the Empire had almost ceased to exist around AD 500, except as episcopal residences, convents, royal castles and the like. The Roman road system was almost unaltered, and so travellers would still 'come to town', which might have preserved a rudimentary market life. But the cities had no aristocracy, bureaucracy, military authority, merchants or artisans of their own and they functioned as local centres almost exclusively in matters concerning the church. The importance of such activities must not be exaggerated, however. The church buildings were modest, and in spite of the continuity of location, and even of street plans, we find very few signs of expansion in for instance Cologne, Mainz, Paris, Tours and other Gallic towns before the 10th century (Hodges & Whitehouse 1983, pp. 82ff). The only townlike settlements existing between AD 400 or 500 and AD 900 are the new late Merovingian and especially Carolingian market centres or emporia, like for instance Dorestad (van Es and Verwers 1980), created by royal power in an attempt to secure deliveries and extra incomes in a period when the Roman taxation of land had long ceased to exist and trade with the Mediterranean areas after AD 600 was insignificant.

In the countryside of the Rhine area we still find villa settlements in the 4th century, at least in the immediate vicinity of the cities (e.g. Bayer 1967, Hinz 1969, pp. 46ff (the chronology of the ceramics is erroneous), Willems 1981). These were abandoned at the end of the 4th century, after which our knowledge of the settlements is negligible. From other sources, as for instance the previously mentioned botanical data, it is clear, though, that west and south Germany suffered a massive contraction of settlement in the 5th century, and an almost totally changed location of the subsequent Merovingian settlements. Our most important material is now the many rich burial finds from the *Reihengräber* (graves in rows) cemeteries; sometimes we also catch a glimpse of villages with independent farmsteads, large buildings in wood and small pit-houses (Christlein 1978, pp. 39ff). But the picture is far from being as complete as in the North Sea region.

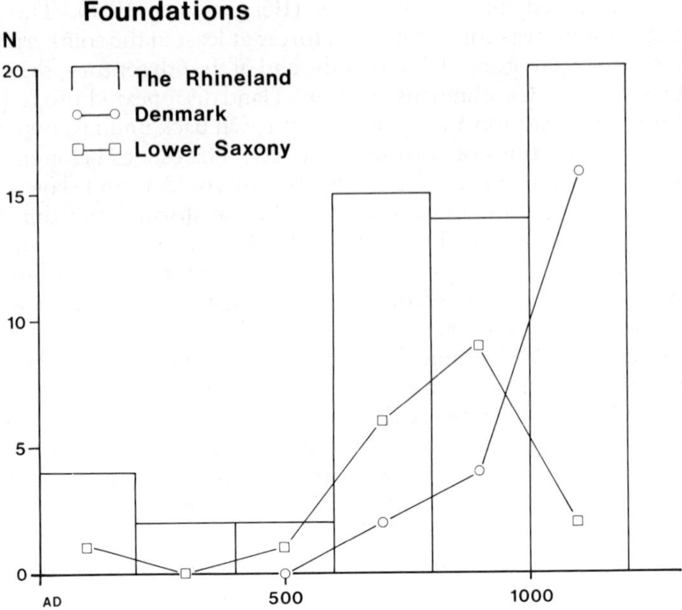

Figure 12.6 Periods of foundation of agrarian settlements of the 12th century AD in the Rhineland, Lower Saxony, and Denmark.

The *Reihengräber* start in the second half of the 5th century and are common all through the 6th century (Christlein 1978, pp. 30ff). With the 7th century they disappear in the Rhine area. These graves show us two things: first, that here also there is equality between the sexes at burial (Donat and Ullrich 1971): in other words, as in Denmark, the lineage makes up the basic structure of the society where rights and inheritance are concerned; and second, the existence of an 'open' society with a high degree of mobility in the period after the Frankish take-over of power. This second point should be amplified: a period rich in grave goods is a sign of a high degree of competition between families as well as between other social groups. The competition is particularly felt at life-crises, which always claim special attention (Randsborg 1982). This kind of competition continued in the Rhine area until the late Merovingian period, when developed private rights were established, leading to decisive checks on the power of the king (Bergengruen 1958). In this connection it is worth noticing that the *Reihengräber* are only found in the Rhine area and in northern Gaul where the Franks made up a large part of the population. In southern Gaul, where the Roman or romanized population was in the majority, since the Frankish hegemony was not followed up by a Frankish settlement, we find few *Reihengräber* (James 1979). Apparently, rights and heritage were so established in the southern regions that demonstrations of the kind common in the north were not needed.

If we look at the archaeological settlement material from the Rhineland, south Germany and adjacent areas, some interesting patterns emerge (see Janssen 1977, pp. 338ff) (Fig. 12.6). Using the flourishing settlements of the 12th century AD as a starting-point, the following picture appears: with the exception of a few sites that more or less fortuitously show traces of settlement before AD 500, a very large proportion of the settlements were founded in the 7th and 8th centuries, relatively fewer in the 9th to 11th centuries, and again a high proportion in the 12th century, which is a phase of expansion in the Rhine area and adjacent regions. As already mentioned, many Merovingian/Carolingian settlements were abandoned during the 9th century (Randsborg 1985, p. 253). If we look at the *Reihengräberfelder*, and thus indirectly at the settlements to which they belonged, we see that in south Germany, for instance, they start in the 5th and 6th centuries, that is before the foundation of those settlements still in existence in the High Middle Ages (Christlein 1978, pp. 30ff). We therefore conclude that the settlements belonging to the feudal society, with its new organization of production and landscape, were mainly founded when the *Reihengräber* were already established or had had their day. These settlements were, in other words, founded precisely when private rights were firmly established. This situation is parallel with the situation in Denmark at the passage from the early to the late Roman period, where the disappearance of the rich graves marks the beginning of new types of village and farm, as at Vorbasse in the 4th century (Randsborg 1982).

In Lower Saxony, north of the Rhine area, a proper kingdom was not as yet established in the Merovingian period. The reason could have been more stable social conditions, the absence of military and political expansion, which would have created at the least a strong military leadership, or monarchy, and lack of incentive to imitate the Romans, as the Franks did. But the Frankish attacks on and conquest of Saxony in the 8th century must have influenced the social structure of the area. In 8th-century Saxony we find richly furnished graves. It even looks as if weapon-graves were particularly common in this phase of increasing Frankish pressure (Stein 1967). It seems that we are concerned with a new warrior group, whose status was stressed at burial. Studying the settlement material, we see that the sites existing in the 12th century in this area were founded in the 8th and especially in the 9th century, and therefore in general later than the weapon-graves (see Jeppesen 1981, pp. 123ff) (Fig. 12.6). In the period AD 900 to 1200 there were only a few new settlement foundations, so the Frankish conquest was contemporary with the transformation and stabilization of the settlement pattern, accompanying what in the Rhine area we have called feudal society.

Towards a state in Denmark

Turning once more to Denmark, we notice in the 10th century a series of rich graves, among them warrior graves with heavy cavalry equipment, not known from the early Viking Age (Randsborg 1980, pp. 126ff, 1981a). These cavalry graves, lying in a belt around Jelling, the mid-Jutland royal centre, are interpreted as burials of a new military caste, dependent on the early, west Danish Jelling state (Randsborg 1980). In the rest of the country, as well as in the preceding centuries, weapons were very seldom put into graves (with the exception of the Baltic island of Bornholm), and we assume that the cavalry graves, which do not seem to continue into the 11th century, mark new norms in society.

The majority of the archaeologically known village sites of the 12th century AD in Denmark were founded in the 11th century and only a few of them have traces of earlier habitation (see Jeppesen 1981, pp. 123) (Fig. 12.6). In the 12th century almost no villages were founded, though foundations resumed in the 13th century. Once again we see that village foundations and a stabilization of the settlement were associated with the final transition from a late barbarian or 'tribal' society to a feudal state, or, in most cases, statelike conditions, and that this followed immediately after a phase with rich graves and increased social mobility, like the Frankish settlement in the Roman provinces near the Rhine.

I have dedicated so much space to these examples because they show the potential of archaeology in the discussion of the transition from tribe to state. The examples also show how the feudalization processes in Western Europe changed Denmark much more profoundly than did contact with the Roman Empire, which only remained a distant influence. First of all, during the Merovingian and Carolingian periods Denmark became engaged in trade in the North Sea Basin, whereby the natural line of communication between the north and the more developed societies in nearby western Europe could be exploited to its fullest capacity. This generated a development, not unlike the development in Free Germania caused by exchange with the Roman Empire, but with a much greater effect; I need only mention Hebedy, the largest Viking Age port-of-trade in the North. And one could add the Viking raids, which expressed the violent forces unleashed when the big incomes derived from the newly inaugurated trade suddenly failed (Randsborg 1981b).

Another thing that happened in Denmark during the Carolingian and the subsequent period (or in Scandinavian terminology, the Viking Age) was that feudal society, and the feudal state as it developed in Europe, was introduced. It is also of interest that state formation in Denmark was not a result of a foreign conquest, but happened through contact and influence. Nevertheless, like the early kingdoms to the south, it was only with the organization and development of the landscape, with the foundation of the medieval village and finally with the development of the provincial towns, that an entity was created which brought about a firm and divisible structure of power and created the economic framework for a further expansion. In this connection it is worth noticing that Denmark in the year AD 1000 was at some points already more developed than the Carolingian Empire, which in spite of its relatively firm organization of the landscape, its emporia, royal castles, bishoprics and monasteries had not as yet developed a network of provincial towns, which through a central market economy could have regulated production and distribution, besides serving as administrative and ecclesiastic centres for the surrounding areas. Though the Danish provincial towns were merely seats, supply centres and investment objects for the élite (Andrén 1985), this concentration of power and means in a systematic pattern encouraged a market economy and diverted attention from the long-distance trade towards the development of the regional resources.

Note

1 In Scandinavia the term 'Iron Age' covers the period from about 500 BC to AD 1000 or 1100, after which the Middle Ages start. The Iron Age has the following sub-divisions: Early Iron Age, from about 500 BC to AD 400; Late Iron Age, from about AD 400 to the end of the period. The Pre-Roman Iron Age is from about 500 BC to 1 BC; the Roman Iron Age from about AD 1 to AD 400. The Viking Age lasted from about AD 800 to AD 1000 or 1100. (The period from about AD 400 to 800 is called in Denmark 'The Germanic Iron Age'; it has various other terms in Sweden and Norway.)

References

Alföldi-Rosenbaum, E. & J. İnan 1979. *Römische und frühbyzantinische Porträtplastik aus der Türkei. Neue Funde.* Mainz: Zabern.

Alföldy, G. 1974. *Noricum.* London: Routledge and Kegan Paul.

Andrén, A. 1985. *Den urbane scenen, städer och samhälle i det medeltida Danmark.* Acta Archaeologica Lundensia Series in 8° Nr 13, Lund.

Balling, A. K. 1984. Møntcirkulationen i jernalderens Danmark. In *Fra Stamme til Stat, Symposium på Sostrup Kloster 23.–25. maj 1984*, 11–21. Højbjerg.

Bayer, H. 1967. Die ländliche Besiedlung Rheinhessens und seiner Randgebieten in römischer Zeit. *Mainzer Zeitschrift* **62**, 125–75.

Becker, B. 1982. *Dendrochronologie und Paläoökologie subfossiler Baumstämme aus Flussablagerungen. Ein Beitrag zur nacheiszeitlichen Auentwicklung im südlich Mitteleuropa.* Mitteilungen der Kommission für Quartärforschung 5. Vienna: Österreichische Akademie der Wissenschaften.

Bechert, T. 1982. *Römisches Germanien zwischen Rhein und Maas. Die Provinz Germania Inferior.* Munich: Hirmer.

Bergengruen, A. 1958. *Adel und Grundherrschaft im Merowingerreich, Siedlungs- und Standesgeschichtliche Studie zu den Anfängen des fränkischen Adels in Nordfrankreich und Belgien.* Vierteljahrschrift für Sozial- und Wirtschaftgeschichte Beiheft 41, Wiesbaden.

Bloemers, J. H. F. 1978. *Rijkswijk (Z.H.), 'De Bult': Eine Siedlung der Cananefaten.* Nederlands Oudheden 8. Amersfoort: Rijksdienst voor het Oudheidkundig Bodemonderzoek.

Bloemers, J. H. F. & H. Safartij 1976. A Roman settlement at De Woerd, Valkenburg (South Holland), Report 1: The potters' stamps. *Berichten van de Rijksdienst voor het Oudheidkundig Bodemonderzoek* **26**, 133–61.

Bülow, G. von 1975. Die Keramikproduktion. In *Die Römer an Rhein und Donau. Zur politischen, wirtschaftlichen und sozialen Entwicklung den römischen Provinzen an Rhein, Mosel und oberer Donau im 3. und 4. Jahrhundert*, R. Günther & H. Köpstein (eds), 230–68. Berlin: Zentralinstitut für alte Geschichte und Archäologie, Akademie der Wissenschaften der DDR.

Christlein, R. 1978. *Die Alamannen, Archäologie eines lebendigen Volkes*. Stuttgart: Konrad Theiss.

Dockès, P. 1982. *Mediaeval slavery and liberation*. Chicago: University of Chicago Press.

Donat, P. & H. Ullrich 1971. Einwohnerzahlen und Siedlungsgrösse der Merowingerzeit: eine methodischer Beitrag zur demographischen Rekonstruktion frühgeschichtlicher Bevölkerungen. *Zeitschrift für Archäologie* **5**, 234–65.

van Es, W. A. 1960. *De romeinse muntvondsten uit de drie noordelijke provincies: een periodisering der relaties*. Groningen: Scripta Academica Groningana.

van Es, W. A. & W. J. H. Verwers 1980. *Excavations at Dorestad*. Vol. 1: *The harbour: Hoogstraat 1*. Nederlands Oudheden 9. Amersfoort: Rijksdienst voor het Oudheidkundig Bodemonderzoek.

Glasbergen, W. 1940–44. Terra sigillata uit de provincie Groningen, Bijdrage tot de geschiedenis van den handel in den romeinschen tijd. *Jaarverslag van de vereeniging voor terpenonderzoek* **25–8**, 317–68.

Goffart, W. A. 1980. *Barbarians and Romans, A.D. 418–584: the techniques of accommodation*. Princeton: Princeton University Press.

Gregory of Tours 1955–6. Gregorii episcopi Turonensis Historiarum Libri Decem. In *Ausgewählte Quellen zur deutschen Geschichte des Mittelalters*, R. Buchner (ed.). Berlin: Rütten & Loening.

Grierson, P. 1981. The Carolingian empire in the eyes of Byzantium. In *Nascita dell'Europa ed Europa Carolingia*, 855–916. Settimane di studio del Centro Italiano di Studi sull'Alto Medioevo 27, Spoleto.

Groenman-van Waateringe, W. 1980. Urbanization and the north-west frontier of the Roman Empire. In *Roman Frontier Studies 1979*, W. S. Hanson & L. J. F. Keppie (eds), 1037–44. British Archaeological Reports International Series 71, Oxford.

Haalebos, J. K. 1977. *Zwammerdam – Nigrum Pullum: ein Auxiliarkastell am niedergermanischen Limes*. Cingula 3. Amsterdam: University of Amsterdam.

Haarnagel, W. 1979. *Die Grabung Feddersen Wierde: Methode, Hausbau, Siedlungs- und Wirtschaftsformen sowie Sozialstruktur*. Feddersen Wierde 2. Wiesbaden: Steiner.

Hansen, U. L. 1976. Das Gräberfled bei Harpelev, Seeland. Studien zur jüngeren römischen Kaiserzeit in der seeländischen Inselgruppe. *Acta Archaeologica* **47**, 91–160.

Hansen, U. L. 1982. Die skandinavischen Terra Sigillata-funde. Zu ihrer Herkunft, Datierung und Relation zu den übrigen römischen Importen der jüngeren Kaiserzeit. *Studien zur Sachsenforschung* **3**, 75–99.

Hinz, H. 1969. *Kreis Bergheim*. Archäologische Funde und Denkmäler des Rheinlandes 2, Düsseldorf.

Hodges, R. & D. Whitehouse 1983. *Muhammad, Charlemagne and the origins of Europe: archaeology and the Pirenne thesis*. London: Duckworth.

Holmqvist, W. 1976. Die Ergebnisse der Grabungen auf Helgø (1954–74). *Prähistorische Zeitschrift* **51**, 127–77.

Hunter, J. R. 1975. Glasses from Scandinavian burials in the first millennium A.D. *World Archaeology* **7**, 79–86.

Hvass, S. 1982. Ländliche Siedlungen der Kaiser- und Völkerwanderungszeit in Dänemark. *Offa* **39**, 189–95.

Ilkjær, J. 1984. Mosefunde i går og i dag. In *Fra Stamme til Stat, Symposium på Sostrup Kloster 23.–25. maj 1984*, 23–31. Højbjerg.

İnan, J. & E. Rosenbaum 1966. *Roman and Early Byzantine portrait sculpture in Asia Minor*. London: British Academy.

James, E. 1979. Cemeteries and the problem of Frankish settlement in Gaul. In *Names, words and graves*, P. H. Sawyer (ed.), 55–89. Leeds: University of Leeds.

Janssen, W. 1977. Dorf und Dorfformen des 7. bis 12. Jahrhunderts im Lichte neuer Ausgrabungen in Mittel- und Nordeuropa. In *Das Dorf der Eisenzeit und des frühen Mittelalters*, H. Jankuhn, R. Schützeichel & F. Schwind (eds), 285–356. Abhandlungen der Akademie der Wissenschaften in Göttingen, Philologisch-historische Klasse, Dritte Folge 101.

Jeppesen, T. G. 1981. *Middelalderlandsbyens opståen, Kontinuitet og brud i den fynske agrarbebyggelse mellem yngre jernalder og tidlig middelalder*. Fynske studier 11, Odense.

Jones, A. H. M. 1966. *The decline of the ancient world*. London: Longman.

Kolendo, J. 1981. Les influences de Rome sur les peuples de l'Europe centrale habitant loin des frontières de l'Empire. L'exemple du territoire de la Pologne. *Klio* **63**, 453–72.

Křížek, F. 1961. Nové nálezy terry sigillaty na Slovensku. *Slovenská Archeológia* **9**, 301–24.

Křížek, F. 1966. Nové nálezy terry sigillaty na Slovensku (II). *Slovenská Archeológia* **14**, 97–145.

Kunow, J. 1983. *Der römische Import in der Germania libera bis zu den Markomannenkrieg, Studien zur Bronze- und Glasgefässen*. Göttinger Schriften zur Vor- und Frühgeschichte 21, Göttingen.

Maioli, M. G. 1983. La ceramica fine da mensa (terra sigillata). In *Ravenna e il porto di Classe: venti anni di richerche archeologiche tra Ravenna e Classe*, G. B. Montanari (ed.), 87–112. Realtà regionale 7, Fonti e Studi, Bologna.

Mosser, S. McA. 1935. *A Bibliography of Byzantine coin hoards*. New York: American Numismatic Society.

Musset, L. 1971. *Les Invasions: le second assaut contre l'Europe chrétienne (VIIe–XIe siècles)*, 2nd edn. Nouvelle Clio 12 bis. Paris: Presses Universitaires de France.

Potter, T. W. 1976. Valleys and settlement: some new evidence. *World Archaeology* **8**, 207–19.

Randsborg, K. 1980. *The Viking Age in Denmark: the formation of a state*. London: Duckworth.

Randsborg, K. 1981a. Burial, succession and early state formation in Denmark. In *The archaeology of death*, R. Chapman, I. Kinnes & K. Randsborg (eds), 105–21. Cambridge: Cambridge University Press.

Randsborg, K. 1981b. Handel, plyndring eller landbrugsekspansion – tre centrale aspekter af Vikingetiden. *Historisk Tidsskrift* **81**, 205–18.

Randsborg, K. 1981c. Les activités internationales des Vikings: raids ou commerce. *Annales (Economies, Sociétés, Civilisations)* **36**, 862–8.

Randsborg, K. 1982. Ranks, rights and resources: an archaeological perspective from Denmark. In *Ranking, resource and exchange*, C. Renfrew & S. Shennan (eds), 132–9. Cambridge: Cambridge University Press.

Randsborg, K. 1984a. The study of slavery in northern Europe: an archaeological approach. *Acta Archaeologica* **55**, 155–60.

Randsborg, K. 1984b. Women in prehistory: the Danish example. *Acta Archaeologica* **55**, 143–54.

Randsborg, K. 1985. Subsistence and settlement in northern temperate Europe in the first millennium A.D. In *Beyond domestication in prehistoric Europe, investigations in subsistence archaeology and social complexity*, G. Barker and C. Gamble (eds), 233–65. London: Academic Press.

Randsborg, K. 1988. Denmark and the Mediterranean in the first millennium AD: an archaeological perspective. In *First millennium papers: western Europe in the first millennium AD*, R. F. J. Jones, J. H. F. Bloemers, S. L. Dyson & M. Biddle (eds), 37–49. British Archaeological Reports International Series 401, Oxford.

Randsborg, K. in preparation. *The first millennium AD: an archaeological approach.*

Rutkowski, B. 1960. *Terra sigillata znalezione w Polsce.* Bibliotheca Antiqua 2, Wrocław.

Sellevold, B. J., U. L. Hansen & J. B. Jørgensen. 1984. *Iron Age man in Denmark. Prehistoric man in Denmark* Vol. III. Nordiske Fortidsminder Series B 8, Copenhagen.

Stein, F. 1967. *Adelsgräber des achten Jahrhunderts in Deutschland.* Germanische Denkmäler der Völkerwanderungszeit, serie A, 9. Berlin: de Gruyter.

Thompson, E. A. 1982. *Romans and barbarians: the decline of the western Empire.* Madison: University of Wisconsin Press.

Thrane, H. (ed.) 1985. *Gudme problemer. Beretning fra et bebyggelses-arkæologisk symposium på Hollufgård afholdtden 24.–25. oktober 1984.* Skrifter fra historisk institut 33, Odense University.

Ward-Perkins, B. 1984. *From classical antiquity to the middle ages: urban public building in northern and central Italy AD 300–850.* Oxford: Oxford University Press.

Wickham, C. 1984. The other transition: from the ancient world to feudalism. *Past and Present* **103**, 3–36.

Willems, W. J. H. 1981. Romans and Batavians: a regional study in the Dutch Eastern River area, I. *Berichten van de Rijksdienst voor het Oudheidkundig Bodemonderzoek* **31**, 7–217.

13 *Great Moravia between the Franconians, Byzantium and Rome*

LUBOMÍR E. HAVLÍK

Introduction

The state of Moravia (Fig. 13.1), in the territory of modern Czechoslovakia, became known in historiography under the name of Great Moravia, although the term did not appear until the work of the Byzantine Emperor Constantine VII about the middle of the 10th century.[1] He applied the term to the late 9th-century empire of King Swentopluk, or, to be more precise, to his domain on the northern and northeastern side of the Danube, including the region around the river Tisa and its tributaries. However, Byzantine historians called countries 'great' provided that they had been the earlier homes of migratory peoples; examples are Great Bulgaria and Great Croatia. The Moravians were first recorded in central Europe after the campaigns of Charlemagne against the Avar Khaganate, when the Franconians became acquainted with the situation in that part of Europe. Recent discoveries in the fields of archaeology, historiography, anthropology, art history, linguistics and literary history enable us to draw a more precise image of Moravia's history, its political and cultural relations with other states, and its rôle and importance in European development in the early Middle Ages.

The Moravians already had some history behind them before they were recorded in central Europe for the first time. They may have come to Moravia between the end of the 7th and the beginning of the 8th centuries. The country was inhabited by some Slav people as early as from the beginning of the 6th century. About 548, they furnished the Langobardic prince Ildigis with an army of 6000 men and granted him asylum in Moravia. Later, they were governed by King Samo (626–61). His kingdom originated in the neighbourhood of the Avar Khaganate. On archaeological evidence, some of the vast cemeteries of southwestern Slovakia originated in the 7th century, whereas others date from the late 7th and the 8th centuries.

Anthropological research carried out in the ancient capital of Moravia (near Mikulčice) has proved that the male population of that place between the 8th and the 10th centuries was of the same type as that of the cemeteries mentioned, but differed from the female population of the capital, and from the male and female of the countryside. The male upper

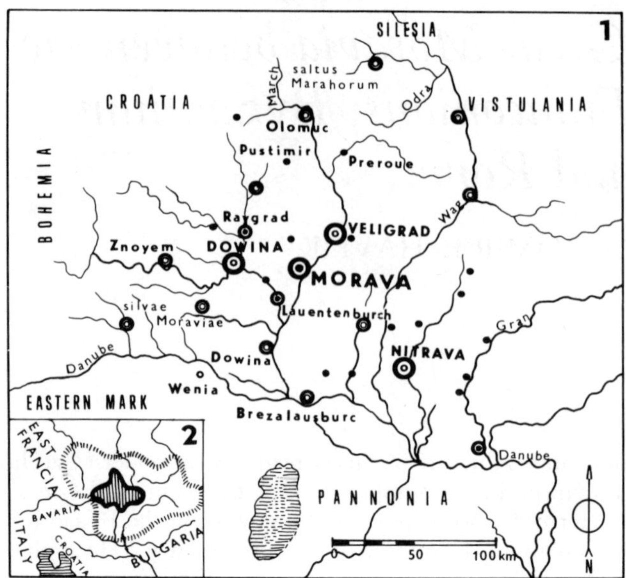

Figure 13.1 (1) The kingdom of Moravia in about the middle of the 9th century. (2) Moravia and surrounding regions in the 9th century.

stratum differed also in clothing. Their boots have been compared to those of Tabaristan. Their jewellery was made in local workshops, but the ornaments and motifs came from the Near East and analogies to them can be found in Syria, Egypt and in the region of Iran. Large buttons had their prototypes in the Caucasian and Iranian area. The type of dwellings was comparable to that of Middle Asia. The origin of the types of horses, cattle and goats bred in Moravia was linked with that region as well. Several elements of the social and political organization of the Moravians also deserve attention. The eastern features of the Moravian (glagolitic) script cannot be denied, either. A presumption, ventured before the recent discoveries were made, suggests the Moymirid dynasty of Moravia was of an Alanic descent.

As far as the upper stratum of the 9th-century Moravians is concerned, that opinion is not contradicted by the facts mentioned above. The men who came to Moravia as Slavs had several links with eastern countries. The population appeared in the Carpathian Basin around the beginning of the 7th century, and after their stay in southwestern Slovakia, they came to Moravia.

The emergence of Moravian power

During the last third of the 8th century, Roman–Franconian elements of Carolingian Christian culture began to penetrate into the upper class of

Moravia. The men who settled down on the banks of the middle Morava at the end of the 7th and in the first half of the 8th centuries organized the construction of a fortified castle and outer defences near Mikulčice. Several extramural but closely attached fortified settlements arose around it. The castle was built in a place inhabited by the Slavs and called Morava (gradŭ Morava), the castle–town of Moravia. Beginning at the end of the 8th century, seven churches and a palace were built in the castle; five other churches have been discovered in the suburbs. A further fortified settlement arose in Moravia in the place known later (because of its large suburb) by the name of Veligrad (Uherské Hradiště and Staré Město of today), as well as several others.

The Bavarian description of the lands situated north of the Danube reports eleven towns and districts (*civitates*) in Moravia between 817 and 843. Moravia proper was situated between the Yesenik Mountains and the Danube, or the Leiser Berge and Manhart, and between the Bohemian–Moravian Highlands and the river Vah; it included the Duchy of Nitra (Slovakia) which became the seat of the minor members of the Moymirids. Prince Pribina (Priwina) of Nitra, who administered the country, was expelled by King Moymir (Moymar) I in 833; Swentopluk, the later King of Moravia, had administered Nitravia before he ascended the throne.

Moravia aroused the interest of Franconian annalists relatively late. Not until 822 did the visit of the Moravian legates to the court of the Emperor Louis the Pious at Frankfurt officially manifest the adherence of Moravia to the Roman Christian universal sphere, the spiritual head of which was the Pope of Rome. Its temporal representatives were the Emperor of the Eastern Roman Empire (Byzantium) and the Emperor of the Western Roman Empire. According to the Bavarian tradition, the Christianization of the Moravians was carried out by the Bishop of Passau in 831. However, the first churches were built in Moravia even earlier. Several of the churches at Morava were founded at the end of the 8th or the beginning of the 9th century, and the church of St. Martin in Nitra (Martin's Hill) was consecrated by the Archbishop of Salzburg about 828.

Several objects from that period indicate Carolingian origin or influence, particularly some girdle-ends and decorated spurs. The Carolingian type of sword also came into use. The sword was a weapon of prominent persons, primarily of the members of the ruling dynasty; it was a sign and symbol of rule and power, in contrast to the typical Moravian battle-axe, which was the most commonly used weapon. In accordance with western European custom, members of the ruling dynasty were buried in the nave of a church. A grave in one particular church at Morava might be that of Moymir I's predecessor, or that of King Moymir I himself, who died before 846. His sword has the mark of the monastery of St. Gall and could have been imported into Moravia before the prohibition of the export of swords to Slav countries in 805. The sword of Blatnica (Nitravia) proves to be of early Carolingian origin as well. However, most of the swords found in Moravia (46) and Nitravia (11) were produced in the country.

The syncretism of the influence of the Carolingian milieu and that of the Near East is to be found for example on girdle-ends from the graves at the capital. Though made in local workshops, they demonstrate the marked influence of Carolingian art styles, and a synthesis of western and eastern motifs and iconography. The influence of Carolingian art had its counterpart in the field of church literature. The Moravian Penitentiary written in Old Slav was composed in Moravia and based on a Latin penitentiary (The Penitentiary of Merseburg). Several prayers and liturgical texts in the Old Slav language of the Moravian type had their origin in the first half of the 9th century.

The consolidation of empire

After the new division of the Western Roman Empire carried out at Verdun in 843, Louis II the German of Eastern Franconia strove to subordinate Moravia and to intervene in its internal affairs. The first round of his attempts finished with his defeat in front of an unidentified Moravian fortress in 855. Louis was pursued across the Danube, and Rostislav, the King of the Moravians (846–870), began to strengthen the internal and foreign political situation of the state of Moravia.

Several churches were built during this period. The variety of their form corresponds to the statement of the biographer of Archbishop Methodius, who wrote that many different teachers of Christianity were in the habit of coming to Moravia from Italy (i.e. from Rome, from the province of the Patriarchate of Grado, and from Dalmatia), from Greece (i.e. from Byzantium and its empire in the Balkans and in the East) and from Germany. They taught various differing forms of Christianity (Franco–Bavarian, Roman, Byzantine, Syrian, Nestorian).

After the strengthening of Moravia's independence in 855, King Rostislav endeavoured to establish the internal affairs of faith, church and law by acquiring persons who could instruct his people in the Moravian vernacular; he also endeavoured to gain an episcopacy for Moravia. All this, including the sanctioning of Moravia's foreign political situation in Europe, Rostislav tried to obtain from Rome. However, Pope Nicholas I, who sided with King Louis the German, the enemy of Moravia, refused King Rostislav's request. Therefore, Rostislav directed the same request to Michael III, the Emperor of the Eastern Roman Empire, in 862.

Byzantium at that time was attempting to subordinate Bulgaria. An alliance with the northwestern neighbour of Bulgaria must have been welcomed. Bulgaria, in order to paralyse Moravia, sought an ally in Eastern Franconia. In the meantime, Byzantium sanctioned Moravia's situation within the Roman universe and the Emperor Michael III pointed to Constantine the Great as the model for Rostislav's life and deeds. The Byzantine legates Constantine the Philosopher, later the monk Cyril (Kyrillos), and his brother Abbot Methodius, the former Byzantine governor Michael, were dispatched to Moravia in order to organize its internal affairs according to the Roman law as modified in Byzantium. The letter of the Emperor (863) granted the privilege of the use of the Moravian vernacular in the liturgy.

The Byzantine mission, backed by the King and nobles, collided with the views of the archipresbyters, the representatives of the Bishop of Passau, and with the Franco-Bavarian clergy who made every effort to enforce the political aims and claims of their king, Louis. In the attempt to stop Rostislav's policy and the activity of the Byzantines aimed against him and the Bavarian clergy, Louis prepared war against Moravia. After having secured the benediction of Pope Nicholas and having joined forces with Khan Boris of Bulgaria at Tulln, he attacked the country in 864. A simultaneous attack by Byzantium prevented Bulgaria from coming to the aid of the German king and compelled that country to accept Christianity and to admit the patronage of the Byzantine Emperor. Louis's attack on Moravia was stopped at Dowina and finished with a peace treaty which in practice confirmed the status quo. The activity of the Byzantines could continue, and they translated several liturgical and Biblical texts from the Greek into the Moravian variety of Old Slav. Constantine is considered to be the author of the 'Civil Law code' based on the Byzantine Eclogue and on native Moravian legal practice. All the literary works were written in the glagolitic script, which legend associates with Constantine and Methodius.

The Byzantine envoys finished their work in Moravia towards the middle of 867. After spending some time in Pannonia at the court of Duke Kotzel, Pribina's son, Constantine and Methodius reached Venice, where the famous dispute with the Latin priests took place. Here, they received the information that the Eastern Roman Imperial throne had been ascended by the new Emperor Basilius I who strove to better Byzantine relations with Rome. This induced Pope Nicholas I to invite the two Byzantines to Rome, where they arrived after the middle of December, 867. They were welcomed by the new Pope Hadrian II, however, who approved the Old Slav glagolitic texts and ordered the ordination of the disciples of the Byzantines. Only after the Byzantine legates had acknowledged Rome's ecclesiastical supremacy over Pannonia and Moravia, and Constantine–Cyril had died in 869, was Methodius ordained archbishop for the restored Church of Pannonia. The new province comprised primarily the state of Moravia, as is confirmed by the Pope's letter addressed to Rostislav, who was named in the first place ahead of Swentopluk (of Nitravia) and Kotzel (of Pannonia). In this way, the original request from Rostislav for a bishop, together with the later one from Kotzel, was fulfilled. But it did not take place until King Rostislav had defeated a renewed attack of Louis the German on Moravia in the middle of 869. His grave losses caused Louis to seek peace, by dispatching his sons and margraves to arrange a settlement with Moravia.

An internal crisis in Moravia in the next year allowed the occupation of Moravia by the Bavarians and Franconians, who took possession of the royal treasure. King Rostislav was captured by his nephew Swentopluk and imprisoned by Louis the German. Later, Swentopluk was interned, too, and the same fate befell Methodius, who was confined by the Bavarian episcopacy. The uprising of the Moravians led by Prince Slavomir, a priest and member of the royal family, won back several towns including the capital. But only the decisive victory of Swentopluk after his release restored the independence of Moravia: the Franco-Bavarian troops were destroyed in front of the capital Morava, and Swentopluk (871–894) ascended the throne. After several other victories over the Franconians, the Bavarians, the Saxons and the Thuringians, the independence of the state of Moravia was secured. The Moravians were able to request Pope John VIII to free Methodius. The Pope punished the Bavarian episcopacy and entrusted Methodius to the care of Swentopluk of Moravia in 873. Methodius, accompanied by the papal legate Bishop Paul of Ancona, came to the capital of Moravia, where 'all the princes' were assembled. That place was appointed as his archiepiscopal see, and he and his successors took their title from this residence. There, the administration of 'all churches in all towns' was conferred upon him by Swentopluk and the nobles of Moravia. The peace negotiations between Louis the German and Swentopluk's chancellor John of Venice took place at Forchheim in 874. However, the annals give no information about the result.

From that time, 'the rule and the realm of the Moravians began to spread and widen over all [the neighbouring] countries' (*Life of Methodius*, Ch. X). The Moravian Empire (Great Moravia) came into being. By 879 it incorporated the country of the Vistulanians, the Silesians, the Slavs of Bohemia (the Croats, the Dudlebs, the Czechs, the Luchans, and the Lemuzians), it adjoined the regions round the Tisa (before 882) and part of Pannonia as far as the Drava (884), and the Sorbs between the Saale and the Elbe paid tribute to Moravia (from 880). The countries were administered by vassal princes or Moravian governors and garrisons. The growth of Swentopluk's power was combined with the Christianization of the neighbouring peoples, a task felt to be incumbent on a Christian king, that was performed by 'the wise and pious' King Swentopluk in collaboration with Archbishop Methodius.

Moravia became a powerful state in Central Europe. King Swentopluk, with the aid of Archbishop Methodius, aspired to consolidate through the establishment of external relations the position which Moravia had gained by its own military power. The request for its official recognition within the Roman Christian universe was presented to Pope John VIII by Methodius in 880. The Pope, 'abandoning all the other temporal sovereigns', granted the direct patronage of St Peter and himself to Swentopluk, his nobles and all the people of the country. The Roman privilege 'Industriae tuae' proclaimed Swentopluk to be 'the only son' of the Papacy: this title was applied only to the Emperors or to the candidates for Imperial rank. The significance of this probably lay in tension between Rome and the Carolingians in the period during which the Western Imperial throne was vacant. The Archiepiscopacy of Moravia was confirmed to Methodius, and the Pope ordained the elected Bishop Wiching of Nitra. A promise was made to create another bishop in order that Methodius could himself ordain other bishops for episcopacies established by the king. The usage of the Old Slav language and script was admitted for Moravia, although the priority of Latin had to be preserved. The first temporal part of the privilege was confirmed by Pope Stephen V in 885. After Swentopluk had succeeded in consolidating his position and that of Moravia in Europe, he and Archbishop Methodius met the new Western Emperor Charles III in 884. Regarding Roman patronage for Moravia from 880, Charles as the temporal head of the Roman universe in the west had no other choice than to recognize Swentopluk's and Moravia's prominent situation within the Roman universe, next to that of the Empire itself. Afterwards, as the King of Eastern Franconia, Charles made a peaceful settlement with King Swentopluk with respect to Pannonia. Archbishop Methodius favoured and carried through the policy of Swentopluk, both in Rome and in Constantinople, which he visited at the invitation of the Emperor Basilius I in 881–882.

During the period 873–885, new churches were built in the Moravian church province, both in Moravia proper, especially at Morava, and elsewhere, as at Prague and Cracow. Several literary works also originated in Moravia during this period, again using the vernacular Slav language and the glagolitic script, e.g. 'The Life and Deeds of Constantine the Philosopher'. Most of the work was done by Methodius, who was himself the author of the Moravian version of the codex of the ecclesiastical law, the *Nomokanon*.

Much jewelry, including large buttons and earrings of gold and silver, has been discovered in the graves of the cemeteries of this period, in the capital Morava, in the suburb of Veligrad, and elsewhere. The objects were produced in local workshops but have an affinity to the style of the Byzantine world and that of the Caucasus and Near East.

The social organization of the state

The sources provide information on the social and political organization of the state of the Moravians, the metropolitan land of the Empire built by them. The supreme rule and dominion (*vlastĭ*), including the right to dispose of all ownership of land, belonged to the king (*kŭnędzĭ*), the chief of all the noblemen. The king was a theocratically ruling monarch of the hereditary dynasty of the Moymirids. He reigned with a council (*sŭvětŭ*) of dukes and noblemen of his court. The state was administered by rich, honourable and well-born noblemen who had the title of *zhupans*. The *zhupans* were the chiefs of 11 (at the beginning of the 9th century) to 30 (in the second half of the 9th century) counties of the state. The minor officials were captains (*kŭmetĭe*), the chiefs of hundreds and village populations. Judges, royal servants (*slugy*) in war and peace who held small possessions in the countryside around castle–towns, and young personal servants (*otroci*) are also recorded. The King's companions (*drudzi*) and warriors (*milites*, *voini*) comprised his retinue – *družina* (*čędĭ*). The commander-in-chief (*vojevoda*) led the troops on horse and on foot during the king's absence. The sources inform us that the largest part of the population was formed by the free common people who were obliged to pay a yearly tax, or public rent (*obrokŭ*), and were compelled to carry out some public service. The yield of portions of this rent was awarded to the sovereign's noblemen. The only real private landed proprietorship was that of the royal dynasty. The ownership of land by the nobles was considered to be a tenancy from the point of view of the sovereign and the state. The actual properties and tenancies consisted of estates and castles. The economy of their lords depended on the work of slaves and bondsmen, who provided only a minor part of the country's production. Several other categories of people are also recorded: debtors, liberated slaves, and church bondsmen.

The income of the sovereign and the state consisted of the feudal public rent and of the taxes and tributes paid by vassal princes or collected by Moravian governors and garrisons in the adjoining princedoms of the Moravian Empire. The primary phase of early feudalism, however, was beginning to change. The villages and estates destroyed during the preceding wars were settled by new people, who finally became serfs bound to their lords. The second phase of early feudalism developed with the weakening of central royal power and the growth of allodial land-holding in the 10th century.

The decline of Moravian power

We have seen that three main directions of international relations prevailed in the history of Moravia: (1) towards the Roman Empire in the west, or towards its kingdom of East Franconia, (2) towards the Roman Empire in the east (Byzantium), (3) towards the Roman Papacy. The last played the leading rôle, even after Methodius's death on 6 April 885. Although Pope Stephen V limited the use of the Slav language in the Mass to the extent permitted by Hadrian II, he urged that the Slav language should be used in other cases. It was not forbidden generally to the church of Moravia. The decline of the literary culture in the vernacular was caused by the expulsion of Methodius's disciples by Bishop Wiching; after Methodius's decease, the Moravian legend 'The Memory and Life of Methodius, the Archbishop of Moravia' was composed. However, Gorazd, the Archbishop designate was deposed by Wiching, who took advantage of King Swentopluk's absence and expelled Methodius's disciples Clement, Nahum, Angelarius, Sava, Laurentius, and Constantine, in all about 200 Slav clergymen. Swentopluk did not subsequently revoke Wiching's action, because, in accordance with his Roman foreign policy, he preferred to have a Latin Church of Moravia. Wiching's action demoted the vernacular literature to a place of lesser importance, though it did not die out.

After King Swentopluk died, probably on 9 March 894, several internal and external events influenced the further history of Moravia. The decline of a strong central power, and changes in the character of proprietorship in favour of private ownership by dukes and nobles weakened the state. The princes of western and southern Bohemia seceded in 895 and sought the protection of Arnulf, the King of East Franconia. The Sorbs followed this example in 897. Swentopluk II, the king's second son, began to quarrel with King Moymir II, the successor of Swentopluk I. In the end, Swentopluk II, a protégé of Arnulf, was compelled to leave the country in 899. In return, Moymir II supported Isanric, the margrave of the Eastern Mark, against Arnulf and protected Isanric's Mark between 899 and 901. With the help of Papal legates, Archbishop John and Bishops Benedictus and Daniel, Moymir restored the Church of Moravia in 900. The legates ordained one archbishop (John) for Moravia proper, and three other bishops: one of them was appointed for Nitra, the second was for Vistulania, while the third bishop may have been for Croatia (East Bohemia), for the Eastern Mark, for Silesia, or for the Hungarians.

Hungarians were permitted by the Moravians to settle within their territory in the basin of the Tisa in 896 because, after their invasion of Bulgaria at the request of Byzantium, the Hungarians had been heavily defeated by the Bulgarians and expelled from their own lands. They had to defend the newly leased settlements against the Bulgarians and to help the Moravians against the Franconians and the Bavarians. This co-operation was realized in a double raid undertaken during the wars between Moravia and Bavaria in 900. After the peace treaty between the two countries in 901, however, the Hungarians turned against Moravia. In 902, they beat the Bavarians who had been entering Moravia, but afterwards they suffered a defeat at the hands of the Moravians. In 906 the Hungarians were again defeated.

The activities of the four Moravian bishops (i.e. archbishop and three bishops) about 910 confirms the conclusion that a state power sufficient to protect the church must have existed in the kingdom of Moravia and in the lands under its supremacy at that time. In the twenties of the 10th century, however, a crisis broke out in the kingdom. Several dukes to the east of the metropolitan land strove for more economic and political recognition, aided by lax enforcement of the king's central power. Some dukes and noblemen even joined the Hungarians who occupied the territory to the east of the lower Vah (southern Nitravia) between 919 and 924. Finally, in order to live on good terms and in peace with the Hungarians, the Moravians began to pay tribute to them. During the crisis, the members of the royal dynasty fled, the archbishop died in 925, and the capital Morava lost its importance. Life disappeared from its castle for one generation and the churches fell to ruins. Veligrad and its suburb met with a similar fate, perhaps, towards the end of the first half of the 10th century. However, there is no evidence that the decline of Moravian towns was caused by the Hungarians. About 1000, Moravia was annexed by Poland, about 1025 the ancient kingdom of Moravia was subjoined by the Přemyslid princes of Bohemia. Spytigneus II of Bohemia imprisoned over 300 of the most prominent representatives of the Moravian nobles in 1055, and took over their estates. He granted them to his nobles, officials and church institutions from Bohemia. This meant a profound change in the social, political, cultural and ethnic life of Moravia, reminiscent of the situation in Anglo-Saxon England after 1066.

Conclusion

In this review of the history of Moravia's external relations, the efforts of Moravia to become a recognized part of the European world of the early Middle Ages appear very clearly. In many respects, however, the Moravians preserved a culture of their own, in spite of assimilating cultural traits from the Western and Eastern Roman Empires. Moravia's social and political organization began to pass from the primary phase of early feudalism to its more progressive second phase in the last third of the 9th century.

The visit to the Western Roman Emperor in 822 represented official acceptance of Moravia into the Roman Christian universe. It had as its consequence the completion of the official Christianization of the ruling nobility and the greater influence of the Latin world. However, this was counteracted by East Franconia's unsuccessful attempts to realize its unilateral claims to Moravia by both military and peaceful means. The effort to establish the external political position of Moravia in Europe led its sovereign to seek the aid of the Papacy and of the Eastern Roman Empire. Such support was a reflection, naturally, of the independence and might of the state of Moravia.

Byzantium's support was evident in the years 863–885, that of the Papacy began from 867–873. The Eastern Roman Emperor acknowledged the foreign political status of Moravia and granted a privileged position to the vernacular in the liturgy. Byzantium opened up the Greek and Eastern cultural world to Moravia and introduced to it the Byzantine version of Roman law. The Papacy established the independent Moravian church province and sanctioned Moravia's independent status within the Roman universe, on a par with that of the Roman Empires. Besides the patronage granted to Moravia in 880, the King of Moravia was entitled to be a candidate to emperorship. Rome sanctioned the use of the vernacular and its script in Moravia, though Latin was given priority. The development of this literary culture remained Moravia's everlasting legacy and contribution to European culture, although, in concordance with the view of the Moravian court, the usage of vernacular in the liturgy was limited in favour of the priority of Latin. The literary heritage of Moravia was transformed to Bulgaria and Kievan Russia and formed the basis of a literary culture there.

Note

1 The historical background to the events discussed in this chapter is described more fully by Boba 1971, Dittrich 1962, Dvornik 1970, Havlík 1978, 1980–81,

1981–82, 1987, and Kučera 1985. The original sources are collected in Havlík 1966–77. For more details of the archaeological evidence, see in particular Dostál 1966, Hrubý 1966, Kučera 1986, Poulík 1975a, 1975b, 1978. See also Poulík *et al.* 1986.

References

Boba, I. 1971. *Moravia's history reconsidered. A reinterpretation of Mediaeval sources.* The Hague: Nijhoff.

Dittrich, Z. R. 1962. *Christianity in Great Moravia.* Groningen: J. B. Wolters.

Dostál, B. 1966. *Slovanská pohřebiště ze střední doby hradištní na Moravě.* Prague: Academia.

Dvornik, F. 1970. *Byzantine missions among the Slavs.* New Brunswick: Rutgers University Press.

Havlík, L. E. (ed.). 1966–77. *Magnae Moraviae fontes historici*, 5 vols. Brno: Purkyně University Press.

Havlík, L. E. 1978. *Morava v 9.–10. století (Moravia in 9th and 10th centuries).* Prague: Academia.

Havlík, L. E. 1980–81. Moravská společnost a stát v 9. století (Moravian society and state in the 9th century). *Slavia Antiqua* **17**, 1–42.

Havlík, L. E. 1981–82. Moravská společnost a stát v 9. století (Moravian society and state in the 9th century). *Slavia Antiqua* **18**, 71–112.

Havlík, L. E. 1987. *Kronika o Velké Moravě (Chronicle of Great Moravia).* Brno: Blok.

Hrubý, V. 1966. *Staré Město – velkomoravský Velehrad.* Prague: Academia.

Kučera, M. 1985. *Velká Morava. Spoločnost, kultura, tradicia.* Bratislava: Osveta.

Kučera, M. 1985. *Postavy velkomoravskej historie.* Bratislava: Osveta.

Poulík, J. 1975a. Mikulčice. Capital of the Lords of Great Moravia. In *Recent Archaeological Excavations in Europe*, R. L. S. Bruce-Mitford (ed.), 1–31. London: Routledge and Kegan Paul.

Poulík, J. 1975b. *Mikulčice – sídlo a pevnost knížat velkomoravských.* Prague: Academia.

Poulík, J. 1978. The origin of Christianity in the countries north of the middle Danube Basin. *World Archaeology* **10**, 138–71.

Poulík, J., B. Chropovský, Z. Klanica, A. Ruttkay, L. E. Havlík, V. Vavřínek, M. Kučera & D. Třeštík 1986. *Grossmähren und die Angfänge der tschechoslowakischen Staatlichkeit.* Prague: Academia.

Index